SCRIPTORUM CLASSICORUM
BIBLIOTHECA OXONIENSIS

OXONII
E TYPOGRAPHEO CLARENDONIANO

ANTIPHONTIS ET ANDOCIDIS
ORATIONES

RECOGNOVERUNT
APPARATU TESTIMONIORUM ORNAVERUNT
ADNOTATIONE CRITICA INSTRUXERUNT

M. R. DILTS
ET
D. J. MURPHY

OXONII
E TYPOGRAPHEO CLARENDONIANO

OXFORD
UNIVERSITY PRESS

Great Clarendon Street, Oxford, OX2 6DP,
United Kingdom

Oxford University Press is a department of the University of Oxford.
It furthers the University's objective of excellence in research, scholarship,
and education by publishing worldwide. Oxford is a registered trade mark of
Oxford University Press in the UK and in certain other countries

First Edition published in 2018

Impression: 1

Published in the United States of America by Oxford University Press
198 Madison Avenue, New York, NY 10016, United States of America

British Library Cataloguing in Publication Data
Data available

Library of Congress Control Number: 2017943300

ISBN 978–0–19–960547–7

Printed and bound by
CPI Group (UK) Ltd, Croydon, CR0 4YY

PREFACE

THIS edition contains the extant speeches attributed to two of the earliest practitioners of Greek rhetoric whose works survive: Antiphon (*c.*480–*c.*411 BCE), reputedly the first to write speeches for clients and publish them (Diod. *apud* Clem. Alex., *Strom.* 1.16.79.3; Ps.-Plut. *X Orat.* 832 C–D; Quint. 3.1.11), and Andocides, a well-born politician and orator (*c.*440–late 390s or 380s BCE). We include the introductory material transmitted in the manuscripts, sc. the *Γένος Ἀντιφῶντος* (*Life of Antiphon*), abridged from the pseudo-Plutarchan life of that orator, and the hypotheses to the speeches (lacking for Antiphon 3.δ, 4.γ, and 4.δ, and for Andocides 1 and 2).[1] The present edition does not include fragments of speeches, nor does it include fragments of the so-called Antiphon the Sophist.[2] For titles of the speeches we use those of the manuscripts but record alternative ancient titles in the critical apparatus.[3] Likewise, we follow the

[1] In this preface, 'we' verbs refer to work done by Dilts and revised by Murphy; 'I' verbs refer to work done subsequently by Murphy. The critical apparatus to the text was drafted by Dilts and checked and revised by Murphy, to whom Latin first-person forms there refer.

[2] A representative defence of the view that the 'Sophist' was not the same man as the speechwriter was made by Pendrick (2002). For the unitarian view, cf. Gagarin (2002) and Darbo-Peschanski (2013).

[3] A few Byzantine commentators err about titles of Antiphon's *Tetralogies*: (*a*) they misunderstand genre terms as titles, sc. (1) *αἱ δευτερολογίαι* (Doxopater, *Hom. in Aphth.* 2.378.9–10 Walz, repeated by Anon. *Schol. in Aphth.* 2.33.29–30 Walz), an error avoided by Greg. Pardus *In Hermogenis Περὶ Μεθόδου Δεινότητος* 7.2.1310.12–19 Walz, Ioan. Sardianus *In Aphthonii Progymnasmata* 94.5–9 Rabe, and Ioan. Diaconus apud Lysiae fr. 115 Carey; (2) *οἱ φονικοί* (Anon. *In Hermog. De Stat.* VII.1.330.15–20 Walz); (*b*) a corrupt gloss on *ἁγνεύετε* (Phot. α 205, *Synagoge* cod. B α 282, *Synagoge*

manuscripts in ordering and numbering the speeches. That the ordering of Antiphon's speeches is ancient is shown by (1) Harpocration's location of a passage in *Tetralogy* A, our Orat. 2, as 'in the second' (Ἀντιφῶν ἐν τῷ β΄, Harp. α 12, cf. Tetr. A.γ.11); (2) Hermogenes' mention of 'the homicide speeches', οἱ φονικοὶ λόγοι, before 'the public discourses and as many as are like these' (*Id.* 2.11.112–13).[4]

Of the speeches contained herein, we consider spurious Andocides 4, *Against Alcibiades*, which bears the marks of being a later rhetorical exercise.[5] The authenticity of Andocides 3, *On the Peace with the Lacedaemonians*, debated since antiquity (cf. Hypothesis 13, Harpocration ϵ 40, ν 13, π 65), has been rejected afresh with strong arguments by E. M. Harris (2000, 2016: 148 n. 12). We do not take a position on this matter. On the other hand, M. Canevaro and Harris (2012) have shown that the decrees and laws inserted into Andocides 1, *On the Mysteries*, are not genuine.[6] As for Antiphon, elements of non-Attic language and law have called into question his authorship of the *Tetralogies*, but the objections are not decisive.[7] Likewise, suspicions that Orat. 6, *On the Chorus Boy*, is vitiated by a large lacuna, or that its opening or ending is not authentic, are not well founded.[8] Authenticity of Orat. 1, *Against the Stepmother*, has not been disputed since the mid-nineteenth century.

aucta α p. 24.1–2), which cites Orat. 2.γ.11, garbles that speech's subtitle as κατηγορία παρασήμου, against κατηγορία φόνου ἀπαράσημος of our MSS.

4 Cf. Gagarin 2002: 52–3.

5 This conclusion was argued in detail by Meier 1836–37; among recent treatments, cf. Gribble 1997. A plausible case for Aeschines of Sphettus as author has been made by Cobetto Ghiggia 1995: 109–21. For a survey of problems of date, authorship, and purpose, cf. Murphy forthcoming.

6 A. Sommerstein's defence (2014) of the Demophantus decree (And. 1.96–98) has been answered by Harris 2014. Against M. Hansen's defences (2015, 2016) of the Patroclides (1.77–9) and Tisamenus decrees (1.83–4), cf. Canevaro and Harris (2016). Accordingly, we do not emend out apparent historical inaccuracies in these inserted documents.

7 Cf. Thiel 1932: 5–19; Decleva Caizzi 1969: 18–21; Gagarin 2002: 52–62.

8 Cf. Barigazzi 1955b: 35–7 and 1954: 182–200.

I. TEXTUAL TRADITION

Two primary manuscripts transmit Antiphon's speeches, and two, speeches of Andocides. Both authors are contained in A, the Codex Crippsianus (British Library Burney 95). A was purchased from Prince Alexander Bano Hantzerli some time after 1802 by John Cripps, having previously belonged to the library of Vatopedi on Mt Athos. A contains Andocides (fos. 3^r–26^v), Isaeus, Dinarchus, Antiphon (fos. 96^v–130^v), Lycurgus, Gorgias, the *Ulysses* of Alcidamus, Lesbonax, and Herodes. A was copied *c.*1312–17 by Michael Klostomalles.[9] For all or part of one or both of our authors, A was collated in situ by Osann, Bekker, Dobson, Sigg, Buermann, Jernstedt, H. Mueller-Struebing and I. H. Ieayes on behalf of Lipsius, MacDowell, and James Zetzel, and it was collated from photographs for the respective speeches by Thalheim, Dalmeyda, Albini, and Cobetto Ghiggia.[10] Moreover, Blass, Thalheim, Lipsius, and Fuhr checked many readings by autopsy.

From A are descended MSS BLMZP (cf. Sigla Codicum). LMP were copied not long after 1492, when Janus Lascaris brought B from Mt Athos to Florence. B is a direct copy of A. LMZ in turn descend from B, copied one from the other in that order, and it is highly probable that M was the model of P.[11]

Almost every page of A contains corrections. Some words are written *in rasura*, others added in the margin or above the line, and others emended by erasure or insertion of letters. The vast majority show the letter forms of the main text. Their ink also displays the same colour range as that of the main text, from a light sepia to almost black. After extensive study, MacDowell (1962: 24–8) confirmed the prevailing view that this corrector, A^1, was the first

[9] Cf. Lamberz 2008: 140–1, who built on work done by Prato 1991: 141–4.

[10] I thank Michael Gagarin for sending me Zetzel's collations of A and Bodl. Auct. T.2.8 (= N) in Antiphon, and I thank Prof. Zetzel for permission to use them.

[11] Cf. Buermann 1882; Buermann 1885; Cinquini 1886: 10–15; Wyse 1904: ii–vii. P, copied in Florence by Michael Suliardus near the end of the 15th c., is not cited by us.

scribe working from the exemplar and restoring its readings, whether *inter scribendum* or on later revision. MacDowell's conclusion has generally been accepted. Having worked in detail with the British Library's high-quality digitization of A, I endorse that conclusion. I assign corrections to A^1 when identification can be made with confidence. When not, I use simply the siglum A^c. I use A^a to distinguish the reading *ante correctionem* from that of A^1 or A^c.

Editors have concluded that most of A^1's activity amounted to restoring readings of his exemplar, although in places it looks as though he worked *suo ingenio* (cf. apparatus at Ant. 2.γ.9, 2.δ.11, 4.α.2, 6.22, And. 1.128 *παιδὶ* A^a : *παιδίω* A^1). We cannot always suppose, in any case, that A^1's reading also stood in the archetype from which A's model descended: cf. Ant. 1.30 *ἀπόλλυνται* M^{im} : *ἀπολοῦνται* A^aN : *ἀπόλωνται* A^1; 4.α.2 *ἀξιωθέντος* AN : *ἀξιωθεὶς* A^1 : *ἀξιωθέντων* Blass; 6.10 *καταψηφίσαισθε* Bekker : *καταψηφίσεσθε* A^aN: *καταψηφίσησθε* A^1 (further examples in Wyse 1904: xxvii). Despite these scattered errors, however, A^1 proves its worth well enough in Antiphon to deserve the nod over A^a when neither is obviously wrong in Andocides 1, where we lack a second primary witness; cf. 1.19 *τε*, 1.26 *ἐξελέγξαι*, 1.45 *ἐξεστρατευμένοι*, 1.85 *πάντες*, 1.103 *τὰ* (*lectio difficilior*; on Andocides' varied structures, cf. Albini 1961: 25–7).

A later corrector, A^2, in a light, yellow-brown ink worked from Isaeus 3 through Dinarchus to Antiphon 5.84 (fo. 123^v top). Although Thalheim (1886: 2) said that A^2 is active also in Lycurgus 70–86 (140^v–141^v), I detect his distinctive strokes and ink only at §80, *δι᾽ ὅπερ* A^2 : *διόπερ* A, and in a few punctuation marks. A^2 worked prior to the late fifteenth century, for his corrections recur in B. A^2's alterations range from minutiae like accents and punctuation to sophisticated emendations such as *εὐρόπως* (Ant. 5.76). Some false corrections of A^2 can be blamed on existing errors in A (e.g. *πεισθέντας* AN : *πεισθέντες* A^2, 3.γ.3, where A^2 was attempting to cope with *ἡγήσησθε*). Others simply lack foundation (e.g. at 1. Hyp. 10, 2.α.3, 2.γ.5–6, 5.61). Most of A^2's interventions may have been his own

conjectures (cf. Wyse 1904: xxvi–xxxv). Still, nineteenth-century scholars were probably right to think that good readings reached A^2 from another manuscript, which was not N (cf. apparatus at 2.α.9, 5.11).

I designate as A^3 the person who used pencil to bracket μεν and thereby create ἐξείη δὲ at Ant. 6.25. Marginal notes on fos. 97–100 (Ant. 1) are Hantzerli's.

Our other primary manuscript of Antiphon is N (Bodleian Auctarium T. 2. 8, Meerman 327, summary catalogue no. 20608; Cataldi Palau 2011: 239–44). Once belonging to the 'collegium Clermontanum' (no. 358A), N was subsequently acquired by Johan Meerman (1751–1815). Today the codex consists of two parts bound together. Only the first part concerns us. Like A, it was copied in the early fourteenth century, but it contains only Dinarchus, Antiphon (23^v–64^v, some leaves out of order), and Lycurgus. We have no copies of N. As A's and N's contents became better known, N's primary status was vindicated against Sauppe (1861), who had contended that N was a copy of A extensively edited by a learned Byzantine.[12]

I follow Thalheim in bundling later corrections under the siglum N^2. We lack grounds to suppose that the corrector/s worked from another manuscript, for these later corrections are either easy ones or false. One of them does find confirmation in PKöln (cf. 2.β.6). Guesswork is likely to have been the source of the mistaken restoration of faded letters on fo. 167^r (5.36 παρέχοντας AN: κατέχοντας N^2).

N was first put to use by Maetzner from collations supplied by John A. Cramer. It was collated anew by Jernstedt, Thalheim, and Zetzel. Having worked only on photographs of N, I rely on Thalheim and Zetzel for distinctions among hands of correctors, and I thank

[12] N's independence was established by Jernstedt (1880: xxxiii–xxxix), Blass (1881: xx–xxv), Graffunder (1882: 35), and Thalheim (1886).

Nigel Wilson for inspecting corrections by autopsy at 1.26, 5.11, 5.19, 6.21, and 6.27.

Andocides 3 and 4 occupy fos. 89^{r-v}, 102^{r}–108^{v}, 111^{r} of a second primary witness, Q (Ambrosianus D 42 sup.). Written on oriental paper between the later thirteenth and earlier fourteenth centuries and bound among other material on western paper, Q also contains Isaeus 1 and 2. Lipsius was the first editor to exploit its readings. Formerly at Grottaferrata, Q came into the Ambrosiana as part of the vast collection of Gian Vincenzo Pinelli. It was collated in Andocides in situ by Lipsius and Cinquini, and from photographs by Cobetto Ghiggia in [And.] 4. Q occupies a further stage from the archetype than does A, for it shows transpositions and other editorial interventions that aim to impart greater clarity and harmony of phrasing.[13]

It has long been held that ANQ are derived from the same archetype.[14] AN or AQ often agree in error. Moreover, AN agree in the inferior reading against PKöln (later second century CE) at 2.β.6 (cf. Hagedorn 1985: 71), and they stand against the indirect tradition in various places (cf. app. crit.).

This archetype probably was sprinkled with variants: (1) supralinear variants appear occasionally in first scribes' hands (N: Ant. 5.81; A: Ant. 4.γ.6, 5.14, 5.46 where A's supralinear variant agrees with N, 5.67, 6.15, And. 1.20; Q: [And.] 4.8); (2) A^1N agree, sometimes in error, against an intelligible variant of A^a (Ant. 2.δ.7, 4.γ.2, 4.γ.5, 4.δ.10, 5.16, 5.19—traces of accents suggest ἕλος stood *in textu*—, 6.28, 6.30, 6.42, 6.47); (3) incongruous alternative readings can be explained on that assumption (e.g. Isaeus 1.15.8, ἀπεμπέμψει Q : ἀπέμεμψεν A^a : ἀπέπεμψεν A^1). Our evidence does not warrant the confidence of Buermann (1885: 395) and others, however, that

[13] Cf. Albini 1964^a: 33–5, 109. I thank Stefano Martinelli Tempesta for verifying ῥαθύμως by autopsy at [And.] 4.23.

[14] Cf. *inter alios* Bienwald 1889: 10–12, Wyse 1904: xxiii–li.

variants laced the archetype on a mass scale.[15] It probably was written in minuscules: Ant. 6.9 εἴπερ Blass : εἰ μὲν AN.[16]

The copyist of N made far fewer errors than did the copyist of A.[17] On the whole, A²N should be followed when they agree. Where the choice between A and N seemingly can go either way, I favour N, as do, among others, Gernet, Decleva Caizzi, and Gagarin. Between A and Q, I favour A.

Of the above-mentioned manuscripts, I have collated B in Antiphon and Andocides, and Q in Andocides 3 and 4, from digitizations provided by their possessor libraries. I have examined thousands of readings in A and hundreds in N, including all corrections noted in the apparatus, using the British Library's digitization and the microfilm made by the Bodleian. I have checked a large number of readings in M from the digitization provided by the British Library, and in L from photographs generously supplied to me by Matilde Malaspina and Sabrina Minuzzi.[18] I examined the editions of Aldus and Stephanus at the Rare Book and Manuscript Library at Columbia University.

Our authors' complete speeches find scant representation in the indirect tradition or in papyri. Quotations by ancient or Byzantine authorities are enumerated above the critical apparatus in this edition. Most of these consist of short passages supplied in lexica. Fragments of manuscripts written on papyrus are the following:

Antiphon

1. 2.β.5–6 κέρδους ... ἀδικήματος: P. Köln 5.213, saec. II. CPF I 1*, 17.3. Cf. Hagedorn 1985.

[15] Cf. Wyse 1904: xxiii–xxviii, Albini 1964ª : 33–4.

[16] Wyse 1904: xlvi–xlvii. A at least was copied from a minuscule manuscript; cf. e.g. Ant. 4.γ.5, 6.15 and see further Wyse 1904: xlvii.

[17] Cf. Ferrante 1972: 24–5. Since Maetzner, the overall superiority of N to A has been recognized by most critics. Graffunder's charge that N regularizes the archetype's word-order was refuted by Bienwald (1889: 20–5).

[18] I thank Ms Malaspina for confirming by autopsy that L contains corrections made *per ras.* at And. 1.51 and 1.146.

2. 4.α.3–4 δυσμένειαν … τοὺς δὲ: PSI inv. 320 ro., saec. II^{ex}–III^{in}. See Lundon 2003.

Andocides

1. 1.70 τῶν … ἱκανῶς: P. Wash. Univ. II 65 (St. Louis, Wash. Univ. inv. 414), saec. III.
2. 1.110 Ἐλευσινίῳ … τεθνάναι and 1.116 ἔπειτα δὲ νόμον … Ἐλευσινίῳ, P. Flor. II 112, fr. C col. II, in Comparetti 1911, no. 112, pp. 16–17, saec. II.

II. EDITIONS

Cf. conspectus below. The speeches of Antiphon and Andocides were first printed as part of the Aldine Attic Orators (Venice, 1513). Working from Florence MS L, the editor, Marcus Musurus, made many corrections and conjectured a number of good emendations.[19]

Beginning with Henri Estienne, known as Stephanus, textual critics for the next two centuries relied on their ingenuity and erudition to improve the text. This process reached its apogee in the monumental work of Johann Jacob Reiske, the critic by far the most frequently represented in the apparatus of subsequent editors. I rely on Reiske for emendations proposed by Scaliger (1540–1609), on Sluiter for those of Valckenaer (1715–85) and Luzac (1746–1807), and on Reiske and Sluiter for emendations made by de Valois (1603–76). Wm. Dobson remains the best source for emendations made as notes by Jeremiah Markland and Peter Paul Dobree, and from Dobson I retrieve conjectures of Conrad Gesner (1516–65) and John Taylor (1704–66).[20] Emendations in And. Orat. 1 that go back to Marc-Antoine Muret (1526–85) are reported by Rosenberg

[19] On L as Musurus' model for the Aldina, cf. Jernstedt 1880: xiv–xviii, Lipsius 1888: xvi.

[20] For Markland, cf. Dobson 1828: I.391–2, and for Dobree, ibid. liii–lxii. Dobson's report is more reliable than those in the printed editions of Dobree.

(1874).[21] Conjectures written in the so-called *schedae Etonenses* can be found in Wyse (1904: lvi–lvii).[22]

Efforts to base the text on a recension of manuscripts began with Bekker, but the text could not be established on scientific principles until, as we noted above, Maetzner had brought Oxford N into parity with the family of the Crippsianus. The ensuing century saw the emergence of a text of greater linguistic polish, as a conception of good Attic oratorical style became established. Cobet, G. A. Hirschig, and van Herwerden led the way towards its restoration, and Blass promoted sensitivity to hiatus and prose rhythm. By the mid-twentieth century, however, currents shifted as the circularity of such an approach to criticism of early prose stylists became apparent. Ten Berge, Barigazzi and Decleva Caizzi for Antiphon, and MacDowell and Albini for Andocides, stood out as defenders of the manuscript tradition when it transmits readings that are intelligible and congruent with the author's habits. As the twentieth century ended, Gagarin and Edwards had brought the text of both authors to a mean between hyper-regularization, with its risk of 'improving' the author, and excessive trust in the accuracy of copyists.

III. PRINCIPLES OF THIS EDITION

This edition adheres more closely to the manuscripts than do those of Blass/Thalheim/Fuhr and the Budé editors. We share the conviction, described above, that it begs the question to form a notion of proper Attic oratorical diction from fourth-century authors and then to emend these two earlier writers in line with that notion. What is more, throughout and even within their works, Antiphon

[21] On Muret as the source of the marginalia copied by Rosenberg, cf. Lipsius 1888: xviii.

[22] Jernstedt (cf. 1880: lxiii) memorialized emendations of August Nauck, and Blass (cf. 1880: vii, 1881: xxvii), emendations of Andreas Weidner and Friedrich Leo.

and Andocides do not maintain consistency of linguistic forms or factual claims. Ionic influence is visible in Antiphon, especially in the Tetralogies, and he ennobles his style through poetical, old-fashioned, or inventive elements.[23] Although Andocides' sentence structure on the whole aspires to greater simplicity, he too makes use of poetical phrasing, archaisms, periphrases, and various stylistic figures.[24] Still, Andocides will indulge in laboured sentence structure, and he is not consistent in word usage or syntax.[25] In general, as long as our manuscripts present an intelligible reading that is not obviously ungrammatical, we retain it. We apply this principle both to linguistic matters and to matters of content, including historical references, for our authors need not always have written what was fact, and to emend out historical difficulties can rest on question-begging assumptions. By the same token, we admit odd-sounding claims in narrative in the manuscripts if they could be true: e.g. that the stepmother enquired about the concubine (*ταύτην ... πυθομένη*, Ant. 1.14) before making a friend of her, or that the wife, after attempting to hang herself, 'was put to bed' (And. 1.125), or that 'others' can be contrasted to 'gods' (And. 1.139). I am slow to emend grammatical outliers for which there is nevertheless evidence in contemporary Greek. For example, I do not emend certain present-stem forms of *φεύγω* to aorist.[26] I follow the manuscripts against most editors in admitting potential and contrary-to-fact constructions without *ἄν*: (1) when *ἄν*'s influence extends from earlier in the discourse (Ant. 5.45, 6.19, And. 1.67); (2) with an impersonal subject (Ant. 1.25, 2.*β*.6); (3) in a direct

[23] Cf. v. Herwerden 1881: 203–4; Rosenthal 1894 *passim*; Gagarin 1997: 25–34.

[24] Cf. e.g. *ἐπίτριπτον κίναδος*, 1.99, with S. Aj. 103, or *οἴχεται πρόρριζον* [sc. *γένος*], 1.146, with S. El. 765. On poetical elements in Andocides, cf. Albini 1961: 29–30, Albini 1964[a] : 28.

[25] 'Andocide è, stilisticamente, capriccioso', Albini 1961: 72. Cf. MacDowell 1962: 19–23; Edwards 1995: 4–6.

[26] Cf. Schoell 1896: 547 n. 5; Redfield 1964: 286.

question ([And.] 4.36; cf. Hermann 1831: 158–9); (4) in an oblique construction ([And.] 4.38; cf. Stahl 1907: 664); (5) when the author may be aiming at a poetic effect ([And.] 4.36, cf. Dover 1962: 36).[27] Moreover, one should not insert ἄν with past indicatives that are not contrary-to-fact (Ant. 2.β.6, 3.β.4, 4.β.2, 6.48). We accept rare words such as εὐρόπως, Ant. 5.76 (*pace* Diggle 1994), or ἐπιπροστίθημι, Ant. 6.17, or middle voice ἀποφαίνοιτο, Ant. 6.30.

Like subsequent editors, we do not follow Blass (1906) in emending ὦ Ἀθηναῖοι in Andocides to ὦ <ἄνδρες> Ἀθηναῖοι. ἄνδρες does seem to have fallen out in Aeschines and Demosthenes when compendia were misread by copyists (cf. Dilts 1997: xix–xx). We do not know that this apostrophe was written *in compendio* in now lost manuscripts of Andocides, however, and ὦ Ἀθηναῖοι prevails in Herodotus, Thucydides, Lycurgus, and Dinarchus.

Some manuscript readings, nevertheless, though intelligible, assault informed judgement: e.g. δειχθῆναι of persons with no further predicate (Ant. 2.α.1, *pace* recent editors); 'my father' at Ant. 5.77, an apparent gloss; ἐδεδοίκει construed as 'was made the object of threats' ([And.] 4.17, *pace* Meier); violent asyndeton at [And.] 4.16 (*pace* Albini). In line with inscriptions, I omit τῶν in expressions like ὁ δῆμος ὁ [τῶν] Ἀθηναίων.[28]

Jernstedt, Blass, and Lipsius systematically corrected the spelling of the manuscripts by drawing on Attic inscriptions, ancient grammarians, and other authors. In inscriptions, however, we encounter a range of forms, sometimes on the same stone, and we have no independent evidence that Antiphon or Andocides spelled consistently.[29] Because Antiphon's *Tetralogies* show Ionic influence, I accept

[27] On omission of ἄν generally, see Frohberger 1863, Gagarin 1997: 27–8, Gerö 2001: 192–3, Murphy 2007: 216–17, 224, 230–1. On οὐκ ἔστιν ὅστις/ὅπως without ἄν, cf. Fraenkel 1950: 310, Barrett 1964: 379–80.

[28] Cf. Müller 1905 and Albini on And. 3.2 and 3.31.

[29] Therefore I follow MS A in δωρειᾷ at And. 1.4 (δωρειά sic A) but δωρεάς at 2.23.

non-Attic forms such as εὗρε.[30] In Antiphon's courtroom speeches and in Andocides, I accept manuscript forms that are not pure Attic when evidence shows that they were in use within a generation of the author, for the spoken language displayed oscillations.[31] Attic inscriptions from late fifth century to early fourth attest accusative first declension masculine names in both η and ην.[32] Likewise, the manuscripts' 1st pers. sing. verb form ἦν is attested in inscriptions (Threatte ii. 587–8). For 1st pers. sing. ᾔδειν, cf. Ar. *V.* 558, 636, *Pax* 1182, Isaeus 9.19 (ed. Roussel), and eight times in Lysias (ed. Carey). Evidence for second pers. sing. βούλῃ over βούλει is good enough that I employ the former as a convention.[33] I adopt the spelling Διπολίεια of the festival (Ant. 2.δ.8, 6.39).[34] Although it is attested in inscriptions, I draw the line, however, at A's τεσσαράκονθ' at And. 3.33, for that speech has 17 instances of -ττ.[35] In the text, I follow present-day conventions for γιγν- forms, accents, breathing marks, nu-moveable, iota subscript, capitalization, and most punctuation. When recording variants in the critical apparatus, however, I report what the copyists wrote. We do not record all trivial manuscript errors or corrections.

In addition to those acknowledged above, other scholars also provided us assistance and advice during the preparation of this volume. We wish to express our gratitude to Angelos Chaniotis,

30 Cf. Decleva Caizzi 1969: 88. On Attic aorists augmented in ηυ-, cf. Mastronarde 1989.

31 Rosenkranz 1930: 148, 152.

32 Threatte ii.173–6. On MS A's Διογένην with Ἀριστομένη at And. 1.13, cf. MacDowell 1962 ad loc., Cominis 1965: 64–5.

33 Kühner-Blass ii. 60, Meisterhans 1900: 165, Threatte ii. 451–2. Because we do not know the date of [And.] 4, I allow λειτουργιῶν to stand at 4.42.

34 Wackernagel 1890, Meisterhans 1900: 55. For uncontracted 'Peiraeus' (And. 1.81) in the 4th c., cf. Meisterhans 1900: 142, Threatte ii. 248–50.

35 In Antiphon, however, we retain the MSS' nine instances of -ττ. On -σσ | -ττ cf. Rosenkranz 1930: 143–5. For Μολοττίαν ([And.] 4.41), cf. Meisterhans 1900: 101, Threatte I. 539–40.

Pietro Cobetto Ghiggia, John Gordan, Edward M. Harris, Leofranc Holford-Strevens, Livio Rossetti, Gerardo Ramírez Vidal, Jordi Redondo Sànchez, and for his help with many aspects of this project, Nigel G. Wilson.

D. J. Murphy
New York

CONSPECTUS EDITIONUM POTIORUM

Albini, U., *Andocide: De Reditu. Introduzione e commento* (Florence, 1961).

Albini, U., *Andocide: De Pace. Introduzione e commento* (Florence, 1964[a]).

Baiter, J. G., and Sauppe, H. (= Turicenses), *Oratores attici*, 2 vols. (Zurich, 1838–43; Zurich, 1850[2]).

Barigazzi, A., *Antifonte: Prima orazione* (Florence, 1955[a]).

Barigazzi, A., *Antifonte: Sesta orazione* (Florence, 1955[b]).

Bekker, E., *Oratores attici* (Oxford, 1822–3, repr. Berlin, 1824; Ant. and And. in vol. i).

Berge, H. M. ten, *Antiphon's zesde rede* (Nijmegen, 1948).

Blass, F., *Andocidis Orationes* (Leipzig, 1871[a]; Leipzig[2], 1880, Leipzig[3], 1906).

Blass, F., *Antiphontis Orationes et Fragmenta* (Leipzig, 1871[b]; Leipzig[2], 1881; Leipzig[3], 1892).

Cobetto Ghiggia, P., *[Andocide:] Contro Alcibiade* (Pisa, 1995).

Dalmeyda, G., *Andocide: Discours* (Paris, 1930, repr.).

Decleva Caizzi, F., *Antiphontis Tetralogiae* (Milan, 1969).

Dobson, W. S., *Oratores Attici et quos sic vocant Sophistae*, 16 vols. (London, 1828; Ant. and And. in vol. i).

Edwards, M., *Andocides* (Warminster, 1995).

Edwards, M., and Usher, S., *Antiphon and Lysias* (Warminster, 1985).

Ferrante, D. *Antifonte. Περὶ του Ἡρώδου Φόνου. Introduzione, testo, traduzione e commentario* (Naples, 1972).

Fuhr = Blass, F., and Fuhr, C., *Andocidis Orationes* (Leipzig, 1913, repr. Stuttgart, 1966).

Gagarin, M., *Antiphon: The Speeches* (Cambridge, 1997).

Gernet, L., *Antiphon; Discours, suivis des fragments d' Antiphon le Sophiste* (Paris, 1923, repr.).

Herwerden, H. van, *Antiphontis Orationes tres scholarum praesertim in usum* (Frankfurt, 1883).

Hickie, W. J., *Andocides: De Mysteriis* (London, 1885).

Jebb, R. C., *Selections from the Attic Orators* (London[2], 1888).

Jernstedt, V., *Antiphontis Orationes* (St Petersburg, 1880).

Lipsius, J. H., *Andocidis Orationes* (Leipzig, 1888).

MacDowell, D., *Andokides: On the Mysteries* (Oxford, 1962).
Maetzner, E., *Antiphontis Orationes XV* (Berlin, 1838).
Maidment, K. J., *Minor Attic Orators, i: Antiphon Andocides* (Cambridge, MA, and London, 1941, repr.).
Makkink, A., *Andokides' Eerste Rede* (Amsterdam, 1932).
Manutius, A., *Orationes horum rhetorum ...* (Venice, 1513).
Marchant, E. C., *Andocides, de Mysteriis and de Reditu* (London, 1889).
Redondo i Sànchez[1], J., *Antifont de Ramnunt. Discursos ...*, 2 vols. (Barcelona, 2003–4).
Redondo i Sànchez[2], J., *Andòcides. Discursos ...*, 2 vols. (Barcelona, 2006–7).
Reiske, J. J., *Oratorum Graecorum ...* 8 vols. (Leipzig, 1770–5; Antiphon in vol. vii, Andocides in vol. iv).
Schiller, K., *Andocidis orationes quattuor* (Leipzig, 1835).
Stephanus, H. (Henri Estienne), *Oratorum veterum orationes* (Geneva, 1575).
Thalheim = Blass, F., and Thalheim, T., *Antiphontis Orationes et Fragmenta* (Leipzig, 1914, repr. Stuttgart, 1966).
Thiel, J. H., *Antiphons erste Tetralogie* (Groningen, 1932).
Ydén, G. M., *Andocidis Oratio de Pace* (Diss. Uppsala, 1872).

CONSPECTUS STUDIORUM

Albini[1]	U. Albini, 'Andocide I, 27', *Maia*, 9 (1957), 154–6.
Albini[2]	U. Albini, rev. of MacDowell 1962, *Gnomon*, 36 (1964[b]), 452–6.
Albini[3]	U. Albini, 'Andocidea', *SIFC* 42 (1970), 259–61.
Albini[4]	U. Albini, 'Noterelle andocidee', in *Studia Florentina Alexandro Ronconi sexagenario oblata* (Rome, 1970), 17–19.
Albini[5]	U. Albini, 'Postille ad [Andocide] IV (contro Alcibiade)', *Estudios Clásicos*, 20 (1984), 305–9.
Bake	J. Bake, 'Antiphontea et andocidea', in *Scholica hypomnemata*, 5 vols. (Leiden, 1837–52), i. 208–28.
Barigazzi[1]	A. Barigazzi. 'Sopra due orazioni di Antifonte', *Athenaeum*, 32 (1954), 159–200.
Barrett	W. S. Barrett, *Euripides: Hippolytos* (Oxford, 1964).
Bienwald	A. Bienwald, *De Crippsiano et Oxoniensi Antiphontis Dinarchi Lycurgi codicibus* (Diss. Görlitz, 1889).
Boeckh[1]	A. Boeckh, *De Areopago dissertatio altera. Prooemium indicis lectionum hibernarum a. MDCCCXXVIII* (Berlin, 1828; repr. *Gesammelte kleine Schriften*, iv. 308–21).
Boeckh[2]	A. Boeckh, *Die Staathaushaltung der Athener*, 3 vols. (Berlin[2], 1851).
Boekmeijer	R. Boekmeijer, *Adnotationes criticae in oratores atticos* (Diss. Groningen, 1895).
Bohlmann	A. Bohlmann, *Antiphontea* (Diss. Breslau, 1882).
Briegleb	E. Briegleb, *Zur Kritik des Antiphon* (Programm. Anclam, 1861).
Buermann 1882	H. Buermann, 'Zur Textkritik des Isaios', *Hermes*, 17 (1882), 385–400.
Buermann 1885	H. Buermann, 'Handschriftliches zu den kleineren attischen Rednern', *RhM*[2] 40 (1885), 387–400.
Canevaro and Harris 2012	M. Canevaro and E. M. Harris, 'The Documents in Andocides' *On the Mysteries*', *CQ*[2] 62 (2012), 98–129.

Canevaro and Harris 2016	M. Canevaro and E. M. Harris, 'The Authenticity of the Documents at Andocides' *On the Mysteries* 77–79 and 83–84', in *Dike* 19 (2016 [2017]), 7–48).
Canter	W. Canter, *De ratione emendandi graecos auctores, syntagma recens auctum* (Antwerp, 1571).
Cataldi Palau	A. Cataldi Palau, *A Catalogue of Greek Manuscripts from the Meerman Collection in the Bodleian Library* (Oxford, 2011).
Cinquini	A. Cinquini, *Andocidis de codicibus qui in bibliotheca Ambrosiana exstant* (Milan, 1886).
Cobet[1]	C. G. Cobet, 'Variae lectiones. Pars secunda', *Mnemosyne,* 4 (1855), 97–144, 233–80, 293–324.
Cobet[2]	C. G. Cobet, *Novae lectiones quibus continentur observationes criticae* (Leiden, 1858).
Cobet[3]	C. G. Cobet. 'De locis nonnullis apud Antiphontem', *Mnemosyne*[2], 8 (1880), 269–91.
Cominis	N. Cominis, 'Varia Graeca', *Acta Classica*, 8 (1965), 53–62.
Comparetti	D. Comparetti, *Papiri greco-egizi*, ii: *Papiri fiorentini. Papiri letterari ed epistolari* (Milan, 1911).
Darbo-Peschanski	C. Darbo-Peschanski, 'Antiphon: la nature "avec" la loi et "sans" l'intérêt personnel', *Philosophie Antique*, 13 (2013), 173–223.
Denniston	J. D. Denniston, 'Varia. II', *CR* 47 (1933), 213–16.
Diggle	J. Diggle, '*Εὐπόρως ἔχειν* and Antiphon, *De Caede Herodis* 76', *ICS* 14 (1994), 81–2.
Dilts	M. R. Dilts, *Aeschines: Orationes* (Stuttgart and Leipzig, 1997).
Dindorf	W. Dindorf, 'Zur erklärung und kritik der schriftsteller', *Philologus*, 12 (1857), 188–92.
Dobree	P. P. Dobree, *Adversaria critica*, ed. C. Scholefield, 2 vols. (Cambridge, 1831; repr. et emend. ed. W. Wagner, Berlin, 1874).
Dover[1]	K. J. Dover, rev. of Albini 1961, *CR*[2] 12 (1962), 35–6.
Dover[2]	Dover, K. J. 'Due problemi testuali in Antifonte', *Maia*, 21 (1969), 123–5 (repr. in English in *The Greeks and Their Legacy, Collected Papers. II* [Oxford and New York, 1988], 36–7).
Droysen	I. Droysen, *De Demophanti Patroclidis Tisameni Populiscitis* (Diss. Berlin, 1873).
Dryander	A. Dryander, *Commentationis de Antiphontis Rhamnusii vita et scriptis selecta capita* (Halle, 1838).

Elter	A. Elter, 'Zu Andokides Myst. 68', *RhM*[2] 69 (1914), 253–4.
Emperius[1]	A. Emperius, rev. of Schiller 1835, in *Opuscula philologica et historica*, ed. F. G. Schneidewin (Göttingen, 1847), 205–15.
Emperius[2]	A. Emperius, rev. of H. Sauppe, *Epistula critica ad Godofredum Hermannum*, in *Opuscula philologica et historica*, ed. F. G. Schneidewin (Göttingen, 1847), 269–85.
Emperius[3]	A. Emperius, 'Adversaria in oratores Atticos. (Ed. I. Bekk.)', in *Opuscula philologica et historica*, ed. F. G. Schneidewin (Göttingen, 1847), 312–18.
Fraenkel	E. Fraenkel, *Aeschylus: Agamemnon*, 3 vols. (Oxford, 1950).
Francke	W. Francke, *De Andocidis oratione quae est de pace* (Diss. Halle, 1876).
Franke	F. Franke, rev. of Maetzner 1838, *N. Jbb. Phil. Päd.* 28 (1840), 52–83.
Frohberger[1]	H. Frohberger, 'Über die Unterordnung mehrerer Verba unter ein ἀπὸ κοινοῦ stehendes ἄν', *Philologus*, 19 (1863), 599–613.
Frohberger[2]	H. Frohberger, 'Annotationes ad oratores Atticos', *Philologus*, 29 (1870), 621–35.
Fuhr[1]	K. Fuhr, *Animadversiones in oratores atticos* (Diss. Bonn, 1877).
Fuhr[2]	K. Fuhr, 'Excurse zu den attischen Rednern', *RhM*[2] 33 (1878), 565–99.
Fuhr[3]	K. Fuhr, rev. of Blass, Andocides[3], *Berl. Philol. Wochenschr.* 27 (1907), 257–61.
Funkhänel	K H. Funkhänel, 'Zu Antiphon', *N. Jbb. Phil. Päd.* 79 (1859), 194–8.
Gagarin	M. Gagarin, *Antiphon the Athenian: Oratory, Law and Justice in the Age of the Sophists* (Austin, 2002).
Gebauer[1]	G. Gebauer, *De praeteritionis formis apud oratores atticos* (Leipzig, 1874).
Gebauer[2]	G. Gebauer, *De hypotacticis et paratacticis argumenti ex contrario formis quae reperiuntur apud oratores Atticos* (Zwickau, 1877).
Gebauer[3]	*G. Gebauer, Ausgewählte Reden des Lysias* (Leipzig, 1880).
Gerö	Gerö, E.-C. '"Irrealis" and Past Tense in Ancient Greek', *Glotta*, 77 (2001), 178–97.
Graffunder	P. Graffunder, *De Crippsiano et Oxoniensi Antiphontis Dinarchi Lycurgi codicibus* (Diss. Berlin, 1882).

Gribble	D. Gribble, 'Rhetoric and History in [Andocides] 4', *CQ*[2] 47 (1997), 367–91.
Hagedorn	D. Hagedorn, 'Antiphon, Tetralogie A *β*, 5–6', in M. Grunewald, .K. Maresch, and W. Schäfer (eds.), *Kölner Papyri (P. Köln)*, v (Papyrologica Coloniensia, 7; Opladen, 1985), no. 213, Inv. 910r, 68–72.
Halbertsma	T. Halbertsma, *Adversaria critica*, ed. H. van Herwerden (Leiden, 1896).
Hansen 2015	M. H. Hansen, 'Is Patrokleides' Decree (Andoc. 1.7–79) a Genuine Document?', *GRBS* 55 (2015), 884–901.
Hansen 2016	M. H. Hansen, 'Is Teisamenos' Decree (Andoc. 1.83–84) a Genuine Document?', *GRBS* 56 (2016), 34–48.
Harris 2000	E. M. Harris, 'The Authenticity of Andokides' *De Pace*. A Subversive Essay', in P. Flensted-Jensen, T. H. Nielsen, and L. Rubenstein (eds.), *Polis & Politics: Studies in Ancient Greek History Presented to Mogens Herman Hansen on his Sixtieth Birthday, August 20, 2000* (Copenhagen, 2000), 479–505.
Harris 2014	E. M. Harris, 'The Authenticity of the Document at Andocides *on the Mysteries* 96–98', *Τεκμήρια*, 12 (2014), 121–52.
Harris 2016	E. M. Harris, 'Alcibiades, the Ancestors, Liturgies, and the Etiquette of Addressing the Athenian Assembly', in V. Litsotakis and S. Farrington (eds.), *The Art of History. Literary Perspectives on Greek and Roman Historiography* (Berlin and Boston, 2016), 145–55.
Hatch	W. Hatch, 'The Use of *ΑΛΙΤΗΡΙΟΣ*, *ΑΛΙΤΡΟΣ*, *ΕΝΑΓΗΣ*, *ΕΝΘΥΜΙΟΣ*, *ΠΑΛΑΜΝΑΙΟΣ*, and *ΠΡΟΣΤΡΟΠΑΙΟΣ*: A Study in Greek Lexicography', *HSCP* 19 (1908), 157–86.
Helbig	W. Helbig, 'Zu Andokides', *N. Jhb. Phil. Päd.* 85 (1862), 679–80.
Hermann	G. Hermann, *De particula ἄν libri iv* (Leipzig, 1831).
Hertlein[1]	F. Hertlein, *Observationes criticae in Xenophontis Historiam Graecam: Particula III* (Wertheim, 1845).
Hertlein[2]	F. Hertlein, 'Zu griechischen Prosaikern', *Hermes*, 12 (1877), 182–8.
Herwerden[1]	H. van Herwerden, 'Antiphontea', *Mnemosyne*[2], 9 (1881), 201–9.

Hirschig[1]	G. A. Hirschig in R. B. and G. A. Hirschig, 'Coniectanea critica (in Aristoph. *Plutum*, Xenophontis *Anabasin*, oratores atticos, Plutarchi *Moralia*)', *Philologus*, 5 (1850), 276–358.
Hirschig[2]	G. A. Hirschig, 'Selectae emendationes et observationes in Antiphontem', *Philologus*, 9 (1854), 728–39.
Hüttner	G. Hüttner, 'Bericht über die auf die attischen Redner bezüglichen literarischen Erscheinungen der Jahre 1882–1885', *(Bursians) Jhbr. kl. Alt.* 46 (1886), 153.
Ignatius	F. Ignatius, *De Antiphontis Rhamnusii elocutione commentatio* (Berlin, 1882).
Jernstedt[1]	V. Jernstedt, *Observationes Antiphonteae* (St Petersburg, 1878).
Kayser[1]	L. Kayser, 'Antiphons Tetralogien', *RhM*[2] 12 (1857), 224–40.
Kayser[2]	L. Kayser, 'Beiträge zur Kritik des Antiphons, Andokides und Anaximenes', *RhM*[2] 16 (1861), 62–81.
Keil	B. Keil, 'Athens Amtsjahre und Kalendarjahre im V. Jahrhundert', *Hermes*, 29 (1894), 32–81.
Kirchhoff	A. Kirchhoff, 'Ueber eine Urkunde der Poleten von Ol. 91, 3', *N. Jhb. Phil. Päd.* 81 (1860), 238–55.
Kirchner	J. Kirchner, 'Beiträge zur attischen Prosopographie', *Hermes*, 31 (1896), 254–63.
Klotz[1]	R. Klotz, *Quaestiones criticae: Liber primus* (Leipzig, 1831).
Klotz[2]	R. Klotz, rev. of Sluiter 1834 and Schiller 1835, *N. Jhb. Phil. Päd.* 13 (1835), 371–98.
Koepke	R. Koepke, *Emendationes andocideae* (Guben, 1869).
Lamberz	E. Lamberz, 'Johannes Kantakuzenos und die Produktion von Luxushandschriften in Konstantinopel in der frühen Palaiologenzeit', in B. Atsalos and N. Tsironi (eds.), *Actes du VIe colloque internationale de paléographie grecque (Drama, 21–27 septembre 2003)* (Athens, 2008), i. 133–57 and iii. 981–1005 (plates).
Linder	K. W. Linder, *De rerum dispositione apud Antiphontem et Andocidem* (Uppsala, 1859).
Lipsius[1]	J. H. Lipsius, 'Über Antiphons Tetralogien', *Sitzb. Sächs. Akad. Leipzig*, 56 (1904), 191–204.
Lundon	J. Lundon, 'Antipho, Tetralogiae *Γ α* 3–4,' *Communicazioni dell'Istituto papirologico 'G. Vitelli'*, 5 (2003), 6–12.
Madvig[1]	J. N. Madvig, *Bemerkungen über einige Punkte der griechischen Wortfügungslehre* (Göttingen, 1848).

Madvig[2]	J. N. Madvig, *Adversaria critica ad scriptores graecos et latinos*, 3 vols. (Copenhagen, 1871–84).
Mastronarde	D. Mastronarde, 'Lautensach's Law and the Augment of Compound-Verbs in *ΕΥ*', *Glotta*, 67 (1989), 101–5.
Meier	M. Meier, *Commentationes quatuor de Andocidis quae vulgo fertur oratione contra Alcibiadem* (Halle, 1836–7, repr. in *Opuscula academica*, 2 vols. ed. F. A. Eckstein and F. Haase, Halle, 1861, i. 74–343 [deest *Comment. tertia*]).
Meisterhans	K. Meisterhans, *Grammatik der attischen Inschriften*, ed. E. Schwyzer. (Berlin[3], 1900).
Meurs, v.	J. van Meurs, *Athenae Atticae. Sive, De praecipuis Athenarum Antiquitatibus* (Leiden, 1624).
Mitford	W. Mitford, *The History of Greece*, 5 vols. (London, 1784–1810, repr.).
Müller	R. Müller, 'De attributo titulorum saeculi V. Atticorum observationes quaedam', *Philologus*, 18 (1905), 554–66.
Murphy 2007	D. J. Murphy, 'Critical Notes on Plato's *Charmides*', *Mnemosyne*, 60 (2007), 213–34.
Murphy forthcoming	D. J. Murphy, 'Socrates in Early Fourth-Century Rhetoric: Polycrates, Isocrates, Lysias and Pseudo-Andocides', in C. Moore (ed.), Brill's *Companion to the Reception of Socrates* (Leiden, forthcoming).
Naber[1]	S. A. Naber, *De fide Andocidis orationis de mysteriis* (Diss. Leiden, 1850).
Naber[2]	S. A. Naber, 'Adnotationes criticae ad Antiphontis Aeschinis Hyperidis Dinarchi orationes', *Mnemosyne*[2], 33 (1905), 157–85.
Naber[3]	S. A. Naber, 'Adnotationes criticae ad Andocidis orationes', *Mnemosyne* [2], 33 (1905), 269–92.
Osann	F. Osann, 'Lectiones andocideae', in *Miscellanea maximam partem critica*, ed. F. Friedemann and J. D. Seebode, 2 vols. (Hildesheim, 1822), i. 702–5.
Packman	Z. Packman, 'Andocides, On the Mysteries', in K. Maresch and Z. Packman (eds). *Papyri from the Washington University Collection St. Louis, Missouri. Part II. (P.Wash.Univ. II)* (Papyrologica Coloniensia, 18; Opladen, 1990), no. 65, Inv. 414, 13–14.
Pahle	F. Pahle, *Die Reden des Antiphon: Eine kritische Untersuchung* (Jever, 1860).
Paoli	U. E. Paoli, *Studi di diritto attico* (Florence, 1930).

Pendrick	G. M. Pendrick, *Antiphon the Sophist: The Fragments* (Cambridge, 2002).
Pertz	A. Pertz, *Quaestionum Lysiacarum caput primum* (Clausthal, 1857).
Petit	S. Petit, *Leges Atticae* (Paris, 1635).
Phabés	B. Phabés, '*Διορθωτικὰ καὶ ἑρμηνευτικά*', *Athêna*, 48 (1938), 184–98.
Pierson	J. Pierson, *Moeridis Atticistae Lexicon Atticum* (Leiden, 1759)
Prato	G. Prato, 'I manoscritti greci dei secoli XIII e XIV: Note paleografiche', in D. Harlfinger and G. Prato. (eds.), *Paleografia e codicologia greca. Atti del II Colloquio internazionale (Berlino-Wolfenbüttel, 17–21 ottobre 1983)* (Alessandria, 1991), i. 131–49 and pls. 1*a*–16*b*.
Radermacher	L. Radermacher, 'Andocideum', *RhM*[2] 56 (1901), 139–41.
Redfield	J. Redfield, rev. of MacDowell 1962, *CP* 59 (1964), 286–8.
Richards[1]	H. Richards, 'Notes on the Attic Orators, (continued)', *CR* 20 (1906), 292–301.
Richards[2]	H. Richards, *Aristophanes and Others* (London, 1909).
Richards[3]	H. Richards, 'Notes on Greek Orators', *CR* 29 (1915), 100–4.
Röhl	H. Röhl, *Zu griechischen Texten. Jahresbericht des Domgymnasiums zu Halberstadt* (Nr. 275) (Halberstadt, 1903).
Rosenberg[1]	E. Rosenberg, 'Altes und Neues zur Kritik des Isäos, Andokides und Lykurgos', *N. Jbb. Phil. Päd.* 109 (1874), 333–44.
Rosenberg[2]	E. Rosenberg, 'Zu Antiphon', *N. Jbb. Phil. Päd.* 111 (1875), 604.
Rosenkranz	B. Rosenkranz, 'Der lokale Grundton und die persönliche Eigenart in der Sprache des Thukydides und der älteren attischen Redner', *IF* 48 (1930), 127–79.
Rosenthal	W. Rosenthal, *De Antiphontis in particularum usu proprietate* (Berlin, 1894).
Rubino	M. Rubino, 'Una nota testuale ad Antipho V 76', *Sileno*, 8 (1982), 55–6.
Sakorraphus	G. M. Sakorraphus, 'Specilegium observationum criticarum ad scriptores graecos', *Mnemosyne*[2], 20 (1892), 301–10.

Sauppe[1]	H. Sauppe, 'Quaestiones antiphonteae', *Index Scholarum publice et privatim in Academia Georgia Augusta … habendarum* (Göttingen, summer 1861).
Sauppe[2]	H. Sauppe, 'Symbolae ad emendandos oratores atticos', *Index Scholarum …* (Göttingen, winter 1874, repr. in *Hermann Sauppes Ausgewählte Schriften*, ed. C. Trieber, Berlin, 1896, 673–85).
Sauppe[3]	H. Sauppe, 'Quaestiones criticae', *Index Scholarum …* (Göttingen, winter 1886, repr. in *Hermann Sauppes Ausgewählte Schriften*, ed. C. Trieber, Berlin, 1896, 782–803).
Schaefer	H. Schaefer, *De nonnullarum particularum apud Antiphontem usu* (Diss. Göttingen, 1877).
Scheibe	K. Scheibe, 'Coniecturae in Antiphontis orationes et quaedam Lysiae fragmenta', *Acta Soc. Graecae*, 2 (1840), 85–98.
Schneider	J. G. Schneider, *Xenophontis de Cyri Disciplina* (Leipzig, 1800; Leipzig[2], 1815).
Schoell[1]	R. Schoell, rev. of Blass 1871*b*, *Jhb. Phil.* 103 (1871), 297–309.
Schoell[2]	R. and F. Schoell, 'Zu Andokides' Mysterienrede', *Jahrb. kl. Philol.* 42 (1896), 545–52.
Schömann[1]	G. F. Schömann, *De comitiis Atheniensium libri tres* (Greifswald, 1819).
Schömann[2]	G. F. Schömann, rev. of Maetzner 1838, *Jhr. f. wissensch. Kritik*, 16/2 (1839), cols. 481–96.
Sluiter	I. O. Sluiter, *Lectiones andocideae* (Leiden, 1804, repr. Leipzig, 1834, with notes by K. Schiller).
Sommerstein	A. Sommerstein, 'The Authenticity of the Demophantus Decree', *CQ*[2] 64 (2014), 49–57.
Spengel[1]	L. Spengel, rev. of Maetzner 1838 and Baiter and Sauppe, *Antiphon* (Zurich, 1838), *Münch. gelehrter Anzeiger*, 7 (1838), cols. 345–52, 368.
Spengel[2]	L. Spengel, 'Ueber die dritte philippische Rede des Demosthenes', *Abhdl. Bayer. Akad.* 3 (1840), 155–206.
Spengel[3]	L. Spengel, 'Antiphon', *RhM* [2] 17 (1862), 161–9.
Stahl	J. Stahl, *Kritisch-historische Syntax des griechischen Verbums der klassischen Zeit* (Heidelberg, 1907).
Sykutris	J. Sykutris, '*Κριτικὰ εἰς Ἀντιφῶντα*', *EEAth* 1 (1925), 109–45.
Thalheim 1886	T. Thalheim, *De Dinarchi codicibus commentatio* (Breslau, 1886).

Thompson — W. Thompson, 'Notes on Andocides', *Acta Classica*, 13 (1970), 141–8.

Threatte — L. Threatte, *The Grammar of Attic Inscriptions*, 2 vols. (Berlin and New York, 1980–96).

Vollgraff — W. Vollgraff, 'Observations sur le sixième discours d'Antiphon', *Mnemosyne*[4], 1 (1948), 257–70 (= *Kleine Schriften* [Göttingen, 1955], ii. 1202–4).

Wackernagel 1890 — J. Wackernagel, 'Dipolia', *RhM*[2] 45 (1890), 480–2 (= *Kleine Schriften* [Göttingen, 1955], ii. 1202–4).

Wackernagel 1907 — J. Wackernagel, 'Hellenistica', *Programm zur akademischen Preisverteilung* (Göttingen, 1907), 3–27 (= *Kleine Schriften* [Göttingen, 1955], ii. 1034–58).

Weil — H. Weil, 'Antiphon, *Meurtre d'Hérode*, §§ 29, 5 et 49', *RPh*[2] 4 (1880), 150.

Wilamowitz[1] — U. von Wilamowitz-Moellendorff, 'Commentariolum grammaticum IV', *Index Scholarum* … (Göttingen, winter 1890), 3–28 (repr. in *Kleine Schriften, IV: Lesefrüchte und Verwandtes*, Berlin, 1962, 660–96).

Wilamowitz[2] — U. von Wilamowitz-Moellendorff, 'Die sechste Rede des Antiphon', *Sitzb. Akad. Berlin* (1900), i. 398–416 (repr. in *Kleine Schriften, III: Griechische Prosa*, Berlin, 1969, 196–217).

Wilamowitz[3] — U. von Wilamowitz-Moellendorff, 'Lesefrüchte', *Hermes*, 44 (1909), 445–6 (repr. in *Kleine Schriften, IV: Lesefrüchte und Verwandtes*, Berlin, 1962, 224–53).

Wilhelm — A. Wilhelm, 'Vermuthungen', *Philologus*[2], 14 (1901), 481–90.

Wyse — W. Wyse, *The Speeches of Isaeus with Critical and Explanatory Notes* (Cambridge, 1904).

SIGLA

A	British Library Burney 95, saec. XIV^1
A^1	librarius primus opus suum corrigens
A^2	corrector atramento clariore utens (cfr. Praef. pp. viii–ix)
A^3	corrector graphide utens (cfr. Praef. p. ix)
N	Oxoniensis Bodleianus Auctarium T.2.4, saec. XIV
N^1	librarius primus opus suum corrigens
N^2	quilibet corrector huius libri (cfr. Praef. p. ix)
B	Florentinus Laurentianus plut. 11.4, saec. XV^4
L	Venetus Marcianus appendix classis VIII.6, saec. XV^{ex}
M	British Library Burney 96, inter annos 1492–6 exaratus
Z	Vratislaviensis olim bibliothecae Magdalenae, nunc bibl. uniuersitatis Magdal. 1069, saec. XV^{ex}
P	Ambrosianus A 99 sup., saec. XV^{ex}
PKöln	P. Köln 5.213. saec. II
PSI	PSI inv. 320r. saec. II ex.–III in.
PFlor	P. Flor. II 112, fr. C col. II, saec. II
Ald.	Editio princeps in aedibus Aldi Manutii Venetiis, anno 1513 cura Marci Musuri
Steph.	Editio oratorum veterum orationum Henrici Stephani Genavae, anno 1575
Sched. Eton.	Schedae Etonenses apud Wysium 1904
Turr.	Editores Turicenses, sc. Baiter et Sauppe

Notae

X^a	prima manus ante correctionem
X^1	prima manus opus suum corrigens
X^c	post correctionem, quis correxerit non liquet
^{sv}	supra versum
^{im}	in margine
^{it}	in textu
stp	sine titulo protulit/-erunt
*	littera erasa

SIGLA

<. . .>	lacuna ab aliquo docto indicata
{ }	verba deleta
< >	verba addita

ΑΝΤΙΦΩΝΤΟΣ
ΛΟΓΟΙ

ΓΕΝΟΣ ΑΝΤΙΦΩΝΤΟΣ

Ἀντιφῶν υἱὸς μὲν ἦν Σοφίλου, φυλῆς δ' Αἰαντίδος, 1
Ῥαμνούσιος τὸν δῆμον. κατὰ δὲ τὰ Περσικὰ γενόμενος 2
συνήκμασε Γοργίᾳ τῷ σοφιστῇ. καὶ διδασκάλῳ τὰ 3
πρῶτα χρησάμενος τῷ πατρὶ διδάσκοντι γράμματα, τῆς
ἡλικίας προβαινούσης τὰ περὶ τοὺς λόγους ἐξεπόνησε·
φυσικῇ ⟨δὲ⟩ δεινότητι τὴν ἐκ τῆς ἀσκήσεως μελέτην 4
προσλαβών, μηδενὸς μὲν ἀκροασάμενος, ὅτι μηδὲ ἦν πώ
τις τότε μήτε λόγων μήτε τεχνῶν ῥητορικῶν συγγραφεὺς
μήτε σοφιστὴς προεστηκὼς διατριβῆς, τοῖς ⟨τῶν⟩ πρὸ
αὐτοῦ δὲ ἐντυχὼν βιβλίοις καὶ τοῖς τῶν ποιητῶν
μάλιστα, εἰς τοσοῦτον προῆλθε δεινότητος, ὥστε
Νέστωρ ἐπεκαλεῖτο διὰ τὴν ἐν τῷ λέγειν ἡδονήν. τοῦ 5
πολιτεύεσθαι δὲ ἀποστὰς νέος ὢν ἐν Κορίνθῳ παρὰ τὴν
ἀγορὰν οἴκημα εἰς ὑποδοχὴν ἀκροατῶν ποιήσας καὶ
ἔξωθεν ἐπιγράψας ὅτι τοὺς λυπουμένους παραμυθεῖται,
εἶτα φιλοχρήματος ὢν καὶ οὐ πολλὰ ἐκ τούτου κερδαίνων 6
τραγῳδίας ἐποίει. ἀποστὰς δὲ καὶ τούτων ἐπὶ ῥητορικὴν 7
ἐτράπετο, καὶ συστησάμενος ἐν Ἀθήναις διατριβὴν
Σωκράτει περὶ τῶν ἐλεγκτικῶν διεφέρετο. πολλοὺς 8
δὲ παιδεύσας ἐπαίδευσε καὶ Θουκυδίδην. ἐν δὲ τῷ 9
Πελοποννησιακῷ πολέμῳ πολλὰ δυνηθεὶς μετέβαλε τὴν
δημοκρατίαν καὶ ἐποίησε τοὺς τετρακοσίους μετὰ τῶν

Tit. AN 1 ἦν A[1] N : om. A[a] 6 add. Sauppe 7 μηδὲ Reiske : μὴ δὲ AN : μηδ' Blass 8 τότε N : om. A 9 add. Blass 12 ἐπεκαλεῖτο N : ἐκαλεῖτο A 14 ὑποδοχὴν N : ἀποδοχὴν A 15 post παραμυθεῖται vac. spat. 3 litt. A : lacunam statuit Blass[2] 17 καὶ A[1sv]N : om. A[a] 21 πελοποννησιακῷ N : πελοπονησιακῶ A 22 τετρακοσίους sic AN

περὶ Ἀρχεπτόλεμον. εἰσαγγελθεὶς δὲ ἑάλω καὶ τοῖς τῶν
10 προδοτῶν ὑπαχθεὶς ἐπιτιμίοις ἄταφος ἐρρίφη. φασὶ δέ
⟨τινες⟩ ἐν Σικελίᾳ αὐτὸν τελευτῆσαι παρὰ Διονυσίου· ἤδη
γὰρ πρεσβύτης ὢν καὶ πρὸς αὐτὸν ἀφικόμενος ἔσκωπτεν
αὐτοῦ τοῦ Διονυσίου τὰς τραγῳδίας, καὶ διὰ τοῦτο,
11 φασίν, ἀχθεσθεὶς ἀπέκτεινεν αὐτόν. ἄλλοι δὲ λέγουσιν
ὅτι οὐ διὰ τοῦτο, ἀλλ' ὑπωπτεύθη, φασί, καταλῦσαι
θέλων τὴν τυραννίδα. ἐρωτηθέντα γάρ φασιν αὐτὸν παρὰ
τοῦ Διονυσίου, ποῖος αὐτῷ χαλκὸς ἀρέσκει, εἰπεῖν, ὅθεν
ἐγένοντο Ἁρμόδιος καὶ Ἀριστογείτων.

23 ἀρχεπτόλεμον AN : ἀρχϊπτόλεμον N^2 25 τινες Ald. : deest in AN 28 φασὶν AN^2 : φησὶν N 29 ὑπωπτεύθη A : ὑποπτεύθη N φασὶ AN^2 : φησι N 30 φασιν AN^2: φησὶν N 31 διονυσίου A^{1}N : διονύσου A^a

1

ΦΑΡΜΑΚΕΙΑΣ ΚΑΤΑ ΤΗΣ ΜΗΤΡΥΙΑΣ

ΥΠΟΘΕΣΙΣ

Φιλόνεώς τις, ἔχων παλλακήν τινα, φίλος ἦν τοῦ πατρὸς τοῦ λέγοντος τὸν λόγον. οὗτος καταγνοὺς τῆς παλλακῆς εἰς πορνεῖον στήσειν ἠπείλησεν. ὁ δὲ πατὴρ τοῦ λέγοντος τὸν λόγον τελευτησάσης αὐτῷ τῆς γυναικὸς μητρυιὰν τῷ παιδὶ ἐπεισήγαγε. κοινολογησαμένης δὲ ταύτης τῇ παλλακῇ διὰ τὸ γείτονας εἶναι καὶ διὰ τὸ μηδὲ αὐτὴν πάνυ ἀγαπᾶσθαι ὑπὸ τοῦ ἀνδρός, ἔδοξεν ἀμφοτέραις φαρμάκῳ ἀνελεῖν τοὺς ἄνδρας. κατασκευασάμεναι δὲ ἑορτῆς οὔσης καὶ κοινῇ τῶν ἀνδρῶν σπενδομένων—φίλοι γὰρ ἦσαν—δεδώκασιν ἀμφοτέροις τὸ φάρμακον ἐν πώματι. καὶ ὁ μὲν Φιλόνεως πλέον λαβὼν παραχρῆμα ἀνῃρέθη, ὁ δὲ τοῦ λέγοντος τὸν λόγον πατὴρ ἔλαττον λαβὼν εἰς νόσον κατέπεσε, καὶ οὕτω τέθνηκεν ἐξ αὐτῆς. ὁ δὲ παῖς γράφεται τὴν μητρυιὰν φαρμακείας. καὶ ἡ μὲν ὑπόθεσις αὕτη, ἡ στάσις δὲ στοχασμός· σημεῖον δὲ τὸ μὴ θέλειν δοῦναι τοὺς οἰκέτας εἰς βάσανον.

Νέος μὲν καὶ ἄπειρος δικῶν ἔγωγε ἔτι, δεινῶς δὲ καὶ 1
ἀπόρως ἔχει μοι περὶ τοῦ πράγματος, ὦ ἄνδρες, τοῦτο μὲν εἰ ἐπισκήψαντος τοῦ πατρὸς ἐπεξελθεῖν τοῖς αὑτοῦ φονεῦσι μὴ ἐπέξειμι, τοῦτο δὲ εἰ ἐπεξιόντι ἀναγκαίως

tit. φαρμακείας κατὰ τῆς μητρυιᾶς AN Arg. tit. ὑπόθεσις ἀντιφῶντος N : ὑπόθεσις τοῦ ἑξῆς A 1–2 παλλακήν … παλλακῆς A : παλακήν … παλακῆς N 5 κοινολογησαμένης A : κοινωλογησαμένης N 6 διὰ τὸ A : om. N 10 πώματι A : πόματι N : ἐκπώματι A^{2sv} 11 πλέον A^{c}N : πλέονα A^{a} 14 alt. ἡ A : om. N 15 AN subiciunt ἀντιφῶντος· φαρμακείας κατὰ τῆς μητρυιᾶς 16 μὲν A^{1} : μεν N : om. A^{a} 17 ἔχει μοι A^{a}N : ἔχοιμι A^{c} 18 αὑτοῦ Steph. : αὐτοῦ AN

ἔχει οἷς ἥκιστα ἐχρῆν ἐν διαφορᾷ καταστῆναι, ἀδελφοῖς
2 ὁμοπατρίοις καὶ μητρὶ ἀδελφῶν. ἡ γὰρ τύχη καὶ αὐτοὶ
οὗτοι ἠνάγκασαν ἐμοὶ πρὸς τούτους αὐτοὺς τὸν ἀγῶνα
καταστῆναι, οὓς εἰκὸς ἦν τῷ μὲν τεθνεῶτι τιμωροὺς
γενέσθαι, τῷ δὲ ἐπεξιόντι βοηθούς. νῦν δὲ τούτων
τἀναντία γεγένηται· αὐτοὶ γὰρ οὗτοι καθεστᾶσιν ἀντί-
3 δικοι καὶ φονῆς, ὡς καὶ ἐγὼ καὶ ἡ γραφὴ λέγει. δέομαι
δ' ὑμῶν, ὦ ἄνδρες, ἐὰν ἐπιδείξω ἐξ ἐπιβουλῆς καὶ
προβουλῆς τὴν τούτων μητέρα φονέα οὖσαν τοῦ ἡμετέρου
πατρός, καὶ μὴ ἅπαξ ἀλλὰ καὶ πολλάκις ἤδη ληφθεῖσαν
τὸν θάνατον τὸν ἐκείνου ἐπ' αὐτοφώρῳ μηχανωμένην,
τιμωρῆσαι πρῶτον μὲν τοῖς νόμοις τοῖς ὑμετέροις, οὓς
παρὰ τῶν θεῶν καὶ τῶν προγόνων διαδεξάμενοι κατὰ τὸ
αὐτὸ ἐκείνοις περὶ τῆς καταψηφίσεως δικάζετε, δεύτερον
δ' ἐκείνῳ τῷ τεθνηκότι καὶ ἅμα ἐμοὶ μόνῳ ἀπολελειμμένῳ
4 βοηθῆσαι. ὑμεῖς γάρ μοι ἀναγκαῖοι. οὓς γὰρ ἐχρῆν τῷ μὲν
τεθνεῶτι τιμωροὺς γενέσθαι, ἐμοὶ δὲ βοηθούς, οὗτοι τοῦ
μὲν τεθνεῶτος φονῆς γεγένηνται, ἐμοὶ δ' ἀντίδικοι
καθεστᾶσι. πρὸς τίνας οὖν ἔλθῃ τις βοηθούς, ἢ ποῖ τὴν
καταφυγὴν ποιήσεται ἄλλοθι ἢ πρὸς ὑμᾶς καὶ τὸ δίκαιον;
5 Θαυμάζω δ' ἔγωγε καὶ τοῦ ἀδελφοῦ, ἥντινά ποτε
γνώμην ἔχων ἀντίδικος καθέστηκε πρὸς ἐμέ, καὶ
εἰ νομίζει τοῦτο εὐσέβειαν εἶναι, τὸ τὴν μητέρα μὴ
προδοῦναι. ἐγὼ δ' ἡγοῦμαι πολὺ ἀνοσιώτερον εἶναι
ἀφεῖναι τοῦ τεθνεῶτος τὴν τιμωρίαν, ἄλλως τε καὶ τοῦ
μὲν ἐκ προβουλῆς ἀκουσίως ἀποθανόντος, τῆς δὲ

24 τῶ δὲ N : τῶ δ' A   26 φονῆς Jernstedt : φονεῖς AN^{2} (in ras. N)   27 ὑμῶν e ras. N^{2} ἐπιδείξω A : ἀποδείξω N   28 προβουλῆς A^{1}N^{c} : προβολῆς A^{a}N^{a} 29 alt. καὶ A : om. N   33 καταψηφίσεως A^{c}N : καταψηφήσεως A^{a} 34 ἀπολελειμμένω A^{1} : ἀπ · · λειμμένω A^{a} : ἀπειλημμένῳ N   37 φονῆς Jernstedt : φονεῖς AN   38 ἔλθῃ N : ἔλθοι A   39 ἄλλοθι AN : ἄλλοσε Hertlein^{1} 45 προβουλῆς A^{1}N^{2} : προβολῆς A^{a}N   δὲ N : δ' A

ἑκουσίως ἐκ προνοίας ἀποκτεινάσης. καὶ πῶς τοῦτό γ' 6
ἐρεῖ, ὡς εὖ οἶδεν ὅτι γ' οὐκ ἀπέκτεινεν ἡ μήτηρ αὐτοῦ
τὸν πατέρα τὸν ἡμέτερον; ἐν οἷς μὲν γὰρ αὐτῷ ἐξουσία
ἦν σαφῶς εἰδέναι, παρὰ τῆς βασάνου, οὐκ ἠθέλησεν·
ἐν οἷς δ' οὐκ ἦν πυθέσθαι, τοῦτο αὐτὸ προὐθυμήθη.
καίτοι αὐτὸ τοῦτο ἐχρῆν, ὃ καὶ ἐγὼ προὐκαλούμην,
προθυμηθῆναι, ὅπως τὸ πραχθὲν ἦν ἀληθῶς ἐπεξελθεῖν.
μὴ γὰρ ὁμολογούντων τῶν ἀνδραπόδων οὗτός τ' εὖ 7
εἰδὼς ἂν ἀπελογεῖτο καὶ ἀντέσπευδε πρὸς ἐμέ, καὶ ἡ
μήτηρ αὐτοῦ ἀπήλλακτο ἂν ταύτης τῆς αἰτίας. ὅπου δὲ
μὴ ἠθέλησεν ἔλεγχον ποιήσασθαι τῶν πεπραγμένων,
πῶς περί γ' ὧν οὐκ ἠθέλησε πυθέσθαι, ἐγχωρεῖ αὐτῷ
περὶ τούτων εἰδέναι; πῶς οὖν περὶ τούτων, ὦ δικάζοντες,
αὐτὸν εἰκὸς εἰδέναι, ὧν γε τὴν ἀλήθειαν οὐκ εἴληφε; τί
ποτε ἀπολογήσεσθαι μέλλει μοι; ἐκ μὲν γὰρ τῆς τῶν 8
ἀνδραπόδων βασάνου εὖ ᾔδει ὅτι οὐχ οἷόν τ' ἦν αὐτῇ
σωθῆναι, ἐν δὲ τῷ μὴ βασανισθῆναι ἡγεῖτο τὴν
σωτηρίαν εἶναι· τὰ γὰρ γενόμενα ἐν τούτῳ ἀφανισθῆναι
ᾠήθησαν. πῶς οὖν εὔορκα ἀντομωμοκὼς ἔσται φάσκων
εὖ εἰδέναι, ὃς οὐκ ἠθέλησε σαφῶς πυθέσθαι ἐμοῦ
ἐθέλοντος τῇ δικαιοτάτῃ βασάνῳ χρήσασθαι περὶ
τούτου τοῦ πράγματος; τοῦτο μὲν γὰρ ἠθέλησα μὲν τὰ 9

46 *καὶ πῶς* Cole apud Gagarinum : *καὶ οὐ* AN : *καίτοι* Thalheim *γ'* AN : om. B, del. Cobet[3] 49 *σαφῶς* A^1N : om. A^a 50 *τοῦτο* N : *τοῦτ'* A 52 *προθυμηθῆναι* del. Sauppe[1] *ἦν ἀληθῶς* Phabés : *ἢ ἀληθές·* AN : *ἦν καὶ τὸ ἀληθὲς* Sauppe[1] : alia alii *ἐπεξελθεῖν* del. Gernet 53 *μὴ* Bekker (qui post *ἐπεξελθεῖν* distinxit) : *μὲν* AN 56 *ἠθέλησεν ἔλεγχον ποιήσασθαι* A : *ἠθέλησε ποιήσασθαι ἔλεγχον* N 58 pr. *περὶ* geminavit pag. fin. causa N 58–9 *πῶς οὖν … εἴληφε* del. Schoell[1], post *ἡμέτερον* l. 48 transp. Thalheim 58–9 *πῶς οὖν … εἰδέναι* om. N 60 *ἀπολογήσεσθαι* A^2, N^2 (*σφάλμα* i.m.) : *ἀπολογήσεται* AN *μέλλει*] *μέλει* Blass[2] (qui *ἀπολογήσεται* tuitus est) 62 *βασανισθῆναι* AN^2 : *βασανιστῆναι* N 64 *εὔορκα* A^cN : *εὔορκα καὶ* A^a *ἀντομωμοκὼς* A^c : *ἀντωμωμοκὼς* A^a : *ἀντομωμοκὸς* N 66 *χρήσασθαι* A^1N : *χρῆσθαι* A^a 67 *ἠθέλησα μὲν* Bake : *ἠθελήσαμεν* AN

τούτων ἀνδράποδα βασανίσαι, ἃ συνῄδει καὶ πρότερον
τὴν γυναῖκα ταύτην, μητέρα δὲ τούτων, τῷ πατρὶ τῷ
ἡμετέρῳ θάνατον μηχανωμένην φαρμάκοις, καὶ τὸν
πατέρα εἰληφότα ἐπ' αὐτοφώρῳ, ταύτην τε οὐκ οὖσαν
ἄπαρνον, πλὴν οὐκ ἐπὶ θανάτῳ φάσκουσαν διδόναι ἀλλ'
10 ἐπὶ φίλτροις. διὰ οὖν ταῦτα ἐγὼ βάσανον τοιαύτην
ἠθέλησα ποιήσασθαι περὶ αὐτῶν, γράψας ἐν γραμ-
ματείῳ ἃ ἐπαιτιῶμαι τὴν γυναῖκα ταύτην, βασανιστάς
τε αὐτοὺς τούτους ἐκέλευον γίγνεσθαι ἐμοῦ παρόντος,
ἵνα μὴ ἀναγκαζόμενοι ἃ ἐγὼ ἐπερωτῴην λέγοιεν, ἀλλ'
ἐξήρκει μοι τοῖς ἐν τῷ γραμματείῳ χρῆσθαι· καὶ αὐτό
μοι τοῦτο τεκμήριον δίκαιον γενέσθαι, ὅτι ὀρθῶς καὶ
δικαίως μετέρχομαι τὸν φονέα τοῦ πατρός· εἰ δὲ ἄπαρνοι
γίγνοιντο ἢ λέγοιεν μὴ ὁμολογούμενα, ⟨ἡ βάσανος⟩
ἀναγκάζοι τὰ γεγονότα κατηγορεῖν· αὕτη γὰρ καὶ τοὺς
τὰ ψευδῆ παρεσκευασμένους λέγειν τἀληθῆ κατηγορεῖν
11 ποιήσει. καίτοι εὖ οἶδά γ', εἰ οὗτοι πρὸς ἐμὲ ἐλθόντες,
ἐπειδὴ τάχιστα αὐτοῖς ἀπηγγέλθη ὅτι ἐπεξίοιμι τοῦ
πατρὸς τὸν φονέα, ἠθέλησαν τὰ ἀνδράποδα ἃ ἦν αὐτοῖς
παραδοῦναι, ἐγὼ δὲ μὴ ἠθέλησα παραλαβεῖν, αὐτὰ ἂν
ταῦτα μέγιστα τεκμήρια παρείχοντο ὡς οὐκ ἔνοχοί εἰσι
τῷ φόνῳ. νῦν δ', ἐγὼ γάρ εἰμι τοῦτο μὲν ὁ θέλων αὐτὸς
βασανιστὴς γενέσθαι, τοῦτο δὲ τούτους αὐτοὺς κελεύων
βασανίσαι ἀντ' ἐμοῦ, ἐμοὶ δήπου εἰκὸς ταὐτὰ ταῦτα

70 μηχανωμένην AN[2] : μηχανωμένη N 71 τὲ N : ras. 2–3 litt. in A 72 διδόναι] δοῦναι Rosenberg[2] 73 τοιαύτην om. A 76 τε N : δὲ A 77 ἐπερωτῴην Jernstedt : ἐπερωτῶ μὴ AN : ἐπερωτῴην μὴ Dobree 79 τοῦτο N : τούτου A γενέσθαι Jernstedt[1] : ἔσται AN 81 <ἡ βάσανος> add. Turr. : <ἡ δίκη> add. Ald. : alia alii 82 ἀναγκάζοι Steph. : ἀναγκάζει AN : ἀναγκάσει Barigazzi[1] : ἀνάγκη εἴη Redondo i Sànchez[1], qui additamenta in l. 81 respuit αὕτη L : αὐτὴ AN 83 ψευδῆ A : ψεύδη N 85 ἀπηγγέλθη N : ἐπηγγέλθη A 87–8 αὐτὰ ἂν ταῦτα Bekker : αὐτὰ ἐνταῦθ' ἂν A[1]N (ἐνταῦθ' ἂν om. ut vid. A[a]) 91 βασανίσαι ἀντ' ἐμοῦ N : ἀντ' ἐμοῦ βασανίσαι A ταὐτὰ ταῦτα Jernstedt : ταῦτα αὐτὰ A : αὐτὰ ταῦτα N

τεκμήρια εἶναι ὡς εἰσὶν ἔνοχοι τῷ φόνῳ. εἰ γὰρ τούτων 12
θελόντων διδόναι εἰς βάσανον ἐγὼ μὴ ἐδεξάμην, τούτοις
ἂν ἦν ταῦτα τεκμήρια. τὸ αὐτὸ οὖν τοῦτο καὶ ἐμοὶ γενέσθω,
εἴπερ ἐμοῦ θέλοντος ἔλεγχον λαβεῖν τοῦ πράγματος αὐτοὶ
μὴ ἠθέλησαν δοῦναι. δεινὸν δ' ἔμοιγε δοκεῖ εἶναι, εἰ ὑμᾶς
μὲν ζητοῦσιν αἰτεῖσθαι ὅπως αὐτῶν μὴ καταψηφίσησθε,
αὐτοὶ δὲ σφίσιν αὐτοῖς οὐκ ἠξίωσαν δικασταὶ γενέσθαι
δόντες βασανίσαι τὰ αὑτῶν ἀνδράποδα. περὶ μὲν οὖν 13
τούτων οὐκ ἄδηλον ὅτι αὐτοὶ ἔφευγον τῶν πραχθέντων
τὴν σαφήνειαν πυθέσθαι· ᾔδεσαν γὰρ οἰκεῖον σφίσι
τὸ κακὸν ἀναφανησόμενον, ὥστε σιωπώμενον καὶ
ἀβασάνιστον αὐτὸ ἐᾶσαι ἐβουλήθησαν. ἀλλ' οὐχ ὑμεῖς γε,
ὦ ἄνδρες, ἔγωγ' εὖ οἶδα, ἀλλὰ σαφὲς ποιήσετε.

Ταῦτα μὲν οὖν μέχρι τούτου· περὶ δὲ τῶν γενομένων πειράσομαι ὑμῖν διηγήσασθαι τὴν ἀλήθειαν· δίκη δὲ κυβερνήσειεν.

Ὑπερῷόν τι ἦν τῆς ἡμετέρας οἰκίας, ὃ εἶχε Φιλόνεως 14
ὁπότ' ἐν ἄστει διατρίβοι, ἀνὴρ καλός τε κἀγαθὸς καὶ
φίλος τῷ ἡμετέρῳ πατρί· καὶ ἦν αὐτῷ παλλακή, ἣν ὁ
Φιλόνεως ἐπὶ πορνεῖον ἔμελλε καταστῆσαι. ταύτην οὖν
πυθομένη ἡ μήτηρ τοῦ ἀδελφοῦ ἐποιήσατο φίλην.
αἰσθομένη δ' ὅτι ἀδικεῖσθαι ἔμελλεν ὑπὸ τοῦ Φιλόνεω, 15
μεταπέμπεται, καὶ ἐπειδὴ ἦλθεν, ἔλεξεν αὐτῇ ὅτι καὶ
αὐτὴ ἀδικοῖτο ὑπὸ τοῦ πατρὸς τοῦ ἡμετέρου· εἰ οὖν
ἐθέλει πείθεσθαι, ἔφη ἱκανὴ εἶναι ἐκείνῃ τε τὸν Φιλόνεων

92–6 εἰ … δοῦναι scholium esse videtur Blassio, del. Gernet   93 θελόντων N : ἐθελόντων A   ἐγὼ N : ἐγώ δὲ A   96 ἠθέλησαν A : ἐθέλησαν N   97 καταψηφίσησθε A[1] : καταψηφίσασθε A[a] : καταψηφίσεσθε N   99 αὑτῶν Steph. : αὐτῶν AN   102 σιωπώμενον A[2]N : σιωπόμενον A   103 ἐᾶσαι in ἐάσαι perperam corr. A[2]   ἐβουλήθησαν A[1]N : ἠβουλήθησαν A[a]   γε A : om. N   109 κἀγαθὸς A : καὶ ἀγαθὸς N (qui etiam post ἀνήρ distinxit)   112 πυθομένη del. Dobree : pro αἰσθομένη posuit Cobet[3]   116 ἐθέλει AN : ἐθέλοι L

φίλον ποιῆσαι καὶ αὑτῇ τὸν ἐμὸν πατέρα, εἶναι φάσκουσα
16 αὑτῆς μὲν τοῦτο εὕρημα, ἐκείνης δ' ὑπηρέτημα. ἠρώτα
οὖν αὐτὴν εἰ ἐθελήσει διακονῆσαί οἱ, καὶ ἣ ὑπέσχετο,
τάχιστα ὡς οἶμαι. μετὰ ταῦτα ἔτυχε τῷ Φιλόνεῳ ἐν
Πειραιεῖ ὄντα ἱερὰ Διὶ Κτησίῳ, ὁ δὲ πατὴρ ὁ ἐμὸς εἰς
Νάξον πλεῖν ἔμελλεν. κάλλιστον οὖν ἐδόκει εἶναι τῷ
Φιλόνεῳ τῆς αὐτῆς ὁδοῦ ἅμα μὲν προπέμψαι εἰς τὸν
Πειραιᾶ τὸν πατέρα τὸν ἐμὸν φίλον ὄντα ἑαυτῷ, ἅμα δὲ
17 θύσαντα τὰ ἱερὰ ἑστιᾶσαι ἐκεῖνον. ἡ οὖν παλλακὴ τοῦ
Φιλόνεω ἠκολούθει τῆς θυσίας ἕνεκα. καὶ ἐπειδὴ ἦσαν ἐν
τῷ Πειραιεῖ, οἷον εἰκός, ἔθυεν. καὶ ἐπειδὴ αὐτῷ ἐτέθυτο
τὰ ἱερά, ἐντεῦθεν ἐβουλεύετο ἡ ἄνθρωπος ὅπως ἂν
αὐτοῖς τὸ φάρμακον δοίη, πότερα πρὸ δείπνου ἢ ἀπὸ
δείπνου. ἔδοξεν οὖν αὐτῇ βουλευομένῃ βέλτιον εἶναι
μετὰ δεῖπνον δοῦναι, ταῖς Κλυταιμήστρας τῆς τούτου
18 μητρὸς ὑποθήκαις ἅμα διακονοῦσαν. καὶ τὰ μὲν ἄλλα
μακρότερος ἂν εἴη λόγος περὶ τοῦ δείπνου ἐμοί τε
διηγήσασθαι ὑμῖν τ' ἀκοῦσαι· ἀλλὰ πειράσομαι τὰ λοιπὰ
ὡς ἐν βραχυτάτοις ὑμῖν διηγήσασθαι, ὡς γεγένηται ἡ
δόσις τοῦ φαρμάκου. ἐπειδὴ γὰρ ἐδεδειπνήκεσαν, οἷον
εἰκός, ὁ μὲν θύων Διὶ Κτησίῳ κἀκεῖνον ὑποδεχόμενος,
ὁ δ' ἐκπλεῖν τε μέλλων καὶ παρ' ἀνδρὶ ἑταίρῳ
αὑτοῦ δειπνῶν, σπονδάς τ' ἐποιοῦντο καὶ λιβανωτὸν ὑπὲρ

117 αὑτῇ N[2] : αὐτῇ A[2]N : αὐτὴ A   118 αὑτῆς Steph. : αὐτῆς AN
119 ἐθελήσει A : ἐθελήσοι N   121 πειραιεῖ A : πειρᾳιεῖ N   post ὄντα
add. θύειν N[2sv]   122 ἔμελλεν A : ἔμελλε N   ἐδόκει εἶναι N : εἶναι
ἐδόκει A   124 πειραιᾶ A : πειραιᾷ N   125 τὰ A : om. N   ἐκεῖνον
A[1]N : ἐκείνων A[a]   126 ἕνεκα Blass[2] : ἕνεκε A : ἕνεκεν A[2]N
127 πειραιεῖ AN[2] : πειραεῖ N   ἔθυεν Orelli apud Turr. : ἔθυον AN   ἐτέθυτο
A : ἐτύ*ετο N : ἐθύ*ετο N[2]   128 ἐβουλεύετο A[1]N : ἐβούλετο A[a]
131 ταῖς A[2] : τῆς AN   Κλυταιμήστρας Gagarin : κλυταιμνήστρας
AN   131–2 τῆς τούτου μητρὸς A[2]N : τοῖς τούτου μητρὸς A : del.
Naber[2]   132 διακονοῦσαν N : διακονοῦσα A   ἄλλα A[1]N : om. A[a]
136 ἐδεδειπνήκεσαν M : ἐδεδειπνήκεισαν AN   139 αὑτοῦ Maetzner :
αὐτοῦ N : om. A

αὐτῶν ἐπετίθεσαν· ἡ δὲ παλλακὴ τοῦ Φιλόνεω τὴν 19
σπονδὴν ἅμα ἐγχέουσα ἐκείνοις εὐχομένοις ἃ οὐκ ἔμελλε
τελεῖσθαι, ὦ ἄνδρες, ἐνέχει τὸ φάρμακον. καὶ ἅμα
οἰομένη δεξιὸν ποιεῖν πλέον δίδωσι τῷ Φιλόνεῳ, ὡς, εἰ
δοίη πλέον, μᾶλλον φιλησομένη ὑπὸ τοῦ Φιλόνεω· οὔπω
γὰρ ᾔδει ὑπὸ τῆς μητρυιᾶς τῆς ἐμῆς ἐξαπατωμένη, πρὶν
ἐν τῷ κακῷ ἤδη ἦν· τῷ δὲ πατρὶ τῷ ἡμετέρῳ ἔλασσον
ἐνέχει. καὶ ἐκεῖνοι ἐπειδὴ ἀπέσπεισαν τὸν ἑαυτῶν 20
φονέα μεταχειριζόμενοι, ἐκπίνουσιν ὑστάτην πόσιν.
ὁ μὲν οὖν Φιλόνεως εὐθέως παραχρῆμα ἀποθνῄσκει,
ὁ δὲ πατὴρ ὁ ἡμέτερος εἰς νόσον ἐμπίπτει, ἐξ ἧς καὶ
ἀπώλετο εἰκοσταῖος. ἀνθ᾿ ὧν ἡ μὲν διακονήσασα καὶ
χειρουργήσασα ἔχει τὰ ἐπίχειρα ὧν ἀξία ἦν, οὐδὲν αἰτία
οὖσα—τῷ γὰρ δημοκοίνῳ τροχισθεῖσα παρεδόθη—ἡ δ᾿
αἰτία τε ἤδη καὶ ἐνθυμηθεῖσα ἕξει, ἐὰν ὑμεῖς τε καὶ οἱ
θεοὶ θέλωσι.

Σκέψασθε οὖν ὅσῳ δικαιότερα ὑμῶν δεήσομαι ἐγὼ ἢ 21
ὁ ἀδελφός. ἐγὼ μέν γε τῷ τεθνεῶτι ὑμᾶς κελεύω καὶ τῷ
ἠδικημένῳ τὸν ἀΐδιον χρόνον τιμωροὺς γενέσθαι· οὗτος
δὲ τοῦ μὲν τεθνεῶτος πέρι οὐδὲν ὑμᾶς αἰτήσεται, ὃς
ἄξιος καὶ ἐλέου καὶ βοηθείας καὶ τιμωρίας παρ᾿ ὑμῶν
τυχεῖν, ἀθέως καὶ ἀκλεῶς πρὸ τῆς εἱμαρμένης ὑφ᾿
ὧν ἥκιστα ἐχρῆν τὸν βίον ἐκλιπών, ὑπὲρ δὲ τῆς 22
ἀποκτεινάσης δεήσεται ἀθέμιτα καὶ ἀνόσια καὶ

141 σπονδὴν A^1N^2 : σποδὴν A^a : σπουδὴν N^a ἐγχέουσα Reiske : ἐκχέουσα AN ἔμελλε A^cN : ἔμελλεν A^a 143 ὡς Bekker, Dobree : ἴσως AN 144 μᾶλλον A^1N : ταχὺ ut vid. A^a 145 ἐμῆς A : ἡμετέρας N 147 ἑαυτῶν A^1N : ἑαυτοῦ A^a 150 ἡμέτερος A^1N : ὑμέτερος A^a 151–2 καὶ χειρουργήσασα huc transp. Blass : post ἐνθυμηθεῖσα l. 154 AN 152 οὐδὲν Steph. : οὐδ᾿ ἐν AN 154 ἕξει A^2N : ἔξει A 156 σκέψασθε AN^2 : σκέψασται N ὑμῶν δεήσομαι N : δεήσομαι ὑμῶν A 157 μέν γε N : μέντοι A 159 πέρι A : περϊ N 160 ἄξιος καὶ A^1N : ἀξίως A^a 163 ἀθέμιτα A^1N : ἀθέμιστα A^a καὶ ἀνόσια om. A

ἀτέλεστα καὶ ἀνήκουστα καὶ θεοῖς καὶ ὑμῖν, δεόμενος ὑμῶν ⟨μὴ τιμωρῆσαι⟩ ἃ αὐτὴ ἑαυτὴν οὐκ ἔπεισε μὴ κακοτεχνῆσαι. ὑμεῖς δ' οὐ τῶν ἀποκτεινάντων ἐστὲ βοηθοί, ἀλλὰ τῶν ἐκ προνοίας ἀποθνῃσκόντων, καὶ ταῦτα ὑφ' ὧν ἥκιστα αὐτοὺς ἐχρῆν ἀποθνῄσκειν. ἤδη οὖν ἐν ὑμῖν ἐστι τοῦτ' ὀρθῶς διαγνῶναι, ὃ καὶ ποιήσατε.

23 *δεήσεται δ' ὑμῶν οὗτος μὲν ὑπὲρ τῆς μητρὸς τῆς αὑτοῦ ζώσης, τῆς ἐκεῖνον διαχρησαμένης ἀβούλως τε καὶ ἀθέως, ὅπως δίκην μὴ δῷ ἂν ὑμᾶς πείθῃ, ὧν ἠδίκηκεν· ἐγὼ δ' ὑμᾶς ὑπὲρ πατρὸς τοὐμοῦ τεθνεῶτος αἰτοῦμαι, ὅπως παντὶ τρόπῳ δῷ. ὑμεῖς δέ, ὅπως διδῶσι δίκην οἱ ἀδικοῦντες, τούτου γε ἕνεκα καὶ δικασταὶ ἐγένεσθε καὶ*

24 *ἐκλήθητε. καὶ ἐγὼ μὲν ἐπεξέρχομαι λέγων, ἵνα δῷ δίκην ὧν ἠδίκηκε καὶ τιμωρήσω τῷ τε πατρὶ τῷ ἡμετέρῳ καὶ τοῖς νόμοις τοῖς ὑμετέροις· ταύτῃ καὶ ἄξιόν μοι βοηθῆσαι ὑμᾶς ἅπαντας, εἰ ἀληθῆ λέγω· οὗτος δὲ τἀναντία, ὅπως ἡ τοὺς νόμους παριδοῦσα μὴ δῷ δίκην ὧν ἠδίκηκε, ταύτῃ*

25 *βοηθὸς καθέστηκε. καίτοι πότερον δικαιότερον τὸν ἐκ προνοίας ἀποκτείναντα δοῦναι δίκην ἢ μή; καὶ πότερον δεῖ οἰκτῖραι μᾶλλον τὸν τεθνεῶτα ἢ τὴν ἀποκτείνασαν; ἐγὼ μὲν οἶμαι τὸν τεθνεῶτα· καὶ γὰρ δικαιότερον καὶ ὁσιώτερον καὶ πρὸς θεῶν καὶ πρὸς ἀνθρώπων γίγνοιτο ὑμῖν. ἤδη οὖν ἐγὼ ἀξιῶ, ὥσπερ κἀκεῖνον ἀνελεημόνως καὶ ἀνοικτίστως αὕτη ἀπώλεσεν, οὕτω καὶ αὐτὴν ταύτην*

165 add. Thalheim, alia alii 168 *αὐτοὺς ἐχρῆν* N : *ἐχρῆν αὐτοὺς* A 169 *ἐστι τοῦτ'* Franke : *ἐστι τοῦ* N : *τοῦτό ἐστιν* A *ποιήσατε* N : *ἐποιήσατε* A : *ποιήσετε* coni. Reiske 170 pr. *τῆς* A : om. N *αὑτοῦ* Maetzner : *αὐτοῦ* AN 171 *διαχρησαμένης* A^1N : *διαχρησαμένοις* A^a *ἀβούλως*] *προβούλως* Dobree 172 *ἠδίκηκεν* A : *ἠδίκηκε* N 173 *δ'* A : om. N *πατρὸς τοὐμοῦ* Franke : *τοῦ πατρός μου* A : *πατρός μου* N 174 *τρόπω* e ras. A^1 (*τρόπον* fuit?) *διδῶσι* A^1N^2 : *δίδωσι* AN : *γρ δώσουσι* N^{2im} 175 *γε* A : om. N 177 et 180 *ἠδίκηκε* A : *ἠδίκησε* N 182 *καὶ* A : *καίτοι* N *πότερον* A^cN : *πρότερον* A^a 183 *δεῖ* Jernstedt : *δικαιότερον* AN *οἰκτῖραι* Blass^2 : *οἰκτεῖραι* A, in ras. N^1 184 *γὰρ* <*ἂν*> Dobree 186 *οὖν ἐγὼ* A : *γοῦν* N

ἀπολέσθαι ὑπό τε ὑμῶν καὶ τοῦ δικαίου. ἡ μὲν γὰρ 26
ἑκουσίως καὶ βουλεύσασα τὸν θάνατον ⟨ἀπέκτεινεν⟩, ὁ δ᾽
ἀκουσίως καὶ βιαίως ἀπέθανε. πῶς γὰρ οὐ βιαίως
ἀπέθανεν, ὦ ἄνδρες; ὅς γ᾽ ἐκπλεῖν ἔμελλεν ἐκ τῆς γῆς
τῆσδε, παρά τε ἀνδρὶ φίλῳ αὑτοῦ εἱστιᾶτο, ἡ δὲ πέμψασα
τὸ φάρμακον καὶ κελεύσασα ἐκείνῳ δοῦναι πιεῖν
ἀπέκτεινεν ἡμῶν τὸν πατέρα. πῶς οὖν ταύτην ἐλεεῖν
ἄξιόν ἐστιν ἢ αἰδοῦς τυγχάνειν παρ᾽ ὑμῶν ἢ ἄλλου του;
ἥτις αὐτὴ οὐκ ἠξίωσεν ἐλεῆσαι τὸν ἑαυτῆς ἄνδρα, ἀλλ᾽
ἀνοσίως καὶ αἰσχρῶς ἀπώλεσεν. οὕτω δέ τοι καὶ ἐλεεῖν 27
ἐπὶ τοῖς ἀκουσίοις παθήμασι μᾶλλον προσήκει ἢ τοῖς
ἑκουσίοις καὶ ἐκ προνοίας ἀδικήμασι καὶ ἁμαρτήμασι.
καὶ ὥσπερ ἐκεῖνον αὕτη οὔτε θεοὺς οὔθ᾽ ἥρωας οὔτ᾽
ἀνθρώπους αἰσχυνθεῖσα οὐδὲ δείσασ᾽ ἀπώλεσεν, οὕτω
καὶ αὐτὴ ὑφ᾽ ὑμῶν καὶ τοῦ δικαίου ἀπολομένη, καὶ μὴ
τυχοῦσα μήτ᾽ αἰδοῦς μήτ᾽ ἐλέου μήτ᾽ αἰσχύνης μηδεμιᾶς
παρ᾽ ὑμῶν, τῆς δικαιοτάτης ἂν τύχοι τιμωρίας.

Θαυμάζω δὲ ἔγωγε τῆς τόλμης τοῦ ἀδελφοῦ καὶ τῆς 28
διανοίας, τὸ διομόσασθαι ὑπὲρ τῆς μητρὸς εὖ εἰδέναι μὴ
πεποιηκυῖαν ταῦτα. πῶς γὰρ ἄν τις εὖ εἰδείη οἷς μὴ
παρεγένετο αὐτός; οὐ γὰρ δήπου μαρτύρων γ᾽ ἐναντίον
οἱ ἐπιβουλεύοντες τοὺς θανάτους τοῖς πέλας μηχανῶνταί
τε καὶ παρασκευάζουσιν, ἀλλ᾽ ὡς μάλιστα δύνανται
λαθραιότατα καὶ ὡς ἀνθρώπων μηδένα εἰδέναι· οἱ δὲ 29

189 add. Reiske 191 ὅς A[1] : ὥς A[a], N (accentus pristinus oblitt. videtur) 192 φίλῳ αὑτοῦ Maetzner : αὑτοῦ φίλῳ Steph. : φίλῳ αὐτοῦ N : αὐτοῦ φίλω A 193 κελεύσασα A : κελεύουσα N 194 ἡμῶν A[1]N : ὑμῶν A[a] 196 αὐτὴ A[1] (inceperat αὕτη scribere) : αὐτὴ, N ἑαυτῆς N : αὑτῆς A 199 ἑκουσίοις Steph. : ἑκουσίως AN 200 αὕτη Reiske : αὐτὴ AN 201 αἰσχυνθεῖσα N : om. A οὐδὲ Maetzner : οὔτε N : om. A δείσασ᾽ N : δείσασα A 202 ἀπολλουμένη ut vid. A[a] 204 τύχοι N : τύχη A 207 πεποιηκυῖαν Cobet[2] : πεποιηκέναι AN 209 μηχανῶνταί τε A[2] N : μηχανῶνται re vera A 210 παρασκευάζουσιν A[1]N : κατασκευάζουσιν ut vid. A[a] 211 μηδένα] η in ras. N[2] δὲ N : δ᾽ A

ἐπιβουλευόμενοι οὐδὲν ἴσασι, πρὶν ἐν αὐτῷ ὦσι τῷ κακῷ γʼ ἤδη καὶ γιγνώσκωσι τὸν ὄλεθρον ἐν ᾧ εἰσί. τότε δέ, ἐὰν μὲν δύνωνται καὶ φθάνωσι πρὶν ἀποθανεῖν, καὶ φίλους καὶ ἀναγκαίους τοὺς σφετέρους καλοῦσι καὶ μαρτύρονται, καὶ λέγουσιν αὐτοῖς ὑφʼ ὧν ἀπόλλυνται, καὶ ἐπισκήπτουσι τιμωρῆσαι σφίσιν αὐτοῖς ἠδικημένοις·

30 ἃ κἀμοὶ παιδὶ ὄντι ὁ πατήρ, τὴν ἀθλίαν καὶ τελευταίαν νόσον νοσῶν, ἐπέσκηπτεν· ἐὰν δὲ τούτων ἁμαρτάνωσι, γράμματα γράφουσι, καὶ οἰκέτας τοὺς σφετέρους αὐτῶν ἐπικαλοῦνται μάρτυρας, καὶ δηλοῦσιν ὑφʼ ὧν ἀπόλλυνται. κἀκεῖνος ἐμοὶ νέῳ ἔτι ὄντι ταῦτα ἐδήλωσε καὶ ἐπέστειλεν, ὦ ἄνδρες, οὐ τοῖς ἑαυτοῦ δούλοις.

31 Ἐμοὶ μὲν οὖν διήγηται καὶ βεβοήθηται τῷ τεθνεῶτι καὶ τῷ νόμῳ· ἐν ὑμῖν δʼ ἐστὶ σκοπεῖν τὰ λοιπὰ πρὸς ὑμᾶς αὐτοὺς καὶ δικάζειν τὰ δίκαια. οἶμαι δὲ καὶ τοῖς θεοῖς τοῖς κάτω μέλειν οἳ ἠδίκηνται.

212 ἴσασι N : ἴσασιν A   213 γʼ ἤδη post πρὶν l. 212 posuit N   γινώσκωσι A^2 : γινώσκουσι A^aN   215 σφετέρους <αὐτῶν> $Hirschig^2$ 216 μαρτύρονται A : μαρτύρωνται N   217 σφίσιν A : φησὶν N   219 καὶ post ἁμαρτάνωσι erasum A   221 ὧν B : ὧν ἂν re vera A, N   222 ἀπόλλυνται M^{im} : ἀπολοῦνται A^aN : ἀπόλωνται A^1 κἀκεῖνος A^1N : καὶ ἐκεῖνος A^a 224 διήγηται A : δεδιήγηται N   βεβοήθηται A^1N : βεβοήθητε A^a 226 τοῖς A : om. N   227 μέλειν A^1N^2 : μέλλειν A^aN   οἳ AN : οἷʼ Boekmeijer

2

ΤΕΤΡΑΛΟΓΙΑ Α

α

ΚΑΤΗΓΟΡΙΑ ΦΟΝΟΥ ΑΠΑΡΑΣΗΜΟΣ

ΥΠΟΘΕΣΙΣ

Πανταχοῦ μὲν τὴν οἰκείαν Ἀντιφῶν ἐνδείκνυται δύναμιν, μάλιστα δ’ ἐν ταύταις ταῖς τετραλογίαις ἐν αἷς αὐτὸς πρὸς αὑτὸν ἀγωνίζεται· δύο γὰρ ὑπὲρ τοῦ κατηγόρου λόγους εἰπὼν δύο καὶ ὑπὲρ τοῦ φεύγοντος ἐμελέτησεν, ὁμοίως ἐν ἀμφοτέροις εὐδοκιμῶν. ἔοικε μὲν οὖν οὗτος ὁ λόγος τῷ Λυσίου λόγῳ τῷ πρὸς Μικίνην γεγραμμένῳ, ἔχει δ’ αὐτῷ τὰ τῆς ὑποθέσεως ὧδε. ἀναχωρῶν τις ἀπὸ δείπνου εὑρέθη σὺν τῷ ἀκολούθῳ συγκεκομμένος. μετὰ τὴν αὐτοῦ τελευτὴν συγγενής τις αὐτοῦ κατηγορεῖ ἐχθροῦ αὐτοῦ ὡς πεποιηκότος τὸν φόνον· ὁ δ’ ἀρνεῖται. ὅθεν στοχασμὸς ἡ στάσις ἀτελής, ἐκ μόνου τοῦ προσώπου συνιστάμενος. ἡ δὲ τοῦ λόγου διαίρεσις αὕτη. ἐν μὲν τοῖς προοιμίοις κατάστασιν ὁ λόγος οὐκ ἔχει, διὰ τὸ μήπω τὴν ὅλην ἠκριβῶσθαι τέχνην. ἀρχόμενος δὲ τῶν ἀγώνων πρώτῃ ἐχρήσατο ἀναιρέσει αἰτιῶν, δι’ ὧν ἀπέδειξεν ὅτι οὐδεὶς αὐτὸν τῶν ὀφειλόντων ὑπονοηθῆναι διέφθειρεν. εἶτα περιίστησι τὸ πρᾶγμα εἰς τὸ δεῖξαι ὅτι ἐξ ἐπιβουλῆς

Antiphontis Orationes 2–4 = Tetralogiae *Α–Γ*. Titulum *τετραλογίαι* testantur Ant. codd. (Arg. A.*α*. l. 2 et inscriptiones subscriptionesve variae) necnon veteres docti Tetr. A. Arg. inscriptio *ὑπόθεσις τῶν ἑξῆς* re vera A, N 1 *ἐνδείκνυται* N : *ἐνδείκτυται* A 2 *πρὸν* ut vid. A, corr. A^2 3 *αὑτὸν* A^2 : *αὐτὸν* AN 4 *ἐμελέτησεν* A : *ἐμελέτησε λόγους* N 5 *οὖν* A : om. N *Λυσίου* A^{1}N^c : *Λυσείω* A^a : *Λυσίω* N^a 6 *μικίνην* A : *μυκήνην* N 7 *ὧδε* A : *ὦδε* N *δείπνου* A : *δείπνων* N 11 pr. *τοῦ* A : om. N 12 *τοῖς* A : om. N post *προοιμίοις* lacunam susp. Blass^2 <*δ’*> *ὁ* Blass^2 15 *αὐτὸν* A^{1}N : *αὐτω* ut vid. A^a

ἀπέθανε, καὶ λοιπὸν ἐμβάλλει εἰς τὴν βούλησιν· τὴν δὲ τῶν ἐλέγχων ἀπαίτησιν λύει τῇ μαρτυρίᾳ τοῦ δούλου. εἶτα παρέκβασις καὶ ἐπίλογος.

1 Ὁπόσα μὲν τῶν πραγμάτων ὑπὸ τῶν ἐπιτυχόντων ἐπιβουλεύεται, οὐ χαλεπὰ ἐλέγχεσθαί ἐστιν· ἂν δ' οἱ ἱκανῶς μὲν πεφυκότες, ἔμπειροι δὲ πραγμάτων ὄντες, ἐν δὲ τούτῳ τῆς ἡλικίας καθεστῶτες ἐν ᾧ κράτιστοι φρονεῖν αὑτῶν εἰσι, πράττωσι, χαλεποὶ καὶ γνωσθῆναι
2 καὶ ἐλεγχθῆναί εἰσι. διὰ γὰρ τὸ μέγεθος τοῦ κινδύνου ἐκ πολλοῦ τὴν ἀσφάλειαν ὧν ἐπιβουλεύουσι σκοποῦντες, οὐ πρότερον ἐπιχειροῦσιν ἢ πάσης ὑποψίας φυλακὴν ποιήσωνται. γιγνώσκοντας οὖν ὑμᾶς χρὴ ταῦτα, κἂν ὁτιοῦν εἰκὸς παραλάβητε, σφόδρα πιστεύειν αὐτῷ. ἡμεῖς δ' οἱ ἐπεξερχόμενοι τὸν φόνον οὐ τὸν αἴτιον
3 ἀφέντες τὸν ἀναίτιον διώκομεν· σαφῶς γὰρ οἴδαμεν ὅτι πάσης τῆς πόλεως μιαινομένης ὑπ' αὐτοῦ, ἕως ἂν διωχθῇ, τό τ' ἀσέβημα ἡμέτερον γίγνεται, τῆς θ' ὑμετέρας ἁμαρτίας ἡ ποινὴ εἰς ἡμᾶς τοὺς μὴ δικαίως διώκοντας ἀναχωρεῖ. ἅπαντος δὲ τοῦ μιάσματος ἀναχωροῦντος εἰς ἡμᾶς, ὡς ἂν δυνώμεθα σαφέστατα ἐξ ὧν γιγνώσκομεν πειρασόμεθα ὑμῖν δηλοῦν ὡς ἀπέκτεινε τὸν ἄνδρα.

⟨Οὔτε γὰρ κακούργους εἰκὸς ἀποκτεῖναι τὸν ἄνθρωπον⟩·
4 οὐδεὶς γὰρ ἂν τὸν ἔσχατον κίνδυνον περὶ τῆς ψυχῆς

19 παρέκβασις A : παρεκβάσεις N Tetr. A.α 1 Inscriptio κατηγορία φόνου ἀπαράσημος AN 22 πραγμάτων N : τῶν πραγμάτων A 24 αὑτῶν N[2] : αὐτῶν AN πράττωσι AN[2] : πράττουσι N : <τι> πράττωσι Kayser[1] γνωσθῆναι A[c] (punctis del. δια), N[2] : διαγνωσθῆναι A[a] : γνωστήναι N 25 ἐλεγχθῆναί Kayser[1] : δειχθῆναί AN 28 ποιήσωνται A : ποιήσονται N 29 παραλάβητε N : παραλάβοιτε A 31 οἴδαμεν AN : ἴσμεν MZ 33 ἡμέτερον AN : ὑμέτερον A[2] 35 δὲ] οὖν ci. Steph. 36 ἡμᾶς A[1]N : ὑμᾶς A[a] ὡς Steph. : ἕως AN 37 ὡς AN : ὃς N[2] 39 ante οὐδεὶς lacuna esse videtur : <οὔτε γὰρ κακούργος εἰκὸς ἀποκτεῖναι τὸν ἄνθρωπον> add. Ald.

κινδυνεύων ἑτοίμην καὶ κατειργασμένην τὴν ὠφέλειαν
ἀφῆκεν· ἔχοντες γὰρ {ἂν} τὰ ἱμάτια εὑρέθησαν. οὐ μὴν
οὐδὲ παροινήσας οὐδεὶς διέφθειρεν αὐτόν· ἐγιγνώσκετο
γὰρ ἂν ὑπὸ τῶν συμποτῶν. οὐδὲ μὴν οὐδ' ἐκ λοιδορίας·
οὐ γὰρ ⟨ἂν⟩ ἀωρὶ τῶν νυκτῶν οὐδ' ἐν ἐρημίᾳ ἐλοιδοροῦντο.
οὐδὲ μὴν ἄλλου στοχαζόμενος ἔτυχε τούτου· οὐ γὰρ ἂν
σὺν τῷ ἀκολούθῳ διέφθειρεν αὐτόν. ἀπολυομένης δὲ 5
τῆς ὑποψίας ἁπάσης αὐτὸς ὁ θάνατος ἐξ ἐπιβουλῆς
ἀποθανόντα μηνύει αὐτόν. Ἐπιθέσθαι δὲ τίνα μᾶλλον
εἰκός ἐστιν, ἢ τὸν μεγάλα μὲν κακὰ προπεπονθότα, ἔτι
δὲ μείζονα ἐπίδοξον ὄντα πάσχειν; ἔστι δ' ὁ διωκόμενος
οὗτος· ἐκ παλαιοῦ γὰρ ἐχθρὸς ὢν αὐτοῦ πολλὰς μὲν καὶ
μεγάλας γραφὰς διώξας οὐδεμίαν εἷλεν, ἔτι δὲ μείζους 6
καὶ πλείους διωχθεὶς οὐδεπώποτ' ἀποφυγὼν ἱκανὸν
μέρος τῶν ὄντων ἀποβέβληκε, τὰ δ' ἄγχιστα ἱερῶν
κλοπῆς δυοῖν ταλάντοιν γεγραμμένος ὑπ' αὐτοῦ,
συνειδὼς μὲν αὑτῷ τὸ ἀδίκημα, ἔμπειρος δ' ὢν τῆς
τούτου δυνάμεως, μνησικακῶν δὲ τῶν ἔμπροσθεν,
εἰκότως μὲν ἐπεβούλευσεν, εἰκότως δ' ἀμυνόμενος τὴν
ἔχθραν ἀπέκτεινε τὸν ἄνδρα. ἥ τε γὰρ ἐπιθυμία τῆς 7
τιμωρίας ἀμνήμονα τῶν κινδύνων καθίστη αὐτόν, ὅ τε
φόβος τῶν ἐπιφερομένων κακῶν ἐκπλήσσων θερμότερον
ἐπιχειρεῖν ἐπῇρε. ἤλπιζέ τε τάδε μὲν δράσας καὶ λήσειν
ἀποκτείνας αὐτὸν καὶ ἀποφεύξεσθαι τὴν γραφήν· οὐδὲ
γὰρ ἐπεξιέναι οὐδένα, ἀλλ' ἐρήμην αὐτὴν ἔσεσθαι· εἴ τε 8

42 del. Reiske *εὑρέθησαν* AN : *ηὑρέθησαν* Jernstedt 45 add. Dobree 48 *τῆς* <*ἄλλης*> Pahle 49 *τίνα* A^2N : *τινα* A 50 *προπεπονθότα* A^1N : *πεπονθότα* A^a 51 *πάσχειν* delere maluit Baiter 54 *οὐδεπώποτ'* A^c : *οὐδὲ πώποτ'* A^a : *οὐπώποτ'* N 57 *τῆς* A^1N : *τοῖς* ut vid. A^a 61 *καθίστη* Reiske : *καθίστησιν* AN 62 *ἐκπλήσσων* A^1N : *ἐμπλήσσων* vel *ἐπιπλήσσων* A^a 63 *ἐπῇρε* $Blass^2$: *ἐπῆρε* N : *ἐπῆρεν* A 64 *ἀποφεύξεσθαι* A^1N^2 : *ἀποφεύξασθαι* A^a, N ut vid. *οὐδὲ* Reiske : *οὔτε* AN 65 *τε* AN : *δὲ* Reiske

καὶ ἁλοίη, τιμωρησαμένῳ κάλλιον ἔδοξεν αὐτῷ ταῦτα πάσχειν, ἢ ἀνάνδρως μηδὲν ἀντιδράσαντα ὑπὸ τῆς γραφῆς διαφθαρῆναι. σαφῶς δ' ᾔδει ἁλωσόμενος αὐτήν· οὐ γὰρ ἂν τόνδε τὸν ἀγῶνα ἐνόμισεν ἀσφαλέστερον εἶναι.

9 Τὰ μὲν βιασάμενα ταῦτά ἐστιν ἀσεβῆσαι αὐτόν.
μάρτυρες δ' εἰ μὲν πολλοὶ παρεγένοντο, πολλοὺς ἂν
παρεσχόμεθα· ἑνὸς δὲ τοῦ ἀκολούθου παραγενομένου, οἳ
τούτου ἤκουον μαρτυρήσουσιν. ἔμπνους γὰρ ἔτι ἀρθείς,
ἀνακρινόμενος ὑφ' ἡμῶν, τοῦτον μόνον ἔφη τῶν παιόντων
γνῶναι αὐτούς. ἐξελεγχόμενος δ' ὑπό τε τῶν εἰκότων
ὑπό τε τῶν παραγενομένων, οὐδενὶ τρόπῳ οὔτε δικαίως
10 οὔτε συμφερόντως ἀπολύοιτ' ἂν ὑφ' ὑμῶν. οἵ τε γὰρ
ἐπιβουλεύοντες ἀνεξέλεγκτοι ἂν εἴησαν, εἰ μήθ' ὑπὸ τῶν
παραγενομένων μήτε ὑπό τῶν εἰκότων ἐξελέγχονται·
ἀσύμφορόν θ' ὑμῖν ἐστὶ τόνδε μιαρὸν καὶ ἄναγνον ὄντα
εἴς ⟨τε⟩ τὰ τεμένη τῶν θεῶν εἰσιόντα μιαίνειν τὴν ἁγνείαν
αὐτῶν, ἐπί τε τὰς αὐτὰς τραπέζας ἰόντα συγκαταπιμπλάναι τοὺς ἀναιτίους· ἐκ γὰρ τούτων αἵ τ' ἀφορίαι
11 γίγνονται δυστυχεῖς θ' αἱ πράξεις καθίστανται. οἰκείαν
οὖν χρὴ τὴν τιμωρίαν ἡγησαμένους, αὐτῷ τούτῳ τὰ τούτου ἀσεβήματα ἀναθέντας, ἰδίαν μὲν τὴν συμφοράν, καθαρὰν δὲ τὴν πόλιν καταστῆσαι.

72 *παρεσχόμεθα* AN^{2} : *παρεσχοίμεθα* N   *τοῦτου* post *δὲ* punctis del. A^{1} *τού* post *οἳ* punctis del. A^{1} 74 *ἡμῶν* A : *ὑμῶν* N   74–5 *τῶν παιόντων γνῶναι* Bekker : *τῶν παρόντων γνῶναι* A : *γνῶναι τῶν παρόντων* N   75 *ἐξελεγχόμενος* A : *ἐλεγχόμενος* N   76 *παραγενομένων* A^{1}N : *γενομένων* A^{a}, et ras. ante *τῶν*   77 *ἀπολύοιτ'* A^{2}N : *ἀπωλύετ'* A   78 *εἴησαν* AN : *εἶεν* Jernstedt   *μήθ'* A : *μήτε* N   79 *ἐξελέγχονται* N^{c} : *ἐξελέγχωνται* AN   80 *θ'* N : om. A   81 add. Blass   83 *τ' ἀφορίαι* N : *τε ἀφορίαι* A^{1} : *τ' ἀναφοραὶ* ut vid. A^{a} 87 subscriptio *κατηγορία φόνου ἀπαράσημος* N

β

ΑΠΟΛΟΓΙΑ ΕΙΣ ΤΟ ΑΥΤΟ ΠΡΑΓΜΑ

ΥΠΟΘΕΣΙΣ

Ὁμολογεῖ μὲν τὴν πρώτην ἔχθραν τὴν πρὸς τὸν τεθνηκότα ὁ ἀπολογούμενος, ἀρνεῖται δὲ τὸν φόνον, καὶ τεκμήριον τοῦ μὴ πεφονευκέναι ποιεῖται τὴν ἔχθραν. λέγει γὰρ ὅτι ἐχθρὸς ὢν ᾔδειν πάντως τὴν αἰτίαν κατ᾽ ἐμαυτοῦ ἥξουσαν· διὰ τοῦτο οὐκ ἂν ἐφόνευον. διαβάλλει δὲ καὶ τὴν μαρτυρίαν τοῦ οἰκέτου, ὡς ἐκ παρασκευῆς γεγονυῖαν τῶν δεσποτῶν. οὐκ ἀπίθανον δέ φησι κακούργους ἀνελόντας αὐτὸν ἀποδῦσαι τὰ ἱμάτια μὴ φθάσαι.

Οὔ μοι δοκῶ ἁμαρτάνειν ἀτυχέστατον ἐμαυτὸν 1
ἡγούμενος εἶναι τῶν πάντων ἀνθρώπων. τῶν μὲν γὰρ
ἄλλων οἱ δυστυχοῦντες, ὁπόταν μὲν ὑπὸ χειμῶνος
πονῶσιν, εὐδίας γενομένης παύονται· ὅταν δὲ νοσήσωσιν,
ὑγιεῖς γενόμενοι σῴζονται· ἐάν τέ τις ἄλλη συμφορὰ
καταλαμβάνῃ αὐτούς, τὰ ἐναντία ἐπιγιγνόμενα ὀνίνησιν.
ἐμοὶ δὲ ζῶν τε ἅνθρωπος ἀνατροπεὺς τοῦ οἴκου ἐγένετο, 2
ἀποθανών τε, κἂν ἀποφύγω, ἱκανὰς λύπας καὶ φροντίδας
προσβέβληκεν. εἰς τοῦτο γὰρ βαρυδαιμονίας ἥκω, ὥστε
οὐκ ἀρκοῦν μοί ἐστιν ἐμαυτὸν ὅσιον καὶ δίκαιον παρέχοντα
μὴ διαφθαρῆναι, ἀλλὰ κἂν μὴ τὸν ἀποκτείναντα εὑρὼν

Tetr. A.β Arg. inscriptio ὑπόθεσις τοῦ (τῶν A) ἑξῆς AN 3 <αὐτὴν> τὴν Jernstedt[1] 4 τοῦτο <οὖν> Blass 5 ἐφόνευον <αὐτόν> dubitanter Decleva Caizzi 5–6 τοῦ οἰκέτου ὡ in ras. A[1] 6 τοῦ οἰκέτου post δεσποτῶν del. A[c] 7–8 ἀποδῦσαι τὰ ἱμάτια μὴ φθάσαι in ras. A[1] 9 inscriptio ἀπολογία εἰς τὸ αὐτὸ πρᾶγμα AN 10 pr. τῶν A[1]N : om. A[a] 11 ὁπόταν A : ὁπότ᾽ ἂν N 12 νοσήσωσιν] ω in ras. N[1] 13 τέ N : δέ A 15 ἅνθρωπος Turr. : ἄνθρωπος AN 17 προσβέβληκεν Sauppe[1] : προβέβληκεν N : ἐμβέβληκεν A : προεμβέβληκεν Decleva Caizzi 18 παρέχοντα AN : παρέχειν τὸ Thalheim 19 κἂν] κὰ in ras. N[1]

ἐξελέγξω, ὃν οἱ τιμωροῦντες αὐτῷ ἀδύνατοι εὑρεῖν εἰσιν,
3 *αὐτὸς καταδοχθεὶς φονεὺς εἶναι ἀνοσίως ἁλώσομαι. καὶ*
ἐμὲ ὡς δεινὸν μὲν παγχάλεπόν φασιν ἐλέγχεσθαι εἶναι, ὡς
δ' ἠλίθιον ἐξ αὐτῶν ὧν ἔπραξα φανερὸν εἶναι ἐργασάμενον
τὸ ἔργον. εἰ γὰρ νῦν διὰ τῆς ἔχθρας τὸ μέγεθος εἰκότως
ὑφ' ὑμῶν καταδοκοῦμαι, πρὶν ἐργάσασθαι εἰκότερον ἦν
προειδότα τὴν νῦν ὑποψίαν εἰς ἐμὲ οὖσαν, καὶ τῶν ἄλλων
εἴ τινα ἔγνων ἐπιβουλεύοντα αὐτῷ, διακωλύειν μᾶλλον ἢ
αὐτὸν ἐργασάμενον εἰς ἑκουσίους καὶ προδήλους ὑποψίας
ἐμπεσεῖν· ἔκ τε γὰρ αὐτοῦ τοῦ ἔργου φανερὸς γενόμενος
ἀπωλλύμην, λαθών τε σαφῶς ᾔδειν τήνδε τὴν ὑποψίαν εἰς
4 *ἐμὲ οὖσαν. ἄθλια μὲν οὖν πάσχω μὴ ἀπολογεῖσθαι μόνον*
βιαζόμενος, ἀλλὰ καὶ τοὺς ἀποκτείναντας φανεροὺς
καταστῆσαι· ὅμως δὲ καὶ τοῦτο ἐπιχειρητέον· οὐδὲν γὰρ
πικρότερον τῆς ἀνάγκης ἔοικεν εἶναι. ἔχω δὲ οὐδαμῶς
ἄλλως ἐλέγχειν ἢ ἐξ ὧν τοὺς ἄλλους ὁ κατήγορος ἀπολύων
αὐτὸν τὸν θάνατόν φησι μηνύειν ἐμὲ τὸν φονέα ὄντα. εἰ
γὰρ τούτων ἀναιτίων δοκούντων εἶναι ἐν ἐμοὶ τἀδίκημα
φανεῖται, τούτων ὑπόπτων ὄντων ἐγὼ δικαίως ⟨ἂν⟩
καθαρὸς δοκοίην εἶναι.

5 *Ἔστι δὲ οὐκ ἀπεικός, ὡς οὗτοί φασιν, ἀλλὰ εἰκὸς ἀωρὶ*
τῶν νυκτῶν πλανώμενον ἐπὶ τοῖς ἱματίοις διαφθαρῆναι.
τὸ γὰρ μὴ ἐκδυθῆναι οὐδὲν σημεῖόν ἐστιν· εἰ γὰρ μὴ
ἔφθησαν περιδύσαντες αὐτόν, ἀλλά τινας προσιόντας

21 *φονεὺς εἶναι*] *ς εἶν* in ras. longiore N[1] 22 *ὡς δεινὸν* post *μὲν* iterat. punctis del. A[1] 25 *ἐργάσασθαι* A[2]N : *ἐργάσθασθαι* A 26 *προειδότα* Kayser[1] : *τὸν εἰδότα* AN : *τὸν* del. Hirschig[2] : *τότ' εἰδότα* Thiel *τὴν νῦν ὑποψίαν* N : *τὴν ὑποψίαν τὴν νῦν* A *οὖσαν* AN : *ἰοῦσαν* Reiske 28 *ὑποψίας* AN : *ἀτυχίας* Thalheim 30 *ἀπωλλύμην* A : *ἀπωλύμην* N *ᾔδειν* N : *ἤδειν* A : *ᾔδη* Jernstedt *τήνδε* A : *τήν τε* N[a] : del. N[c] 31 *οὖσαν* AN : *ἰοῦσαν* Reiske 38 *δικαίως* N : *δ' εἰκότως* A add. Blass 40 *δὲ* A[1]N : *δὴ* A[a] *εἰκὸς* A[1]N : om. A[a] 42 *ἐκδυθῆναι* A[c]N : *ἐκδυνηθῆναι* A[a] *μὴ* AN[2] : om. N

φοβηθέντες ἀπέλιπον, ἐσωφρόνουν καὶ οὐκ ἐμαίνοντο
τὴν σωτηρίαν τοῦ κέρδους προτιμῶντες. εἰ δὲ μὴ καὶ ἐπὶ 6
τοῖς ἱματίοις διεφθάρη, ἀλλ' ἑτέρους ἰδὼν ἄλλο τι
κακουργοῦντας, ἵνα μὴ μηνυτὴς τοῦ ἀδικήματος
γένηται, ἀπέθανεν ὑπ' αὐτῶν, τίς οἶδε; τοὺς δὲ μὴ πολὺ
ἧσσον ἐμοῦ μισοῦντας αὐτόν—ἦσαν δὲ πολλοί — πῶς
οὐκ εἰκὸς ἦν ἐμοῦ μᾶλλον διαφθεῖραι αὐτόν; ἐκείνοις
μὲν γὰρ φανερὰ ἦν ἡ ὑποψία εἰς ἐμὲ οὖσα, ἐγὼ δὲ
ὑπὲρ ἐκείνων ὑπαίτιος ἐσόμενος σαφῶς ᾔδειν. τοῦ δὲ 7
ἀκολούθου ἡ μαρτυρία πῶς ἀξία πιστεύεσθαί ἐστιν;
ὑπό τε γὰρ τοῦ κινδύνου ἐκπεπληγμένον αὐτὸν οὐκ εἰκὸς
ἦν τοὺς ἀποκτείναντας γνῶναι, ὑπό τε τῶν κυρίων
ἀναγιγνωσκόμενον ἐπινεῦσαι ἦν εἰκός. ἀπιστουμένων
δὲ καὶ τῶν ἄλλων δούλων ἐν ταῖς μαρτυρίαις—οὐ γὰρ ἂν
ἐβασανίζομεν αὐτούς—πῶς δίκαιον τούτῳ μαρτυροῦντι
πιστεύσαντας διαφθεῖραί με; εἰ δέ τις τὰ εἰκότα 8
ἀληθέσιν ἴσα ἡγεῖται καταμαρτυρῆσαί μου, ταὐτὸν
ἀντιλογισάσθω ὅτι με εἰκότερον ἦν τὴν ἀσφάλειαν τῆς
ἐπιβουλῆς τηροῦντα φυλάξασθαι καὶ μὴ παραγενέσθαι
τῷ ἔργῳ μᾶλλον ἢ τοῦτον σφαττόμενον ὀρθῶς γνῶναι.
ὡς δὲ τόνδε τὸν κίνδυνον οὐκ ἀσφαλέστερον τοῦ ἀπὸ 9
τῆς γραφῆς ἡγούμην εἶναι, ἀλλὰ πολλαπλάσιον, εἰ μὴ
παρεφρόνουν, διδάξω. ἁλοὺς μὲν γὰρ τὴν γραφὴν τῆς

7 *ἀναγιγνωσκόμενον* stp Harp. α 107 s.v. Phot. α 1419 Suda α 1824 Lex Vind α 6 [Zonar.] α p. 196 l. 15

---

47 *κακουργουντας* PKöln (cfr. A.γ.2) : *κακὸν ποιοῦντας* AN *μὴ* AN[2] PKöln : om. N 48 post *οἶδε* distinxit A[2] *τοὺς δὲ* L : *τούσδε* AN 49 *δὲ* A[2]N : om. A 50 *ἦν* A : *ἂν ἦν* A[2] : *ἦν ἂν* N 51 *οὖσα* AN : *ἰοῦσα* Reiske 52 *ᾔδειν* N : *ἤδειν* A : *ᾔδη* Jernstedt *δὲ* A[2]N : om. A 60 *ταυτὸν* AN : *τοῦτ' αὖ* Gernet 63 *σφαττόμενον* AN : *σφαζόμενον* Jernstedt 64 *τόνδε* Dobree : *οὐδὲ* AN 65 *μὴ* A[1]N : om. A[a] 66 *γὰρ* A[1]N : om. A[a]

μὲν οὐσίας ᾔδειν ἐκστησόμενος, τοῦ δὲ σώματος καὶ
τῆς πόλεως οὐκ ἀπεστερούμην, περιγενόμενος δὲ καὶ
λειφθείς, κἂν ἔρανον παρὰ τῶν φίλων συλλέξας, οὐκ ἂν
εἰς τὰ ἔσχατα κακὰ ἦλθον· ἐὰν δὲ νῦν καταληφθεὶς
ἀποθάνω, ἀνόσια ὀνείδη τοῖς παισὶν ὑπολείψω, ἢ φυγὼν
γέρων καὶ ἄπολις ὢν ἐπὶ ξενίας πτωχεύσω.
10 Οὕτω μὲν ἃ κατηγόρηταί μου, πάντα ἄπιστά ἐστιν·
ἀπολύεσθαι δὲ ὑφ᾽ ὑμῶν, εἰ καὶ εἰκότως μὲν ὄντως δὲ
μὴ ἀπέκτεινα τὸν ἄνδρα, πολὺ μᾶλλον δίκαιός εἰμι. ἐγώ
τε γὰρ φανερὸν ὅτι μεγάλα ἀδικούμενος ἠμυνόμην· οὐ
γὰρ ἂν εἰκότως ἐδόκουν ἀποκτεῖναι αὐτόν· τούς τε
ἀποκτείναντας καὶ οὐ τοὺς αἰτίαν ἔχοντας ἀποκτεῖναι
11 ὀρθῶς ἂν καταλαμβάνοιτε. ἐκ δὲ παντὸς τρόπου
ἀπολυόμενος τῆς αἰτίας ἔγωγε οὔτε εἰς τὰ τεμένη εἰσιὼν
τὴν ἁγνείαν τῶν θεῶν μιανῶ, οὔτε ὑμᾶς πείθων ἀπολῦσαί
με ἀνόσια πράττω. οἱ δὲ διώκοντες μὲν ἐμὲ τὸν ἀναίτιον,
τὸν δὲ αἴτιον ἀφιέντες, τῆς τε ἀφορίας αἴτιοι γίγνονται,
ὑμᾶς τε ἀσεβεῖς εἰς τοὺς θεοὺς πείθοντες καταστῆναι
πάντων ὧν ἐμὲ ἄξιόν φασι παθεῖν εἶναι δίκαιοί εἰσι
12 τυγχάνειν. τούτους μὲν οὖν τούτων ἀξίους ὄντας
ἀπίστους ἡγεῖσθε· ἐμὲ δὲ ἔκ τε τῶν προειργασμένων
γνώσεσθε οὔτε ἐπιβουλεύοντα οὔτε τῶν οὐ προσηκόντων
ὀρεγόμενον, ἀλλὰ τἀναντία τούτων πολλὰς μὲν καὶ
μεγάλας εἰσφορὰς εἰσφέροντα, πολλὰ δὲ τριηραρχοῦντα,

67 *ᾔδειν* N: *ἤδειν* A : *ᾔδη* Jernstedt 67–8 *τοῦ δὲ σώματος καὶ τῆς πόλεως* N : *τῆς δὲ πόλεως καὶ τοῦ σώματος* A 68 *ἀπεστερούμην* N : *ἐστερούμην* A 69 *λειφθεὶς* N : *ληφθεὶς* A 70 *καταληφθεὶς* A[2]N : *καταλειφθεὶς* A 76 *ἠμυνόμην* Kayser[1] : *ἠμυνάμην* AN 77 *εἰκότως ἐδόκουν* N : *ἐδόκουν εἰκότως* A 79 *καταλαμβάνοιτε* N : *καταλαμβάνητε* A 82 *πράττω* AN : *πράσσω* Blass 83 *δὲ* N : *δ᾽* A 84 *ἀσεβεῖς* A : *ἀσεβεῖς τε* N 86 *οὖν* A[1]N : om. A[a] 87 *ἔκ τε*] *ἔκ γε* Franke *προειργασμένων* N : *προειργαμένων* A 89 *τἀναντία* A : *τὰ ἐναντία* N

λαμπρῶς δὲ χορηγοῦντα, πολλοὺς δὲ ἐρανίζοντα, μεγάλας
δὲ ὑπὲρ πολλῶν ἐγγύας ἀποτίνοντα, τήν τε οὐσίαν οὐ
δικαζόμενον ἀλλ' ἐργαζόμενον κεκτημένον, φιλοθύτην
τε καὶ νόμιμον ὄντα. τοιούτου δὲ ὄντος μου μηδὲν ἀνόσιον
μηδ' αἰσχρὸν καταγνῶτε. εἰ δὲ ὑπὸ ζῶντος ἐδιωκόμην, 13
οὐκ ἂν μόνον ὑπὲρ ἐμαυτοῦ ἀπελογούμην, ἀλλ' αὐτόν τε
τοῦτον καὶ τοὺς τούτῳ μὲν βοηθοῦντας, παρ' ἐμοῦ δὲ
ὠφελεῖσθαι ζητοῦντας ἐφ' οἷς κατηγορεῖτέ μου, ἐπέδειξα
ἂν ἀδικοῦντας. ταῦτα μὲν οὖν ἐπιεικέστερον ἢ δικαιότερον
παρήσω· δέομαι δ' ὑμῶν, ὦ ἄνδρες τῶν μεγίστων κριταὶ
καὶ κύριοι, ἐλεήσαντας τὴν ἀτυχίαν μου ἰατροὺς γενέσθαι
αὐτῆς, καὶ μὴ συνεπιβάντας τῇ τούτων ἐπιθέσει περιιδεῖν
ἀδίκως καὶ ἀθέως διαφθαρέντα με ὑπ' αὐτῶν.

92 *τήν τε*] *τὴν δὲ* Schaefer   93 *καὶ* post *ἐργαζόμενον* punctis del. A[1]   94 *τὲ καὶ* sic N : *δὲ καὶ* A   95 *μηδ'* N : *μὴ δὲ* A   *αἰσχρὸν*] *ισχρὸ* in ras. N[1]   98 *κατηγορεῖτέ* A : *κατηγορεῖτε* N : *κατηγορεῖταί* Ald.   *ἐπέδειξα* N : *ἀπέδειξα* A   103 *με* post *περιιδεῖν* l. 102 N   subscriptio *ἀπολογία φόνου ἀπαρασήμου* N[2] (*ἀπαρασίμου* N)

γ

ΕΚ ΚΑΤΗΓΟΡΙΑΣ Ο ΥΣΤΕΡΟΣ

ΥΠΟΘΕΣΙΣ

Τὰ εἰρημένα ὑπὸ τοῦ κατηγορουμένου λύει ἐνταῦθα, ὡς οὔτε ἄπιστος ἡ μαρτυρία τοῦ οἰκέτου, οὔτε ἀπίθανον πλούσιον ὄντα καὶ ἔνδοξον ποιῆσαι τὸν φόνον, διακινδυνεύειν μέλλοντα ὑπ᾽ αὐτοῦ τὴν οὐσίαν ἀπολέσαι. τὰς προτάσεις δὲ λύει κατὰ περιτροπήν· ἐκείνου γὰρ εἰπόντος ὅτι ἀτυχής εἰμι, περιτρέπει λέγων ὅτι ἡ ἀτυχία παρ᾽ αὐτοῦ ἀδικεῖται.

1 *Ἥ τε ἀτυχία ἀδικεῖται ὑπ᾽ αὐτοῦ, ἣν προϊστάμενος τῆς κακουργίας ἀφανίσαι τὴν αὑτοῦ μιαρίαν ζητεῖ· ὑπό τε ὑμῶν οὐκ ἄξιος ἐλεεῖσθαί ἐστιν, ἀκούσιον μὲν τῷ παθόντι περιθεὶς τὴν συμφοράν, ἑκουσίως δὲ αὐτὸς εἰς τοὺς κινδύνους καταστάς. ὡς μὲν οὖν ἀπέκτεινε τὸν ἄνδρα, ἐν τῷ προτέρῳ λόγῳ ἀπεδείξαμεν· ὡς δὲ οὐκ ὀρθῶς ἀπελογήθη, νῦν πειρασόμεθα ἐλέγχοντες.*

2 *Εἴτε γὰρ προσιόντας τινὰς προϊδόντες οἱ ἀποκτείναντες αὐτοὺς ἀπολιπόντες ᾤχοντο φεύγοντες πρότερον ἢ ἀπέδυσαν, οἱ ἐντυχόντες ἂν αὐτοῖς, εἰ καὶ τὸν δεσπότην τεθνεῶτα εὗρον, τόν γε θεράποντα, ὃς ἔμπνους ἀρθεὶς ἐμαρτύρει, ἔτι ἔμφρονα εὑρόντες, σαφῶς ἀνακρίναντες τοὺς ἐργασαμένους ἤγγειλαν ἂν ἡμῖν, καὶ οὐχ οὗτος ἂν τὴν αἰτίαν εἶχεν· εἴτε ἄλλοι τινὲς ἕτερόν τι τοιοῦτον*

1 *ἀπελογήθη* stp Pollux 2.119

Arg. inscr. *ὑπόθεσις τοῦ ἑξῆς* AN 1 *κατηγορουμένου* A[1]N : *κατηγόρου* A[a] 4 *ἀπολέσαι* A[1]N : *ἀπολέσθαι* A[a] 6 *ἀτυχία* A[1]N : *ἀδικία**** A[a] Inscriptio *κατηγορία ὕστερος* AN 8 *αὑτοῦ* Steph. : *αὐτοῦ* AN 14 *προιδόντες* N : *ἰδόντες* A 16 *αὐτοῖς* Reiske : *αὐτῷ* N : *αὐτῶ* A 17 *εὗρον* AN : *ηὗρον* Jernstedt 17–18 *ὃς … ἐμαρτύρει* del. Seume apud Sauppium[3] 19 alt. *ἂν* N: om. A

κακουργοῦντες ὀφθέντες ὑπ' αὐτῶν, ἵνα μὴ γνωσθῶσι
διέφθειραν αὐτούς, ἅμα τῷ τούτων φόνῳ τὸ κακούργημα
ἂν ἐκηρύσσετο καὶ εἰς τούτους ἂν ἡ ὑποψία ἧκεν. οἵ τε 3
ἧσσον κινδυνεύοντες τῶν μᾶλλον ἐν φόβῳ ὄντων οὐκ
οἶδ' ὅπως ἂν μᾶλλον ἐπεβούλευσαν αὐτῷ. τοὺς μὲν γὰρ
ὅ τε φόβος ἥ τε ἀδικία ἱκανὴ ἦν παῦσαι τῆς προμηθίας,
τοῖς δὲ ὅ τε κίνδυνος ἥ τε αἰσχύνη μείζων οὖσα τῆς
διαφορᾶς, εἰ καὶ διενοήθησαν ταῦτα πρᾶξαι, ἀρκοῦσα
ἦν σωφρονίσαι τὸ θυμούμενον τῆς γνώμης. οὐκ ὀρθῶς 4
δὲ τὴν τοῦ ἀκολούθου μαρτυρίαν ἄπιστον λέγουσιν
εἶναι. οὐ γὰρ ἐπὶ ταῖς τοιαύταις μαρτυρίαις βασανί-
ζονται, ἀλλ' ἐλεύθεροι ἀφίενται· ὁπόταν δὲ ἢ κλέψαντες
ἀπαρνῶνται ἢ συγκρύπτωσι τοῖς δεσπόταις, τότε
βασανίζοντες ἀξιοῦμεν τἀληθῆ λέγειν αὐτούς. οὐδὲ μὴν 5
ἀπογενέσθαι ἢ παραγενέσθαι εἰκότερον αὐτόν ἐστιν. εἰ
γὰρ ἀπεγένετο, τὸν μὲν κίνδυνον τὸν αὐτὸν ἔμελλε καὶ
παρὼν κινδυνεύειν—πᾶς γὰρ αὐτῶν ληφθεὶς τοῦτον ἂν
τὸν ἐπιβουλεύσαντα ἤλεγχεν ὄντα—τὸ δ' ἔργον ἧσσον
πράσσειν· οὐδεὶς γὰρ ὅστις τῶν παρόντων οὐκ ἂν
ὀκνηρότερος εἰς τὴν πρᾶξιν ἦν. ὡς δ' οὐκ ἐλάσσω ἀλλὰ 6
πολὺ μείζω τὸν ἀπὸ τῆς γραφῆς κίνδυνον ἢ τόνδε ἡγεῖτο
εἶναι, διδάξω. τὸ μὲν ἁλῶναι καὶ ἀποφυγεῖν ἀμφοτέρας
τὰς διώξεις ἐν ἴσαις ἐλπίσι θῶμεν αὐτῷ εἶναι. μὴ
παραχθῆναι δὲ τὴν γραφὴν οὐδεμίαν ἐλπίδα εἶχε τούτου
γε ζῶντος· οὐ γὰρ ἂν ἐπείθετο αὐτῷ· εἰς δὲ τόνδε τὸν
ἀγῶνα ἥξειν οὐκ ἤλπισε· λήσειν γὰρ ἐδόκει ἀποκτείνας

23 *οἵ τε* AN : *οἱ δὲ* Schaefer 26 *προμηθίας* Bekker : *προθυμίας* AN 29 *σωφρονίσαι* A : *σωφρονῆσαι* N 32 *ἢ* in ras N^1 33 *ἢ* $\mathrm{A}^2\mathrm{N}$: *εἰ* vel *οἱ* A 34 *τἀληθῆ* Weidner : *ἀληθῆ* AN 36 *μὲν* $\mathrm{A}^1\mathrm{N}$: om. A *τὸν αὐτὸν* AN : *οὐ τὸν αὐτὸν* A^2 37 *πᾶς* N : *πῶς* A *αὐτῶν ληφθεὶς* AN : *ἂν αὐτῶν ὁ λειφθεὶς* A^2 41 *τόνδε* A^2 : *τόδε* A : *τότε* N 44–5 *εἶχε τούτου γε* N : *γ' εἶχε τούτου* A 45 *ἐπείθετο*] *ἐπέθετο* Dobree 46 *ἀγῶνα* N : *κίνδυνον* A

7 αὐτόν. ἀξιῶν δὲ διὰ τὸ φανερὰν εἶναι τὴν ὑποψίαν
αὐτῷ μὴ καταδοκεῖσθαι ὑφ' ὑμῶν, οὐκ ὀρθῶς ἀξιοῖ.
εἰ γὰρ τοῦτον ἐν τοῖς μεγίστοις κινδύνοις ὄντα ἱκανὴ
ἦν ἡ ὑποψία ἀποστρέψαι τῆς ἐπιθέσεως, οὐδείς γ'
ἂν ἐπεβούλευσεν αὐτῷ· πᾶς γὰρ ἄν τις τῶν ἧσσον
κινδυνευόντων, τὴν ὑποψίαν μᾶλλον τοῦ κινδύνου
8 φοβούμενος, ἧσσον ἢ οὗτος ἡγεῖτο αὐτῷ. αἱ δ' εἰσφοραὶ
καὶ χορηγίαι εὐδαιμονίας μὲν ἱκανὸν σημεῖόν ἐστι,
τοῦ δὲ μὴ ἀποκτεῖναι τἀναντία· περὶ γὰρ αὐτῆς τῆς
εὐδαιμονίας τρέμων μὴ ἀποστερηθῇ, εἰκότως μὲν
ἀνοσίως δὲ ἀπέκτεινε τὸν ἄνδρα. φάσκων δὲ οὐ τοὺς
εἰκότως ἀλλ' ὄντως ἀποκτείναντας φονέας εἶναι, περὶ
μὲν τῶν ἀποκτεινάντων ὀρθῶς λέγει, εἴπερ ἐγένετο
φανερὸν ἡμῖν τίνες ἦσαν οἱ ἀποκτείναντες αὐτόν· μὴ
δεδηλωμένων δὲ τῶν ἀποκτεινάντων, ὑπὸ τῶν εἰκότων
ἐλεγχόμενος οὗτος ἂν καὶ οὐδεὶς ἕτερος ἀποκτείνας
αὐτὸν εἴη. οὐ γὰρ ἐπὶ μαρτύρων ἀλλὰ κρυπτόμενα
πράσσεται τὰ τοιαῦτα.

9 Οὕτω δὲ φανερῶς ἐκ τῆς αὐτοῦ ἀπολογίας ἐλεγχθεὶς
διαφθείρας αὐτόν, οὐδὲν ἕτερον ὑμῶν δεῖται ἢ τὴν
αὑτοῦ μιαρίαν εἰς ὑμᾶς αὐτοὺς ἐκτρέψαι. ἡμεῖς δὲ
ὑμῶν δεόμεθα μὲν οὐδέν, λέγομεν δ' ὑμῖν, εἰ μήτε ἐκ
τῶν εἰκότων μήτε ἐκ τῶν μαρτυρουμένων οὗτος νῦν

47 *φανερὰν* A^{c}N : *μὴ φανερὰν* A^{a} 48 *μὴ* A^{1}N : om. A^{a} 49 *εἰ* Reiske : *οὐ* AN 50 *ἀποστρέψαι*] *ἀποτρέψαι* Reiske 50–1 *γ' ἂν* Reiske : *γὰρ* AN : *γὰρ* <*ἂν*> Thiel 51 *ἐπεβούλευσεν* A^{1}N : *ἐπεβούλευεν* A^{a} *ἧσσον* A^{1}N : *ἥσσων* A^{a} 53 *ἡγεῖτο* AN : *ἐπέθετο* Maetzner; lacuna (*ἐπιθετέον* vel sim.) aut ante *ἡγεῖτο*, ut censuit Reiske, aut post *αὐτῷ*, ut censuit Maidment, statuenda est 54 *εὐδαιμονίας μὲν ἱκανὸν* N : *ἱκανὸν μὲν εὐδαιμονίας* A 58 *ἀλλ' ὄντως* Funkhänel : *ἀλλὰ τοὺς* AN : *ἀλλὰ τοὺς* <*ὄντως*> Reiske 61 *εἰκότων* A^{1}N : *εἰκότως* A^{a} 62 *ἀποκτείνας* AN : *ἁποκτείνας* Ignatius : <*ὁ*> *ἀποκτείνας* Weidner 63 *εἴη* A^{1}N : *ἂν εἴη* A^{a} *ἐπὶ* Ald. : *ὑπὸ* AN 64 *τὰ τοιαῦτα* N : *ταῦτα* A 65 *φανερῶς* A^{1} : *φανερὸς* A^{a}N *αὑτοῦ* Steph. : *αὐτου* AN 67 *αὑτοῦ* Steph. : *αὐτοῦ* AN 68 *ὑμῶν* e ras. A^{1}

ἐλέγχεται, οὐκ ἔστιν ἔτι τῶν διωκομένων ἔλεγχος οὐδείς.
ἀδίκως δ᾽ ἀπολυομένου τούτου ὑφ᾽ ὑμῶν, ἡμῖν μὲν 10
προστρόπαιος ὁ ἀποθανὼν οὐκ ἔσται, ὑμῖν δὲ ἐνθύμιος
γενήσεται. σαφῆ μὲν γὰρ τὸν θάνατον γιγνώσκοντες,
φανερῶς δὲ τὰ ἴχνη τῆς ὑποψίας εἰς τοῦτον φέροντα,
πιστῶς δὲ τοῦ ἀκολούθου μαρτυροῦντος, πῶς ἂν δικαίως
ἀπολύοιτε αὐτόν; ταῦτα οὖν εἰδότες βοηθεῖτε μὲν τῷ 11
ἀποθανόντι, τιμωρεῖσθε δὲ τὸν ἀποκτείναντα, ἁγνεύετε
δὲ τὴν πόλιν. τρία γὰρ ἀγαθὰ πράξετε· ἐλάσσους μὲν
τοὺς ἐπιβουλεύοντας καταστήσετε, πλείους δὲ τοὺς τὴν
εὐσέβειαν ἐπιτηδεύοντας, ἀπολύεσθε δ᾽ αὐτοὶ τῆς ὑπὲρ
τούτου μιαρίας.

10 ὁ ἀποθανὼν—γενήσεται Herennius *de divers. verb. signif.* ε 82.4 s.vv. ἐνθύμιον καὶ ἐνθύμημα [Ammon.] *de adfin. vocab. diff.* 171.3 *EtGud* ε p. 475.5 11 ἁγνεύετε τὴν πόλιν Harp. α 12 s.v.

---

71 ἀπολυομένου A^{1}N : ἀπολουμένου A^{a} ἡμῖν A^{1}N : ὑμῖν A^{a} 72 ὁ ἀποθανὼν οὐκ ἔσται] τεθνεὼς οὗτος lexica δὲ] om. lexica 73–6 σαφῆ μὲν ... αὐτόν post οὐδείς l. 70, transp. Jernstedt[1] 73 μὲν A^{1}N : om. A^{a} 78 δὲ] om. Harp. 80 ἀπολύεσθε AN : ἀπολύσεσθε Sauppe subscriptio ἐκ κατηγορίας ὁ ὕστερος N

δ

ΕΞ ΑΠΟΛΟΓΙΑΣ Ο ΥΣΤΕΡΟΣ

ΥΠΟΘΕΣΙΣ

Ἰδού, φησίν, ἐγὼ καί ἡ ἀτυχία μου. δεικτικῶς δὲ λέγει, ἑαυτὸν αἰνιττόμενος.—οὗτος, φησίν, ἐγὼ παραδίδωμι ἐμαυτὸν καὶ τῇ ἀτυχίᾳ μου καὶ τῇ τούτων κακουργίᾳ. τεκμήριον τοῦ μὴ πεποιηκέναι τίθησιν ὁ ἀπολογούμενος τὸ μηδαμοῦ προελθεῖν ἐκείνης τῆς νυκτός, καὶ περὶ τούτου πάντας τοὺς παῖδας εἰς βάσανον παραδίδωσιν.

1 *Ἰδοὺ ἐγὼ τῇ τε ἀτυχίᾳ, ἣν οὐ δικαίως αἰτιῶμαι, ὡς οὗτοί φασιν, ἑκὼν ἐμαυτὸν ἐγχειρίζω, τῇ τε τούτων ἔχθρᾳ, δεδιὼς μὲν τὸ μέγεθος τῆς διαβολῆς αὐτῶν, πιστεύων δὲ τῇ ὑμετέρᾳ γνώμῃ τῇ τε ἀληθείᾳ τῶν ἐξ ἐμοῦ πραχθέντων. ἀποστερούμενος δὲ ὑπ' αὐτῶν μηδὲ τὰς παρούσας ἀτυχίας ἀνακλαύσασθαι πρὸς ὑμᾶς, ἀπορῶ εἰς ἥντινα ἄλλην σωτηρίαν χρή με καταφυγεῖν.*
2 *καινότατα γὰρ δή, εἰ χρὴ καινότατα μᾶλλον ἢ κακουργότατα εἰπεῖν, διαβάλλουσί με. κατήγοροι γὰρ καὶ τιμωροὶ φόνου προσποιούμενοι εἶναι, ὑπεραπολογούμενοι τῆς ἀληθοῦς ὑποψίας ἁπάσης, διὰ τὴν ἀπορίαν τοῦ ἀποκτείναντος αὐτόν, ἐμὲ φονέα φασὶν εἶναι· δρῶντες δὲ τἀναντία ὧν προστέτακται αὐτοῖς, φανερὸν ὅτι ἀδίκως ἐμὲ μᾶλλον ἀποκτεῖναι ζητοῦσιν ἢ*
3 *τὸν φονέα τιμωρεῖσθαι. ἐμὲ δὲ προσῆκεν οὐδὲν ἄλλο ἢ πρὸς τὴν μαρτυρίαν τοῦ ἀκολούθου ἀπολογηθῆναι· οὐ γὰρ μηνυτὴς οὐδ' ἐλεγκτὴρ τῶν ἀποκτεινάντων εἰμί,*

Arg. inscriptio *ἡ* (art. om. A) *ὑπόθεσις τοῦ ἐξ ἀπολογίας ὑστέρου τοῦ ἑξῆς* AN 1–3 *Ἰδού ... κακουργίᾳ* e schol. censuit Blass 3 *δὲ* ante *τοῦ* add. A^2 7 *τῇ* A^2 : *ᾗ* AN 16 *προσποιούμενοι* A^{1}N : *ποιούμενοι* A^a 17 *ἀληθοῦς ὑποψίας ἁπάσης* N : *ὑποψίας πάσης τῆς ἀληθοῦς* A 23 *οὐδ'* A : *οὐδὲ* N

ἀλλὰ διωκόμενος, ἀποκρίνομαι. ὅμως δὲ περιεργαστέον,
ἵνα ἐκ παντὸς τρόπου τούτους τε ἐπιβουλεύοντάς μοι
ἐμαυτόν τε ἀπολυόμενον ἐπιδείξω τῆς ὑποψίας. τὴν μὲν 4
οὖν ἀτυχίαν ᾗ με διαβάλλουσιν, εἰς εὐτυχίαν αἰτοῦμαι
μεταστῆναι· ἀξιῶ δ' ὑμᾶς ἀπολύσαντάς με μακαρίσαι
μᾶλλον ἢ καταλαβόντας ἐλεῆσαι.

Φασὶ δὲ τῶν μὲν ἐντυχόντων παιομένοις αὐτοῖς οὐδένα
ὅντινα οὐκ εἰκότερον εἶναι σαφῶς πυθόμενον τοὺς
διαφθείραντας αὐτοὺς εἰς οἶκον ἀγγεῖλαι, ἢ ἀπολιπόντα
οἴχεσθαι. ἐγὼ δὲ οὐδένα οὕτω θερμὸν καὶ ἀνδρεῖον 5
ἄνθρωπον εἶναι δοκῶ, ὅντινα οὐκ ἂν ἀωρὶ τῶν νυκτῶν
νεκροῖς ἀσπαίρουσι συντυχόντα πάλιν ὑποστρέψαντα
φεύγειν μᾶλλον ἢ πυνθανόμενον τοὺς κακούργους περὶ
τῆς ψυχῆς κινδυνεῦσαι. τούτων δὲ μᾶλλον ἃ εἰκὸς ἦν
δρασάντων, οἱ μὲν ἐπὶ τοῖς ἱματίοις διαφθείραντες αὐ-
τοὺς οὐκ ἂν ἔτι εἰκότως ἀφίοιντο, ἐγὼ δὲ ἀπήλλαγμαι
τῆς ὑποψίας. εἰ δὲ ἐκηρύσσοντο ἢ μὴ ἄλλοι τινὲς 6
κακοῦργοι ἅμα τῷ τούτων φόνῳ, τίς οἶδεν; οὐδενὶ γὰρ
ἐπιμελὲς ἦν σκοπεῖν ταῦτα. ἀφανοῦς δὲ ὄντος τοῦ
κηρύγματος, οὐδὲ ὑπὸ τούτων τῶν κακούργων ἄπιστον
διαφθαρῆναι αὐτόν. τοῦ δὲ θεράποντος πῶς χρὴ 7
πιστοτέραν τὴν μαρτυρίαν ἢ τῶν ἐλευθέρων ἡγεῖσθαι;
οἱ μὲν γὰρ ἀτιμοῦνταί τε καὶ χρήμασι ζημιοῦνται, ἐὰν
μὴ τἀληθῆ δοκῶσι μαρτυρῆσαι· ὁ δὲ οὐκ ἔλεγχον
παρασχὼν οὐδὲ βάσανον ποῦ δίκην δώσει; ἢ τίς ἔλεγχος

25 μοι A^{c} : μου A^{a}N   28 μεταστῆναι N : μεσταστῆναι A
30 ἐντυχόντων A^{1}N : ἀτυχόντων ut vid. A^{a} παιομένοις A^{1im}N : om. A^{a}
32 αὐτοὺς A^{1}N : αὐτὸς A^{a} ἀπολιπόντα Gesner : ἀπολιπόντας AN
34 τῶν νυκτῶν N : τῆς νυκτὸς A   35 ἀσπαίρουσι N : ἀσπαίρουσιν A
39 ἀφίοιντο A^{2} : ἀφίωντο A : ἀφίοντο N   40–1 ἐκηρύσσετο ἢ μὴ ἄλλο τι κακούργημα ci. Jernstedt   46 ἐὰν e ras. A^{1} 48 παρασχὼν A, N ut vid. : παρασχόμενος N^{2} ποῦ Reiske : οὐ A : τι οὐ N : τινα οὐ N^{2} ἢ τίς Reiske : εἴ τις AN

ἔσται; ἀκινδύνως τε οὗτός γε μέλλων μαρτυρεῖν οὐδὲν θαυμαστὸν ἔπαθεν ὑπὸ τῶν κυρίων ἐχθρῶν μοι ὄντων πεισθεὶς καταψεύδεσθαί μου· ἐγώ τε ἀνόσι' ἂν πάσχοιμι, εἰ μὴ πιστῶς καταμαρτυρηθεὶς διαφθαρείην ὑφ' ὑμῶν.

8 *μὴ παραγενέσθαι δέ με τῷ φόνῳ ἀπιστότερον ἢ παραγενέσθαι φασὶν εἶναι. ἐγὼ δ' οὐκ ἐκ τῶν εἰκότων ἀλλ' ἔργῳ δηλώσω οὐ παραγενόμενος. ὁπόσοι γὰρ δοῦλοί μοι ἢ δοῦλαί εἰσι, πάντας παραδίδωμι βασανίσαι· καὶ ἐὰν μὴ φανῶ ταύτῃ τῇ νυκτὶ ἐν οἴκῳ καθεύδων ἢ ἐξελθών που, ὁμολογῶ φονεὺς εἶναι. ἡ δὲ νὺξ οὐκ*

9 *ἄσημος· τοῖς γὰρ Διπολιείοις ὁ ἀνὴρ ἀπέθανε. περὶ δὲ τῆς εὐδαιμονίας, ἧς ἕνεκα τρέμοντά μέ φασιν εἰκότως ἀποκτεῖναι αὐτόν, πολὺ τἀναντία ἐστί. τοῖς μὲν γὰρ ἀτυχοῦσι νεωτερίζειν συμφέρει· ἐκ γὰρ τῶν μεταβολῶν ἐπίδοξος ἡ δυσπραγία μεταβάλλειν αὐτῶν ἐστι· τοῖς δ' εὐτυχοῦσιν ἀτρεμίζειν καὶ φυλάσσειν τὴν παροῦσαν εὐπραγίαν. μεθισταμένων γὰρ τῶν πραγμάτων*

10 *δυστυχεῖς ἐξ εὐτυχούντων καθίστανται. ἐκ δὲ τῶν εἰκότων προσποιούμενοί με ἐλέγχειν, οὐκ εἰκότως ἀλλ' ὄντως φονέα μέ φασι τοῦ ἀνδρὸς εἶναι. τὰ δὲ εἰκότα ἄλλα πρὸς ἐμοῦ μᾶλλον ἀποδέδεικται ὄντα. ὅ τε γὰρ καταμαρτυρῶν μου ἄπιστος ἐλήλεγκται ὤν, ὅ τε ἔλεγχος οὐκ ἔστι· τά τε τεκμήρια ἐμά, οὐ τούτου ὄντα ἐδήλωσα· τά τε ἴχνη τοῦ φόνου οὐκ εἰς ἐμὲ φέροντα, ἀλλ'*

49 *τε* N : *τὲ* A : *δὲ* mal. Reiske : *γε* Decleva Caizzi : del. Gernet *οὗτός* A : *οὗτος* N : *τοῦτό* Dobree *γε* AN : *τε* mal. Reiske 50 *κυρίων* A^{a} : *κυρίως* A^{1}N 52 *ὑμῶν*] *φ ὑμ* e ras. A^{1} (fort. *αὐτῶν* A^{a}) 55 *ὁπόσοι* A^{c}N : *ὁπόσαι* A^{a} et fort. N^{a} 56 *δοῦλοι* A^{1}N : *δοῦδοι* ut vid. A^{a} *μοι ἢ δοῦλαι* N : *ἢ δοῦλαι μοι* A 57 *καθεύδων*] *παθεύδων* ut vid. A, corr. A^{2} 58 *που* AN : *ποι* Reiske 59 *Διπολιείοις* scripsi (cfr. praef. n. 34) : *διιπολείοις* A^{a}N : *διιπολίοις* A^{c} *δὲ* A^{1}N : om. A^{a} 61 *μὲν* N : om. A 62 *ἀτυχοῦσι νεωτερίζειν* Ald. : *ἀτυχοῦσι ἑταιρίζειν* AN 63 *μεταβάλλειν αὐτῶν* AN : *μεταβαλεῖν αὐτοῖς* Reiske 65 *γὰρ* N : *δὲ* A *πραγμάτων* Steph. : *πραγματειῶν* AN 69 *ἄλλα* AN : *ἀλλὰ* Sauppe 71 *τούτου*] *τούτων* Jernstedt

εἰς τοὺς ἀπολυομένους ἀποδέδεικται ὑπ᾽ αὐτῶν. Πάντων δὲ τῶν κατηγορηθέντων ἀπίστων ἐλεγχθέντων, οὐκ ἐὰν ἀποφύγω οὐκ ἔστιν ἐξ ὧν ἐλεγχθήσονται οἱ κακουργοῦντες, ἀλλ᾽ ἐὰν ληφθῶ, οὐδεμία ἀπολογία τοῖς διωκομένοις ἀρκοῦσά ἐστιν.

Οὕτω δὲ ἀδίκως διώκοντές με, αὐτοὶ μὲν ἀνοσίως 11 ἀποκτεῖναι ζητοῦντες καθαροί φασιν εἶναι, ἐμὲ δὲ ὃς εὐσεβεῖν ὑμᾶς πείθω, ἀνόσια δρᾶν λέγουσιν. ἐγὼ δὲ καθαρὸς ὢν πάντων τῶν ἐγκλημάτων ὑπὲρ ἐμαυτοῦ ἐπισκήπτω αἰδεῖσθαι τὴν τῶν μηδὲν ἀδικούντων εὐσέβειαν, ὑπὲρ δὲ τοῦ ἀποθανόντος ἀναμιμνῄσκων τὴν ποινὴν παραινῶ ὑμῖν, μὴ τὸν ἀναίτιον καταλαβόντας τὸν αἴτιον ἀφεῖναι· ἀποθανόντος γὰρ ἐμοῦ οὐδεὶς ἔτι τὸν αἴτιον ζητήσει. ταῦτα οὖν σεβόμενοι ὁσίως καὶ 12 δικαίως ἀπολύετέ με, καὶ μὴ μετανοήσαντες τὴν ἁμαρτίαν γνῶτε· ἀνίατος γὰρ ἡ μετάνοια τῶν τοιούτων ἐστίν.

11 μὴ—αἴτιον stp Suda κ 607.3 s.v. καταλαβεῖν   12 ἁμαρτίαν—ἐστίν stp parum accurate Phot. α 1992 s.v. ἀνίατον, sc. ἀνίατος ἡ ἁμαρτία ἐστίν

---

76 ληφθῶ Bekker : ἐλεγχθῶ A^{2}N : ἐλεγχῶ A : καταληφθῶ Blass coll. disput. Spengelii^3 79 ὃς A^1 : ὡς AN   81 ὑπὲρ AN : ὑπὲρ <μὲν> Bekker : ὑπέρ <τε> Blass   83 δὲ AN : τε Blass   83–5 ἀναμιμνῄσκων ... ἀποθανόντος om. N   84 τὸν A : om. Suda   καταλαβόντας A^1 : καταλαβόντες Suda : καταβαλόντας A^a 88 subscriptio ὁ ὕστερος τῆς ἀπολογίας N

3

ΤΕΤΡΑΛΟΓΙΑ Β

α

ΚΑΤΗΓΟΡΙΑ ΦΟΝΟΥ ΑΚΟΥΣΙΟΥ

ΥΠΟΘΕΣΙΣ

Δύο παῖδες ἐν γυμνασίοις ἠκόντιζον, συνέβη δὲ τὸν μὲν ἐντέχνως ἀφεῖναι τὸ βέλος, τὸν δ' ἕτερον ὑπὸ τὴν φορὰν τοῦ ἀκοντίου δραμόντα πληγῆναι. τελευτήσαντος δὲ τοῦ παιδὸς ὁ τούτου πατὴρ κατηγορεῖ τοῦ βαλόντος ὡς ἀνδροφόνου· ὁ δὲ μετατίθησι τὴν αἰτίαν τῆς πληγῆς ἐπὶ τὸν δραμόντα. ὅθεν οἱ μὲν ἀντέγκλημα τὴν στάσιν, οἱ δὲ μετάστασιν λέγουσιν.

Τὰ μὲν ὁμολογούμενα τῶν πραγμάτων ὑπό τε τοῦ νόμου 1
κατακέκριται ὑπό τε τῶν ψηφισαμένων, οἳ κύριοι πάσης
τῆς πολιτείας εἰσίν· ἐὰν δέ τι ἀμφισβητήσιμον ᾖ, τοῦτο
ὑμῖν, ὦ ἄνδρες πολῖται, προστέτακται διαγνῶναι. οἶμαι
μὲν οὖν οὐδὲ ἀμφισβητήσειν πρὸς ἐμὲ τὸν διωκόμενον·
ὁ γὰρ παῖς μου ἐν γυμνασίῳ ἀκοντισθεὶς διὰ τῶν
πλευρῶν ὑπὸ τούτου τοῦ μειρακίου παραχρῆμα
ἀπέθανεν. ἑκόντα μὲν οὖν οὐκ ἐπικαλῶ ἀποκτεῖναι,
ἄκοντα δέ. ἐμοὶ δὲ οὐκ ἐλάσσω τοῦ ἑκόντος ἄκων 2
τὴν συμφορὰν κατέστησε. τῷ δὲ ἀποθανόντι αὐτῷ μὲν
οὐδὲν ἐνθύμιον, τοῖς δὲ ζῶσι προσέθηκεν. ὑμᾶς δὲ ἀξιῶ

Arg. Inscriptio ὑπόθεσις τῆς ἑξῆς τετραλογίας AN 1 γυμνασίοις] γυμνασίῳ ci. Maetzner 6 ἀντέγκλημα A^{1}N : ἀντέκλημα A 7 Inscriptio κατηγορία φόνου ἀκουσίου AN 11 οὖν A^{1}N : omiserat ut vid. A^{a} οὐδὲ A : oblitteratum in N 15 ἐλάσσω A^{1}N : ἐλάσσων A^{a} 16–17 τῷ δὲ ... προσέθηκεν del. Gernet ἐλεοῦντας μὲν τὴν ἀπαιδίαν τῶν γονέων, οἰκτίροντας δὲ τὴν ἄωρον τοῦ ἀποθανόντος τελευτήν, εἴργοντας ὧν ὁ νόμος εἴργει τὸν ἀποκτείναντα μὴ περιορᾶν ἅπασαν τὴν πόλιν ὑπὸ τούτου μιαινομένην.

18 οἰκτίροντας Blass² : οἰκτείροντας AN 19 εἴργοντας A¹ ut vid., N : εἵργοντας Aᵃ 20 εἴργει A¹ : εἴργειν N : εἵργει Aᵃ Subscriptio κατηγορία φόνου ἀκουσίου N

β

ΑΠΟΛΟΓΙΑ ΦΟΝΟΥ ΑΚΟΥΣΙΟΥ

ΥΠΟΘΕΣΙΣ

Ὁ τοῦ ἀκοντίσαντος πατὴρ ἑαυτῷ φησιν αἴτιον γενέσθαι τὸν ἀποθανόντα τοῦ φόνου· φερομένου γὰρ τοῦ ἀκοντίου ὑποδραμεῖν ὑπὸ τὸν σκοπόν, ὅθεν ἂν αὐτὸν ἑαυτοῦ φονέα νομίζεσθαι. ἔστιν οὖν ἡ στάσις μετάστασις, οὐ συγγνώμη ὥς τινες ἐνόμιζον.

Νῦν δὴ φανερόν μοι ὅτι αὗται αἱ συμφοραὶ καὶ χρεῖαι 1
τούς τε ἀπράγμονας εἰς ἀγῶνας τούς τε ἡσυχίους τολμᾶν
τά τε ἄλλα παρὰ φύσιν λέγειν καὶ δρᾶν βιάζονται. ἐγὼ
γὰρ ἥκιστα τοιοῦτος ὢν καὶ βουλόμενος εἶναι, εἰ μὴ
πολύ γε ἔψευσμαι, ὑπ' αὐτῆς τῆς συμφορᾶς ἠναγκάσθην
νῦν παρὰ τὸν ἄλλον τρόπον ὑπὲρ πραγμάτων
ἀπολογεῖσθαι, ὧν ἐγὼ χαλεπῶς μὲν τὴν ἀκρίβειαν
ἔγνων, ἔτι δὲ ἀπορωτέρως διάκειμαι ὡς χρὴ ὑμῖν
ἑρμηνεῦσαι ταῦτα. ὑπὸ δὲ σκληρᾶς ἀνάγκης βιαζόμενος, 2
καὶ αὐτὸς εἰς τὸν ὑμέτερον ἔλεον, ὦ ἄνδρες δικασταί,
καταπεφευγὼς δέομαι ὑμῶν, ἐὰν ἀκριβέστερον ἢ ὡς
σύνηθες ὑμῖν δόξω εἰπεῖν, μὴ διὰ τὰς προειρημένας
τύχας ἀποδεξαμένους μου τὴν ἀπολογίαν δόξῃ καὶ μὴ
ἀληθείᾳ τὴν κρίσιν ποιήσασθαι· ἡ μὲν γὰρ δόξα τῶν

Arg. Inscriptio ὑπόθεσις τοῦ ἑξῆς AN 3 ὑποδραμεῖν Jernstedt^1 : ὑπέδραμεν AN ὅθεν <δικαίως> Maetzner 4 οὖν N : om. A ἡ A^1N : ὁ A^a 6 Inscriptio ἀπολογία φόνου ἀκουσίου AN μοι A^1N : om. A^a 7 ἀγῶνας <καταστῆναι> Reiske 8 ἄλλα <καὶ> Sauppe, Scheibe 10 αὐτῆς τῆς A^1, N^1 (τῆς τ in ras.) : τῆς om. A^a 11 νῦν Jernstedt : ἂν re vera A^a, N : ras. A^c πραγμάτων A^cN : τῶν πραγμάτων A^a 13 ἀπορωτέρως A, N^1 (alt. ω in ras.) ὡς AN : ὅπως Blass 15 καὶ A^1 : κἂν A^aN 17 ὑμῖν A^1N : om. A^a 18 <δυσχερῶς> ἀποδεξαμένους Gebauer^3

πραχθέντων πρὸς τῶν λέγειν δυναμένων ἐστίν, ἡ δὲ ἀλήθεια πρὸς τῶν δίκαια καὶ ὅσια πρασσόντων.

3 Ἐδόκουν μὲν οὖν ἔγωγε ταῦτα παιδεύων τὸν υἱὸν ἐξ
ὧν μάλιστα τὸ κοινὸν ὠφελεῖται, ἀμφοῖν τι ἡμῖν ἀγαθὸν
ἀποβήσεσθαι· συμβέβηκε δέ μοι πολὺ παρὰ γνώμην
τούτων. τὸ γὰρ μειράκιον οὐχ ὕβρει οὐδὲ ἀκολασίᾳ,
ἀλλὰ μελετῶν μετὰ τῶν ἡλίκων ἀκοντίζειν ἐν τῷ
γυμνασίῳ, ἔβαλε μὲν, οὐκ ἀπέκτεινε δὲ οὐδένα κατά γε
τὴν ἀλήθειαν ὧν ἔπραξεν, ἄλλου δ᾽ εἰς αὑτὸν ἁμαρτόντος
4 εἰς ἀκουσίους αἰτίας ἦλθεν. εἰ μὲν γὰρ τὸ ἀκόντιον ἔξω
τῶν ὅρων τῆς αὑτοῦ πορείας ἐπὶ τὸν παῖδα ἐξενεχθὲν
ἔτρωσεν αὐτόν, οὐδεὶς ἡμῖν λόγος ὑπελείπετο μὴ
φονεῦσιν εἶναι· τοῦ δὲ παιδὸς ὑπὸ τὴν τοῦ ἀκοντίου
φορὰν ὑποδραμόντος καὶ τὸ σῶμα προστήσαντος, ⟨ὁ
μὲν ἐκωλύθη⟩ τοῦ σκοποῦ τυχεῖν, ὁ δὲ ὑπὸ τὸ ἀκόντιον
ὑπελθὼν ἐβλήθη, καὶ τὴν αἰτίαν οὐχ ἡμετέραν οὖσαν
5 προσέβαλεν ἡμῖν. διὰ δὲ τὴν ὑποδρομὴν βληθέντος
τοῦ παιδός, τὸ μὲν μειράκιον οὐ δικαίως ἐπικαλεῖται,
οὐδένα γὰρ ἔβαλε τῶν ἀπὸ τοῦ σκοποῦ ἀφεστώτων· ὁ
δὲ παῖς εἴπερ ἑστὼς φανερὸς ὑμῖν ἐστι μὴ βληθείς,
ἑκουσίως ⟨δ᾽⟩ ὑπὸ τὴν φορὰν τοῦ ἀκοντίου ὑπελθών,
ἔτι σαφεστέρως δηλοῦται διὰ τὴν αὑτοῦ ἁμαρτίαν
ἀποθανών· οὐ γὰρ ἂν ἐβλήθη ἀτρεμίζων καὶ μὴ
6 διατρέχων. ἀκουσίου δὲ τοῦ φόνου ἐξ ἀμφοῖν ὑμῖν
ὁμολογουμένου γενέσθαι, ἐκ τῆς ἁμαρτίας, ὁποτέρου
αὐτῶν ἐστίν, ἔτι δὲ σαφέστερον ⟨ἂν⟩ ὁ φονεὺς ἐλεγχθείη.

22 *μὲν οὖν* A^1 : *μὲν* A^a : *γοῦν* N 24 *ἀποβήσεσθαι* A^1N : *ἀποβήσεται* A^a 26 *ἐν* M : *ἐπὶ* AN 27 *οὐκ ἀπέκτεινε δὲ οὐδένα* A^1N : *οὐκ ἀπέκτεινα δὲ* A^a : *οὐδένα οὐδ᾽ ἀπέκτεινε* Blass^2 28 *ἄλλου δ᾽ εἰς αὑτὸν* A^1 ut vid. : *ἀλλ᾽ οὐδ᾽ εἰς αὐτὸν* A^aN 30 *αὑτοῦ* Steph. : *αὐτοῦ* AN 31 *οὐδεὶς* <*ἂν*> Dobree 32 *φονεῦσιν* Bekker : *φονεὺς* AN 33–4 add. Reiske 38 *τῶν* A^1N : *τὸν* A^a 39 *φανερὸς* A^1 : *φανερῶς* A^aN 40 add. Blass 41 *αὑτοῦ* Steph. : *αὐτοῦ* AN 45 *δὲ* AN : *γε* Sauppe : del. Dobree add. Dobree

οἵ τε γὰρ ἁμαρτάνοντες ὧν ἂν ἐπινοήσωσί τι δρᾶσαι,
οὗτοι πράκτορες τῶν ἀκουσίων εἰσίν· οἵ τε ἀκούσιόν
τι δρῶντες ἢ πάσχοντες, οὗτοι τῶν παθημάτων αἴτιοι
γίγνονται. τὸ μὲν τοίνυν μειράκιον περὶ οὐδένα οὐδὲν 7
ἥμαρτεν. οὔτε γὰρ ἀπειρημένον ἀλλὰ προστεταγμένον
ἐξεμελέτα, οὔτε ἐν γυμναζομένοις ἀλλ᾽ ἐν τῇ τῶν
ἀκοντιζόντων τάξει ἠκόντιζεν, οὔτε τοῦ σκοποῦ
ἁμαρτών, εἰς τοὺς ἀφεστῶτας ἀκοντίσας, τοῦ παιδὸς
ἔτυχεν, ἀλλὰ πάντα ὀρθῶς ὡς ἐπενόει δρῶν ἔδρασε μὲν
οὐδὲν ἀκούσιον, ἔπαθε δὲ διακωλυθεὶς τοῦ σκοποῦ
τυχεῖν. ὁ δὲ παῖς βουλόμενος προδραμεῖν, τοῦ καιροῦ 8
διαμαρτὼν ἐν ᾧ διατρέχων οὐκ ἂν ἐπλήγη, περιέπεσεν
οἷς οὐκ ἤθελεν, ἀκουσίως δὲ ἁμαρτὼν εἰς ἑαυτὸν
οἰκείαις συμφοραῖς κέχρηται, τῆς δ᾽ ἁμαρτίας
τετιμωρημένος ἑαυτὸν ἔχει τὴν δίκην, οὐ συνηδομένων
μὲν οὐδὲ συνεθελόντων ἡμῶν, συναλγούντων δὲ καὶ
συλλυπουμένων. τῆς δὲ ἁμαρτίας εἰς τοῦτον ἡκούσης,
τὸ ἔργον οὐχ ἡμέτερον ἀλλὰ τοῦ ἐξαμαρτόντος ἐστί, τό
τε πάθος εἰς τὸν δράσαντα ἐλθὸν ἡμᾶς μὲν ἀπολύει τῆς
αἰτίας, τὸν δὲ δράσαντα δικαίως ἅμα τῇ ἁμαρτίᾳ
τετιμώρηται. ἀπολύει δὲ καὶ ὁ νόμος ἡμᾶς, ᾧ πιστεύων, 9
εἴργοντι μήτε ἀδίκως μήτε δικαίως ἀποκτείνειν, ὡς
φονέα με διώκει. ὑπὸ μὲν γὰρ τῆς αὐτοῦ τοῦ τεθνεῶτος
ἁμαρτίας ὅδε ἀπολύεται μηδὲ ἀκουσίως ἀποκτεῖναι
αὐτόν· ὑπὸ δὲ τοῦ διώκοντος οὐδ᾽ ἐπικαλούμενος ὡς

46 *ὧν* AN : *ὡς* Wilamowitz[1] 47 *οἵ τε* Spengel[2] : *οἱ δὲ* AN *ἀκούσιόν* Pahle : *ἑκούσιόν* AN 48 *ἢ πάσχοντες* del. Spengel[2] : *καὶ πάσχοντες* Cole apud Gagarinum 49–50 *οὐδὲν ἥμαρτεν* N : *ἥμαρτεν οὐδὲν* A 51 *ἐξεμελέτα* A : *ἐμελέτα* N 53 *ἁμαρτὼν* A^aN : *ἁμαρτὸν* A^c *ἀφεστῶτας* A^2N : *ἐφεστῶτας* A 54 *πάντα* A^1N : *πάντας* A^a 56 *καιροῦ* Spengel[2] : *χώρου* AN : *χρόνου* Reiske 61 *συνεθελόντων* A^1N : *συνεθελότων* A^a 62 *τοῦτον* Reiske : *τοῦτο* AN 63 pr. *τὸ* AN : *τό* <*τ'*> Spengel[2] 67 *εἴργοντι* A^1N : *εἵργοντι* A^a 68 *φονέα με* AN : *φονέας* Lipsius[1] : an *φονέας ἡμᾶς*? Blass[2] *τῆς αὐτοῦ* in ras A^1 70 *οὐδ᾽ ἐπικαλούμενος ὡς* A^1N : *ὡς ἐπικαλούμενος* A^a

ἑκὼν ἀπέκτεινεν, ἀμφοῖν ἀπολύεται τοῖν ἐγκλημάτοιν,
10 ⟨μήτ' ἄκων⟩ μήθ' ἑκὼν ἀποκτεῖναι. ἀπολυόμενος δὲ ὑπό τε τῆς ἀληθείας τῶν πραχθέντων ὑπό τε τοῦ νόμου καθ' ὃν διώκεται, οὐδὲ τῶν ἐπιτηδευμάτων ἕνεκα δίκαιοι τοιούτων κακῶν ἀξιοῦσθαί ἐσμεν. οὗτός τε γὰρ ἀνόσια πείσεται τὰς οὐ προσηκούσας φέρων ἁμαρτίας, ἐγώ τε μᾶλλον μὲν οὐδέν, ὁμοίως δὲ τούτῳ ἀναμάρτητος ὤν, εἰς πολλαπλασίους τούτου συμφορὰς ἥξω· ἐπί τε γὰρ τῇ τούτου διαφθορᾷ ἀβίωτον τὸ λειπόμενον τοῦ βίου διάξω, ἐπί τε τῇ ἐμαυτοῦ ἀπαιδίᾳ ζῶν ἔτι κατορυχθήσομαι.

11 Ἐλεοῦντες οὖν τοῦδε μὲν τοῦ νηπίου τὴν ἀναμάρτητον συμφοράν, ἐμοῦ δὲ τοῦ γηραιοῦ καὶ ἀθλίου τὴν ἀπροσδόκητον κακοπάθειαν, μὴ καταψηφισάμενοι δυσμόρους ἡμᾶς καταστήσητε, ἀλλ' ἀπολύοντες εὐσεβεῖτε. ὅ τε γὰρ ἀποθανὼν συμφοραῖς περιπεσὼν οὐκ ἀτιμώρητός ἐστιν, ἡμεῖς τε οὐ δίκαιοι τὰς τούτων
12 ἁμαρτίας συμφέρειν ἐσμέν. τήν τε οὖν εὐσέβειαν τούτων τῶν πραχθέντων καὶ τὸ δίκαιον αἰδούμενοι ὁσίως καὶ δικαίως ἀπολύετε ἡμᾶς, καὶ μὴ ἀθλιωτάτω δύο πατέρα καὶ παῖδα ἀώροις συμφοραῖς περιβάλητε.

11 *γηραιοῦ* stp Pollux 2.13 (item 4.*α*.2)

---

72 add. Ald. *μήθ'* A : *μήτε* N 73 *τῶν πραχθέντων ὑπό τε τοῦ νόμου* A[1]N : *τοῦ νόμου ὑπό τε τῶν πραχθέντων* A[a] 74 *ἕνεκα* Ald. : *εἵνεκα* AN 80 *διάξω* A[c]N : *διδάξω* A[a] 80–1 *ἔτι κατορυχθήσομαι* Reiske : *ἐπικατορυχθήσομαι* AN 82 *οὖν* A : *μὲν οὖν* N *τοῦδε* AN[2] : *οὐδὲ* N 86 *ἀποθανὼν*] *ἁμαρτὼν* Sched. Eton. 90 *ἡμᾶς* N : *ὑμᾶς* A *δύο* A[a]N : *δύω* A[1] 91 *περιβάλητε* N : *περιβάλοιτε* A subscriptio *ἀπολογία φόνου ἀκουσίου* N

γ

ΕΚ ΚΑΤΗΓΟΡΙΑΣ Ο ΥΣΤΕΡΟΣ

Ὅτι μὲν αὐτὴ ἡ χρεία παρὰ φύσιν καὶ λέγειν καὶ δρᾶν 1
ἅπαντας ἀναγκάζει, ἔργῳ καὶ οὐ λόγῳ δοκεῖ μοι σημαίνειν οὗτος· ἥκιστα γὰρ ἔν γε τῷ ἔμπροσθεν χρόνῳ ἀναιδὴς καὶ τολμηρὸς ὤν, νῦν ὑπ' αὐτῆς τῆς συμφορᾶς ἠνάγκασται λέγειν οἷα οὐκ ἄν ποτε ᾤμην ἐγὼ τοῦτον
εἰπεῖν. ἐγώ τε γὰρ πολλῇ ἀνοίᾳ χρώμενος οὐκ ἂν 2
ὑπέλαβον τοῦτον ἀντειπεῖν· οὐδὲ γὰρ ἂν ἕνα λόγον ἀντὶ δυοῖν λέξας τὸ ἥμισυ τῆς κατηγορίας ἐμαυτὸν ἂν ἀπεστέρησα· οὗτός τε μὴ τολμῶν οὐκ ἂν προεῖχε τῷ διπλασίῳ μου, ἕνα μὲν πρὸς ἕνα λόγον ἀπολογηθείς,
ἃ δὲ κατηγόρησεν ἀναποκρίτως εἰπών. τοσοῦτον δὲ 3
προέχων ἐν τοῖς λόγοις ἡμῶν, ἔτι δὲ ἐν οἷς ἔπρασσε πολλαπλάσια τούτων, οὗτος μὲν οὐκ ὁσίως δεῖται ὑμῶν συχνῶς τὴν ἀπολογίαν ἀποδέχεσθαι αὐτοῦ· ἐγὼ δὲ δράσας μὲν οὐδὲν κακόν, παθὼν δὲ ἄθλια καὶ δεινά, καὶ νῦν ἔτι δεινότερα τούτων ἔργῳ καὶ οὐ λόγῳ, εἰς τὸν ὑμέτερον ἔλεον καταπεφευγὼς δέομαι ὑμῶν, ὦ ἄνδρες ἀνοσίων ἔργων τιμωροί, ὁσίων δὲ διαγνώμονες, μὴ ἔργα φανερὰ ὑπὸ πονηρᾶς λόγων ἀκριβείας πεισθέντας,
ψευδῆ τὴν ἀλήθειαν τῶν πραχθέντων ἡγήσασθαι· ἡ 4
μὲν γὰρ πιστότερον ἢ ἀληθέστερον σύγκειται, ἡ δ' ἀδολώτερον καὶ ἀδυνατώτερον λεχθήσεται. τῷ μὲν

Inscriptio *ὁ ὕστερος ἐκ κατηγορίας* AN 3 *γε* A[c]N : *τε* A[a] 7–8 *ἀντὶ δυοῖν λέξας* Reiske : *ἀντιδοὺς ἢ λέξας* AN : *ἀντιδοὺς* {*ἢ λέξας*} Maetzner 11 *ἀναποκρίτως* A[1]N : *ἀποκρίτως* A[a] 14–15 *δὲ δράσας* Reiske : *δ' ἔδρασα* AN 19 *ἔργα φανερὰ* AN : secl. Franke : <*παρὰ τὰ*> *ἔργα φανερὰ* Gernet : <*πρὸς*> *ἔργα φανερὰ* Schoell[1] : *ἔργα φανερὰ* <*παραλαβόντας*> Thalheim *πεισθέντας* AN : *πεισθέντες* A[2] : *πεισθέντας* <*ἀφανίσαι*> dubitanter Sauppe 20 *ἡγήσασθαι* N : *ἡγήσασθε* A[a] : *ἡγήσησθε* A[1]

οὖν δικαίῳ πιστεύων ὑπερορῶ τῆς ἀπολογίας· τῇ δὲ σκληρότητι τοῦ δαίμονος ἀπιστῶν ὀρρωδῶ, μὴ οὐ μόνον τῆς χρείας τοῦ παιδὸς ἀποστερηθῶ, ἀλλὰ καὶ αὐθέντην
5 *προσκαταγνωσθέντα ὑφ' ὑμῶν ἐπίδω αὐτόν. εἰς τοῦτο γὰρ τόλμης καὶ ἀναιδείας ἥκει, ὥστε τὸν μὲν βαλόντα καὶ ἀποκτείναντα οὔτε τρῶσαι οὔτε ἀποκτεῖναί φησι, τὸν δὲ οὔτε ψαύσαντα τοῦ ἀκοντίου οὔτε ἐπινοήσαντα ἀκοντίσαι, ἁπάσης μὲν γῆς ἁμαρτόντα, πάντων δὲ σωμάτων, διὰ τῶν ἑαυτοῦ πλευρῶν διαπῆξαι τὸ ἀκόντιον λέγει. ἐγὼ δὲ ἑκουσίως κατηγορῶν ἀποκτεῖναι αὐτὸν πιστότερος ἄν μοι δοκῶ εἶναι ἢ οὗτος, ⟨ὃς⟩ μήτε βαλεῖν*
6 *μήτε ἀποκτεῖναί φησι τὸ μειράκιον. ὁ μὲν γὰρ ἐν τούτῳ τῷ καιρῷ καλούμενος ὑπὸ τοῦ παιδοτρίβου, ὃς ὑπεδέχετο τοῖς ἀκοντίζουσι τὰ ἀκόντια ἀναιρεῖσθαι, διὰ τὴν τοῦ βαλόντος ἀκολασίαν πολεμίῳ τῷ τούτου βέλει περιπεσών, οὐδὲν οὐδ' εἰς ἕν' ἁμαρτών, ἀθλίως ἀπέθανεν· ὁ δὲ περὶ τὸν τῆς ἀναιρέσεως καιρὸν πλημμελήσας, οὐ τοῦ σκοποῦ τυχεῖν ἐκωλύθη, ἀλλ' ἄθλιον καὶ πικρὸν σκοπὸν ἐμοὶ ἀκοντίσας, ἑκὼν μὲν οὐκ ἀπέκτεινε, μᾶλλον δὲ ἑκὼν ἢ οὔτε ἔβαλεν οὔτε ἀπέκτεινεν.*

7 *Ἀκουσίως δὲ οὐχ ἧσσον ἢ ἑκουσίως ἀποκτείναντός μου τὸν παῖδα, τὸ παράπαν δὲ ἀρνουμένου μὴ ἀποκτεῖναι*

27 *ἥκει* A^1N : *ἥκω* A^a 28 *ἀποκτείναντα* A : *ἀκοντίσαντα* N 29 *ψαύσαντα* A^1N : *ψαύσατα* A^a 31–2 *τὸ ἀκόντιον λέγει* N : *λέγει τὸ ἀκόντιον* A 33 add. Ald. 34 *φησι* A : *φασι* N : *φάσκων* (*ὃς* omisso) Weidner 35 *καλούμενος* AN : *κελευόμενος* Maidment *ὃς ὑπεδέχετο* AN : *ᾧ ὑπεδέχετο* Thalheim : *ὡς ὑπεδέχοιτο* Blass[2] 36 *ἀναιρεῖσθαι* del. Franke 38 *ἕν'* Franke : *ἓν* AN *ἀπέθανεν* A : *ἀπέθανε* N 40 *ἐκωλύθη* A^2N : *ἐκωλήθη* ut vid. A^1 : *ἐβουλήθη* ut vid. A^a 41 *ἑκὼν* A : *ἐκὼν* N 42 *ἢ* eras. in A 43 *ἀκουσίως … ἑκουσίως* A^2 : *ἑκουσίως … ἀκουσίως* AN *ἧσον* A, corr. A^2 *ἀποκτείναντός* AN : *ἀπέκτεινέ* A^2 44 post *παῖδα* lacunam susp. Sykutris *δὲ* del. Jernstedt *ἀρνουμένου* AN : *ἀρνούμενος* A^2

αὐτόν, οὐδ' ὑπὸ τοῦ νόμου καταλαμβάνεσθαί φησιν, ὃς ἀπαγορεύει μήτε δικαίως μήτε ἀδίκως ἀποκτείνειν. ἀλλὰ τίς ὁ βαλών; εἰς τίν' ὁ φόνος ἀνήκει; εἰς τοὺς θεωμένους ἢ εἰς τοὺς παιδαγωγούς, ὧν οὐδεὶς οὐδὲν κατηγορεῖ; οὐ γὰρ ἀφανὴς ἀλλὰ καὶ λίαν φανερὸς ἔμοιγε αὐτοῦ ὁ θάνατός ἐστιν. ἐγὼ δὲ τὸν νόμον ὀρθῶς ἀγορεύειν φημὶ τοὺς ἀποκτείναντας κολάζεσθαι· ὅ τε γὰρ ἄκων ἀποκτείνας ἀκουσίοις κακοῖς περιπεσεῖν δίκαιός ἐστιν, ὅ τε διαφθαρεὶς οὐδὲν ἧσσον ἀκουσίως ἢ ἑκουσίως βλαφθεὶς ἀδικοῖτ' ἂν ἀτιμώρητος γενόμενος.

οὐ δίκαιος δὲ ἀποφυγεῖν ἐστι διὰ τὴν ἀτυχίαν τῆς 8
ἁμαρτίας. εἰ μὲν γὰρ ὑπὸ μηδεμιᾶς ἐπιμελείας τοῦ θεοῦ ἡ ἀτυχία γίγνεται, ἁμάρτημα οὖσα τῷ ἁμαρτόντι συμφορὰ δικαία γενέσθαι ἐστίν· εἰ δὲ δὴ θεία κηλὶς τῷ δράσαντι προσπίπτει ἀσεβοῦντι, οὐ δίκαιον τὰς θείας προσβολὰς διακωλύειν γίγνεσθαι. ἔλεξαν δὲ καὶ ὡς οὐ 9
πρέπει χρηστὰ ἐπιτηδεύοντας αὐτοὺς κακῶν ἀξιοῦσθαι· ἡμεῖς δὲ πῶς ἂν πρέποντα πάσχοιμεν, εἰ μηδὲν ὑποδεέστερα τούτων μελετῶντες θανάτῳ ζημιούμεθα; φάσκων δὲ ἀναμάρτητος εἶναι, καὶ ἀξιῶν τὰς συμφορὰς τῶν ἁμαρτόντων εἶναι καὶ μὴ εἰς τοὺς ἀναμαρτήτους ἐκτρέπεσθαι, ὑπὲρ ἡμῶν λέγει. ὅ τε γὰρ παῖς μου εἰς οὐδένα οὐδὲν ἁμαρτών, ὑπὸ τούτου τοῦ μειρακίου ἀποθανών, ἀδικοῖτ' ἂν ἀτιμώρητος γενόμενος· ἐγώ τε τοῦδε μᾶλλον ἀναμάρτητος ὢν δεινὰ πείσομαι, ἃ ὁ

47 ὁ βαλών; ἐς τίν' ὁ φόνος ἀνήκει; Bekker (t. 5, p. 695) : ὁ βάλλων (βαλὼν A^{2}) ἐστὶν· ὁ φόνος ὃν ἀνήκει, A : ὁ βάλλων ἐστιν· ὁ φόνος, ὃν ἀνήκει N : ὁ βαλών; εἰς τίν' ὁ φόνος ἂν ἀνήκοι; Decleva Caizzi   49 γὰρ A^{1}N : ** A^{a} (δὲ fuit?)   53 διαφθαρεὶς A^{2} : δὲ φθαρεὶς AN   53–4 ἀκουσίως ἢ ἑκουσίως A^{2} : ἑκουσίως ἢ ἀκουσίως AN   55 ἐστι N : ἐστιν A   56 ὑπὸ <μηδενὸς δαίμονος> Thalheim   μηδεμιᾶς A^{2} : μὴ δὲ δϊ post quae vac. spat. 5–6 litt. N : μηδὲ **** A   58 εἰ δὲ δὴ θεία Blass^{2} : εἰ δὲ θεία A^{2} : ἡ δὲ ἀλήθεια AN   60 οὐ A^{1sv} : om. A^{a}N

10 νόμος ἀποδίδωσί μοι μὴ τυχὼν παρ᾽ ὑμῶν. ὡς δὲ οὐδὲ τῆς ἁμαρτίας οὐδὲ τοῦ ἀκουσίως ἀποκτεῖναι, ἐξ ὧν αὐτοὶ λέγουσιν, ἀπολύεται, ἀλλὰ κοινὰ ἀμφότερα ταῦτα ἀμφοῖν αὐτοῖν ἐστι, δηλώσω. εἴπερ ὁ παῖς διὰ τὸ ὑπὸ τὴν φορὰν τοῦ ἀκοντίου ὑπελθεῖν καὶ μὴ ἀτρέμας ἑστάναι φονεὺς αὐτὸς αὑτοῦ δίκαιος εἶναί ἐστιν, οὐδὲ τὸ μειράκιον καθαρὸν τῆς αἰτίας ἐστίν, ἀλλ᾽ εἴπερ τούτου μὴ ἀκοντίζοντος ἀλλ᾽ ἀτρέμα ἑστῶτος ἀπέθανεν ὁ παῖς. ἐξ ἀμφοῖν δὲ τοῦ φόνου γενομένου, ὁ μὲν παῖς εἰς αὑτὸν ἁμαρτὼν μᾶλλον ἢ κατὰ τὴν ἁμαρτίαν ἑαυτὸν τετιμώρηται, τέθνηκε γάρ, ὁ δὲ συλλήπτωρ καὶ κοινωνὸς εἰς τοὺς οὐ προσήκοντας τῆς ἁμαρτίας γενόμενος πῶς δίκαιος ἀζήμιος ἀποφυγεῖν ἐστιν;

11 Ἐκ δὲ τῆς αὐτῶν τῶν ἀπολογουμένων ἀπολογίας μετόχου τοῦ μειρακίου τοῦ φόνου ὄντος, οὐκ ἂν δικαίως οὐδὲ ὁσίως ἀπολύοιτε αὐτόν. οὔτε γὰρ ἡμεῖς, οἱ διὰ τὴν τούτων ἁμαρτίαν διαφθαρέντες, αὐθένται καταγνωσθέντες ὅσια ἀλλ᾽ ἀνόσι᾽ ἂν πάθοιμεν ὑφ᾽ ὑμῶν· οὔθ᾽ οἱ θανατώσαντες ἡμᾶς μὴ εἰργόμενοι τῶν προσηκόντων εὐσεβοῖντ᾽ ἂν ὑπὸ τῶν ἀπολυσάντων τοὺς ἀνοσίους. πάσης δ᾽ ὑπὲρ πάντων τῆς κηλῖδος εἰς ὑμᾶς ἀναφερομένης, πολλὴ εὐλάβεια ὑμῖν τούτων ποιητέα ἐστί· καταλαβόντες μὲν γὰρ αὐτὸν καὶ εἵρξαντες ὧν ὁ νόμος εἵργει καθαροὶ τῶν ἐγκλημάτων ἔσεσθε,

70 ἀποδίδωσί N : δίδωσι A : δίδωσί A^{2} μοι A^{1}N : om. A^{a} 71 οὐδὲ τοῦ Sauppe : τοῦδε τοῦ AN : τοῦδε τῶ A^{2} 73 εἴπερ] εἰ γὰρ Ald. 74 ὑπελθεῖν N : ἐλθεῖν A 75 αὑτοῦ AN^{c} : αὐτοῦ N^{a} 79 αὑτὸν A^{1}N^{c} : αὐτὸν A^{a}N^{a} ἑαυτὸν A : αὑτὸν N 82 πῶς A^{1}N : πῶν A^{a} 84 τοῦ φόνου ὄντος N : ὄντος τοῦ φόνου A 85 ἀπολύοιτε A^{1}N : ἀπολύεται A^{a} 88 εἰργόμενοι A^{2}N : εἱργόμενοι A 89 προσηκόντων A^{2}N : **προσηκο**των A (quid fuerit non liquet) 91 ὑμᾶς A^{2}N : ἡμᾶς A εὐλάβεια ὑμῖν A^{2} : εὐσέβεια ὑμῖν N : εὐσέβεια ἡμῖν A 92 εἵρξαντες A^{2}N : εἴρξαντες A 93 εἵργει A^{2}N : εἴργει A

ἀπολύσαντες δὲ ὑπαίτιοι καθίστασθε. τῆς οὖν ὑμετέρας 12
εὐσεβείας ἕνεκα καὶ τῶν νόμων ἀπάγοντες τιμωρεῖσθε αὐτόν. αὐτοί τε μὴ μεταλάβητε τῆς τούτου μιαρίας, ἡμῖν τε τοῖς γονεῦσιν, οἳ ζῶντες κατορωρύγμεθα ὑπ' αὐτοῦ, δόξῃ γοῦν ἐλαφροτέραν τὴν συμφορὰν καταστήσατε.

94 ὑμετέρας A^2N : ἡμετέρας A 95 τιμωρεῖσθε A^2N : τιμωρεῖσθαι A 96 <καὶ> αὐτοὶ Blass 97 κατορωρύγμεθα Ald. : κατωρύγμεθα AN subscriptio ὁ ὕστερος ἐκ κατηγορίας N

δ

ΕΞ ΑΠΟΛΟΓΙΑΣ Ο ΥΣΤΕΡΟΣ

1 *Τοῦτον μὲν εἰκὸς πρὸς τὴν ἑαυτοῦ κατηγορίαν
προσέχοντα τὸν νοῦν μὴ μαθεῖν τὴν ἀπολογίαν μου,
ὑμᾶς δὲ χρὴ γιγνώσκειν ὅτι ἡμεῖς μὲν οἱ ἀντίδικοι
κατ' εὔνοιαν κρίνοντες τὸ πρᾶγμα εἰκότως δίκαια
ἑκάτεροι αὑτοὺς οἰόμεθα λέγειν, ὑμᾶς δὲ ὁσίως ὁρᾶν*
2 *προσήκει τὰ πραχθέντα· ἐκ τῶν λεγομένων γὰρ ἡ
ἀλήθεια σκεπτέα αὐτῶν ἐστίν. ἐγὼ δέ, εἰ μέν τι ψεῦδος
εἴρηκα, ὁμολογῶ καὶ τὰ ὀρθῶς εἰρημένα προσδιαβάλλειν
ἄδικα εἶναι· εἰ δὲ ἀληθῆ μέν, λεπτὰ δὲ καὶ ἀκριβῆ, οὐκ
ἐγὼ ὁ λέγων ἀλλ' ὁ πράξας τὴν ἀπέχθειαν αὐτῶν δίκαιος
φέρεσθαί ἐστι.*

3 *Θέλω δὲ πρῶτον ὑμᾶς μαθεῖν, ὅτι οὐκ ἐάν τις φάσκῃ
ἀποκτεῖναι, τοῦτ' ἔστιν, ἀλλ ἐάν τις ἐλεγχθῇ. οὗτος δὲ
ὁμολογῶν τὸ ἔργον ὡς ἡμεῖς λέγομεν γενέσθαι, ὑπὲρ
τοῦ ἀποκτείναντος ἀμφισβητεῖ, ὃν ἀδύνατον ἀλλαχόθεν*
4 *ἢ ἐκ τῶν πραχθέντων δηλοῦσθαι. σχετλιάζει δὲ κακῶς
ἀκούειν φάσκων τὸν παῖδα, εἰ μήτε ἀκοντίσας μήτε
ἐπινοήσας αὐθέντης ὢν ἀποδείκνυται, καὶ οὐ πρὸς τὰ
λεγόμενα ἀπολογεῖται. οὐ γὰρ ἀκοντίσαι οὐδὲ βαλεῖν
αὑτόν φημι τὸν παῖδα, ἀλλ' ὑπὸ τὴν πληγὴν τοῦ ἀκοντίου
ὑπελθόντα οὐχ ὑπὸ τοῦ μειρακίου ἀλλ' ὑφ' ἑαυτοῦ*

Inscriptio *ἐξ ἀπολογίας ὁ ὕστερος* AN 2 *ἀπολογίαν* A¹N : *ἀπογίαν* Aᵃ 3 *χρὴ γινώσκειν*, A² : *χρὴ γινωσκοντας* AN : post *χρὴ* lacunam posuit Thalheim 4 *κρίνοντες* A¹N : *κρίνοντας* Aᵃ 5 *αὑτοὺς* A² : *αὐτοὺς* AN 9 *ἄδικα εἶναι* del. Hüttner 10 *ἀπέχθειαν* A : *ἐπάχθειαν* N 11 *ἐστι* A²Nᶜ : *ἐστιν* ANᵃ 12 *πρῶτον ὑμᾶς* N : *ὑμᾶς πρῶτον* A 14 *ὑπὲρ*] *περὶ* Blass 17–18 *μήτε ἐπινοήσας* N : *μήτ' ἐπινοήσας* A¹ : *μηθ' ὑπονοήσας* Aᵃ 18 *ἀποδείκνυται* N : *ἀποδέδεικται* A 20 *αὑτὸν* A² : *αὐτὸν* AN 21 *ὑπελθόντα* A¹ e ras., N

διαφθαρῆναι· οὐ γὰρ ἀτρεμίζων ἀπέθανε. τῆς δὲ
διαδρομῆς αἰτίας ταύτης γενομένης, εἰ μὲν ὑπὸ τοῦ
παιδοτρίβου καλούμενος διέτρεχεν, ὁ παιδοτρίβης ἂν
ἀποκτείνας αὐτὸν εἴη, εἰ δ’ ὑφ’ ἑαυτοῦ πεισθεὶς ὑπῆλθεν,
αὐτὸς ὑφ’ ἑαυτοῦ διέφθαρται. θέλω δὲ μὴ πρότερον ἐπ’ 5
ἄλλον λόγον ὁρμῆσαι, ἢ τὸ ἔργον ἔτι φανερώτερον
καταστῆσαι, ὁποτέρου αὐτῶν ἐστί. τὸ μὲν μειράκιον
οὐδενὸς μᾶλλον τῶν συμμελετώντων ἐστὶ τοῦ σκοποῦ
ἁμαρτόν, οὐδὲ τῶν ἐπικαλουμένων τι διὰ τὴν αὑτοῦ
ἁμαρτίαν δέδρακεν· ὁ δὲ παῖς οὐ ταὐτὰ τοῖς συνθεω-
μένοις δρῶν, ἀλλ’ εἰς τὴν ὁδὸν τοῦ ἀκοντίου ὑπελθών,
σαφῶς δηλοῦται παρὰ τὴν αὑτοῦ ἁμαρτίαν περισσο-
τέροις ἀτυχήμασι τῶν ἀτρεμιζόντων περιπεσών. ὁ μὲν
γὰρ ἀφεὶς οὐδὲν ἂν ἥμαρτε, μηδενὸς ὑπὸ τὸ βέλος
ὑπελθόντος· αὐτὸς δ’ οὐκ ἂν ἐβλήθη μετὰ τῶν θεωμένων
ἑστώς. ὡς δ’ οὐδενὸς μᾶλλον τῶν συνακοντιζόντων 6
μέτοχός ἐστι τοῦ φόνου, διδάξω. εἰ γὰρ διὰ τὸ τοῦτον
ἀκοντίζειν ὁ παῖς ἀπέθανε, πάντες ἂν οἱ συμμελετῶντες
συμπράκτορες εἴησαν τῆς αἰτίας· οὗτοι γὰρ οὐ διὰ τὸ μὴ
ἀκοντίζειν οὐκ ἔβαλον αὐτόν, ἀλλὰ διὰ τὸ μηδενὶ ὑπὸ τὸ
ἀκόντιον ὑπελθεῖν· ὁ δὲ νεανίσκος οὐδὲν περισσὸν
τούτων ἁμαρτών, ὁμοίως τούτοις οὐκ ἂν ἔβαλεν αὐτὸν
ἀτρέμα σὺν τοῖς θεωμένοις ἑστῶτα. ἔστι δὲ οὐδὲ τὸ 7
ἁμάρτημα τοῦ παιδὸς μόνον, ἀλλὰ καὶ ἡ ἀφυλαξία. ὁ
μὲν γὰρ οὐδένα ὁρῶν διατρέχοντα, πῶς ἂν ἐφυλάξατο
μηδένα βαλεῖν; ὁ δ’ ἰδὼν τοὺς ἀκοντίζοντας, εὐπετῶς ἂν

22 <ἂν> ἀτρεμίζων Franke 23 γενομένης Blass : γινομένης AN 24 καλούμενος A[2] : καλούμενον AN 25 ἀποκτείνας AN : ἁποκτείνας Ignatius 30 τί re vera A[c]N : τίς A[a] αὑτοῦ M[1] : αὐτοῦ AN 32 ὑπελθών A[2]N[2] : ἐπελθών A : ὑπελθόν N 33 αὑτοῦ N[2]M : αὐτοῦ AN[a] 34 ἀτυχήμασι A[2] : ἁμαρτήμασι AN : παθήμασι Jernstedt περιπεσὼν AN[2] : περιπεσὸν N 35 ἥμαρτε N : ἥμαρτεν A 40 εἴησαν AN : εἶεν Thalheim τῆς αἰτίας] καὶ συναίτιοι Gernet, qui εἶεν probavit 41 μηδενὶ Reiske : μηδένα AN 44 ἔστι A[1]N : ἔτι A[a]

ἐφυλάξατο μὴ βληθῆναι· ἐξῆν γὰρ αὐτῷ ἀτρέμα
8 ἑστάναι. τὸν δὲ νόμον ὃν παραφέρουσιν, ἐπαινεῖν δεῖ.
ὀρθῶς γὰρ καὶ δικαίως τοὺς ἀκουσίως ἀποκτείναντας
ἀκουσίοις παθήμασι κολάζει. τὸ μὲν οὖν μειράκιον
ἀναμάρτητον ὄν, οὐκ ἂν δικαίως ὑπὲρ τοῦ ἁμαρτόντος
κολάζοιτο· ἱκανὸν γάρ αὐτῷ ἐστι τὰς αὑτοῦ ἁμαρτίας
φέρειν· ὁ δὲ παῖς ταῖς αὑτοῦ ἁμαρτίαις διαφθαρείς, ἅμα
ἥμαρτέ τε καὶ ὑφ' ἑαυτοῦ ἐκολάσθη. κεκολασμένου δὲ
τοῦ ἀποκτείναντος, οὐκ ἀτιμώρητος ὁ φόνος ἐστίν.
9 ἔχοντός γε δὴ τὴν δίκην τοῦ φονέως, οὐκ ἐὰν ἀπολύσητε
ἡμᾶς, ἀλλ' ἐὰν καταλάβητε, ἐνθύμιον ὑπολείψεσθε. ὁ
μὲν γὰρ αὐτὸς τὰς αὑτοῦ ἁμαρτίας φέρων, οὐδενὶ οὐδὲν
προστρόπαιον καταλείψει· ὁ δὲ καθαρὸς τῆς αἰτίας
ὢν ἐὰν διαφθαρῇ, τοῖς καταλαμβάνουσι μεῖζον τὸ
ἐνθύμιον γενήσεται. εἰ δὲ αὐθέντης ἐκ τῶν λεγομένων
ἐπιδείκνυται, οὐχ ἡμεῖς αὐτῷ οἱ λέγοντες αἴτιοί ἐσμεν,
10 ἀλλ' ἡ πρᾶξις τῶν ἔργων. ὀρθῶς δὲ τῶν ἐλέγχων
ἐλεγχόντων τὸν παῖδα αὐθέντην ὄντα, ὁ νόμος ἀπολύων
ἡμᾶς τῆς αἰτίας τὸν ἀποκτείναντα καταλαμβάνει. μήτε
οὖν ἡμᾶς εἰς μὴ προσηκούσας συμφορὰς ἐμβάλητε,
μήτε αὐτοὶ ταῖς τούτων ἀτυχίαις βοηθοῦντες ἐναντία
τοῦ δαίμονος γνῶτε, ἀλλ' ὥσπερ ὅσιον καὶ δίκαιον,
μεμνημένοι τοῦ πάθους ὅτι διὰ τὸν ὑπὸ τὴν φορὰν τοῦ
ἀκοντίου ὑπελθόντα ἐγένετο, ἀπολύετε ἡμᾶς· οὐ γὰρ
αἴτιοι τοῦ φόνου ἐσμέν.

48 *μὴ βληθῆναι* Kayser[1] : *μηδένα μὴ βαλεῖν* AN : *μὴ διαδραμεῖν* Wilamowitz[1] : alii alia 53 *αὑτοῦ* M : *αὐτοῦ* AN 54 *αὑτοῦ* Steph. : *αὐτοῦ* AN 56 *ἐστίν* A : *ἐστί* N 57 *δὴ* N : om. A *ἐὰν*] *ἐὰν οὖν* A[2] 58 *καταλάβητε* N : *καταλάβοιτε* A *ὑπολείψεσθε* AN : *ὑπολήψεσθε* Decleva Caizzi 59 *γὰρ* A : om. N *αὑτοῦ* A : *ἑαυτοῦ* N 61 *ὢν* Scheibe : *ὃς δὲ* A[a]N : *ὃς* A[2], ut mihi vid. *διαφθαρῇ* A[2] : *φθαρῇ* AN 71 *ἐγένετο,* A[2] : *ἐγένετο ἀπολέσθαι* AN subscriptio *ὁ ὕστερος ἐξ ἀπολογίας* N

4

ΤΕΤΡΑΛΟΓΙΑ Γ

α

ΦΟΝΟΥ ΚΑΤΗΓΟΡΙΑ ΚΑΤΑ ΤΟΥ ΛΕΓΟΝΤΟΣ ΑΜΥΝΑΣΘΑΙ

ΥΠΟΘΕΣΙΣ

Νέος καὶ πρεσβύτης ἐκ λοιδορίας ἀλλήλοις συμπεσόντες ἐμάχοντο, ἰσχυρότερον δὲ τοῦ νέου πλήξαντος τέθνηκεν ὁ πρεσβύτης· καὶ περὶ τούτου κατηγορεῖ τις τοῦ νέου ὡς τὸν φόνον πεποιηκότος. ὁ δὲ πρῶτον τὸν πρεσβύτην ἀδίκων ἄρξαι λέγει χειρῶν. ὅθεν ἀντέγκλημα ἡ στάσις γίνεται.

Νενόμισται μὲν ὀρθῶς τὰς φονικὰς δίκας περὶ πλείστου 1
τοὺς κρίνοντας ποιεῖσθαι διώκειν τε καὶ μαρτυρεῖν
κατὰ τὸ δίκαιον, μήτε τοὺς ἐνόχους ἀφιέντας μήτε τοὺς
καθαροὺς εἰς ἀγῶνα καθιστάντας. ὅ τε γὰρ θεὸς 2
βουλόμενος ποιῆσαι τὸ ἀνθρώπινον φῦλον τοὺς πρῶτον
γενομένους ἔφυσεν ἡμῶν, τροφέας τε παρέδωκε τὴν
γῆν καὶ τὴν θάλασσαν, ἵνα μὴ σπάνει τῶν ἀναγκαίων
προαποθνῄσκοιμεν τῆς γηραιοῦ τελευτῆς. ὅστις οὖν

2 *γηραιοῦ* stp Pollux 2.13.2 (item 3.*β*.11)

Arg. inscr. *ὑπόθεσις τῆς ἑξῆς τετραλογίας* AN, *περὶ φόνου ὃν ὡς ἀμυνόμενος ἔδρασεν* add. N   1 *ἀλλήλοις συμπεσόντες* N : *συμπεσόντες ἀλλήλοις* A   5 *ἀντέγκλημα* N : *ἀντέκλημα* A   Inscriptio *φόνου κατηγορία* (*κατηγορία φόνου* A) *κατὰ τοῦ λέγοντος ἀμύνασθαι* AN   8 *ἀφιέντας* A^{1}N : *ἀφιέντες* A^{a} 9 *καθιστάντας* AN^{a} : *καθιέντας* N^{c} <*ὁ*> *θεὸς* Thalheim, qui Spengelii *ὅτε* accepit   10 *φῦλον* N : *γένος* A   *πρῶτον* A : *πρώτους* N   11 *τε* A^{c} : *τε καὶ* A^{a}N : lacunam postea susp. nonnulli   12 *τὴν* om. N

τούτων ὑπὸ τοῦ θεοῦ ἀξιωθέντος τοῦ βίου ἡμῶν ἀνόμως
τινὰ ἀποκτείνει, ἀσεβεῖ μὲν περὶ τοὺς θεούς, συγχεῖ
3 δὲ τὰ νόμιμα τῶν ἀνθρώπων. ὅ τε γὰρ ἀποθανών,
στερόμενος ὧν ὁ θεὸς ἔδωκεν αὐτῷ, εἰκότως θεοῦ
τιμωρίαν ὑπολείπει τὴν τῶν ἀλιτηρίων δυσμένειαν,
ἣν οἱ παρὰ τὸ δίκαιον κρίνοντες ἢ μαρτυροῦντες,
συνασεβοῦντες τῷ ταῦτα δρῶντι, οὐ προσῆκον μίασμα
4 εἰς τοὺς ἰδίους οἴκους εἰσάγονται· ἡμεῖς τε οἱ τιμωροὶ
τῶν διεφθαρμένων, εἰ δι' ἄλλην τινὰ ἔχθραν τοὺς
ἀναιτίους διώκοιμεν, τῷ μὲν ἀποθανόντι οὐ τιμωροῦντες
δεινοὺς ἀλιτηρίους ἕξομεν τοὺς τῶν ἀποθανόντων
προστροπαίους, τοὺς δὲ καθαροὺς ἀδίκως ἀποκτείνοντες
ἔνοχοι τοῦ φόνου τοῖς ἐπιτιμίοις ἐσμέν, ὑμᾶς τε ἄνομα
δρᾶν πείθοντες καὶ τοῦ ὑμετέρου ἁμαρτήματος ὑπαίτιοι
5 γιγνόμεθα. ἐγὼ μὲν οὖν δεδιὼς ταῦτα, εἰς ὑμᾶς παράγων
τὸν ἀσεβήσαντα καθαρὸς τῶν ἐγκλημάτων εἰμί· ὑμεῖς
δὲ ἀξίως τῶν προειρημένων τῇ κρίσει προσέχοντες τὸν
νοῦν, ἀξίαν δίκην τοῦ πάθους τῷ εἰργασμένῳ ἐπιθέντες,
ἅπασαν τὴν πόλιν καθαρὰν τοῦ μιάσματος καταστήσετε.
6 εἰ μὲν γὰρ ἄκων ἀπέκτεινε τὸν ἄνδρα, ἄξιος ἂν ἦν
συγγνώμης τυχεῖν τινός· ὕβρει δὲ καὶ ἀκολασίᾳ
παροινῶν εἰς ἄνδρα πρεσβύτην, τύπτων τε καὶ πνίγων
ἕως τῆς ψυχῆς ἀπεστέρησεν αὐτόν, ὡς μὲν ἀποκτείνας
τοῦ φόνου τοῖς ἐπιτιμίοις ἔνοχός ἐστιν, ὡς δὲ συγχέων

4 *ἐπιτιμίοις* stp Pollux 8.21 (item δ.7)

---

14 *τούτων ... ἀξιωθέντος* A[a] (*ἀξιωθεὶς* A[1]) N : *τῶν ... ἀξιωθέντων* Blass 17 *ὧν* AN[2] : *ὢν* N 18 *ἀλιτηρίων* A[2]N : *ἁλιτηρίων* A 21 *ἰδίους* AN : om. PSI *εἰσάγοντα* sic PSI *ἡμεῖς* A[2]N PSI : *ὑμεῖς* A 22 *δι' ἄλλην*] *δι αιαλλην* sic PSI 23 *διώκοιμεν* AN[1] PSI : *διώκομεν* N[a] 24 *ἀλιτηρίους* A[2]N : *ἁλιτηρίους* A 25 *προστροπαίους* A[1]N PSI : *προτροπαίους* A[a] 26 *τε* AN : *δὲ* Schaefer 30 *προσέχοντες* A : *προσεχόντες* N : *προσσχόντες* Nauck 31 *τοῦ πάθους* A[1]N : om. A[a] *τῷ εἰργασμένῳ* N : *τῶ εἰργασμένω* A[1]N : *τῶν εἰργασμένων* A[a] 33 *τὸν* N : *τὸ* sic A

ἅπαντα τῶν γεραιτέρων τὰ νόμιμα οὐδενὸς ἁμαρτεῖν,
οἷς οἱ τοιοῦτοι κολάζονται, δίκαιός ἐστιν. ὁ μὲν τοίνυν 7
νόμος ὀρθῶς ὑμῖν τιμωρεῖσθαι παραδίδωσιν αὐτόν·
τῶν δὲ μαρτύρων ἀκηκόατε, οἳ παρῆσαν παροινοῦντι
αὐτῷ. ὑμᾶς δὲ χρὴ τῇ τε ἀνομίᾳ τοῦ παθήματος
ἀμύνοντας, τήν τε ὕβριν κολάζοντας ἀξίως τοῦ πάθους,
τὴν βουλεύσασαν ψυχὴν ἀνταφελέσθαι αὐτόν.

38 *τῶν γεραιτέρων* Gernet : *τῶν γεραιρετέρων* $\mathrm{A^a}$: *τῶν γεραιοτέρων* $\mathrm{A^c}$: *τὸν γηραιότερον* N   39–40 *ὁ … νόμος* AN : *οἱ … νόμοι* $\mathrm{N^2}$ 40 *παραδίδωσιν* A : *παραδιδοῦσιν* N   subscriptio *φόνου κατηγορία κατὰ τοῦ λέγοντος ἀμύνασθαι* N

β

ΑΠΟΛΟΓΙΑ ΦΟΝΟΥ, ΩΣ ΑΜΥΝΟΜΕΝΟΣ ΑΠΕΚΤΕΙΝΕΝ

ΥΠΟΘΕΣΙΣ

Ἡ στάσις μετάστασις· μεταφέρει γὰρ ἐπὶ τὸν θεραπεύσαντα ἰατρὸν τὸν φόνον. τὸ γὰρ ἀντεγκληματικὸν ὡς παρεπόμενον ἔλαβεν.

1 Ὅτι μὲν βραχεῖς τοὺς λόγους ἐποιήσαντο, οὐ θαυμάζω
αὐτῶν· οὐ γὰρ ὡς μὴ πάθωσιν ὁ κίνδυνος αὐτοῖς ἐστιν,
ἀλλ' ὡς ἐμὲ μὴ δικαίως δι' ἔχθραν διαφθείρωσιν.
ὅτι δ' ἐξισοῦν τοῖς μεγίστοις ἐγκλήμασιν ἤθελον τὸ
πρᾶγμα, οὗ ὁ ἀποθανὼν αὐτῷ αἴτιος καὶ μᾶλλον ἢ ἐγὼ
ἐγένετο, εἰκότως ἂν ἀγανακτεῖν μοι δοκῶ. ἄρχων γὰρ
χειρῶν ἀδίκων, καὶ παροινῶν εἰς ἄνδρα πολὺ αὑτοῦ
σωφρονέστερον, οὐχ αὑτῷ μόνον τῆς συμφορᾶς, ἀλλὰ
2 καὶ ἐμοὶ τοῦ ἐγκλήματος αἴτιος ἐγένετο. οἶμαι μὲν οὖν
ἔγωγε οὔτε δίκαια τούτους οὔθ' ὅσια δρᾶν ἐγκαλοῦντας
ἐμοί. τὸν γὰρ ἄρξαντα τῆς πληγῆς, εἰ μὲν σιδήρῳ ἢ λίθῳ
ἢ ξύλῳ ἠμυνάμην αὐτόν, ἠδίκουν μὲν οὐδ' οὕτως—οὐ
γὰρ ταὐτὰ ἀλλὰ μείζονα καὶ πλείονα δίκαιοι οἱ ἄρχοντες
ἀντιπάσχειν εἰσί· ταῖς δὲ χερσὶ τυπτόμενος ὑπ'
αὐτοῦ, ταῖς χερσὶν ἅπερ ἔπασχον ἀντιδρῶν, πότερα
3 ἠδίκουν; εἶεν· ἐρεῖ δέ "Ἀλλ' ὁ νόμος εἴργων μήτε δικαίως
μήτε ἀδίκως ἀποκτείνειν ἔνοχον τοῦ φόνου τοῖς
ἐπιτιμίοις ἀποφαίνει σε ὄντα· ὁ γὰρ ἀνὴρ τέθνηκεν".

Arg. inscriptio τοῦ (τῶν A) ἑξῆς ὑπόθεσις AN Inscriptio ἀπολογία φόνου, ὃν ὡς ἀμυνόμενος ἀπέκτεινεν (-νε N) AN : ὃν del. Sauppe 8 αὑτῷ A^2N : αὐτῷ A^1 : om. A^a 10 αὑτοῦ Ald. : αὐτοῦ AN 12 τοῦ ἐγκλήματος αἴτιος ἐγένετο N : αἴτιος τοῦ ἐγκλήματος γέγονεν A 14 ἐμοί A^1N : ἐμοῦ ut vid. A^a 15 οὐδ' <ἂν> Blass^3, qui antea <ἂν> οὐδ' scripserat 16 ταὐτὰ, A : ταυτὰ N 17 ὑπ' in ras. A^1 19 ἠδίκουν A^c : ἂν ἠδίκουν A^aN εἴργων A^2N : εἵργων A

ἐγὼ δὲ δεύτερον καὶ τρίτον οὐκ ἀποκτεῖναί φημι. εἰ μὲν
γὰρ ὑπὸ τῶν πληγῶν ὁ ἀνὴρ παραχρῆμα ἀπέθανεν, ὑπ'
ἐμοῦ μὲν δικαίως δ' ἂν ἐτεθνήκει—οὐ γὰρ ταὐτὰ ἀλλὰ
μείζονα καὶ πλείονα οἱ ἄρξαντες δίκαιοι ἀντιπάσχειν
εἰσί· νῦν δὲ πολλαῖς ἡμέραις ὕστερον μοχθηρῷ ἰατρῷ 4
ἐπιτρεφθεὶς διὰ τὴν τοῦ ἰατροῦ μοχθηρίαν καὶ οὐ διὰ
τὰς πληγὰς ἀπέθανε. προλεγόντων γὰρ αὐτῷ τῶν
ἄλλων ἰατρῶν, εἰ ταύτην τὴν θεραπείαν θεραπεύσοιτο,
ὅτι ἰάσιμος ὢν διαφθαρήσοιτο, δι' ὑμᾶς τοὺς συμβούλους
διαφθαρεὶς ἐμοὶ ἀνόσιον ἔγκλημα προσέβαλεν.
ἀπολύει δέ με καὶ ὁ νόμος καθ' ὃν διώκομαι. τὸν γὰρ 5
ἐπιβουλεύσαντα κελεύει φονέα εἶναι. ἐγὼ μὲν οὖν πῶς
ἂν ἐπιβουλεύσαιμι αὐτῷ, εἰ μὴ καὶ ἐπεβουλεύθην ὑπ'
αὐτοῦ; τοῖς γὰρ αὐτοῖς ἀμυνόμενος αὐτὸν καὶ τὰ αὐτὰ
δρῶν ἅπερ ἔπασχον, σαφὲς ὅτι τὰ αὐτὰ ἐπεβούλευσα
καὶ ἐπεβουλεύθην. εἰ δέ τις ἐκ τῶν πληγῶν τὸν θάνατον 6
οἰόμενος γενέσθαι φονέα με αὐτοῦ ἡγεῖται εἶναι,
ἀντιλογισάσθω ὅτι διὰ τὸν ἄρξαντα αἱ πληγαὶ γενόμεναι
τοῦτον αἴτιον τοῦ θανάτου καὶ οὐκ ἐμὲ ἀποφαίνουσιν
ὄντα· οὐ γὰρ ἂν ἠμυνάμην μὴ τυπτόμενος ὑπ' αὐτοῦ.
ἀπολυόμενος δὲ ὑπό τε τοῦ ⟨νόμου ὑπό τε τοῦ⟩ ἄρξαντος
τῆς πληγῆς, ἐγὼ μὲν οὐδενὶ τρόπῳ φονεὺς αὐτοῦ εἰμι, ὁ
δὲ ἀποθανών, εἰ μὲν ἀτυχίᾳ τέθνηκε, τῇ ἑαυτοῦ ἀτυχίᾳ
κέχρηται—ἠτύχησε γὰρ ἄρξας τῆς πληγῆς—εἰ δ'
ἀβουλίᾳ τινί, τῇ ἑαυτοῦ ἀβουλίᾳ διέφθαρται· οὐ γὰρ εὖ
φρονῶν ἔτυπτέ με.

22 δεύτερον AN : καὶ δεύτερον A[2] 24 ταὐτὰ N[2] : ταυτὰ A[2] : ταῦτα AN 26 μοχθηρῷ N : πονηρῷ A 29 εἰ A : εἰς N 31 ἔγκλημα A : om. N 32–7 ἀπολύει ... ἐπεβουλήθην post ὑπ' αὐτοῦ, l. 41, transp. Thalheim 33 ἐπιβουλεύσαντα A[1]N : ἐπιβουλεύοντα A[a] φονέα] φον in ras. A[1] 34 ἐπιβουλεύσαιμι] ἐπεβούλευσα Kayser[1] εἰ AN : ὅτι Schoell[1] 36 ἐπεβούλευσα A : ἐβούλευσα N 38 εἶναι A : om. N 42 pr. τε del. N[2] add. Reiske ἄρξαντος A[2]N : ἄρξατος A

7 *Ὡς μὲν οὖν οὐ δικαίως κατηγοροῦμαι, ἐπιδέδεικταί μοι· ἐθέλω δὲ τοὺς κατηγοροῦντάς μου πᾶσιν οἷς ἐγκαλοῦσιν ἐνόχους αὐτοὺς ὄντας ἀποδεῖξαι. καθαρῷ μέν μοι τῆς αἰτίας ὄντι φόνον ἐπιβουλεύοντες, ἀποστεροῦντες δέ με τοῦ βίου ὃν ὁ θεὸς παρέδωκέ μοι, περὶ τὸν θεὸν ἀσεβοῦσιν· ἀδίκως δὲ θάνατον ἐπιβουλεύοντες τά τε νόμιμα συγχέουσι φονεῖς τέ μου γίγνονται· ἀνοσίως δ' ἀποκτεῖναι ὑμᾶς με πείθοντες καὶ τῆς ὑμετέρας εὐσεβείας αὐτοὶ φονεῖς εἰσί.*

8 *Τούτοις μὲν οὖν ὁ θεὸς ἐπιθείη τὴν δίκην· ὑμᾶς δὲ χρὴ τὸ ὑμέτερον σκοποῦντας ἀπολῦσαί με μᾶλλον ἢ καταλαβεῖν βούλεσθαι. ἀδίκως μὲν γὰρ ἀπολυθείς, διὰ τὸ μὴ ὀρθῶς ὑμᾶς διδαχθῆναι ἀποφυγών, τοῦ μὴ διδάξαντος καὶ οὐχ ὑμέτερον τὸν προστρόπαιον τοῦ ἀποθανόντος καταστήσω· μὴ ὀρθῶς δὲ καταληφθεὶς ὑφ' ὑμῶν, ὑμῖν καὶ οὐ τούτῳ τὸ μήνιμα τῶν ἀλιτηρίων*
9 *προστρίψομαι. ταῦτ' οὖν εἰδότες, τουτοισὶ τὸ ἀσέβημα τοῦτο ἀναθέντες, αὐτοί τε καθαροὶ τῆς αἰτίας γένεσθε ἐμέ τε ὁσίως καὶ δικαίως ἀπολύετε· οὕτω γὰρ ἂν καθαρώτατοι πάντες οἱ πολῖται εἴημεν.*

49 *μου* A[1]N : om. A[a]   50 *αὐτοὺς* A : om. N   *μέν*] *μὲν* <*γάρ*> Reiske : *γάρ* maluit Thalheim   *μοι* A : *τοι* N   51 *ἐπιβουλεύοντες* A : *ἐπιβολεύοντες* N : *ἐπικαλοῦντες* Kayser[1]   51–2 *δέ με* N : *δέ μου* A   54 *φονεῖς* AN et mox l. 56 : *φονῆς* Jernstedt et mox l. 56   55 *ὑμᾶς* A[1]N : *ἡμᾶς* A[a]   56 *αὐτοὶ*] *αὑτοὶ* Blass[2]   58 *ὑμέτερον* A[2]N : *ἡμέτερον* A   60 *ὑμᾶς διδαχθῆναι* N : *διδα*χθῆναι ὑμᾶς* A   alt. *μὴ* del. Jernstedt[1] : *μὴ* <*ὀρθῶς*> Ignatius   65 *γένεσθε* AN[2] : *γενέσθε* N   subscriptio *ἀπολογία φόνου ὃν ὡς ἀμυνόμενος ἀπέκτεινεν* N

γ

ΕΚ ΚΑΤΗΓΟΡΙΑΣ Ο ΥΣΤΕΡΟΣ

ΥΠΟΘΕΣΙΣ

Ἐν τούτῳ φησὶ {θαυμάζω} ὅτι οὐκ εἰκὸς ἄρξαι χειρῶν ἀδίκων τὸν πρεσβύτερον. εἶτα ὅτι εἰ καὶ οὕτως ἔχει, ὁ μέχρι φόνου ἀμυνόμενος ὑπεύθυνος. καὶ περὶ τοῦ ἰατροῦ, ὡς δι᾽ ἀπειρίαν ἐσφάλη, ἀνεύθυνος ὤν.

Τοῦτόν τε οὐ θαυμάζω ἀνόσια δράσαντα ὅμοια οἷς 1
εἴργασται λέγειν, ὑμῖν τε συγγιγνώσκω βουλομένοις τὴν ἀκρίβειαν τῶν πραχθέντων μαθεῖν τοιαῦτα ἀνέχεσθαι ἀκούοντας αὐτοῦ, ἃ ἐκβάλλεσθαι ἄξιά ἐστι. τὸν γὰρ ἄνδρα ὁμολογῶν τύπτειν τὰς πληγὰς ἐξ ὧν ἀπέθανεν, αὐτὸς μὲν τοῦ τεθνηκότος οὔ φησι φονεὺς εἶναι, ἡμᾶς δὲ τοὺς τιμωροῦντας αὐτῷ ζῶν τε καὶ βλέπων φονέας αὑτοῦ φησιν εἶναι. θέλω δὲ καὶ τὰ ἄλλα παραπλήσια ἀπολογηθέντα τούτοις ἐπιδεῖξαι αὐτόν.

Εἶπε δὲ πρῶτον μέν, εἰ καὶ ἐκ τῶν πληγῶν ἀπέθανεν 2
ὁ ἀνήρ, ὡς οὐκ ἀπέκτεινεν αὐτόν· τὸν γὰρ ἄρξαντα τῆς πληγῆς, τοῦτον αἴτιον τῶν πραχθέντων γενόμενον καταλαμβάνεσθαι ὑπὸ τοῦ νόμου, ἄρξαι δὲ τὸν ἀποθανόντα. μάθετε δὴ πρῶτον μὲν ὅτι ἄρξαι καὶ παροινεῖν τοὺς νεωτέρους τῶν πρεσβυτέρων εἰκότερόν ἐστι· τοὺς μὲν γὰρ ἥ τε μεγαλοφροσύνη τοῦ γένους ἥ τε ἀκμὴ τῆς ῥώμης ἥ τε ἀπειρία τῆς μέθης ἐπαίρει τῷ θυμῷ χαρίζεσθαι, τοὺς δὲ ἥ τε ἐμπειρία τῶν

Arg. inscriptio *ὑπόθεσις τῶν ἑξῆς* A : *ἡ ὑπόθεσις* N 1 *ἐν τούτῳ* A : *ἐκ τούτων* N del. censuit Sauppe *ὅτι* A^{1}N : om. A^{a} Inscriptio *ἐκ κατηγορίας ὁ ὕστερος* AN 8 *ἀκούοντας* A^{1}N : *ἀκούαντας* A^{a} 10 *φησι* N : *φησιν* A 12 *αὑτοῦ* Steph. : *αὐτοῦ* AN *τὰ ἄλλα* N : *τἄλλα* e corr. A^{1} (*τὰ* scripserat A^{a}) 14–15 *εἶπε … αὐτόν* om. A^{a}, add. A^{1im} 21 *ῥώμης* A^{1}N : *ὥρας* A^{a}

παροινουμένων ἥ τε ἀσθένεια τοῦ γήρως ἥ τε δύναμις
3 τῶν νέων φοβοῦσα σωφρονίζει. ὡς δὲ οὐδὲ τοῖς αὐτοῖς
ἀλλὰ τοῖς ἐναντιωτάτοις ἠμύνατο αὐτόν, αὐτὸ τὸ ἔργον
σημαίνει. ὁ μὲν γὰρ ἀκμαζούσῃ τῇ ῥώμῃ τῶν χειρῶν
χρώμενος ἀπέκτεινεν· ὁ δὲ ἀδυνάτως τὸν κρείσσονα
ἀμυνόμενος, οὐδὲ σημεῖον οὐδὲν ὧν ἠμύνετο ὑπολιπὼν
ἀπέθανεν. εἰ δὲ ταῖς χερσὶν ἀπέκτεινε καὶ οὐ σιδήρῳ,
ὅσον αἱ χεῖρες οἰκειότεραι τοῦ σιδέρου τούτῳ εἰσί,
4 τοσούτῳ μᾶλλον φονεύς ἐστιν. ἐτόλμησε δὲ εἰπεῖν ὡς
ὁ ἄρξας τῆς πληγῆς καὶ μὴ διαφθείρας μᾶλλον τοῦ
ἀποκτείναντος φονεύς ἐστι· τοῦτον γὰρ βουλευτὴν τοῦ
θανάτου φησὶ γενέσθαι. ἐγὼ δὲ πολὺ τἀναντία τούτων
φημί. εἰ γὰρ αἱ χεῖρες ἃ διανοούμεθα ἑκάστῳ ἡμῶν
ὑπουργοῦσιν, ὁ μὲν πατάξας καὶ μὴ ἀποκτείνας τῆς
πληγῆς βουλευτὴς ἐγένετο, ὁ δὲ θανασίμως τύπτων τοῦ
θανάτου· ἐκ γὰρ ὧν ἐκεῖνος διανοηθεὶς ἔδρασεν, ὁ ἀνὴρ
τέθνηκεν. ἔστι δὲ ἡ μὲν ἀτυχία τοῦ πατάξαντος, ἡ δὲ
συμφορὰ τοῦ παθόντος. ὁ μὲν γὰρ ἐξ ὧν ἔδρασεν
ἐκεῖνος διαφθαρείς, οὐ τῇ ἑαυτοῦ ἁμαρτίᾳ ἀλλὰ τῇ τοῦ
πατάξαντος χρησάμενος ἀπέθανεν· ὁ δὲ μείζω ὧν ἤθελε
πράξας, τῇ ἑαυτοῦ ἀτυχίᾳ ὃν οὐκ ἤθελεν ἀπέκτεινεν.
5 ὑπὸ δὲ τοῦ ἰατροῦ φάσκων αὐτὸν ἀποθανεῖν, θαυμάζω
ὅτι ὑφ᾽ ἡμῶν τῶν συμβουλευσάντων ἐπιτρεφθῆναί
φησιν αὐτὸν διαφθαρῆναι. καὶ γὰρ ἂν εἰ μὴ ἐπετρέψαμεν,
ὑπ᾽ ἀθεραπείας ἂν ἔφη διαφθαρῆναι αὐτόν. εἰ δέ τοι
καὶ ὑπὸ τοῦ ἰατροῦ ἀπέθανεν, ὡς οὐκ ἀπέθανεν, ὁ μὲν

23 *παροινουμένων* Reiske : *παρανομουμένων* AN 24 *οὐδὲ* N : *οὐ* A 28 *ὧν ἠμύνετο ὑπολιπὼν* scripsi : *ὧν ἠμύνετο ὑπολείπων* N : *ὑπολιπὼν ὧν ἠμύνατο* A : *ὧν ἠμύνατο ὑπολιπὼν* Blass 30 *οἰκειότεραι τοῦ σιδήρου* N : *τοῦ σιδήρου οἰκειότεραι* A *εἰσὶ* A^1 : *εἰσι* N : *ἐστὶ* A^a 37 *βουλευτῆς* A, corr. A^2 38 *θάνου* ut vid. A^a, corr. A^1 42 *ἀπέθανεν* A : *ἔπαθεν* N 45 *ὑφ᾽* A^a : *οὐχ ὑφ᾽* A^{1}N *ἡμῶν* A^{1}N : *ὑμῶν* A^a 46 *ἐπετρέψαμεν* AN^2 : *ἐπιτρέψαμεν* N

ἰατρὸς οὐ φονεὺς αὐτοῦ ἐστιν, ὁ γὰρ νόμος ἀπολύει
αὐτόν, διὰ δὲ τὰς τούτου πληγὰς ἐπιτρεψάντων ἡμῶν
αὐτῷ, πῶς ἂν ἄλλος τις ἢ ὁ βιασάμενος ἡμᾶς χρῆσθαι
αὐτῷ φονεὺς εἴη ἄν;

Οὕτω δὲ φανερῶς ἐκ παντὸς τρόπου ἐλεγχόμενος 6
ἀποκτεῖναι τὸν ἄνδρα, εἰς τοῦτο τόλμης καὶ ἀναιδείας
ἥκει, ὥστ' οὐκ ἀρκοῦν αὐτῷ ἐστιν ὑπὲρ τῆς αὑτοῦ
ἀσεβείας ἀπολογεῖσθαι, ἀλλὰ καὶ ἡμᾶς, οἳ τὸ τούτου
μίασμα ἐπεξερχόμεθα, ἀθέμιστα καὶ ἀνόσια δρᾶν φησι.
τούτῳ μὲν οὖν πρέπει καὶ ταῦτα καὶ ἔτι τούτων 7
δεινότερα λέγειν, τοιαῦτα δεδρακότι· ἡμεῖς δὲ τὸν
θάνατον φανερὸν ἀποδεικνύντες, τήν τε πληγὴν
ὁμολογουμένην ἐξ ἧς ἀπέθανε, τόν τε νόμον εἰς τὸν
πατάξαντα τὸν φόνον ἀνάγοντα, ἀντὶ τοῦ παθόντος
ἐπισκήπτομεν ὑμῖν, τῷ τούτου φόνῳ τὸ μήνιμα τῶν
ἀλιτηρίων ἀκεσαμένους πᾶσαν τὴν πόλιν καθαρὰν τοῦ
μιάσματος καταστῆσαι.

6 *ἀθέμιστα καὶ ἀνόσια δρᾶν* stp Phot. *α* 458 s.vv. (*εἶπε καὶ Ἀντιφῶν* Fuhr recte, apud Thalheimium : *εἶπε καὶ Ξενοφῶν* Photii libri)

---

53 *οὕτω* Pahle : *οὕτως* A^{sv} : *οὗτος* A^{it}N *δὲ* in ras. A^{1} *ἐκ παντὸς τρόπου ἐλεγχόμενος* N : *ἐλεγχόμενος ἐκ παντὸς τρόπου* A 55 *αὑτοῦ* Steph. : *αὐτοῦ* AN 57 *φησί* N : *φησὶ* A^{1}: *φασὶ* A^{a} 60 *τε* ante *θάνατον* add. Blass 61 *ὁμολογουμένην* A^{1}N : *ὁμολογοῦμεν* A^{a} 62 *παθόντος* A : *ἀποθανόντος* N 63 *ὑμῖν* A^{1}N : *ἡμῖν* A^{a} 64 *ἀλιτηρίων* N : *ἁλιτηρίων* A Subscriptio *ἐκ κατηγορίας ὁ ὕστερος* N

δ

ΕΞ ΑΠΟΛΟΓΙΑΣ Ο ΥΣΤΕΡΟΣ

1 Ὁ μὲν ἀνήρ, οὐ καταγνοὺς αὐτὸς αὑτοῦ, ἀλλα τὴν σπουδὴν τῶν κατηγόρων φοβηθείς, ὑπαπέστη· ἡμῖν δὲ τοῖς φίλοις ζῶντι ἢ ἀποθανόντι εὐσεβέστερον ἀμύνειν αὐτῷ. ἄριστα μὲν οὖν αὐτὸς ἂν ὑπὲρ αὑτοῦ ἀπελογεῖτο· ἐπεὶ δὲ τάδε ἀκινδυνότερα ἔδοξεν εἶναι, ἡμῖν, οἷς μέγιστον ἂν πένθος γένοιτο στερηθεῖσιν αὐτοῦ, ἀπολογητέον.

2 Δοκεῖ δέ μοι περὶ τὸν ἄρξαντα τῆς πληγῆς τὸ ἀδίκημα εἶναι. ὁ μὲν οὖν διώκων οὐκ εἰκόσι τεκμηρίοις χρώμενος τοῦτον τὸν ἄρξαντά φησιν εἶναι. εἰ μὲν γὰρ ὥσπερ βλέπειν μὲν τοῖν ὀφθαλμοῖν, ἀκούειν δὲ τοῖς ὠσίν, οὕτω κατὰ φύσιν ἦν ὑβρίζειν μὲν τοὺς νέους, σωφρονεῖν δὲ τοὺς γέροντας, οὐδὲν ἂν τῆς ὑμετέρας κρίσεως ἔδει· αὐτὴ γὰρ ἡ ἡλικία τῶν νέων κατέκρινε· νῦν δὲ πολλοὶ μὲν νέοι σωφρονοῦντες, πολλοὶ δὲ πρεσβῦται παροινοῦντες, οὐδὲν μᾶλλον τῷ διώκοντι ἢ τῷ φεύγοντι
3 τεκμήριον γίγνονται. κοινοῦ δὲ τοῦ τεκμηρίου ἡμῖν ὄντος τούτῳ, τῷ παντὶ προέχομεν· οἱ γὰρ μάρτυρες τοῦτόν φασιν ἄρξαι τῆς πληγῆς. ἄρξαντος δὲ τούτου, καὶ τῶν ἄλλων ἁπάντων ⟨τῶν⟩ κατηγορουμένων ἀπολύεται τῆς αἰτίας. εἴ τε γὰρ ὁ πατάξας, διὰ τὴν πληγὴν βιασάμενος ὑμᾶς ἐπιτρεφθῆναι ἰατρῷ, μᾶλλον τοῦ ἀποκτείναντος φονεύς ἐστιν, ὁ ἄρξας τῆς πληγῆς φονεὺς γίγνεται. οὗτος γὰρ ἠνάγκασε τόν τε ἀμυνόμενον

Inscriptio ἐξ ἀπολογίας ὁ ὕστερος AN   5 εἶναι, ἡμῖν Hirschig^2 : ἡμῖν εἶναι A^{1}N : ὑμῖν εἶναι A^a 11 μὲν A : om. N   τοῖν ὀφθαλμοῖν N : τοῖς ὀφθαλμοῖς A   14 τῶν νέων AN : τὸν νέον A^2 18 <καὶ> τούτῳ Blass^2 20 add. Bekker   κατηγορουμένων] κατηγορημένων Fuhr^2 21 εἴ τε AN : εἴπερ Ignatius

ἀντιτύπτειν τόν τε πληγέντα ἐπὶ τὸν ἰατρὸν ἐλθεῖν.
ἀνόσια γὰρ ⟨ἂν⟩ ὁ διωκόμενος πάθοι, εἰ μήτε ἀποκτείνας
ὑπὲρ τοῦ ἀποκτείναντος μήτε ἄρξας ὑπὲρ τοῦ ἄρξαντος
φονεὺς ἔσται. ἔστι δὲ οὐδὲ ὁ ἐπιβουλεύσας οὐδὲν μᾶλλον 4
ὁ διωκόμενος τοῦ διώκοντος. εἰ γὰρ ὁ μὲν ἄρξας τῆς
πληγῆς τύπτειν καὶ μὴ ἀποκτείνειν διενοήθη, ὁ δὲ
ἀμυνόμενος ἀποκτεῖναι, οὗτος ἂν ὁ ἐπιβουλεύσας εἴη.
νῦν δὲ καὶ ὁ ἀμυνόμενος τύπτειν καὶ οὐκ ἀποκτεῖναι
διανοηθεὶς ἥμαρτεν, εἰς ἃ οὐκ ἐβούλετο πατάξας. τῆς 5
μὲν οὖν πληγῆς βουλευτὴς ἐγένετο, τὸν δὲ θάνατον πῶς
ἂν ἐπεβούλευσεν, ὅς γε ἀκουσίως ἐπάταξεν; οἰκεῖον δὲ
καὶ τὸ ἁμάρτημα τῷ ἄρξαντι μᾶλλον ἢ τῷ ἀμυνομένῳ
ἐστίν. ὁ μὲν γὰρ ἃ ἔπασχεν ἀντιδρᾶν ζητῶν, ὑπ᾽ ἐκείνου
βιαζόμενος ἐξήμαρτεν· ὁ δὲ διὰ τὴν αὑτοῦ ἀκολασίαν
πάντα δρῶν καὶ πάσχων, καὶ τῆς ἑαυτοῦ καὶ τῆς ἐκείνου
ἁμαρτίας ⟨αἴτιος ὢν⟩ δίκαιος φονεὺς εἶναί ἐστιν. ὡς 6
δὲ οὐδὲ κρεισσόνως ἀλλὰ πολὺ ὑποδεεστέρως ὧν
ἔπασχεν ἠμύνετο, διδάξω. ὁ μὲν ὑβρίζων καὶ παροινῶν
πάντ᾽ ἔδρα καὶ οὐδὲν ἠμύνατο· ὁ δὲ μὴ πάσχειν ἀλλ᾽
ἀπωθεῖσθαι ζητῶν, ἅ τε ἔπασχεν ἀκουσίως ἔπασχεν,
ἅ τ᾽ ἔδρασε τὰ παθήματα βουλόμενος διαφυγεῖν
ἐλασσόνως ἢ κατ᾽ ἀξίαν τὸν ἄρξαντα ἠμύνετο, καὶ οὐκ
ἔδρα. εἰ δὲ κρείσσων ὢν τὰς χεῖρας κρεισσόνως ἠμύνετο 7
ἢ ἔπασχεν, οὐδ᾽ οὕτω δίκαιος ὑφ᾽ ὑμῶν καταλαμβάνεσθαί
ἐστι. τῷ μὲν γὰρ ἄρξαντι πανταχοῦ μεγάλα ἐπιτίμια

26 add. Turr.   ὁ Reiske : ὅ τε N : ὅτε A^a : ὅ γε A^c 27 ὑπὲρ A^2: ὑπὸ AN   28 μᾶλλον A^c : μᾶλλον ἢ A^{a}N   32 pr. καὶ A^{1}N : om. A^a 33 ἐβούλετο A : ἠβούλετο N   34 βουλευτῆς A, corr. A^2 35 ὅς Sauppe : ὅν AN   36 καὶ N : om. A   38 αὑτοῦ A : ἑαυτοῦ N   39 καὶ τῆς ἑαυτοῦ A : om. N   40 add. Maetzner : <αἴτιος> Steph.   41 κρεισσόνως Reiske : κρεῖσσον ὢν A^{a}N : κρείσσων ὢν A^2 ὑποδεεστέρως Reiske : ὑποδεέστερος AN   43 ἠμύνατο AN : ἠμύνετο maluit Sauppe   ἀλλ᾽ N : ἀλλὰ A   44 ἀκουσίως A^{1}N : ἑκουσίως A^a 47 εἰ δὲ A^{1}N : οὐδὲ A^a

ἐπίκειται, τῷ δὲ ἀμυνομένῳ οὐδαμοῦ οὐδὲν ἐπιτίμιον
8 γέγραπται. πρὸς δὲ τὸ μήτε δικαίως μήτε ἀδίκως ἀποκτείνειν ἀποκέκριται· οὐ γὰρ ὑπὸ τῶν πληγῶν ἀλλ' ὑπὸ τοῦ ἰατροῦ ὁ ἀνὴρ ἀπέθανεν, ὡς οἱ μάρτυρες μαρτυροῦσιν. ἔστι δὲ καὶ ἡ τύχη τοῦ ἄρξαντος καὶ οὐ τοῦ ἀμυνομένου. ὁ μὲν γὰρ ἀκουσίως πάντα δράσας καὶ παθὼν ἀλλοτρίᾳ τύχῃ κέχρηται· ὁ δὲ ἑκουσίως πάντα πράξας, ἐκ τῶν αὑτοῦ ἔργων τὴν τύχην προσαγόμενος, τῇ αὑτοῦ ἀτυχίᾳ ἥμαρτεν.

9 Ὡς μὲν οὖν οὐδενὶ ἔνοχος τῶν κατηγορημένων ὁ διωκόμενός ἐστιν, ἀποδέδεικται. εἰ δέ τις κοινὴν μὲν τὴν πρᾶξιν κοινὴν δὲ τὴν ἀτυχίαν αὐτῶν ἡγούμενος εἶναι, μηδὲν ἀπολύσιμον μᾶλλον ἢ καταλήψιμον ἐκ τῶν λεγομένων γιγνώσκει αὐτὸν ὄντα, καὶ οὕτως ἀπολύειν μᾶλλον ἢ καταλαμβάνειν δίκαιός ἐστι. τόν τε γὰρ διώκοντα οὐ δίκαιον καταλαμβάνειν, μὴ σαφῶς διδάξαντα ὅτι ἀδικεῖται· τόν τε φεύγοντα ἀνόσιον
10 ἁλῶναι, μὴ φανερῶς ἐλεγχθέντα ἃ ἐπικαλεῖται. οὑτωσὶ δὲ ἐκ παντὸς τρόπου τῶν ἐγκλημάτων ἀπολυομένου τοῦ ἀνδρός, ἡμεῖς ὁσιώτερον ὑμῖν ἐπισκήπτομεν ὑπὲρ αὐτοῦ, μὴ τὸν φονέα ζητοῦντας κολάζειν τὸν καθαρὸν ἀποκτείνειν. ὅ τε γὰρ ⟨μὴ⟩ ἀποκτείνας τοῦ ἀποθανόντος

7 ἐπιτίμιον stp Pollux 8.21 (item α.4)

51 μήτε δικαίως Reiske : μὴ δικαίως AN 57 προσαγόμενος Reiske : προαγόμενος AN 59 οὖν A : om. N 63 post ὄντα add. καὶ οὐ τοῦ ἀπολύειν ἢ καταλήψιμον ἐκ τῶν λεγομένων γινώσκει αὐτὸν ὄντα N, quae del. N^{c} οὕτως A^{2} : οὐ τοῦ AN 64 post ἢ add. καταλαμβάνειν δίκαιόν ἐστι γινώσκει αὐτὸν ὄντα A^{a}, quae A^{1} mutavit in καταλήψιμον ἐκ τῶν λεγομένων γινώσκει αὐτὸν ὄντα, deinde delevit δίκαιός N : δίκαιόν A 68 δὲ in ras. A^{1} 69 ὑπὲρ A^{1}N : περὶ A^{a} 71 ἀποκτείνειν A^{a} : ζητεῖν ἀποκτείνειν A^{1}N <μὴ> ἀποκτείνας Sykutris : ἀποκτείνας AN : ἀλιτήριος Thalheim : ἀποθανὼν $Emperius^{2}$ τοῦ AN : τούτου Sauppe : del. $Emperius^{2}$ ἀποθανόντος AN : καταληφθέντος Jernstedt : κατακριθέντος Hatch : del. $Emperius^{2}$

οὐδὲν ἧσσον τοῖς αἰτίοις προστρόπαιός ἐστιν, οὗτός τε
ἀνοσίως διαφθαρεὶς διπλάσιον καθίστησι τὸ μίασμα
τῶν ἀλιτηρίων τοῖς ἀποκτείνασιν αὐτόν. ταῦτα οὖν 11
δεδιότες, τὸν μὲν καθαρὸν ὑμέτερον ἡγεῖσθε εἶναι
ἀπολύειν τῆς αἰτίας, τὸν δὲ μιαρὸν τῷ χρόνῳ ἀποδόντες
φῆναι τοῖς ἔγγιστα τιμωρεῖσθαι ὑπολείπετε· οὕτω γὰρ
ἂν δικαιότατα καὶ ὁσιώτατα πράξαιτ' ἄν.

72 *ἐστιν*] *ἔσται* Kayser^1 73 *μίασμα* AN : *μήνιμα* Briegleb 74 *ἀλιτηρίων* A^{2}N : *ἁλιτηρίων* A 75 *τὸν* A : *τὸ* N *ἡγεῖσθε* A^2 : *ἡγεῖσθαι* AN 77 *ἔγγιστα* A^{1}N : *ἔγγυστα* A^a *ὑπολείπετε* A^{1}N : *ὑπολίπετε* A^a 78 *ἂν* N : om. A subscriptio *τέλος τῶν τετραλογιῶν* N

5

ΠΕΡΙ ΤΟΥ ΗΡΩΙΔΟΥ ΦΟΝΟΥ

ΥΠΟΘΕΣΙΣ

Ἕλος τις Μιτυληναῖος ἀνὴρ ἐξ Ἀθηνῶν κατὰ ταὐτὸν ἀνήγετο Ἡρῴδῃ εἰς τὴν Αἶνον· ὡς δὲ πλέοντες ἐγένοντο ἐν τῇ Μηθύμνῃ τῆς Λέσβου, ἐπειδὴ ἀστέγαστον ἦν τὸ πλοῖον, εὑρόντες ἕτερον ἐστεγασμένον μετέβησαν. εἰσελθόντων δὲ αὐτῶν ἐν αὐτῷ ἐξῆλθε περὶ τὴν ἑσπέραν ὁ Ἡρῴδης καὶ οὐκέτι εἰσῆλθεν. ἐπανελθόντος οὖν αὐτοῦ τοῦ Ἕλου μόνου, οἱ συγγενεῖς τοῦ τελευτήσαντος ἐγράψαντο μὲν τὸν Ἕλον ὡς κακοῦργον, ἐν δὲ τῷ δικαστηρίῳ ἀγωνιζόμενοι εἶπον ὅτι καὶ ἀπέκτεινεν αὐτόν. ὁ δὲ τὸ μὲν τῆς κακουργίας ἔγκλημα ἀπολύεται παραγραφικῶς, λέγων κακούργους εἶναι τοὺς κλέπτας καὶ λωποδύτας, ὧν οὐδὲν ἀπέδειξάν με ποιήσαντα· μεταβαίνει δ' ἐπὶ τὴν ὑπὲρ τοῦ φόνου ἀπολογίαν, καὶ στοχαστικῶς ἀγωνίζεται. τὰ δὲ ἀπ' ἀρχῆς ἄχρι τέλους κοινά.

Ἐβουλόμην μέν, ὦ ἄνδρες, τὴν δύναμιν τοῦ λέγειν καὶ 1
τὴν ἐμπειρίαν τῶν πραγμάτων ἐξ ἴσου μοι καθεστάναι
τῇ τε συμφορᾷ καὶ τοῖς κακοῖς τοῖς γεγενημένοις· νῦν
δὲ τοῦ μὲν πεπείραμαι πέρα τοῦ προσήκοντος, τοῦ δὲ
ἐνδεής εἰμι μᾶλλον τοῦ συμφέροντος. οὗ μὲν γάρ με ἔδει 2
κακοπαθεῖν τῷ σώματι μετὰ τῆς αἰτίας τῆς οὐ προσ-
ηκούσης, ἐνταυθοῖ οὐδέν με ὠφέλησεν ἡ ἐμπειρία· οὗ δέ

Tit. περὶ τοῦ Ἡρώδου φόνου AN Harp. δ 60, φ 26 Arg. inscriptio ὑπόθεσις τοῦ ἡρώδου φόνου AN 11 λωποδύτας A : λωποδίτας N inscriptio ἀντιφῶντος ὑπὲρ τοῦ ἡρώδου φόνου N : deest in A 14 μὲν <ἂν> Cobet[3] 17 πέρα τοῦ προσήκοντος A[1]N : τοῦ προσήκοντος πέρα A[a] 18 γάρ A[2]N : γαρ A ἔδει <μὴ> dubitanter Gernet

με δεῖ σωθῆναι μετὰ τῆς ἀληθείας εἰπόντα τὰ γενόμενα,
3 ἐν τούτῳ με βλάπτει ἡ τοῦ λέγειν ἀδυνασία. πολλοὶ μὲν
γὰρ ἤδη τῶν οὐ δυναμένων λέγειν ἄπιστοι γενόμενοι
τοῖς ἀληθέσιν, αὐτοῖς τούτοις ἀπώλοντο, οὐ δυνάμενοι
δηλῶσαι αὐτά· πολλοὶ δὲ τῶν λέγειν δυναμένων πιστοὶ
γενόμενοι τῷ ψεύδεσθαι, τούτῳ ἐσώθησαν, διότι
ἐψεύσαντο. ἀνάγκη οὖν, ὅταν τις ἄπειρος ᾖ τοῦ
ἀγωνίζεσθαι, ἐπὶ τοῖς τῶν κατηγόρων λόγοις εἶναι
μᾶλλον ἢ ἐπ' αὐτοῖς τοῖς ἔργοις καὶ τῇ ἀληθείᾳ τῶν
4 πραγμάτων. ἐγὼ οὖν, ὦ ἄνδρες, αἰτήσομαι ὑμᾶς οὐχ
ἅπερ οἱ πολλοὶ τῶν ἀγωνιζομένων ἀκροᾶσθαι σφῶν
αὐτῶν αἰτοῦνται, σφίσι μὲν αὐτοῖς ἀπιστοῦντες, ὑμῶν
δὲ προκατεγνωκότες ἄδικόν τι—εἰκὸς γὰρ ἐν ἀνδράσι
γε ἀγαθοῖς καὶ ἄνευ τῆς αἰτήσεως τὴν ἀκρόασιν
ὑπάρχειν τοῖς φεύγουσιν, οὗπερ καὶ οἱ διώκοντες ἔτυχον
5 ἄνευ αἰτήσεως—τάδε δὲ δέομαι ὑμῶν, τοῦτο μὲν ἐάν τι
τῇ γλώσσῃ ἁμάρτω, συγγνώμην ἔχειν μοι, καὶ ἡγεῖσθαι
ἀπειρίᾳ αὐτὸ μᾶλλον ἤ ἀδικίᾳ ἡμαρτῆσθαι, τοῦτο
δὲ ἐάν τι ὀρθῶς εἴπω, ἀληθείᾳ μᾶλλον ἢ δεινότητι
εἰρῆσθαι. οὐ γὰρ δίκαιον οὔτ' ἔργῳ ἁμαρτόντα διὰ
ῥήματα σωθῆναι, οὔτ' ἔργῳ ὀρθῶς πράξαντα διὰ

2 *ἀδυνασία* stp Phot. *α* 394 s.v. *ἀδυναμία* *Synagoge aucta* *α* I.32.24–25 Bachmann = Anec. Bekk. I.345.26–27 *Synagoge vers. B* *α* 384   5 *οὐ δίκαιον—γνώμης* stp Stob. *Anth.* 4.5.65 (qui *γὰρ* omisit)

---

21 *μετὰ τῆς ἀληθείας* geminat. postea delet. in N   22 *λέγειν* A[1]N : *λέγοντος* A[a]   *ἀδυνασία* Sauppe[1] coll. lexicis : *ἀδυναμία* AN   *μὲν* N : om. A   24–5 *οὐ δυνάμενοι δηλῶσαι αὐτά* del. Dobree   25 *τῶν λέγειν δυναμένων* A[2] : *τῶν λέγειν* AN[a] : *τῶι λέγειν* N[c] : *τῶν λέγειν* <*ἐπισταμένων*> vel *τῶν* <*δεινῶν*> *λέγειν* Fuhr[1]   26 <*αὐτῷ*> *τούτῳ* maluit Baiter   30 *αἰτήσομαι* A[c] : *αἰτήσομαι δὲ* A[a]N   36 *τάδε δὲ* A[2] : *τάδε* AN   37 *γλώσσῃ* A[2]N : *γλώσῃ* A   *συγγνώμην ἔχειν μοι* huc transp. censuit Baiter : ante *τοῦτο μὲν* l. 36 AN   38 *αὐτὸ μᾶλλον* N : *μᾶλλον αὐτὸ* A   40 *γὰρ* AN : om. Stob.   *οὔτ'* AN : *οὔτε* Stob. 40–1 *διὰ ῥήματα* AN : *ῥήματι* Stob.   41 *οὔτ'* AN : *οὔτε* Stob.

*ῥήματα ἀπολέσθαι· τὸ μὲν γὰρ ῥῆμα τῆς γλώσσης
ἁμάρτημά ἐστι, τὸ δὲ ἔργον τῆς γνώμης. ἀνάγκη δὲ* 6
*κινδυνεύοντα περὶ αὑτῷ καί πού τι καὶ ἐξαμαρτεῖν.
οὐ γὰρ μόνον τῶν λεγομένων ἀνάγκη ἐνθυμεῖσθαι,
ἀλλὰ καὶ τῶν ἐσομένων· ἅπαντα γὰρ τὰ ἐν ἀδήλῳ
ἔτ' ὄντα ἐπὶ τῇ τύχῃ μᾶλλον ἀνάκειται ἢ τῇ προνοίᾳ.
ταῦτ' οὖν ἔκπληξιν πολλὴν παρέχειν ἀνάγκη ἐστὶ τῷ
κινδυνεύοντι. ὁρῶ γὰρ ἔγωγε καὶ τοὺς πάνυ ἐμπείρους* 7
*τοῦ ἀγωνίζεσθαι πολλῷ χεῖρον ἑαυτῶν λέγοντας,
ὅταν ἔν τινι κινδύνῳ ὦσιν· ὅταν δ' ἄνευ κινδύνων τι
διαπράσσωνται, μᾶλλον ὀρθουμένους. ἡ μὲν οὖν αἴτησις,
ὦ ἄνδρες, καὶ νομίμως καὶ ὁσίως ἔχουσα, καὶ ἐν τῷ
ὑμετέρῳ δικαίῳ οὐχ ἧσσον ἢ ἐν τῷ ἐμῷ· περὶ δὲ τῶν
κατηγορημένων ἀπολογήσομαι καθ' ἕκαστον.*

Πρῶτον μὲν οὖν, ὡς παρανομώτατα καὶ βιαιότατα εἰς 8
*τόνδε τὸν ἀγῶνα καθέστηκα, τοῦτο ὑμᾶς διδάξω, οὐ τῷ
φεύγειν ἂν τὸ πλῆθος τὸ ὑμέτερον, ἐπεὶ κἂν ἀνωμότοις
ὑμῖν καὶ μὴ κατὰ νόμον μηδένα ἐπιτρέψαιμι περὶ
τοῦ σώματος τοῦ ἐμοῦ διαψηφίσασθαι, ἕνεκά γε τοῦ
πιστεύειν ἐμοί τε μηδὲν ἐξημαρτῆσθαι εἰς τόδε τὸ
πρᾶγμα καὶ ὑμᾶς γνώσεσθαι τὰ δίκαια, ἀλλ' ἵνα ᾖ
τεκμήρια ὑμῖν καὶ τῶν ἄλλων πραγμάτων {καὶ} τῶν
εἰς ἐμὲ ἡ τούτων βιαιότης καὶ παρανομία. πρῶτον μὲν* 9
*γὰρ κακοῦργος ἐνδεδειγμένος φόνου δίκην φεύγω,
ὃ οὐδεὶς πώποτ' ἔπαθε τῶν ἐν τῇ γῇ ταύτῃ. καὶ ὡς μὲν
οὐ κακοῦργός εἰμι οὐδ' ἔνοχος τῷ τῶν κακούργων νόμῳ,
αὐτοὶ οὗτοι τούτου γε μάρτυρες γεγένηνται. περὶ γὰρ
τῶν κλεπτῶν καὶ λωποδυτῶν ὁ νόμος κεῖται, ὧν οὐδὲν*

42 *ῥήματα* AN : *ῥῆμα* Stob. *ἀπολέσθαι* A[2] Stob. : *ἀπολεῖσθαι* AN *γλώσσης* A[2]N : *γνώσσης* A 43 pr. *δὲ* N Stob. : *δ'* A 44 *αὑτῷ* N : *αὐτῶ* A[1] : *αὐτῶ* A[a] 52 *διαπράσσωνται* A[1] : *διαπράσσονται* A[a]N *ὀρθουμένους* A[2]N : *ὀρθωμένους* A 63 *ὑμῖν* A[1]N : *ἐμοὶ* A[a] del. Sauppe 68 *γε* N : om. A

ἐμοὶ προσὸν ἀπέδειξαν. οὕτως εἴς γε ταύτην τὴν ἀπαγωγὴν νομιμωτάτην καὶ δικαιοτάτην πεποιήκασιν
10 *ὑμῖν τὴν ἀποψήφισίν μου. φασὶ δὲ αὖ τό γε ἀποκτείνειν μέγα κακούργημα εἶναι, καὶ ἐγὼ ὁμολογῶ μέγιστόν γε, καὶ τὸ ἱεροσυλεῖν καὶ τὸ προδιδόναι τὴν πόλιν· ἀλλὰ χωρὶς περὶ αὐτῶν ἑκάστου οἱ νόμοι κεῖνται. ἐμοὶ δὲ πρῶτον μέν, οὗ τοῖς ἄλλοις εἴργεσθαι προαγορεύουσι τοῖς τοῦ φόνου φεύγουσι τὰς δίκας, ἐνταυθοῖ πεποιήκασι τὴν κρίσιν ἐν τῇ ἀγορᾷ· ἔπειτα τίμησίν μοι ἐποίησαν, ἀνταποθανεῖν τοῦ νόμου κειμένου τὸν ἀποκτείναντα, οὐ τοῦ ἐμοὶ συμφέροντος ἕνεκα, ἀλλὰ τοῦ σφίσιν αὐτοῖς λυσιτελοῦντος, καὶ ἐνταῦθα ἔλασσον ἔνειμαν τῷ τεθνηκότι τῶν ἐν τῷ νόμῳ κειμένων· οὗ δ' ἕνεκα,*
11 *γνώσεσθε προϊόντος τοῦ λόγου. ἔπειτα δέ, ὃ πάντας οἶμαι ὑμᾶς ἐπίστασθαι, ἅπαντα τὰ δικαστήρια ἐν ὑπαίθρῳ δικάζει τὰς δίκας τοῦ φόνου, οὐδενὸς ἄλλου ἕνεκα ἢ ἵνα τοῦτο μὲν οἱ δικασταὶ μὴ ἴωσιν εἰς τὸ αὐτὸ τοῖς μὴ καθαροῖς τὰς χεῖρας, τοῦτο δὲ ὁ διώκων τὴν δίκην τοῦ φόνου ἵνα μὴ ὁμωρόφιος γίγνηται τῷ αὐθέντῃ. σὺ δὲ τοῦτο μὲν παρελθὼν τοῦτον τὸν νόμον τοὐναντίον τοῖς ἄλλοις πεποίηκας· τοῦτο δὲ δέον σε διομόσασθαι ὅρκον τὸν μέγιστον καὶ ἰσχυρότατον, ἐξώλειαν σαυτῷ καὶ γένει καὶ οἰκίᾳ τῇ σῇ ἐπαρώμενον, ἦ μὴν μὴ ἄλλα κατηγορήσειν ἐμοῦ ἢ εἰς αὐτὸν τὸν φόνον, ὡς*

70 *προσὸν* A^{c}N : *πρὸς ὃν* A^{a} *γε* A^{2}N : *τε* A   72 *ἀποψήφισίν* A^{c}N : *ἀποψήφησίν* A^{a} *γε* Sauppe : *τε* AN   73 *μέγα* Ald. : *με* AN   76 *πρῶτον* A^{1}N : *πρὸς* A^{a} *οὗ* A^{2} : *οὐ* AN   *εἴργεσθαι* A^{2}N : *εἵργεσθαι* A   78 *κρίσιν* in ras. A^{1} 79 *ἀνταποθανεῖν* post *ἀποκτείναντα* l. 79 transp. A^{2} 81 *ἔνειμαν* A^{2} : *ἔνειμαν ἂν* N : *ἂν ἔνειμαν ἂν* A   82 *κειμένων* susp. Jernstedt : del. Blass^{3} 84 *ἅπαντα τὰ δι* in ras. N^{1} 85 *ὑπαίθρω* A^{2}N : *ὑπέρθρω* A   88 *ἵνα* del. Herwerden^{1} 91 *ἰσχυρότατον* AN^{2} : *ἰσχυρώτατον* N   *ἐξώλειαν* A^{2}N^{2} : *ἐξωλίαν* AN   *σαυτῶ* N : *αὐτῶ* A   92 *οἰκία* AN^{2} : *οἰκεία* N   *ἦ* A^{2}N^{2} : *ἢ* AN

ἔκτεινα, ἐν ᾧ οὔτ᾽ ἂν κακὰ πολλὰ εἰργασμένος ἡλισκόμην ἄλλῳ ἢ αὐτῷ τῷ πράγματι, οὔτ᾽ ἂν πολλὰ ἀγαθὰ εἰργασμένος τούτοις ἂν ἐσῳζόμην τοῖς ἀγαθοῖς· ἃ σὺ 12 παρελθών, αὐτὸς σεαυτῷ νόμους ἐξευρών, ἀνώμοτος μὲν αὐτὸς ἐμοῦ κατηγορεῖς, ἀνώμοτοι δὲ οἱ μάρτυρες καταμαρτυροῦσι, δέον αὐτοὺς τὸν αὐτὸν ὅρκον σοὶ διομοσαμένους καὶ ἁπτομένους τῶν σφαγίων καταμαρτυρεῖν ἐμοῦ. ἔπειτα κελεύεις τοὺς δικαστὰς ἀνωμότοις πιστεύσαντας τοῖς μαρτυροῦσι φόνου δίκην καταγνῶναι, οὓς σὺ αὐτὸς ἀπίστους κατέστησας παρελθὼν τοὺς κειμένους νόμους, καὶ ἡγῇ χρῆναι αὐτοῖς τὴν σὴν παρανομίαν κρείσσω γενέσθαι αὐτῶν τῶν νόμων.

Λέγεις δὲ ὡς οὐκ ἂν παρέμεινα εἰ ἐλελύμην, ἀλλ᾽ 13 ᾠχόμην ἂν ἀπιών, ὡσπερεὶ ἄκοντά με ἀναγκάσας εἰσελθεῖν εἰς τὴν γῆν ταύτην. καίτοι ἐμοὶ εἰ μηδὲν διέφερε στέρεσθαι τῆσδε τῆς πόλεως, ἴσον ἦν μοι καὶ προσκληθέντι μὴ ἐλθεῖν, ἀλλ᾽ ἐρήμην ὀφλεῖν τὴν δίκην, τοῦτο δὲ ἀπολογησαμένῳ τὴν προτέραν ἐξεῖναι ἐξελθεῖν· ἅπασι γὰρ τοῦτο κοινόν ἐστι. σὺ δέ, ὃ τοῖς ἄλλοις Ἕλλησι κοινόν ἐστιν, ἰδίᾳ ζητεῖς με μόνον ἀποστερεῖν, αὐτὸς σαυτῷ νόμον θέμενος. καίτοι τούς γε νόμους οἳ κεῖνται 14 περὶ τῶν τοιούτων, πάντας ἂν οἶμαι ὁμολογῆσαι κάλλιστα νόμων ἁπάντων κεῖσθαι καὶ ὁσιώτατα. ὑπάρχει μέν γε αὐτοῖς ἀρχαιοτάτοις εἶναι ἐν τῇ γῇ

94 ἐν ᾧ AN[2] : ἐγὼ N κακὰ A[2] : κἆτα A : δεινὰ ut vid. N[c], quid fuerit non liquet 95 ἂν AN : αὖ Reiske 96–7 σὺ παρελθών A : συμπαρελθών N 97 ἐξευρὼν A : εὑρὼν N 102 ἀνωμότοις A[2]N : ἀνομότοις A 104 ἡγῇ Dryander : εἴ γε A : ἤ γε N : λέγων Ald. 105 αὐτοῖς AN : αὖθις Gernet 108 ἂν ἀπιὼν A[2] : ἀνάπτων AN 109–10 στέρεσθαι A[2]N : στερέσθαι A 110 μοι] οἶμαι Weidner 111 ὀφλεῖν Maetzner : ὄφλειν A[1]N : ὤφλειν εἶναι A[a] τὴν δίκην A : om. N §14 cfr. Orat. VI.2 115–26 τούς … οὕτως del. Sauppe[2] 117 ἁπάντων del. Sakorraphus

ταύτῃ, ἔπειτα τοὺς αὐτοὺς ἀεὶ περὶ τῶν αὐτῶν, ὅπερ μέγιστόν ἐστι σημεῖον νόμων καλῶς κειμένων· ὁ γὰρ χρόνος καὶ ἡ ἐμπειρία τὰ μὴ καλῶς ἔχοντα ἐκδιδάσκει τοὺς ἀνθρώπους. ὥστε οὐ δεῖ ὑμᾶς ἐκ τῶν τοῦ κατηγόρου λόγων τοὺς νόμους καταμανθάνειν, εἰ καλῶς ὑμῖν κεῖνται ἢ μή, ἀλλ' ἐκ τῶν νόμων τοὺς τοῦ κατηγόρου λόγους, εἰ ὀρθῶς καὶ νομίμως ὑμᾶς διδάσκουσι τὸ
15 πρᾶγμα ἢ οὔ. οὕτως οἵ γε νόμοι κάλλιστα κεῖνται οἱ περὶ φόνου, οὓς οὐδεὶς πώποτε ἐτόλμησε κινῆσαι· σὺ δὲ μόνος δὴ τετόλμηκας γενέσθαι νομοθέτης ἐπὶ τὰ πονηρότερα, καὶ ταῦτα παρελθὼν ζητεῖς με ἀδίκως ἀπολέσαι. ἃ δὲ σὺ παρανομεῖς, αὐτὰ ταῦτά μοι μέγιστα μαρτύριά ἐστιν· εὖ γὰρ ᾔδεις ὅτι οὐδεὶς ἂν ἦν σοι ὃς ἐκεῖνον τὸν ὅρκον διομοσάμενος ἐμοῦ κατεμαρτύρησεν.
16 ἔπειτα δὲ οὐχ ὡς πιστεύων τῷ πράγματι ἀναμφισβητήτως ἕνα τὸν ἀγῶνα περὶ τοῦ πράγματος ἐποιήσω, ἀλλὰ ἀμφισβήτησιν καὶ λόγον ὑπελίπου ὡς καὶ τοῖσδε τοῖς δικασταῖς ἀπιστήσων. ὥστε μηδέν μοι ἐνθάδε {μηδὲ} πλέον εἶναι μηδ' ἀποφυγόντι, ἀλλ' ἐξεῖναί σοι λέγειν ὅτι κακοῦργος ἀπέφυγον, ἀλλ' οὐ τοῦ φόνου τὴν δίκην· ἑλὼν δ' αὖ ἀξιώσεις με ἀποκτεῖναι ὡς τοῦ φόνου τὴν δίκην ὠφληκότα. καίτοι πῶς ἂν εἴη τούτων δεινότερα μηχανήματα, εἰ ὑμῖν μὲν ἅπαξ τουτουσὶ πείσασι κατείργασται ἃ βούλεσθε, ἐμοὶ δ' ἅπαξ
17 ἀποφυγόντι ὁ αὐτὸς κίνδυνος ὑπολείπεται; ἔτι δὲ μάλ'

122 ὑμᾶς A : ἡμᾶς N   τοῦ κατηγόρου A^{sv}N : τῶν κατηγόρων A^{it} 125 διδάσκουσι Reiske : διδάξουσι A : διδάξει N   126 ἢ] ex corr. A^{1} (ο fuit?)   129 πονηρότερα N : πονηρότατα A   130 παρανομεῖς A : παρονομεῖς N   μέγιστα AN : μεγίστη N^{2} 131 μαρτύρια A : μαρτυρία N   ᾔδεις A^{2}N : ἤδεις A : ᾔδησθα Jernstedt   135 ἐποίησω A, corr. A^{2} ὑπελίπου A^{c} : ὑπελείπου A^{a}N   136 τοῖσδε τοῖς Pahle : τοῖς τότε AN : τότε τοῖς Denniston   137 del. Reiske   139 αὖ Bekker : ἂν AN   ἀξιώσεις A^{2} : ἀξιώσῃς AN   143 ὑπολείπεται A^{a} : ἀπολείπεται A^{1}N

ἐδέθην, ὦ ἄνδρες, παρανομώτατα ἁπάντων ἀνθρώπων. ἐθέλοντος γάρ μου ἐγγυητὰς τρεῖς καθιστάναι κατὰ τὸν νόμον, οὕτως οὗτοι διεπράξαντο τοῦτο ὥστε μὴ ἐγγενέσθαι μοι ποιῆσαι. τῶν δὲ ἄλλων ξένων ὅστις πώποτε ἠθέλησε καταστῆσαι ἐγγυητάς, οὐδεὶς πώποτ' ἐδέθη. καίτοι οἱ ἐπιμεληταὶ τῶν κακούργων τῷ αὐτῷ χρῶνται νόμῳ τούτῳ. ὥστε καὶ οὗτος κοινὸς τοῖς ἄλλοις πᾶσιν ὢν ἐμοὶ μόνῳ ἐπέλιπε μὴ ὠφελῆσαι. τούτοις γὰρ 18
ἦν τοῦτο συμφέρον, πρῶτον μὲν ἀπαρασκευότατον γενέσθαι με, μὴ δυνάμενον διαπράσσεσθαι αὐτὸν τἀμαυτοῦ πράγματα, ἔπειτα κακοπαθεῖν τῷ σώματι, τούς τε φίλους προθυμοτέρους ἔχειν τοὺς ἐμαυτοῦ τούτοις τὰ ψευδῆ μαρτυρεῖν ἢ ἐμοὶ τἀληθῆ λέγειν, διὰ τὴν τοῦ σώματος κακοπάθειαν. ὄνειδός τε αὐτῷ τε ἐμοὶ περιέθεσαν καὶ τοῖς ἐμοῖς προσήκουσιν εἰς τὸν βίον ἅπαντα.

Οὑτωσὶ μὲν δὴ πολλοῖς ἐλασσωθεὶς τῶν νόμων τῶν 19
ὑμετέρων καὶ τοῦ δικαίου καθέστηκα εἰς τὸν ἀγῶνα· ὅμως μέντοι γε καὶ ἐκ τούτων πειράσομαι ἐμαυτὸν ἀναίτιον ἐπιδεῖξαι. καίτοι χαλεπόν γε τὰ ἐκ πολλοῦ κατεψευσμένα καὶ ἐπιβεβουλευμένα, ταῦτα παραχρῆμα ἀπελέγχειν· ἃ γάρ τις μὴ προσεδόκησεν, οὐδὲ φυλάξασθαι ἐγχωρεῖ.

145 καθιστάναι N : καθιστᾶναι A[2] : καθεστάναι A 146 τοῦτο, ὥστε sic AN : ὥστε τοῦτο maluit Reiske 147 μοι A : με N 147–8 ὅστις πώποτε A : ὅστίς ποτε N 148 πώποτ' A : πώποτε N 149 ἐδέθη e ras. A[1] 150 ὥστε A[1]N : ὅστε A[a] 151 ἐπέλιπε A[1] : ἐπέλειπε N : ὑπέλειπε A[a] ὠφελῆσαι Gernet : ὠφελῆσαι τοῦδε κόσμου AN : ὠφελῆσθαι τοῦδε τοῦ νόμου A[2] : ἀπολῦσαι τοῦ δεσμοῦ Thalheim 153 αὐτὸν Bekker : ἐμαυτὸν AN 156 τούτοις A[2] : τοῖς AN λέγειν del. Jernstedt 156–7 διὰ … κακοπάθειαν damnavit Dobree 157 alt. τε Reiske : γε AN 160 ἐλασσωθεὶς A[a], N[1] (accentus supra pr. ε eras.) : ἔλος σωθεὶς A[1], fort. N[a]

20 Ἐγὼ δὲ τὸν μὲν πλοῦν ἐποιησάμην ἐκ τῆς Μυτιλήνης, ὦ ἄνδρες, ἐν τῷ πλοίῳ πλέων ᾧ Ἡρῴδης οὗτος, ὅν φασιν ὑπ' ἐμοῦ ἀποθανεῖν· ἐπλέομεν δὲ εἰς τὴν Αἶνον, ἐγὼ μὲν ὡς τὸν πατέρα—ἐτύγχανε γὰρ ἐκεῖ ὢν τότε—ὁ δ' Ἡρῴδης ἀνδράποδα Θρᾳξὶν ἀνθρώποις ἀπολύσων. συνέπλει δὲ τά τε ἀνδράποδα ἃ ἔδει αὐτὸν ἀπολῦσαι, καὶ οἱ Θρᾷκες οἱ λυσόμενοι. τούτων δ' ὑμῖν τοὺς μάρτυρας παρέξομαι.

ΜΑΡΤΥΡΕΣ

21 Ἡ μὲν πρόφασις ἑκατέρῳ τοῦ πλοῦ αὕτη· ἐτύχομεν δὲ χειμῶνί τινι χρησάμενοι, ὑφ' οὗ ἠναγκάσθημεν κατασχεῖν εἰς τῆς Μηθυμναίας τι χωρίον, οὗ τὸ πλοῖον ὥρμει τοῦτο εἰς ὃ μετεκβάντα φασὶν ἀποθανεῖν αὐτόν {τὸν Ἡρῴδην}. καὶ πρῶτον μὲν αὐτὰ ταῦτα σκοπεῖτε, ὅτι ⟨οὐ τῇ ἐ⟩μῇ προνοίᾳ μᾶλλον ἐγίγνετο ἢ τύχῃ. οὔτε γὰρ πείσας τὸν ἄνδρα οὐδαμοῦ ἀπελέγχομαι σύμπλουν μοι γενέσθαι, ἀλλ' αὐτὸς καθ' αὑτὸν τὸν πλοῦν πεποιημένος
22 ἕνεκα πραγμάτων ἰδίων· οὔτ' αὖ ἐγὼ ἄνευ προφάσεως ἱκανῆς φαίνομαι τὸν πλοῦν ποιησάμενος εἰς τὴν Αἶνον, οὔτε κατασχόντες εἰς τὸ χωρίον τοῦτο ἀπὸ παρασκευῆς οὐδεμιᾶς, ἀλλ' ἀνάγκῃ χρησάμενοι· οὔτ' αὖ ἐπειδὴ ὡρμισάμεθα, ἡ μετέκβασις ἐγένετο εἰς τὸ ἕτερον πλοῖον οὐδενὶ μηχανήματι οὐδ' ἀπάτῃ, ἀλλ' ἀνάγκῃ καὶ τοῦτο ἐγίγνετο. ἐν ᾧ μὲν γὰρ ἐπλέομεν, ἀστέγαστον ἦν τὸ

167 Μυτιλήνης Jernstedt : μιτυλήνης AN et sic propemodum ubique (sed vid. §24) 171 ἀπολύσων e corr. A^1 (ἀπολύων inceperat scribere) 178 μηθυμναίας A : μεθυμναίας N 179 μετεκβάντα A^{1}N : μεταβάντα A^a φασὶν A^2 : φησὶν AN 179–80 del. Reiske 180 σκοπεῖτε] alt. ε in ras. N^2 ὅτι AN : εἰ Thalheim 181 <οὐ τῇ ἐ>μῇ Jebb : μὴ AN : μοι Thalheim : οὐ Maetzner 183 καθ' αὑτὸν Steph. : κατ' αὐτὸν AN 184 αὖ A^c : αὖ τ' AN 187 αὖ e ras. N^2 188 ὡρμισάμεθα AN^2 : ὡρμησάμεθα N μετέκβασις A^{1}N : μετάβασις A^a

πλοῖον, εἰς ὃ δὲ μετέβημεν, ἐστεγασμένον· τοῦ δὲ ὑετοῦ ἕνεκα ταῦτ᾽ ἦν. τούτων δ᾽ ὑμῖν μάρτυρας παρέξομαι.

ΜΑΡΤΥΡΕΣ

Ἐπειδὴ δὲ μετεξέβημεν εἰς τὸ ἕτερον πλοῖον, ἐπίνομεν. 23
καὶ ὁ μέν ἐστι φανερὸς ἐκβὰς ἐκ τοῦ πλοίου καὶ οὐκ εἰσβὰς πάλιν· ἐγὼ δὲ τὸ παράπαν οὐκ ἐξέβην ἐκ τοῦ πλοίου τῆς νυκτὸς ἐκείνης. τῇ δ᾽ ὑστεραίᾳ, ἐπειδὴ ἀφανὴς ἦν ὁ ἀνήρ, ἐζητεῖτο οὐδέν τι μᾶλλον ὑπὸ τῶν ἄλλων ἢ καὶ ὑπ᾽ ἐμοῦ· καὶ εἴ τῳ τῶν ἄλλων ἐδόκει δεινὸν εἶναι, καὶ ἐμοὶ ὁμοίως. καὶ εἴς τε τὴν Μυτιλήνην ἐγὼ αἴτιος ἦν πεμφθῆναι ἄγγελον, καὶ τῇ ἐμῇ γνώμῃ ἐπέμπετο· καὶ ἄλλου οὐδενὸς ἐθέλοντος βαδίζειν, 24
οὔτε τῶν ἀπὸ τοῦ πλοίου οὔτε τῶν αὐτῷ τῷ Ἡρῴδῃ συμπλεόντων, ἐγὼ τὸν ἀκόλουθον τὸν ἐμαυτοῦ πέμπειν ἕτοιμος ἦν· καίτοι οὐ δήπου γε κατ᾽ ἐμαυτοῦ μηνυτὴν ἔπεμπον εἰδώς. ἐπειδὴ δὲ ὁ ἀνὴρ οὔτε ἐν τῇ Μυτιλήνῃ ἐφαίνετο ζητούμενος οὔτ᾽ ἄλλοθι οὐδαμοῦ, πλοῦς τε ἡμῖν ἐγίγνετο, καὶ τἆλλ᾽ ἀνήγετο πλοῖα ἅπαντα, ᾠχόμην κἀγὼ πλέων. τούτων δ᾽ ὑμῖν τοὺς μάρτυρας παρασχήσομαι.

ΜΑΡΤΥΡΕΣ

Τὰ μὲν γενόμενα ταῦτ᾽ ἐστίν· ἐκ δὲ τούτων ἤδη σκοπεῖτε 25
τὰ εἰκότα. πρῶτον μὲν γὰρ πρὶν ἀνάγεσθαί με εἰς τὴν

192 *μάρτυρας* Reiske : *μαρτυρίας* AN   194 *μετεξέβημεν* A : *μετέβημεν* N   195 *ἐκ* A : om. N   196 *παράπαν* A[1]N : *πάπαν* A[a]   197 *ἐκ* N : om. A   201 *ἦν*] *ᾖ* Jernstedt   203 pr. *τῶν* AN[2] : fort. *τοῦ* N   204 *ἀκόλουθον* A[1]N : *ἀκούλοθον* A[a]   *πέμπειν* A[1]N : *πέμπτειν* A[a]   205 *ἦν*] *ᾖ* Jernstedt   *οὐ δήπου γε* N : *γε οὐ δήπου* A   206 *Μυτιλήνῃ* Jernstedt : *μιτυλήνη* A : *μυτυλήνη* N   208 *τἆλλ᾽* re vera A : *τἄλλα* N   209 *πλέων* A[2]N : *πλέον* A

Αἶνον, ὅτε ἦν ἀφανὴς ὁ ἀνήρ, οὐδεὶς ᾐτιάσατό με
ἀνθρώπων, ἤδη πεπυσμένων τούτων τὴν ἀγγελίαν· οὐ
γὰρ ἄν ποτε ᾠχόμην πλέων. ἀλλ' εἰς μὲν τὸ παραχρῆμα
κρεῖσσον ἦν τὸ ἀληθὲς καὶ τὸ γεγενημένον τῆς τούτων
αἰτιάσεως, καὶ ἅμα ἐγὼ ἔτι ἐπεδήμουν· ἐπειδὴ δ' ἐγώ
τε ᾠχόμην πλέων καὶ οὗτοι ἐξ ἐπιβουλῆς συνέθεσαν
ταῦτα καὶ ἐμηχανήσαντο κατ' ἐμοῦ, τότε ᾐτιάσαντο.
26 λέγουσι δὲ ὡς ἐν μὲν τῇ γῇ ἀπέθανεν ὁ ἀνήρ, κἀγὼ λίθον
αὐτῷ ἐνέβαλον εἰς τὴν κεφαλήν, ὃς οὐκ ἐξέβην τὸ
παράπαν ἐκ τοῦ πλοίου. καὶ τοῦτο μὲν ἀκριβῶς οὗτοι
ἴσασιν· ὅπως δ' ἠφανίσθη ὁ ἀνήρ, οὐδενὶ λόγῳ εἰκότι
δύνανται ἀποφαίνειν. δῆλον γὰρ ὅτι ἐγγύς που τοῦ
λιμένος εἰκὸς ἦν τοῦτο γίγνεσθαι, τοῦτο μὲν μεθύοντος
τοῦ ἀνδρός, τοῦτο δὲ νύκτωρ ἐκβάντος ἐκ τοῦ πλοίου·
οὔτε γὰρ αὑτοῦ κρατεῖν ἴσως ἂν ἐδύνατο, οὔτε τῷ
ἀπάγοντι νύκτωρ μακρὰν ὁδὸν ἡ πρόφασις ἂν εἰκότως
27 ἐγίγνετο· ζητουμένου δὲ τοῦ ἀνδρὸς δύο ἡμέρας καὶ ἐν
τῷ λιμένι καὶ ἄπωθεν τοῦ λιμένος, οὔτε ὀπτὴρ οὐδεὶς
ἐφάνη οὔθ' αἷμα οὔτ' ἄλλο σημεῖον οὐδέν. κᾆτ' ἐγὼ
συγχωρῶ τῷ τούτων λόγῳ, παρεχόμενος μὲν τοὺς
μάρτυρας ὡς οὐκ ἐξέβην ἐκ τοῦ πλοίου; εἰ δὲ καὶ ὡς
μάλιστα ἐξέβην ἐκ τοῦ πλοίου, οὐδενὶ τρόπῳ εἰκὸς
ἦν ἀφανισθέντα λαθεῖν τὸν ἄνθρωπον, εἴπερ γε μὴ
28 πάνυ πόρρω ἀπῆλθεν ἀπὸ τῆς θαλάσσης. ἀλλ' ὡς
κατεποντώθη λέγουσιν. ἐν τίνι πλοίῳ; δῆλον γὰρ ὅτι ἐξ

25 *αἰτιάσεως* stp Pollux 3.136 (item 89.3, 6.6.11) **27** *ὀπτὴρ* stp Pollux 2.57.4

---

215 *πεπυσμένων* A : *πεπυσμένον* e ras. N[2] 218 *δ'* N : *δὲ* e compendio A 219 *συνέθεσαν*] *σαν* in ras. A[1] 222 *αὐτῷ ἐνέβαλον* N : *ἐνέβαλον αὐτῷ* A *οὐκ* A[1]N : om. A[a] 226 pr. *τοῦτο* A : *αὐτὸ* N 228 *αὑτοῦ* Taylor, Reiske : *αὐτοῦ* AN 230 *καὶ ἐν* N : *ἐν* A 231 *ἄπωθεν* A : *ἄποθεν* N *ὀπτὴρ* A[2]N Pollux : *ὀππὴρ* A 232 *οὔθ'* … *οὔτ'* A : *οὔτε* … *οὔτε* N 233 *μὲν*] om. B, del. Halbertsma 234–5 *εἰ δὲ* … *πλοίου* in mg. N 236 *γε* N : om. A 238 *ἐν τίνι* A[2] : *ἔν τινι* AN

αὐτοῦ τοῦ λιμένος ἦν τὸ πλοῖον. πῶς ἂν οὖν οὐκ ἐξηυρέθη; καὶ μὴν εἰκός γε ἦν καὶ σημεῖόν τι γενέσθαι ἐν τῷ πλοίῳ ἀνδρὸς τεθνεῶτος καὶ ἐκβαλλομένου νύκτωρ. νῦν δ' ἐν μὲν ᾧ ἔπινε πλοίῳ καὶ ἐξ οὗ ἐξέβαινεν, ἐν τούτῳ φασὶν εὑρεῖν σημεῖα, ἐν ᾧ αὐτοὶ μὴ ὁμολογοῦσιν ἀποθανεῖν τὸν ἄνδρα· ἐν ᾧ δὲ κατεποντώθη, οὐχ ηὗρον οὔτ' αὐτὸ τὸ πλοῖον οὔτε σημεῖον οὐδέν. τούτων δ' ὑμῖν τοὺς μάρτυρας παρασχήσομαι.

ΜΑΡΤΥΡΕΣ

Ἐπειδὴ δὲ ἐγὼ μὲν φροῦδος ἦν πλέων εἰς τὴν Αἶνον, τὸ 29
δὲ πλοῖον ἧκεν εἰς τὴν Μυτιλήνην ἐν ᾧ ἐγὼ καὶ ὁ Ἡρῴδης
ἐπίνομεν, πρῶτον μὲν εἰσβάντες εἰς τὸ πλοῖον ἠρεύνων,
καὶ ἐπειδὴ τὸ αἷμα ηὗρον, ἐνταῦθα ἔφασαν τεθνάναι τὸν
ἄνδρα· ἐπειδὴ δὲ αὐτοῖς τοῦτο οὐκ ἐνεχώρει, ἀλλ'
ἐφαίνετο τῶν προβάτων ὂν αἷμα, ἀποτραπόμενοι τούτου
τοῦ λόγου συλλαβόντες ἐβασάνιζον τοὺς ἀνθρώπους.
καὶ ὃν μὲν τότε παραχρῆμα ἐβασάνισαν, οὗτος μὲν 30
οὐδὲν εἶπε περὶ ἐμοῦ φλαῦρον· ὃν δ' ἡμέραις ὕστερον
πολλαῖς ἐβασάνισαν, ἔχοντες παρὰ σφίσιν αὐτοῖς τὸν
πρόσθεν χρόνον, οὗτος ἦν ὁ πεισθεὶς ὑπὸ τούτων καὶ
καταψευσάμενος ἐμοῦ. παρέξομαι δὲ τούτων τοὺς
μάρτυρας.

29 φροῦδος Harp. φ 26 s.v.

---

240 ἐξηυρέθη Jernstedt : ἐξευρέθη AN 241 τεθνεῶτος <ἐντιθεμένου> Blass 242 δ' ἐν μὲν ᾧ N : δὲ μὲν ᾧ A : δὲ ἐν ᾧ μὲν A^2 243 ὁμολογοῦσιν A^1 : ὁμολογῶσιν A^{a}N 244 ηὗρον Jernstedt : εὗρον AN 246 παρασχήσομαι Bekker : παραστήσομαι AN 248 μὲν φροῦδος N : φροῦδος μὲν A ἦν] ἦ Jernstedt 249 ὁ N : om. A 250 ἐπίνομεν Weil : ἐπλέομεν AN 251 ηὗρον Jernstedt : εὗρον AN 253 τῶν del. Reiske 258 καὶ A^{1}N : om. A^a : post παρέξομαι δὲ transp. Reiske

ΜΑΡΤΥΡΕΣ

31 Ὡς μὲν ὕστερον τοσούτῳ χρόνῳ ὁ ἀνὴρ ἐβασανίσθη,
μεμαρτύρηται ὑμῖν· προσέχετε δὲ τὸν νοῦν αὐτῇ τῇ
βασάνῳ, οἵα γεγένηται. ὁ μὲν γὰρ δοῦλος, ᾧ ἴσως οὗτοι
τοῦτο μὲν ἐλευθερίαν ὑπέσχοντο, τοῦτο δ᾽ ἐπὶ τούτοις
ἦν παύσασθαι κακούμενον αὐτόν, ἴσως ὑπ᾽ ἀμφοῖν
πεισθεὶς κατεψεύσατό μου, τὴν μὲν ἐλευθερίαν ἐλπίσας
οἴσεσθαι, τῆς δὲ βασάνου εἰς τὸ παραχρῆμα βουλόμενος
32 ἀπηλλάχθαι. οἶμαι δ᾽ ὑμᾶς ἐπίστασθαι τοῦτο, ὅτι ἐφ᾽
οἷς ἂν τὸ πλεῖστον μέρος τῆς βασάνου, πρὸς τούτων
εἰσὶν οἱ βασανιζόμενοι λέγειν ὅσ᾽ ἂν ἐκείνοις μέλλωσι
χαριεῖσθαι· ἐν τούτοις γὰρ αὑτοῖς ἐστιν ἡ ὠφέλεια,
ἄλλως τε κἂν μὴ παρόντες τυγχάνωσιν ὧν ἂν
καταψεύδωνται. εἰ μὲν γὰρ ἐγὼ ἐκέλευον αὐτὸν
στρεβλοῦν ὡς οὐ τἀληθῆ λέγοντα, ἴσως ἂν ἐν αὐτῷ
τούτῳ ἀπετρέπετο μηδὲν κατ᾽ ἐμοῦ καταψεύδεσθαι,
νῦν δὲ αὑτοὶ ἦσαν καὶ βασανισταὶ καὶ ἐπιτιμηταὶ
33 τῶν σφίσιν αὐτοῖς συμφερόντων. ἕως μὲν οὖν μετὰ
χρηστῆς ἐλπίδος ἐγίγνωσκέ μου καταψευσάμενος,
τούτῳ διισχυρίζετο τῷ λόγῳ· ἐπειδὴ δὲ ἐγίγνωσκεν
ἀποθανούμενος, ἐνταῦθ᾽ ἤδη τῇ ἀληθείᾳ ἐχρῆτο, καὶ
ἔλεγεν ὅτι πεισθείη ὑπὸ τούτων ἐμοῦ καταψεύδεσθαι.

262 τοσούτῳ Reiske : τούτω τῶ AN   264 γὰρ A^{1}N : om. A^{a} 266 ὑπ᾽ A^{2}N : ἐπ᾽ A   270 πλεῖστον <ᾖ> Reiske   271 ὅσ᾽ ἂν Thalheim : ὅταν AN : ὅ, τι ἂν Ald.   272 τούτοις AN : τούτῳ maluit Sauppe αὑτοῖς scripsi : αὐτοῖς AN   273 τυγχάνωσιν A^{1}N : στύγχανουσιν A^{a} 274 καταψεύδωνται A^{1}N : κατάψωται A^{a} εἰ μὲν γὰρ ἐγὼ Gebauer^{3} : εἰ γὰρ ἐγὼ μὲν A^{a}N : εἰ γὰρ ἐγὼ A^{c} 275 οὐ τἀληθῆ A^{c}N^{c} : οὔτ᾽ ἀληθῆ A^{a}N^{a} 277 αὑτοὶ Blass^{2} : αὐτοὶ AN   278 σφίσιν A : σφίσι N   279 ἐλπίδος N : τῆς ἐλπίδος A καταψευσάμενος AN^{2} : κατεψευσάνενος N^{a} 281 ἐνταῦθ᾽ A^{2}N : ἐνταῦτ᾽ A   282 πεισθείη AN^{2} : πειθείη N καταψεύδεσθαι A : κατεψεύδεσθαι N

διαπειραθέντα δ' αὐτὸν τὰ ψευδῆ λέγειν, ὕστερον δὲ 34
τἀληθῆ λέγοντα, οὐδέτερα ὠφέλησεν, ἀλλ' ἀπέκτειναν
ἄγοντες τὸν ἄνδρα, τὸν μηνυτήν, ᾧ πιστεύοντες ἐμὲ
διώκουσι, τοὐναντίον ποιήσαντες ἢ οἱ ἄλλοι ἄνθρωποι.
οἱ μὲν γὰρ ἄλλοι τοῖς μηνυταῖς τοῖς μὲν ἐλευθέροις
χρήματα διδόασι, τοὺς δὲ δούλους ἐλευθεροῦσιν·
οὗτοι δὲ θάνατον τῷ μηνυτῇ τὴν δωρεὰν ἀπέδοσαν,
ἀπαγορευόντων τῶν φίλων τῶν ἐμῶν μὴ ἀποκτείνειν
τὸν ἄνδρα πρὶν {ἂν} ἐγὼ ἔλθοιμι. δῆλον οὖν ὅτι οὐ τοῦ 35
σώματος αὐτοῦ χρεία ἦν αὐτοῖς, ἀλλὰ τῶν λόγων· ζῶν
μὲν γὰρ ὁ ἀνὴρ διὰ τῆς αὐτῆς βασάνου ἰὼν ὑπ' ἐμοῦ
κατήγορος ἂν ἐγίγνετο τῆς τούτων ἐπιβουλῆς,
τεθνεὼς δὲ τὸν μὲν ἔλεγχον τῆς ἀληθείας ἀπεστέρει
δι' αὐτοῦ τοῦ σώματος ἀπολλυμένου, τοῖς δὲ λόγοις
τοῖς ἐψευσμένοις ὑπ' ἐκείνου ὡς ἀληθέσιν οὖσιν ἐγὼ
ἀπόλλυμαι. τούτων δὲ μάρτυράς μοι κάλει.

⟨ΜΑΡΤΥΡΕΣ⟩

Ἐχρῆν μὲν γὰρ αὐτούς, ὡς ἐγὼ νομίζω, ἐνθάδε 36
παρέχοντας τὸν μηνυτὴν αὐτὸν ἀπελέγχειν ἐμέ, καὶ
αὐτῷ τούτῳ χρῆσθαι ἀγωνίσματι, ἐμφανῆ παρέχοντας
τὸν ἄνδρα καὶ κελεύοντας βασανίζειν, ἀλλὰ μὴ
ἀποκτεῖναι. φέρε γὰρ δὴ ποτέρῳ νῦν χρήσονται τῶν
λόγων; πότερα ᾧ πρῶτον εἶπεν ἢ ᾧ ὕστερον; καὶ πότερ'
ἀληθῆ ἐστιν, ὅτ' ἔφη με εἰργάσθαι τὸ ἔργον ἢ ὅτ' οὐκ

283 alt. δὲ A^{1}N : μὲν A^{a} 284 ὠφέλησεν Reiske : ὠφέλησαν AN 286 ἄθρωποι A, corr. A^{2} 289 δωρεὰν AN : δωρειὰν Jernstedt 290 ἀπαγορευόντων N : ἀπογορευόντων A 291 del. Dobree : ἢ Weidner 292 αὐτοῦ A^{1}N : om. A^{a} 293 αὐτῆς] η in ras N^{1} 297–8 ἐγὼ ἀπόλλυμαι in ras. A^{1} 299 tit. add. Reiske 300 μὲν A : om. N 301 παρέχοντας AN : κατέχοντας N^{2} 304 τῶν A^{2}N : τῶ A 305 πότερα A^{c}N : πρότερα A^{a} ᾧ N : ὧ A^{1} : om. A^{a}

37 ἔφη; εἰ μὲν γὰρ ἐκ τοῦ εἰκότος ἐξετασθῆναι δεῖ τὸ πρᾶγμα, οἱ ὕστεροι λόγοι ἀληθέστεροι φαίνονται. ἐψεύδετο μὲν γὰρ ἐπ' ὠφελείᾳ τῇ ἑαυτοῦ, ἐπειδὴ δὲ ⟨διὰ⟩ τὸ ψεύδεσθαι ἀπώλλυτο, ἡγήσατο τἀληθῆ κατειπὼν διὰ τοῦτο σωθῆναι ἄν. τῆς μὲν οὖν ἀληθείας οὐκ ἦν αὐτῷ τιμωρὸς οὐδείς· οὐ γὰρ παρὼν ἐγὼ ἐτύγχανον, ᾧπερ σύμμαχος ἦν ἡ ἀλήθεια τῶν ὑστέρων λόγων· τοὺς δὲ προτέρους λόγους τοὺς κατεψευσμένους ἦσαν οἱ ἀφανιοῦντες ὥστε μηδέποτε εἰς τὸ ἀληθὲς καταστῆναι.

38 καὶ οἱ μὲν ἄλλοι, καθ' ὧν ἂν μηνύῃ τις, οὗτοι κλέπτουσι τοὺς μηνύοντας κᾆτ' ἀφανίζουσιν· αὐτοὶ δὲ οὗτοι οἱ ἀπάγοντες καὶ ζητοῦντες τὸ πρᾶγμα τὸν κατ' ἐμοῦ μηνυτὴν ἠφάνισαν. καὶ εἰ μὲν ἐγὼ τὸν ἄνδρα ἠφάνισα ἢ μὴ ἤθελον ἐκδοῦναι τούτοις ἢ ἄλλον τινὰ ἔφευγον ἔλεγχον, αὐτοῖς ἂν τούτοις ἰσχυροτάτοις εἰς τὰ πράγματα ἐχρῶντο, καὶ ἦν ταῦτα αὐτοῖς μέγιστα τεκμήρια κατ' ἐμοῦ· νῦν δέ, ὁπότε αὐτοὶ οὗτοι προκαλουμένων τῶν φίλων τῶν ἐμῶν ταῦτ' ἔφυγον, ἐμοὶ δήπου κατὰ τούτων εἶναι χρὴ ταὐτὰ ταῦτα τεκμήρια, ὡς οὐκ ἀληθῆ τὴν αἰτίαν ἐπέφερον ἣν ᾐτιῶντο.

39 Ἔτι δὲ καὶ τάδε λέγουσιν, ὡς ὡμολόγει ὁ ἄνθρωπος βασανιζόμενος συναποκτεῖναι τὸν ἄνδρα. ἐγὼ δέ φημι ταῦτα μὲν οὐ λέγειν αὐτόν, ὅτι δὲ ἐξάγοι ἐμὲ καὶ τὸν ἄνδρα ἐκ τοῦ πλοίου, καὶ ὅτι ἤδη τεθνεῶτα αὐτὸν ὑπ'

307 εἰκότος A^{c}N : εἰκότως A^{a} 309–10 <διὰ> τὸ mendo felici in sua adnotatiuncula Reiske, ci. Jernstedt : τὸ AN : τῷ A^{2} : <διὰ> τοῦ Steph. 311 τοῦτο AN : τούτου A^{2} 313 σύμαχος A^{a}, corr. A^{1} ἡ A^{1}N : om. A^{a} 316 ἂν μηνύῃ τις N : μηνύῃ ἂν τίς A (ἄν τις A^{2}) οὗτοι Reiske : αὐτοὶ AN 317 κᾆτ' N : κᾆτα A 321 αὐτοῖς ἂν Spengel^{1} : αὐτοὶ δὴ AN : alii ἂν post τούτοις vel πράγματα addiderunt 325 ταὐτὰ ταῦτα Fuhr^{1} : ταῦτα τὰ AN 326 ᾐτιῶντο Dobree: ᾤοντο A^{2}N : ὤοντο A 327 ὡμολόγει A : ὁμολογεῖ N 329 ἐξάγοι A^{c} : ἐξάγει A^{a}N : ἐξαγάγοι Baiter

ἐμοῦ συνανελὼν καὶ ἐνθεὶς εἰς τὸ πλοῖον καταποντώσειε.
καίτοι σκέψασθε ὅτι πρῶτον μέν, πρὶν ἐπὶ τὸν τροχὸν 40
ἀναβῆναι, ὁ ἀνὴρ μέχρι τῆς ἐσχάτης ἀνάγκης τῇ ἀληθείᾳ
ἐχρῆτο καὶ ἀπέλυέ με τῆς αἰτίας· ἐπειδὴ δὲ ἐπὶ τὸν
τροχὸν ἀνέβη, τῇ ἀνάγκῃ χρώμενος ἤδη κατεψεύδετό
μου, βουλόμενος ἀπηλλάχθαι τῆς βασάνου· ἐπειδὴ 41
δὲ ἐπαύσατο βασανιζόμενος, οὐκέτι ἔφη με τούτων
εἰργάσθαι οὐδέν, ἀλλὰ τὸ τελευταῖον ἀπῴμωξεν ἐμέ τε
καὶ αὑτὸν ὡς ἀδίκως ἀπολλυμένους, οὐ χάριτι τῇ ἐμῇ—
πῶς γάρ; ὅς γε κατεψεύσατο—ἀλλ᾽ ἀναγκαζόμενος ὑπὸ
τοῦ ἀληθοῦς καὶ βεβαιῶν τοὺς πρώτους λόγους ὡς
ἀληθεῖς εἰρημένους. ἔπειτα δὲ ὁ ἕτερος ἄνθρωπος, 42
ὁ ἐν τῷ αὐτῷ πλοίῳ πλέων καὶ παρὼν διὰ τέλους καὶ
συνών μοι, τῇ αὐτῇ βασάνῳ βασανιζόμενος τοῖς μὲν
πρώτοις καὶ τοῖς ὕστερον λόγοις τοῖς τοῦ ἀνθρώπου
συνεφέρετο ὡς ἀληθέσιν εἰρημένοις, διὰ τέλους γάρ με
ἀπέλυε, τοῖς δὲ ἐπὶ τοῦ τροχοῦ λεγομένοις, οὓς ἐκεῖνος
ἀνάγκῃ μᾶλλον ἢ ἀληθείᾳ ἔλεγε, τούτοις δὲ διεφέρετο. ὁ
μὲν γὰρ ἐκβάντα μ᾽ ἔφη ἐκ τοῦ πλοίου ἀποκτεῖναι τὸν
ἄνδρα, καὶ αὐτὸς ἤδη τεθνεῶτα συνανελεῖν μοι· ὁ δὲ
τὸ παράπαν ἔφη οὐκ ἐκβῆναί με ἐκ τοῦ πλοίου. καίτοι 43
τὸ εἰκὸς σύμμαχόν μοί ἐστιν. οὐ γὰρ δήπου οὕτω
κακοδαίμων ἐγώ, ὥστε τὸ μὲν ἀποκτεῖναι τὸν ἄνδρα
προὐνοησάμην μόνος, ἵνα μοι μηδεὶς συνειδείη, ἐν ᾧ μοι
ὁ πᾶς κίνδυνος ἦν, ἤδη δὲ πεπραγμένου μοι τοῦ ἔργου
μάρτυρας καὶ συμβούλους ἐποιούμην. καὶ ἀπέθανε μὲν 44

331 *συνανελὼν* Maetzner : *συνελὼν* N : om. A   *καὶ* A^{a}N : eras. A^{c} *καταποντώσειε* AN^{c} : *καταποντώσειεν* N^{a} 332 *πρῶτον μὲν* A^{1}N : om. A^{a} 339 *αὑτὸν* M : *αὐτὸν* AN   *ἀδίκως* A : *ἀδίκους* N   343 *ὁ* om. A   *διὰ τέλους* A^{2}N : *διατέλους* A^{a} 346 *εἰρημένοις* N : *οὖσι* A^{1} : *ὦσι* A^{a} *διὰ τέλους* A^{2}N : *διατέλους* A^{a} 347 *δὲ* N : *δ᾽* A   349 *μ᾽* N : *με* A   350 *συνανελεῖν* A : *συνελεῖν* N   351 *ἔφη οὐκ ἐκβῆναι με* L^{1} (*ἐμβῆναι* L^{a}) : *ἔφη, οὐ κ᾽ ἐκβῆναι με* A : *οὐδ᾽ ἐκβῆναι μ᾽ ἔφη* N   354 *μόνος* in ras. A^{1}

ὁ ἀνὴρ οὑτωσὶ ἐγγὺς τῆς θαλάσσης καὶ τῶν πλοίων, ὡς ὁ τούτων λόγος ἐστίν· ὑπὸ δὲ ἑνὸς ἀνδρὸς ἀποθνῄσκων οὔτε ἀνέκραγεν οὔτ' αἴσθησιν οὐδεμίαν ἐποίησεν οὔτε τοῖς ἐν τῇ γῇ οὔτε τοῖς ἐν τῷ πλοίῳ; καὶ μὴν πολλῷ ⟨ἐπὶ⟩ πλέον γε ἀκούειν ἔστι νύκτωρ ἢ μεθ' ἡμέραν, ἐπ' ἀκτῆς ἢ κατὰ πόλιν· καὶ μὴν ἔτι ἐγρηγορότων φασὶν ἐκβῆναι
45 τὸν ἄνδρα ἐκ τοῦ πλοίου. ἔπειτα ἐν τῇ γῇ μὲν ἀποθανόντος, ἐντιθεμένου δὲ εἰς τὸ πλοῖον, οὔτε ἐν τῇ γῇ σημεῖον οὐδὲ αἷμα ἐφάνη οὔτε ἐν τῷ πλοίῳ, νύκτωρ μὲν ἀναιρεθέντος, νύκτωρ δ' ἐντιθεμένου εἰς τὸ πλοῖον. ἢ δοκεῖ ἂν ὑμῖν ἄνθρωπος δύνασθαι ἐν τοιούτῳ πράγματι ὢν τά τε ἐν τῇ γῇ ὄντα ἀναξύσαι καὶ τὰ ἐν τῷ πλοίῳ ἀνασπογγίσαι, ἃ οὐδὲ μεθ' ἡμέραν τις οἷός τε ἐγένετο, ἔνδον ὢν αὑτοῦ καὶ μὴ πεφοβημένος, τὸ παράπαν ἀφανίσαι; ταῦτα, ὦ ἄνδρες, πῶς εἰκότα ἐστίν;
46 ὃ δὲ ⟨δεῖ⟩ καὶ μάλιστα ἐνθυμεῖσθαι—καὶ μή μοι ἄχθεσθε, ἂν ὑμᾶς πολλάκις ταὐτὰ διδάξω· μέγας γὰρ ὁ κίνδυνός ἐστι, καθ' ὅ τι δ' ἂν ὑμεῖς ὀρθῶς γνῶτε, κατὰ τοῦτο σῴζομαι, καθ' ὅ τι δ' ἂν ψευσθῆτε τἀληθοῦς, κατὰ τοῦτο ἀπόλλυμαι—μὴ οὖν ἐξέληται τοῦτο ὑμῶν μηδείς, ὅτι τὸν μηνυτὴν ἀπέκτειναν, καὶ διετείναντο αὐτὸν μὴ εἰσελθεῖν εἰς ὑμᾶς, μηδ' ἐμοὶ ἐγγενέσθαι παρόντι ἄξαι τὸν ἄνδρα καὶ βασανίσαι αὐτόν· καίτοι

46 διετείναντο Harp. δ 60 s.v., ac stp Phot. δ 558; Suda δ 972 necnon [Zonar.] δ 546.19 imperfectum tradunt

---

357 ὁ N : om. A οὑτωσὶ Blass : οὑτοσὶ AN 359 ἀνέγκραγεν A^{a} 360 πλοίῳ; N : πλοίω· A 360–1 <ἐπὶ> πλέον γε ἀκούειν $Schömann^{2}$: πλέον γε ἀγνοεῖν AN : <ἐπὶ> πλέον γεγωνεῖν $Cobet^{1}$ 368 τε N : τ' A 369 ἀνασπογγίσαι N : ἀποσπογγίσαι A <ἄν> τις maluit Baiter 370 αὑτοῦ A : αὐτοῦ N πεφοβημένος $A^{1}N$: πεφομένος A^{a} 372 add. Thalheim ἐνθυμεῖσθαι A^{it} : ἐνθυμεῖσθε A^{sv} (sed ϵ supra αι eras.), N : δεῖ ἐνθυμεῖσθαι A^{2} 373 ταὐτὰ Reiske : ταῦτα AN 374 ἔστι A : ἐστιν N 376 ἐξέληται A^{2} : ἐξελεῖται AN 377 διετείναντο AN et procul dubio Harp. ipse: διετείνοντο Harp. codd. Suda [Zonar.] : διετείνετο perperam Phot. cod. 379 ἄξαι re vera AN : ἐξαιτεῖν Baiter : ἐλέγξαι Dobree

πρὸς τούτων ἦν τοῦτο. νῦν δὲ πριάμενοι τὸν ἄνδρα, ἰδίᾳ 47 ἐπὶ σφῶν αὐτῶν ἀπέκτειναν, τὸν μηνυτήν, οὔτε τῆς πόλεως ψηφισαμένης, οὔτε αὐτόχειρα ὄντα τοῦ ἀνδρός. ὃν ἐχρῆν δεδεμένον αὐτοὺς φυλάσσειν, ἢ τοῖς φίλοις τοῖς ἐμοῖς ἐξεγγυῆσαι, ἢ τοῖς ἄρχουσι τοῖς ὑμετέροις παραδοῦναι, καὶ ψῆφον περὶ αὐτοῦ γενέσθαι. νῦν δὲ αὐτοὶ καταγνόντες τὸν θάνατον τοῦ ἀνδρὸς ἀπεκτείνατε· ὃ οὐδὲ πόλει ἔξεστιν, ἄνευ Ἀθηναίων οὐδένα θανάτῳ ζημιῶσαι. καὶ τῶν μὲν ἄλλων λόγων τῶν ἐκείνου τουτουσὶ κριτὰς ἠξιώσατε γενέσθαι, τῶν δὲ ἔργων αὐτοὶ δικασταὶ γίγνεσθε. καίτοι οὐδὲ οἱ τοὺς δεσπότας 48 ἀποκτείναντες, ἐὰν ἐπ' αὐτοφώρῳ ληφθῶσιν, οὐδ' οὗτοι ἀποθνῄσκουσιν ὑπ' αὐτῶν τῶν προσηκόντων, ἀλλὰ παραδιδόασιν αὐτοὺς τῇ ἀρχῇ κατὰ νόμους ὑμετέρους πατρίους. εἴπερ γὰρ καὶ μαρτυρεῖν ἔξεστι δούλῳ κατὰ τοῦ ἐλευθέρου τὸν φόνον, καὶ τῷ δεσπότῃ, ἂν δοκῇ, ἐπεξελθεῖν ὑπὲρ τοῦ δούλου, καὶ ἡ ψῆφος ἴσον δύναται τῷ δοῦλον ἀποκτείναντι καὶ τῷ ἐλεύθερον, εἰκός τοι καὶ ψῆφον γενέσθαι περὶ αὐτοῦ ἦν, καὶ μὴ ἄκριτον ἀποθανεῖν αὐτὸν ὑφ' ὑμῶν. ὥστε πολλῷ ἂν ὑμεῖς δικαιότερον κρίνοισθε ἢ εγὼ νῦν φεύγω ὑφ' ὑμῶν ἀδίκως.

Σκοπεῖτε δή, ὦ ἄνδρες, καὶ ἐκ τοῖν λόγοιν τοῖν ἀνδροῖν 49 ἑκατέροιν τοῖν βασανισθέντοιν τὸ δίκαιον καὶ τὸ εἰκός. ὁ μὲν γὰρ δοῦλος δύο λόγω ἔλεγε· τοτὲ μὲν ἔφη με εἰργάσθαι τὸ ἔργον, τοτὲ δὲ οὐκ ἔφη· ὁ δὲ ἐλεύθερος οὐδέπω νῦν εἴρηκε περὶ ἐμοῦ φλαῦρον οὐδέν, τῇ αὐτῇ βασάνῳ βασανιζόμενος. τοῦτο μὲν γὰρ οὐκ ἦν αὐτῷ 50

390 γίγνεσθε] ἐγένεσθε Schoell[1] 392 ἀποθνῄσκουσιν N : θνῄσκουσιν A 397 alt. τῷ Reiske : τὸν AN 399–400 ὑμεῖς δικαιότερον A : δικαιότερον ὑμεῖς N κρίνοισθε Ald. : κρίνεσθε AN 404 δύο N : δύω A 404–5 τοτὲ … τοτὲ A[2]N : τότε … τότε A

ἐλευθερίαν προτείνοντας ὥσπερ τὸν ἕτερον πεῖσαι·
τοῦτο δὲ μετὰ τοῦ ἀληθοῦς ἐβούλετο κινδυνεύων
πάσχειν ὅ τι δέοι· ἐπεὶ τό γε συμφέρον καὶ οὗτος
ἠπίστατο, ὅτι τότε παύσοιτο στρεβλούμενος, ὁπότε
εἴποι τὰ τούτοις δοκοῦντα. ποτέρῳ οὖν εἰκός ἐστι
πιστεῦσαι, τῷ διὰ τέλους τὸν αὐτὸν ἀεὶ λόγον λέγοντι,
ἢ τῷ τοτὲ μὲν φάσκοντι τοτὲ δ' οὔ; ἀλλὰ καὶ ἄνευ
βασάνου τοιαύτης οἱ τοὺς αὐτοὺς αἰεὶ περὶ τῶν αὐτῶν
λόγους λέγοντες πιστότεροί εἰσι τῶν διαφερομένων
51 σφίσιν αὐτοῖς. ἔπειτα δὲ καὶ ἐκ τῶν λόγων τῶν
τοῦ ἀνθρώπου μερὶς ἑκατέρῳ ἴση ἐστί, τούτοις μὲν τὸ
φάσκειν, ἐμοὶ δὲ τὸ μὴ φάσκειν, ἔκ τε ἀμφοῖν τοῖν
ἀνδροῖν τοῖν βασανισθέντοιν· ὁ μὲν γὰρ ἔφησεν, ὁ δὲ διὰ
τέλους ἔξαρνος ἦν. καὶ μὲν δὴ τὰ ἐξ ἴσου γενόμενα τοῦ
φεύγοντός ἐστι μᾶλλον ἢ τοῦ διώκοντος, εἴπερ γε καὶ
τῶν ψήφων ὁ ἀριθμὸς ἐξ ἴσου γενόμενος τὸν φεύγοντα
μᾶλλον ὠφελεῖ ἢ τὸν διώκοντα.

52 Ἡ μὲν βάσανος, ὦ ἄνδρες, τοιαύτη ἐγένετο, ᾗ οὗτοι
πιστεύοντες εὖ εἰδέναι φασὶν ὑπ' ἐμοῦ ἀποθανόντα
τὸν ἄνδρα. καίτοι τὸ παράπαν ἔγωγ' ἂν εἴ τι συνῄδειν
ἐμαυτῷ καὶ εἴ τι ἐμοὶ τοιοῦτον εἴργαστο, ἠφάνισ' ἂν τὼ
ἀνθρώπω, ὅτε ἐπ' ἐμοὶ ἦν τοῦτο μὲν εἰς τὴν Αἶνον
ἀπάγειν ἅμα ἐμοί, τοῦτο δὲ εἰς τὴν ἤπειρον διαβιβάσαι,
καὶ μὴ ὑπολείπεσθαι μηνυτὰς κατ' ἐμαυτοῦ τοὺς

408 *προτείνοντας* AN : *προτείναντας* Reiske 410 *πάσχειν* A^{1}N : *παρασχεῖν* A^{a} 411 *παύσοιτο* Madvig[1] : *παύσαιτο* AN 413 *ἀεὶ* A^{1}N : om. A^{a}, del. censuit Sauppe[1] 415 *αὐτῶν* A^{1}N : *ἄλλων* A^{a} 418 *ἑκατέρῳ* N : *ἑκατέρω* A : *ἑκατέροις* Weidner : *ἑκατέρων* Redondo i Sànchez[1] *ἴση ἐστὶ·* A^{2} : *ἴσον εἰ*** A : *ἶσον, εἰ* N : *ἴση ἂν εἴη* Thalheim *τούτοις μὲν τὸ* A^{2} : *τοῦτον μέντοι* AN 419–21 *ἐκ … ἦν* secl. Hirschig[2] 423 *γενόμενος* A : *γιγνόμενος* N 425 *ἐγένετο* A : *γεγένηται* N 427 *συνῄδειν* A^{2} : *συνήδειν* AN : *συνῄδη* Jernstedt 428 *εἴ τι ἐμοὶ* re vera A^{2} : *εἴ τ' ἐμοὶ* AN 430 *ἀπάγειν* A^{2} : *ἀπάγων* AN *ἅμα* A^{1}N : om. A^{a}

συνειδότας. φασὶ δὲ γραμματείδιον εὑρεῖν ἐν τῷ πλοίῳ, 53
ὃ ἔπεμπον ἐγὼ Λυκίνῳ, ὡς ἀποκτείναιμι τὸν ἄνδρα.
καίτοι τί ἔδει με γραμματείδιον πέμπειν, αὐτοῦ
συνειδότος τοῦ τὸ γραμματείδιον φέροντος; ὥστε τοῦτο
μὲν σαφέστερον αὐτὸς ἔμελλεν ἐρεῖν ὁ εἰργασμένος,
τοῦτο δὲ οὐδὲν ἔδει κρύπτειν αὐτόν· ἃ γὰρ μὴ οἷόν τε
εἰδέναι τὸν φέροντα, ταῦτ᾽ ἄν τις μάλιστα συγγράψας
πέμψειεν. ἔπειτα δὲ ὅ τι μὲν μακρὸν εἴη πρᾶγμα, τοῦτο 54
μὲν ἄν τις ἀναγκασθείη γράψαι τῷ μὴ διαμνημονεύειν
τὸν ἀπαγγέλλοντα ὑπὸ πλήθους· τοῦτο δὲ βραχὺ ἦν
ἀπαγγεῖλαι, ὅτι τέθνηκεν ὁ ἀνήρ. ἔπειτα ἐνθυμεῖσθε
ὅτι διάφορον ἦν τὸ γραμματείδιον τῷ βασανισθέντι,
διάφορος δ᾽ ὁ ἄνθρωπος τῷ γραμματειδίῳ· ὁ μὲν
γὰρ βασανιζόμενος αὐτὸς ἔφη ἀποκτεῖναι, τὸ δὲ
γραμματείδιον ἀνοιχθὲν ἐμὲ τὸν ἀποκτείναντα ἐμήνυε.
καίτοι ποτέρῳ χρὴ πιστεῦσαι; τὸ μὲν γὰρ πρῶτον οὐχ 55
ηὗρον ἐν τῷ πλοίῳ ζητοῦντες τὸ γραμματείδιον, ὕστερον
δέ. τότε μὲν γὰρ οὔπω οὕτως ἐμεμηχάνητο αὐτοῖς·
ἐπειδὴ δὲ ὁ ἄνθρωπος ὁ πρότερος βασανισθεὶς οὐδὲν
ἔλεγε κατ᾽ ἐμοῦ, τότε εἰσβάλλουσιν εἰς τὸ πλοῖον
τὸ γραμματείδιον, ἵνα ταύτην ἔχοιεν ἐμοὶ τὴν αἰτίαν
ἐπιφέρειν· ἐπειδὴ δὲ ἀνεγνώσθη τὸ γραμματείδιον 56
καὶ ὁ ὕστερος βασανιζόμενος οὐ συνεφέρετο τῷ

432 *γραμματείδιον* Bekker : *γραμματίδιον* A[1]N : *γραματίδιον* A[a] 434 *γραμματείδιον*] *γραμματίδιον* AN ubique 435 post *φέροντος* AN habent *τίνος γε δὲ ἕνεκα … ἐμοὶ κἀκείνῳ;* quae ad §57 init. transposuit Ald. 436 *αὐτὸς* maluit Reiske : *αὐτοῖς* AN *ἐρεῖν* A : *εὑρεῖν* N 437 *αὐτόν* Ald. : *αὐτά* AN 439 *πέμψειεν* A[1]N : *πέμπειεν* A[a] *τοῦτο* A[2] : *τούτου* AN 440 *μὲν* N : om. A *τῷ* A[2] : *τοῦ* AN 443 *διάφορον* Reiske : *διαφέρον* AN 444 *διάφορος … γραμματειδίῳ* secl. Gernet *γραμματειδίῳ* Blass (-*τιδίῳ* Reiske) : *γραμματείω* N : *γραμματίω* A 447 *ποτέρω* A[1]N : *προτέρω* A[a] 448 *ηὗρον* Jernstedt : *εὗρον* AN *ζητοῦντες* A[1]N : *ζημιοῦντες* A[a] 449 *οὕτως* A : *οὕτω* N 450 *πρότερος* N : *πρότερον* A 452 *ταύτην*] *ταύτῃ γ᾽* Jernstedt[1] 454 *συνεφέρετο* A[1]N : *συνέφερε* A[a]

γραμματειδίῳ, οὐκέτι οἷόν τ᾽ ἦν ἀφανίσαι τὰ ἀναγνωσθέντα. εἰ γὰρ ἡγήσαντο τὸν ἄνδρα πείσειν ἀπὸ πρώτης καταψεύδεσθαί μου, οὐκ ἄν ποτ᾽ ἐμηχανήσαντο τὰ ἐν τῷ γραμματειδίῳ. καί μοι μάρτυρας τούτων κάλει.

ΜΑΡΤΥΡΕΣ

57 Τίνος γε δὴ ἕνεκα τὸν ἄνδρα ἀπέκτεινα; οὐδὲ γὰρ ἔχθρα
οὐδεμία ἦν ἐμοὶ κἀκείνῳ. λέγειν δὲ τολμῶσιν ὡς ἐγὼ
χάριτι τὸν ἄνδρα ἔκτεινα. καὶ τίς πώποτε χαριζόμενος
ἑτέρῳ τοῦτο εἰργάσατο; οἶμαι μὲν γὰρ οὐδένα, ἀλλὰ δεῖ
μεγάλην τὴν ἔχθραν ὑπάρχειν τῷ τοῦτο μέλλοντι
ποιήσειν, καὶ τὴν πρόνοιαν ἐκ πολλῶν φανερὰν εἶναι
ἐπιβουλευομένην. ἐμοὶ δὲ κἀκείνῳ οὐκ ἦν ἔχθρα
58 οὐδεμία. εἶεν, ἀλλὰ δείσας περὶ ἐμαυτοῦ μὴ αὐτὸς παρ᾽
ἐκείνου τοῦτο πάθοιμι; καὶ γὰρ ἂν τῶν τοιούτων ἕνεκά
τις ἀναγκασθείη τοῦτο ἐργάσασθαι. ἀλλὰ οὐδέν μοι
τοιοῦτον ὑπῆρκτο εἰς αὐτόν. ἀλλὰ χρήματα ἔμελλον
59 λήψεσθαι ἀποκτείνας αὐτόν; ἀλλ᾽ οὐκ ἦν αὐτῷ. ἀλλὰ σοὶ
μᾶλλον ἐγὼ τὴν πρόφασιν ταύτην ἔχοιμ᾽ ἂν εἰκότως
μετὰ τῆς ἀληθείας ἀναθεῖναι, ὅτι χρημάτων ἕνεκα
ζητεῖς ἐμὲ ἀποκτεῖναι, μᾶλλον ἢ σὺ ἐμοὶ ἐκεῖνον· καὶ
πολὺ ἂν δικαιότερον ἁλοίης ⟨σὺ⟩ τοῦ φόνου ἐμὲ
ἀποκτείνας ὑπὸ τῶν ἐμοὶ προσηκόντων, ἢ ἐγὼ ὑπὸ σοῦ
καὶ τῶν ἐκείνου ἀναγκαίων. ἐγὼ μὲν γάρ σου φανερὰν

455 *οὐκέτι* N : *οὐκέτ᾽* A   455–6 *ἀναγνωσθέντα*] *γν* in ras. A^1 457 *καταψεύδεσθαι* AN^1 : *κατεσψεύδεσθαι* ut vid. N^a 460–1 *τίνος γε δὲ ἕνεκα … ἐμοὶ κἀκείνῳ* transposuit ex §53 l. 435 Ald.   460 *οὐδὲ* Ald. : *οὔτε* AN   461 *κἀκείνω* N : *καὶ ἐκείνω* A   462 *ἔκτεινα* AN : *ἀπέκτεινα* Weidner   465 *πολλῶν*] *πολλοῦ* Pahle   *φανερὰν εἶναι* N : *εἶναι φανερὰν* A   469 *ἀλλὰ* N : *ἀλλ᾽* A   470–1 *ἀλλὰ … αὐτῷ* huc transposuit Dobree : ante *εἶεν* §58 l. 467 habent AN   474 *σὺ ἐμοὶ* A^c : *σὺν ἐμοὶ* A^aN 475 add. Ald. : *τοῦ* del. Maetzner   477 *γάρ σου* Jernstedt : *γάρ σοι* AN : *γὰρ σοῦ* $Blass^2$

τὴν πρόνοιαν εἰς ἐμὲ ἀποδείκνυμι, σὺ δέ με ἐν ἀφανεῖ λόγῳ ζητεῖς ἀπολέσαι.

Ταῦτα μὲν ὑμῖν λέγω, ὡς αὐτῷ μοι πρόφασιν οὐδεμίαν 60
ἔχει ἀποκτεῖναι τὸν ἄνδρα· δεῖ δέ με καὶ ὑπὲρ Λυκίνου
ἀπολογήσασθαι, ὡς ἔοικεν, ἀλλ' οὐχ ὑπὲρ αὑτοῦ μόνον,
ὡς οὐδ' ἐκεῖνον εἰκότως αἰτιῶνται. λέγω τοίνυν ὑμῖν ὅτι
ταὐτὰ ὑπῆρχεν αὐτῷ εἰς ἐκεῖνον ἅπερ ἐμοί· οὔτε γὰρ
χρήματα ἦν αὐτῷ ὁπόθεν ἂν ἔλαβεν ἀποκτείνας ἐκεῖνον,
οὔτε κίνδυνος αὐτῷ ὑπῆρχεν οὐδεὶς ὅντινα διέφευγεν
ἀποθανόντος ἐκείνου. τεκμήριον δὲ μέγιστον ὡς οὐκ 61
ἐβούλετο αὐτὸν ἀπολέσαι· ἐξὸν γὰρ αὐτῷ ἐν ἀγῶνι καὶ
κινδύνῳ μεγάλῳ καταστήσαντι μετὰ τῶν νόμων τῶν
ὑμετέρων ἀπολέσαι ἐκεῖνον, εἴπερ προωφείλετο αὐτῷ
κακόν, καὶ τό τε ἴδιον τὸ αὑτοῦ διαπράξασθαι καὶ τῇ
πόλει τῇ ὑμετέρᾳ χάριν καταθέσθαι, εἰ ἐπέδειξεν
ἀδικοῦντα ἐκεῖνον, οὐκ ἠξίωσεν, ἀλλ' οὐδ' ἦλθεν ἐπὶ
τοῦτον. καίτοι καλλίων γε ἦν ὁ κίνδυνος αὐτῷ <. . .>

ΜΑΡΤΥΡΕΣ

Ἀλλὰ γὰρ ἐνταῦθα μὲν ἀφῆκεν αὐτόν· οὗ δὲ ἔδει 62
κινδυνεύειν αὐτὸν περί τε αὑτοῦ καὶ περὶ ἐμοῦ, ἐνταῦθα
δ' ἐπεβούλευεν, ἐν ᾧ γνωσθεὶς ἂν ἀπεστέρει μὲν ἐμὲ τῆς
πατρίδος, ἀπεστέρει δ' ἑαυτὸν ἱερῶν καὶ ὁσίων καὶ τῶν
ἄλλων ἅπερ μέγιστα καὶ περὶ πλείστου ἐστὶν ἀνθρώποις.

478 δέ με AN : δ' ἐμὲ Blass[2] 481 ἔχει ἀποκτεῖναι AN : ἔχει <τὸ> ἀποκτεῖναι Gernet : εἶχε ἀποκτεῖναι Edwards : εἶχε τὸ ἀποκτεῖναι Kayser[2] δέ A : om. N 482 αὑτοῦ A[1]N : αὐτοῦ A[a] 483 οὐδ' A : οὐδὲ N 485 αὐτῷ susp. Nauck, del. Gernet 494 τοῦτον AN : τοῦτο A[2] καλλίων A : καλλίω N post αὐτῷ lacunam indicavit Blass : tit. l. 495 del. dubitanter Gagarin 496 οὗ δὲ Blass[2] : οὐδὲ N : οὐ γὰρ A 497 alt. περὶ N : om. A 498–500 ἐν ᾧ ... ἀνθρώποις secl. Gernet 498 γνωσθεὶς] καταγνωσθεὶς Frohberger[2] 499 δ' ἑαυτὸν re vera AN

Ἔπειτα δ' εἰ καὶ ὡς μάλιστα ἐβούλετο αὐτὸν ὁ Λυκῖνος τεθνάναι—εἶμι γὰρ καὶ ἐπὶ τὸν τῶν κατηγόρων λόγον—οὗ αὐτὸς οὐκ ἠξίου αὐτόχειρ γενέσθαι, τοῦτο τὸ ἔργον

63 ἐγώ ποτ' ἂν ἐπείσθην ἀντ' ἐκείνου ποιῆσαι; πότερα ὡς ἐγὼ μὲν ἦν τῷ σώματι ἐπιτήδειος διακινδυνεύειν, ἐκεῖνος δὲ χρήμασι τὸν ἐμὸν κίνδυνον ἐκπρίασθαι; οὐ δῆτα· τῷ μὲν γὰρ οὐκ ἦν χρήματα, ἐμοὶ δὲ ἦν· ἀλλ' αὐτὸ τοὐναντίον ἐκεῖνος τοῦτο θᾶσσον ἂν ὑπ' ἐμοῦ ἐπείσθη κατά γε τὸ εἰκὸς ἢ ἐγὼ ὑπὸ τούτου, ἐπεὶ ἐκεῖνός γ' ἑαυτὸν οὐδ' ὑπερήμερον γενόμενον ἑπτὰ μνῶν δυνατὸς ἦν λύσασθαι, ἀλλ' οἱ φίλοι αὐτὸν ἐλύσαντο. καὶ μὲν δὴ καὶ τῆς χρείας τῆς ἐμῆς καὶ τῆς Λυκίνου τοῦτο ὑμῖν μέγιστον τεκμήριόν ἐστιν, ὅτι οὐ σφόδρα ἐχρώμην ἐγὼ Λυκίνῳ φίλῳ, ὡς πάντα ποιῆσαι ἂν τὰ ἐκείνῳ δοκοῦντα· οὐ γὰρ δήπου ἑπτὰ μὲν μνᾶς οὐκ ἀπέτεισα ὑπὲρ αὐτοῦ δεδεμένου καὶ λυμαινομένου, κίνδυνον δὲ τοσοῦτον ἀράμενος ἄνδρα ἀπέκτεινα δι' ἐκεῖνον.

64 Ὡς μὲν οὖν οὐκ αὐτὸς αἴτιός εἰμι τοῦ πράγματος οὐδὲ ἐκεῖνος, ἀποδέδεικται καθ' ὅσον ἐγὼ δύναμαι μάλιστα. τούτῳ δὲ χρῶνται πλείστῳ λόγῳ οἱ κατήγοροι, ὅτι ἀφανής ἐστιν ὁ ἀνήρ, καὶ ὑμεῖς ἴσως περὶ τούτου αὐτοῦ ποθεῖτε ἀκοῦσαι. εἰ μὲν οὖν τοῦτο εἰκάζειν με δεῖ, ἐξ ἴσου τοῦτό ἐστι καὶ ὑμῖν καὶ ἐμοί· οὔτε γὰρ ὑμεῖς αἴτιοι τοῦ ἔργου ἐστὲ οὔτε ἐγώ· εἰ δὲ δεῖ τοῖς ἀληθέσι χρῆσθαι,

502 τεθνᾶναι N, corr. N^2 505 ἦν] ἦ Jernstedt 506 ἐκπρίασθαι A^{2}N^2 : ἐκπριᾶσθαι AN 507 τῷ μὲν ... ἦν post τούτου l. 509 transp. Reiske, del. Dobree 508 τοὐναντίον Sauppe^1 : τοῦτο ἐναντίον AN : τὸ ἐναντίον A^2 : τούτου τὸ ἐναντίον Edwards 510 ὑπερήμερον A^1 (sed accentus mutavit A^2) N : ὑπὲρ ἡμέτερον A^a 512 tert. τῆς del. Cobet^3, coll. Lysia 8.16 515 ἀπέτεισα Blass^2 : ἀπέτισα A : ἐπέτισα N ὑπὲρ Meier : περὶ AN 518 εἰμι A^{1}N : μοι A^a 519 δύναμαι A^{1}N : δύνωμαι A^a 520 <τῷ> λόγῳ Frohberger^2 521 αὐτοῦ] αὐτοὶ Reiske 522 με δεῖ N : δεῖ με A

τῶν εἰργασμένων τινὰ ἐρωτώντων· ἐκείνου γὰρ ἄριστ᾽
ἂν πύθοιντο. ἐμοὶ μὲν γὰρ τῷ μὴ εἰργασμένῳ τοσοῦτον 65
τὸ μακρότατον τῆς ἀποκρίσεώς ἐστιν, ὅτι οὐκ εἴργασμαι·
τῷ δὲ ποιήσαντι ῥᾳδία ἐστὶν ἡ ἀπόδειξις, καὶ μὴ
ἀποδείξαντι εὖ εἰκάσαι. οἱ μὲν γὰρ πανουργοῦντες ἅμα τε
πανουργοῦσι καὶ πρόφασιν εὑρίσκουσι τοῦ ἀδικήματος·
τῷ δὲ μὴ εἰργασμένῳ χαλεπὸν περὶ τῶν ἀφανῶν
εἰκάζειν. οἶμαι δ᾽ ἂν καὶ ὑμῶν ἕκαστον, εἴ τίς τινα ἔροιτο
ὅ τι μὴ τύχοι εἰδώς, τοσοῦτον ἂν εἰπεῖν, ὅτι οὐκ οἶδεν·
εἰ δέ τις περαιτέρω τι κελεύοι λέγειν, ἐν πολλῇ ἂν
ἔχεσθαι ὑμᾶς ἀπορίᾳ δοκῶ. μὴ τοίνυν ἐμοὶ νείμητε τὸ 66
ἄπορον τοῦτο, ἐν ᾧ μηδ᾽ ἂν αὐτοὶ εὐποροῖτε· μηδὲ ἐὰν
εὖ εἰκάζω, ἐν τούτῳ μοι ἀξιοῦτε τὴν ἀπόφευξιν εἶναι,
ἀλλ᾽ ἐξαρκείτω μοι ἐμαυτὸν ἀναίτιον ἀποδεῖξαι τοῦ
πράγματος. ἐν τούτῳ οὖν ἀναίτιός εἰμι, οὐκ ἐὰν {μὴ}
ἐξεύρω ὅτῳ τρόπῳ ἀφανής ἐστιν ἢ ἀπόλωλεν ἁνήρ, ἀλλ᾽
εἰ μὴ προσήκει μοι μηδὲν ὥστ᾽ ἀποκτεῖναι αὐτόν. ἤδη 67
δ᾽ ἔγωγε καὶ πρότερον ἀκοῇ ἐπίσταμαι γεγονός, τοῦτο
μὲν τοὺς ἀποθανόντας, τοῦτο δὲ τοὺς ἀποκτείναντας
οὐχ εὑρεθέντας· οὔκουν ἂν καλῶς ἔχοι, εἰ τούτων δέοι
τὰς αἰτίας ὑποσχεῖν τοὺς συγγενομένους. πολλοὶ δέ γ᾽
ἤδη σχόντες ἑτέρων πραγμάτων αἰτίας, πρὶν τὸ σαφὲς
αὐτῶν γνωσθῆναι, προαπώλοντο. αὐτίκα Ἐφιάλτην τὸν 68
ὑμέτερον πολίτην οὐδέπω νῦν ηὕρηνται οἱ ἀποκτείναντες·

525–6 ἄριστ᾽ ἂν Hirschig[2] : ἄριστα AN : ἂν ἄριστα Dobree 527 μακρότατον N : μακρότερον A 531 εἰργασμένω A : ἐργασαμένῳ N 533 εἰπεῖν A[2] : εἶπεν AN 534 τι N : om. A κελεύοι Reiske : κελεύει AN 535 ἔχεσθαι ὑμᾶς N : ὑμᾶς ἔχεσθαι A 536 εὐποροῖτε A : εὐπορῆτε N[1] : εὐπορ*ιτε N[a] 537 μοι A[1]N : με A[a] ἀξιοῦτε A[2]N : ἀξιοῦται A[a] 539 del. Reiske 540 ἐξεύρω A[1]N : om. A[a] ἁνήρ Sauppe : ἀνὴρ AN 541 προσήκει A : προσήσκει N : προσῆκε Stahl 544 οὔκουν A[2] : οὐκοῦν AN ἔχοι A[sv]N : ἔχη A[it] 545 δέ AN[2] : δὲ N 547 προαπώλοντο A[c]N : προσαπώλοντο A[a] 548 ὑμέτερον] υ in ras. N[1] <καὶ> νῦν Weil ηὕρηνται Jernstedt : εὕρηνται AN

εἰ οὖν τις ἠξίου τοὺς συνόντας ἐκείνῳ εἰκάζειν οἵτινες ἦσαν οἱ ἀποκτείναντες Ἐφιάλτην, εἰ δὲ μή, ἐνόχους εἶναι τῷ φόνῳ, οὐκ ἂν καλῶς εἶχε τοῖς συνοῦσιν. ἔπειτα οἵ γε Ἐφιάλτην ἀποκτείναντες οὐκ ἐζήτησαν τὸν νεκρὸν ἀφανίσαι, οὐδ' ἐν τούτῳ κινδυνεύειν μηνῦσαι τὸ πρᾶγμα, ὥσπερ οἵδε φασὶν ἐμὲ τῆς μὲν ἐπιβουλῆς οὐδένα κοινωνὸν ποιήσασθαι τοῦ θανάτου, τῆς δ' ἀναιρέσεως.
69 τοῦτο δ' ἐντὸς οὐ πολλοῦ χρόνου παῖς ἐζήτησεν οὐδὲ δώδεκα ἔτη γεγονὼς τὸν δεσπότην ἀποκτεῖναι· καὶ εἰ μὴ φοβηθείς, ὡς ἀνεβόησεν, ἐγκαταλιπὼν τὴν μάχαιραν ἐν τῇ σφαγῇ ᾤχετο φεύγων, ἀλλ' ἐτόλμησε μεῖναι, ἀπώλοντ' ἂν οἱ ἔνδον ὄντες ἅπαντες· οὐδεὶς γὰρ ἂν ᾤετο τὸν παῖδα τολμῆσαί ποτε τοῦτο· νῦν δὲ συλληφθεὶς αὐτὸς ὕστερον κατεῖπεν αὑτοῦ. τοῦτο δὲ περὶ χρημάτων αἰτίαν ποτὲ σχόντες οὐκ οὖσαν, ὥσπερ ἐγὼ νῦν, οἱ Ἑλληνοταμίαι οἱ ὑμέτεροι, ἐκεῖνοι μὲν ἅπαντες ἀπέθανον ὀργῇ μᾶλλον ἢ γνώμῃ, πλὴν ἑνός, τὸ δὲ πρᾶγμα ὕστερον
70 καταφανὲς ἐγένετο. τοῦ δ' ἑνὸς τούτου—Σωσίαν ὄνομά φασιν αὐτῷ εἶναι—κατέγνωστο μὲν ἤδη θάνατος, ἐτεθνήκει δὲ οὔπω· καὶ ἐν τούτῳ ἐδηλώθη, τῷ τρόπῳ ἀπωλώλει τὰ χρήματα, καὶ ὁ ἀνὴρ ἀπελύθη ὑπὸ τοῦ δήμου τοῦ ὑμετέρου παραδεδομένος ἤδη τοῖς ἕνδεκα,
71 οἱ δ' ἄλλοι ἐτέθνασαν οὐδὲν αἴτιοι ὄντες. ταῦθ' ὑμῶν αὐτῶν ἐγὼ οἶμαι μεμνῆσθαι τοὺς πρεσβυτέρους, τοὺς

70 ἀπελύθη stp Pollux 8.68

549 ἠξίου A[2]N : ἥξει οὐ A 550 Ἐφιάλτην del. Dobree 559 ἐν N : om. A 560 ὄντες N : om. A 561 τολμῆσαι ποτε τοῦτο N : ποτε τοῦτο τολμῆσαι A 562 αὑτοῦ A[2] : αὐτοῦ AN 564 ἐκεῖνοι AN : ἔκειντο Dover[2] ἀπέθανον A[2] : ἀποθανόντες AN 566 τούτου A[1]N : om. A[a] 568 τῷ AN : ὅτῳ Hirschig[2] 569 ἀπωλώλει A : ἀπολώλει N ἀπελύθη Kayser[2] (coll. Polluce) : ἀπήχθη A[c]N : ἀπήγχθη A[a] 571 ἐτέθνασαν A[2]N : ἐτέθνησαν A

δὲ νεωτέρους πυνθάνεσθαι ὥσπερ ἐμέ. οὕτως ἀγαθόν
ἐστι μετὰ τοῦ χρόνου βασανίζειν τὰ πράγματα. καὶ
τοῦτ' ἴσως ἂν φανερὸν γένοιτ' ἂν ὕστερον, ὅτῳ τρόπῳ
τέθνηκεν ὁ ἄνθρωπος. μὴ οὖν ὕστερον τοῦτο γνῶτε,
ἀναίτιόν με ὄντα ἀπολέσαντες, ἀλλὰ πρότερόν γ' εὖ
βουλεύσασθε, καὶ μὴ μετ' ὀργῆς καὶ διαβολῆς, ὡς
τούτων οὐκ ἂν γένοιντο ἕτεροι πονηρότεροι σύμβουλοι.
οὐ γὰρ ἔστιν ὅ τι ἂν ὀργιζόμενος ἄνθρωπος εὖ γνοίη· 72
αὐτὸ γὰρ ᾧ βουλεύεται, τὴν γνώμην διαφθείρει τοῦ
ἀνθρώπου. μέγα τοι ἡμέρα παρ' ἡμέραν γιγνομένη
γνώμην, ὦ ἄνδρες, ἐξ ὀργῆς μεταστῆσαι καὶ τὴν ἀλήθειαν
εὑρεῖν τῶν γεγενημένων. εὖ δὲ ἴστε ὅτι ἐλεηθῆναι 73
ὑφ' ὑμῶν ἄξιός εἰμι μᾶλλον ἢ δίκην δοῦναι· δίκην μὲν
γὰρ εἰκός ἐστι διδόναι τοὺς ἀδικοῦντας, ἐλεεῖσθαι δὲ
τοὺς ἀδίκως κινδυνεύοντας. κρεῖσσον δὲ χρὴ γίγνεσθαι
ἀεὶ τὸ ὑμέτερον δυνάμενον ἐμὲ δικαίως σῴζειν, ἢ τὸ
τῶν ἐχθρῶν βουλόμενον ἀδίκως με ἀπολλύναι. ἐν μὲν
γὰρ τῷ ἐπισχεῖν ἔστι καὶ τὰ δεινὰ ταῦτα ποιῆσαι ἃ
οὗτοι κελεύουσιν· ἐν δὲ τῷ παραχρῆμα οὐκ ἔστιν ἀρχὴν
ὀρθῶς βουλεύεσθαι.

Δεῖ δέ με καὶ ὑπὲρ τοῦ πατρὸς ἀπολογήσασθαι. 74
καίτοι γε πολλῷ μᾶλλον εἰκὸς ἦν ἐκεῖνον ὑπὲρ ἐμοῦ

72 *οὐ—ἀνθρώπου* stp Stob. *Anth.* 3.20.43, quem secutus est Mich. Apost. *Ep.* 125.76–8 (qui *βούλεται* scripsit cum deterioribus Stobaei libris pro *βουλεύεται*)

---

573 *πυνθάνεσθαι* A : *πυνθάνασθαι* N 575 *ἂν* A : om. N *ὅτω* e ras. N^{1} : *καὶ ὅτω* A 578 *μὴ μετ'* Ald. : *μήτε μετ'* AN 580 *οὐ γὰρ* AN : *οὐκ* Stob. *ἂν* Stob. : om. AN *εὖ* Stob. : *ἂν* AN 581 *ᾧ* in ras. N^{1} : *ὧ* A : *ὃ* N^{a} Stob. *βουλεύεται* e ras. $A^{1}N^{1}$ Stob. : *βουλεύο*ται* A^{a} (N^{a} non liquet) 582 *τοι* N : *τι* A *ἡμέρα … γιγνομένη* Steph. : *ἡμέραν … γιγνομένην* AN 583 *ὦ ἄνδρες* A : *ω ἀνδρὸς* N *μεταστῆσαι* Steph. : *μεταστήσειν* AN 587 *ἀδίκως* A^{1}N : *κακῶς* ut vid. A^{a} *δὲ* A : *δὴ* N 587–8 *γίγνεσθαι ἀεὶ* N : *ἀεὶ γίγνεσθαι* A 589 *ἐχθρῶν*] *θ* in ras. A^{1} 591 *οὗτοι* A^{1}N : *οὔτοι* A^{a} *ἀρχὴν* Ald. : *ἀρχὴ, ἢ* re vera AN 594 *γε* post *πολλῷ* transp. vel del. maluit Jernstedt

ἀπολογήσασθαι πατέρα ὄντα· ὁ μὲν γὰρ πολλῷ
πρεσβύτερός ἐστι τῶν ἐμῶν πραγμάτων, ἐγὼ δὲ πολλῷ
νεώτερος τῶν ἐκείνῳ πεπραγμένων. καὶ εἰ μὲν ἐγὼ
τούτου ἀγωνιζομένου κατεμαρτύρουν ἃ μὴ σαφῶς ᾔδειν
ἀκοῇ δὲ ἠπιστάμην, δεινὰ ἂν ἔφη πάσχειν ὑπ' ἐμοῦ·
75 νῦν δὲ ἀναγκάζων ἐμὲ ἀπολογεῖσθαι ὧν ἐγὼ πολλῷ
νεώτερός εἰμι καὶ λόγῳ οἶδα, ταῦτα οὐ δεινὰ ἡγεῖται
εἰργάσθαι. ὅμως μέντοι καθ' ὅσον ἐγὼ οἶδα, οὐ προδώσω
τὸν πατέρα κακῶς ἀκούοντα ἐν ὑμῖν ἀδίκως. καίτοι
τάχ' ἂν σφαλείην, ἃ ἐκεῖνος ὀρθῶς ἔργῳ ἔπραξε, ταῦτ'
ἐγὼ λόγῳ μὴ ὀρθῶς εἰπών· ὅμως δ' οὖν κεκινδυνεύσεται.
76 πρὶν μὲν γὰρ τὴν ἀπόστασιν τὴν Μυτιληναίων γενέσθαι,
ἔργῳ τὴν εὔνοιαν ἐδείκνυε τὴν εἰς ὑμᾶς· ἐπειδὴ δὲ ἡ
πόλις ὅλη κακῶς ἐβουλεύσατο ἀποστᾶσα καὶ ἥμαρτε
τῆς ὑμετέρας γνώμης, μετὰ τῆς πόλεως ὅλης ἠναγκάσθη
συνεξαμαρτεῖν. τὴν μὲν οὖν γνώμην ἔτι καὶ ἐν ἐκείνοις
ὅμοιος ἦν εἰς ὑμᾶς, τὴν δὲ εὔνοιαν οὐκέτι ἦν ἐπ' ἐκείνῳ
τὴν αὐτὴν εἰς ὑμᾶς παρέχειν. οὔτε γὰρ ἐκλιπεῖν τὴν
πόλιν εὐρόπως εἶχεν αὐτῷ· ἱκανὰ γὰρ ἦν τὰ ἐνέχυρα
ἃ εἴχετο αὐτοῦ, οἵ τε παῖδες καὶ τὰ χρήματα· τοῦτο δ'
αὖ μένοντι πρὸς τὴν πόλιν αὐτῷ ἀδυνάτως εἶχεν
77 ἰσχυρίζεσθαι. ἐπεὶ δ' ὑμεῖς τοὺς αἰτίους τούτων
ἐκολάσατε, ἐν οἷς οὐκ ἐφαίνετο ὢν ὁ ἐμὸς πατήρ, τοῖς δ'
ἄλλοις Μυτιληναίοις ἄδειαν ἐδώκατε οἰκεῖν τὴν σφετέραν
αὑτῶν, οὐκ ἔστιν ὅ τι ὕστερον αὐτῷ ἡμάρτηται,

598 ᾔδειν AN : ᾔδη Jernstedt 605 κεκινδυνεύσεται A[2] : καὶ κινδυνεύσεται AN 606 τὴν Μυτιλ. Blass[2] : τῶν Μιτυλ. AN : <τὴν> τῶν Μυτιλ. Gernet 608–9 ἀποστᾶσα ... γνώμης secl. Hirschig[2] 611 δὲ N : δ' A ἐπ' in ras. A[1] 612 παρέχειν] παρέχεσθαι Hirschig[2] 613 εὐρόπως A[2] : εὖ ρ' ὅπως AN : εὐπόρως Schömann[2] 614 εἴχετο AN : ἔκειτο Rubino 618 ἐδώκατε AN : ἔδοτε Herwerden[1]

{τῷ ἐμῷ πατρί,} οὐδ' ὅ τι οὐ πεποίηται τῶν δεόντων,
οὐδ' ἧς τινος λητουργίας ἡ πόλις ἐνδεὴς γεγένηται, οὔτε
ἡ ὑμετέρα οὔτε ἡ Μυτιληναίων, ἀλλὰ καὶ χορηγίας
ἐχορήγει καὶ τέλη κατατίθησιν. εἰ δ' ἐν Αἴνῳ χωροφιλεῖ, 78
τοῦτο οὐκ ἀποστερῶν γε τῶν εἰς τὴν πόλιν ἑαυτὸν
οὐδενὸς οὐδ' ἑτέρας πόλεως πολίτης γεγενημένος,
ὥσπερ ἑτέρους ὁρῶ τοὺς μὲν εἰς τὴν ἤπειρον ἰόντας, καὶ
οἰκοῦντας ἐν τοῖς πολεμίοις τοῖς ὑμετέροις, ⟨τοὺς δὲ⟩
καὶ δίκας ἀπὸ ξυμβόλων ὑμῖν δικαζομένους, οὐδὲ
φεύγων τὸ πλῆθος τὸ ὑμέτερον, τοὺς δ' οἵους ὑμεῖς
μισῶν συκοφάντας. ἃ μὲν οὖν μετὰ τῆς πόλεως ὅλης 79
ἀνάγκῃ μᾶλλον ἢ γνώμῃ ἔπραξε, τούτων οὐ δίκαιός
ἐστιν ὁ ἐμὸς πατὴρ ἰδίᾳ δίκην διδόναι. ἅπασι γὰρ
Μυτιληναίοις ἀείμνηστος ἡ τότε ἁμαρτία γεγένηται·
ἠλλάξαντο μὲν γὰρ πολλῆς εὐδαιμονίας πολλὴν
κακοδαιμονίαν, ἐπεῖδον δὲ τὴν ἑαυτῶν πατρίδα
ἀνάστατον γενομένην. ἃ δὲ ἰδίᾳ οὗτοι διαβάλλουσι
τὸν ἐμὸν πατέρα, μὴ πείθεσθε· χρημάτων γὰρ ἕνεκα
ἡ πᾶσα παρασκευὴ γεγένηται ἐπ' ἐμοὶ κἀκείνῳ. πολλὰ
δ' ἐστὶ τὰ συμβαλλόμενα τοῖς βουλομένοις τῶν ἀλλοτρίων
ἐφίεσθαι. γέρων μὲν ἐκεῖνος ὥστ' ἐμοὶ βοηθεῖν, νεώτερος
δ' ἐγὼ πολλῷ ἢ ὥστε δύνασθαι ἐμαυτῷ τιμωρεῖν
ἱκανῶς. ἀλλ' ὑμεῖς βοηθήσατέ μοι, καὶ μὴ διδάσκετε 80
τοὺς συκοφάντας μεῖζον ὑμῶν αὐτῶν δύνασθαι. ἐὰν
μὲν γὰρ εἰσιόντες εἰς ὑμᾶς ἃ βούλονται πράσσωσι,

78 χωροφιλεῖ stp Pollux 9.13

620 del. Dobree 621 λητουργίας Blass[2] : λειτουργίας AN 623 ἐχορήγει AN : χορηγεῖ Blass κατατίθησιν N : κατετίθει A χωροφιλεῖ A[2] : χωροφίλει AN 624 τοῦτο <ποιεῖ> Reiske ἑαυτὸν geminatum del. A[1] 627 add. Reiske 629 ὑμέτερον A[2]N : ἡμέτερον A 632 ἰδίᾳ A[1], N ut vid. (δια paene oblit.) : om. A[a] 634 πολλῆς N : πολῆς A 637 πείθεσθε AN[1] : πείθεσθαι N[a] 638 ἐπ' A : ὑπ' N 639 δ' ἐστὶ N : δ' ἐστι re vera A 640 ὥστ' ἐμοὶ Bekker : ὥστε μοι AN

δεδειγμένον ἔσται τούτους μὲν πείθειν, τὸ δ' ὑμέτερον πλῆθος φεύγειν· ἐὰν δὲ εἰσιόντες εἰς ὑμᾶς πονηροὶ μὲν αὐτοὶ δοκῶσιν εἶναι, πλέον δ' αὐτοῖς μηδὲν γένηται, ὑμετέρα ἡ τιμὴ καὶ ἡ δύναμις ἔσται, ὥσπερ καὶ τὸ δίκαιον ἔχει. ὑμεῖς οὖν ἐμοί τε βοηθεῖτε καὶ τῷ δικαίῳ.

81 Ὅσα μὲν οὖν ἐκ τῶν ἀνθρωπίνων τεκμηρίων καὶ μαρτυριῶν οἷά τε ἦν ἀποδειχθῆναι, ἀκηκόατε· χρὴ δὲ καὶ τοῖς ἀπὸ τῶν θεῶν σημείοις γενομένοις εἰς τὰ τοιαῦτα οὐχ ἥκιστα τεκμηραμένους ψηφίζεσθαι. καὶ γὰρ τὰ τῆς πόλεως κοινὰ τούτοις μάλιστα πιστεύοντες ἀσφαλῶς διαπράσσεσθε, τοῦτο μὲν τὰ εἰς τοὺς κινδύνους
82 ἥκοντα, τοῦτο δὲ εἰς τὰ ἔξω τῶν κινδύνων. χρὴ δὲ καὶ εἰς τὰ ἴδια ταῦτα μέγιστα καὶ πιστότατα ἡγεῖσθαι. οἶμαι γὰρ ὑμᾶς ἐπίστασθαι ὅτι πολλοὶ ἤδη ἄνθρωποι μὴ καθαροὶ χεῖρας ἢ ἄλλο τι μίασμα ἔχοντες συνεισβάντες εἰς τὸ πλοῖον συναπώλεσαν μετὰ τῆς αὑτῶν ψυχῆς τοὺς ὁσίως διακειμένους τὰ πρὸς τοὺς θεούς· τοῦτο δὲ ἤδη ἑτέρους ἀπολομένους μὲν οὔ, κινδυνεύσαντας δὲ τοὺς ἐσχάτους κινδύνους διὰ τοὺς τοιούτους ἀνθρώπους· τοῦτο δὲ ἱεροῖς παραστάντες πολλοὶ δὴ καταφανεῖς ἐγένοντο οὐχ ὅσιοι ὄντες, καὶ διακωλύοντες τὰ ἱερὰ μὴ γίγνεσθαι τὰ νομιζόμενα.
83 ἐμοὶ τοίνυν ἐν πᾶσι τούτοις τὰ ἐναντία ἐγένετο. τοῦτο μὲν γὰρ ὅσοις συνέπλευσα, καλλίστοις ἐχρήσαντο πλοῖς·

645 *δεδειγμένον* AN : *δεδιδαγμένον* Gernet : *δεδογμένον* Jernstedt   649 *τε* A^{1}N : om. A^a 652 *τῶν* post *τοῖς* punctis del. A^1 ut vid.   653 *τεκμηραμένους* AN^{it} : *τεκμαιρομένους* N^{sv} 655 *διαπράσσεσθε* A : *διαπράσεσθε* N   656 *εἰς* del. Bekker   *τῶν* ex corr. N^1 (fort. *τοῦ* fuit)   659 <*τὰς*> *χεῖρας* Fuhr^1 660 *τὸ* del. Dobree   661 *αὑτῶν* Steph. : *αὐτῶν* AN   662 *ἀπολομένους* A^{c}N : *ἀπολουμένους* A^a *οὔ*, sic interpunxit A^2 : *οὐ* AN   664 *τοῦτο δὲ* A : *τοῦ δὲ* N   665 *καὶ* del. censuit Sauppe^1 666 *γίγνεσθαι* A^{2}N^1 : *γίνεσθαι* N^a : *γίγνεσθε* A   668 *ὅσοις* A^{2}N : *ὁσίοις* A

τοῦτο δὲ ὅπου ἱεροῖς παρέστην, οὐκ ἔστιν ὅπου οὐχὶ κάλλιστα τὰ ἱερὰ ἐγένετο. ἃ ἐγὼ ἀξιῶ μεγάλα μοι τεκμήρια εἶναι τῆς αἰτίας, ὅτι οὐκ ἀληθῆ μου οὗτοι κατηγοροῦσι. ⟨καί μοι ἀνάβητε⟩ τούτων μάρτυρες.

ΜΑΡΤΥΡΕΣ

84 Ἐπίσταμαι δὲ καὶ τάδε, ὦ ἄνδρες δικασταί, ὅτι εἰ μὲν ἐμοῦ κατεμαρτύρουν οἱ μάρτυρες, ὥς τι ἀνόσιον γεγένηται ἐμοῦ παρόντος ἐν πλοίῳ ἢ ἐν ἱεροῖς, αὐτοῖς γε τούτοις ἰσχυροτάτοις ἂν ἐχρῶντο, καὶ πίστιν τῆς αἰτίας ταύτην σαφεστάτην ἀπέφαινον, τὰ σημεῖα τὰ ἀπὸ τῶν θεῶν· νῦν δὲ τῶν τε σημείων ἐναντίων τοῖς τούτων λόγοις γιγνομένων, τῶν τε μαρτύρων ἃ μὲν ἐγὼ λέγω μαρτυρούντων ἀληθῆ εἶναι, ἃ δ᾽ οὗτοι κατηγοροῦσι ψευδῆ, τοῖς μὲν μαρτυροῦσιν ἀπιστεῖν ὑμᾶς κελεύουσι, τοῖς δὲ λόγοις οὓς αὐτοὶ λέγουσι πιστεύειν ὑμᾶς φασι χρῆναι. καὶ οἱ μὲν ἄλλοι ἄνθρωποι τοῖς ἔργοις τοὺς λόγους ἐλέγχουσιν, οὗτοι δὲ τοῖς λόγοις τὰ ἔργα ζητοῦσιν ἄπιστα καθιστάναι.

85 Ὅσα μὲν οὖν ἐκ τῶν κατηγορηθέντων μέμνημαι, ὦ ἄνδρες, ἀπολελόγημαι· οἶμαι δὲ καὶ ὑμῶν <...> ἀποψηφίσασθαι. ταὐτὰ γὰρ ἐμέ τε σῴζει, καὶ ὑμῖν νόμιμα καὶ εὔορκα γίγνεται. κατὰ γὰρ τοὺς νόμους ὠμόσατε δικάσειν· ἐγὼ δὲ καθ᾽ οὓς μὲν ἀπήχθην, οὐκ ἔνοχός εἰμι τοῖς νόμοις, ὧν δ᾽ ἔχω τὴν αἰτίαν, ἀγών

670 ἐγένετο AN^1 : ἐγίνετο N^a 672 add. Steph. : lacunam indicavit Blass 679 ἐναντίων A^{2}N : ἐναντίον A 680 γιγνομένων A^{1}N : γιγνομένοις A^a 682 ὑμᾶς A^{2}N : ἡμᾶς A 683–4 φασὶ χρῆναι N : χρῆναι φασὶ A 685–6 τὰ ἔργα ζητοῦσιν N : ζητοῦσι τὰ ἔργα A 688 καὶ A : om. N lacunam post ὑμῶν statuit Reiske : δέομαι pro οἶμαι ci. Dobree : alii aliter 689 ταὐτὰ Bekker : ταυτὰ Ald. : ταῦτα AN 691 ὠμόσατε A^{2}N : ὡμόσατε A 692 ἔχω A^{1}N : ἐγὼ A^a

μοι νόμιμος ὑπολείπεται. εἰ δὲ δύο ἐξ ἑνὸς ἀγῶνος γεγένησθον, οὐκ ἐγὼ αἴτιος, ἀλλ᾽ οἱ κατήγοροι. καίτοι οὐ δήπου οἱ μὲν ἔχθιστοι οἱ ἐμοὶ δύο ἀγῶνας περὶ ἐμοῦ πεποιήκασιν, ὑμεῖς δὲ οἱ τῶν δικαίων ἴσοι κριταὶ προκαταγνώσεσθέ μου ἐν τῷδε τῷ ἀγῶνι τὸν φόνον.

86 μὴ ὑμεῖς γε, ὦ ἄνδρες· ἀλλὰ δότε τι καὶ τῷ χρόνῳ, μεθ᾽ οὗ ὀρθότατα εὑρίσκουσιν οἱ τὴν ἀκρίβειαν ζητοῦντες τῶν πραγμάτων. ἠξίουν μὲν γὰρ ἔγωγε περὶ τῶν τοιούτων, ὦ ἄνδρες, εἶναι τὴν δίκην κατὰ τοὺς νόμους, κατὰ μέντοι τὸ δίκαιον ὡς πλειστάκις ἐλέγχεσθαι. τοσούτῳ γὰρ ἄμεινον ἂν ἐγιγνώσκετο· οἱ γὰρ πολλοὶ ἀγῶνες τῇ μὲν ἀληθείᾳ σύμμαχοί εἰσι, τῇ δὲ διαβολῇ

87 πολεμιώτατοι. φόνου γὰρ δίκη καὶ μὴ ὀρθῶς γνωσθεῖσα ἰσχυρότερον τοῦ δικαίου καὶ τοῦ ἀληθοῦς ἐστιν· ἀνάγκη γάρ, ἐὰν ὑμεῖς μου καταψηφίσησθε, καὶ μὴ ὄντα φονέα μηδ᾽ ἔνοχον τῷ ἔργῳ χρῆσθαι τῇ δίκῃ καὶ τῷ νόμῳ· καὶ οὐδεὶς ἂν τολμήσειεν οὔτε τὴν δίκην τὴν δεδικασμένην παραβαίνειν πιστεύσας αὑτῷ ὅτι οὐκ ἔνοχός ἐστιν, οὔτε ξυνειδὼς αὑτῷ τοιοῦτον ἔργον εἰργασμένῳ μὴ οὐ χρῆσθαι τῷ νόμῳ· ἀνάγκη δὲ τῆς δίκης νικᾶσθαι παρὰ τὸ ἀληθές, αὐτοῦ τε τοῦ ἀληθοῦς, ἄλλως τε καὶ ἐὰν μὴ ᾖ

88 ὁ τιμωρήσων. αὐτῶν δὲ τούτων ἕνεκα οἵ τε νόμοι καὶ αἱ διωμοσίαι καὶ τὰ τόμια καὶ αἱ προρρήσεις, καὶ τἆλλα ὅσα γίγνεται τῶν δικῶν ἕνεκα τοῦ φόνου, πολὺ διαφέροντά ἐστιν ἢ {καὶ} ἐπὶ τοῖς ἄλλοις, ὅτι καὶ αὐτὰ τὰ πράγματα, περὶ ὧν οἱ κίνδυνοι, περὶ πλείστου ἐστὶν

696 *ἴσοι* A : *ἶσοι* N *κριταὶ* N : *κριτοὶ* A 697 *προκαταγνώσεσθέ* A^1N : *προκαταγνώσεσθαί* A^a *μου* A : *με* N *ἀγῶνι* Maetzner : *λόγῳ* AN 700 alt. *τῶν* A^1N : om. A^a 702 *μέντοι* <*τούτους*> dubitanter Sauppe 703 *ἄμεινον ἂν* N : *ἂν ἄμεινον* A §§87–89 cfr. 6.3–6 710 *αὑτῷ* Ald. : *αὐτῶ* AN 711 *αὑτῷ* A^1N : *αὐτῶ* A^a 714 *ἕνεκα* A : *εἵνεκα* N 715 *τἆλλα* Gernet : *τἄλλα* N : *τἄλλ᾽* A 716 *ὅσα* N : *ὁπόσα* A 717 del. Maetzner

ὀρθῶς γιγνώσκεσθαι· ὀρθῶς μὲν γὰρ γνωσθέντα
τιμωρία ἐστὶ τῷ ἀδικηθέντι, φονέα δὲ τὸν μὴ αἴτιον
ψηφισθῆναι ἁμαρτία καὶ ἀσέβειά ἐστιν εἴς τε τοὺς
θεοὺς καὶ εἰς τοὺς νόμους. καὶ οὐκ ἴσον ἐστὶ τόν τε **89**
διώκοντα μὴ ὀρθῶς αἰτιάσασθαι καὶ ὑμᾶς τοὺς
δικαστὰς μὴ ὀρθῶς γνῶναι. ἡ μὲν γὰρ τούτων αἰτίασις
οὐκ ἔχει τέλος, ἀλλ᾽ ἐν ὑμῖν ἐστι καὶ τῇ δίκῃ· ὅ τι δ᾽ ἂν
ὑμεῖς ἐν αὐτῇ τῇ δίκῃ μὴ ὀρθῶς γνῶτε, τοῦτο οὐκ ἔστιν
ὅποι ἄν τις ἀνενεγκὼν τὴν ἁμαρτίαν ἀπολύσαιτο.
πῶς ἂν οὖν ὀρθῶς δικάσαιτε περὶ αὐτῶν; εἰ τούτους **90**
τε ἐάσετε τὸν νομιζόμενον ὅρκον διομοσαμένους
κατηγορῆσαι, κἀμὲ περὶ αὐτοῦ τοῦ πράγματος
ἀπολογήσασθαι. πῶς δὲ ἐάσετε; ἐὰν νυνὶ ἀποψηφίσησθέ
μου. διαφεύγω γὰρ οὐδ᾽ οὕτω τὰς ὑμετέρας γνώμας,
ἀλλ᾽ ὑμεῖς ἔσεσθε οἱ κἀκεῖ περὶ ἐμοῦ διαψηφιζόμενοι.
καὶ φεισαμένοις μὲν ὑμῖν ἐμοῦ νῦν ἔξεστι τότε χρῆσθαι
ὅ τι ἂν βούλησθε, ἀπολέσασι δὲ οὐδὲ βουλεύσασθαι ἔτι
περὶ ἐμοῦ ἐγχωρεῖ. καὶ μὴν εἰ δέοι ἁμαρτεῖν τι, τὸ **91**
ἀδίκως ἀπολῦσαι ὁσιώτερον ἂν εἴη τοῦ μὴ δικαίως
ἀπολέσαι· τὸ μὲν γὰρ ἁμάρτημα μόνον ἐστί, τὸ δὲ

89 *αἰτίασις* stp Pollux 3.136 (item 26.7, 6.6.11) **91** *εἰ—ἀσέβημα* stp Stob. *Anth.* 4.5.19, quem secutus est Arsen. *Apophth.* cent. 6.68a

---

723 *αἰτιάσασθαι* N : *αἰτιασασθαι* A[1] : *αἰτιᾶσθαι* A[a] 727 *ὅποι ἄν* Ald. : *ὁπόι άν* N : *ὁποίαν* A *ἀνενεγκὼν* A[1]N : *ἐνεγκὼν* A[a] *ἁμαρτίαν*] *αἰτίαν* Thalheim ex 6.6 728 *δικάσαιτε* Bekker : *δικάσητε* AN 729 *διομοσαμένους* A : *διομοσομένους* N[1] : *διωμοσομένους* N[a] 733 *ὑμεῖς*] *ο* in *υ* per ras. corr. A[c] *ἔσεσθε* AN[1] : *ἔσεσθαι* N[a] *κἀκεῖ* Ald. : *κακοὶ* AN 734 *φεισαμένοις* N : *ψηφισαμένοις* A 735 *ἂν βούλησθε, ἀπολέσασι δὲ* Dobree : *ἃ δὴ βούλεσθαι* (*βούλεσθε* A[a]), *ἀπολογήσασθαι* A[1]N 736 *ἁμαρτεῖν τι, τὸ* maluit Maetzner : *ἁμαρτεῖν ἐπὶ τῷ* AN : *τι ἁμαρτεῖν, τὸ* Stob. 737 *ἂν εἴη* Dobree : *ἂν ᾖ* AN : *ἢ* Stob. *τοῦ* Stob. Ald. : *τὸ* AN Stob.[c] *μὴ δικαίως* AN : *ἀδίκως* Stob. 738 *ἁμάρτημα μόνον* N : *μόνον ἁμάρτημα* A : *ἁμάρτημα* Stob.

ἕτερον καὶ ἀσέβημα. ἐν ᾧ χρὴ πολλὴν πρόνοιαν ἔχειν,
μέλλοντας ἀνήκεστον ἔργον ἐργάζεσθαι. ἐν μὲν γὰρ
ἀκεστῷ πράγματι καὶ ὀργῇ χρησαμένους καὶ διαβολῇ
πιθομένους ἔλαττόν ἐστιν ἐξαμαρτεῖν· μεταγνοὺς γὰρ
ἔτι ἂν ὀρθῶς βουλεύσαιτο· ἐν δὲ τοῖς ἀνηκέστοις πλέον
βλάβος τὸ μετανοεῖν καὶ γνῶναι ἐξημαρτηκότας. ἤδη δέ
τισιν ὑμῶν καὶ μετεμέλησεν ἀπολωλεκόσι. καίτοι ὅπου
ὑμῖν τοῖς ἐξαπατηθεῖσι μετεμέλησεν, ἦ καὶ πάνυ τοι
92 χρὴ τούς γε ἐξαπατῶντας ἀπολωλέναι. ἔπειτα δὲ τὰ
μὲν ἀκούσια τῶν ἁμαρτημάτων ἔχει συγγνώμην, τὰ δὲ
ἑκούσια οὐκ ἔχει. τὸ μὲν γὰρ ἀκούσιον ἁμάρτημα, ὦ
ἄνδρες, τῆς τύχης ἐστί, τὸ δὲ ἑκούσιον τῆς γνώμης.
ἑκούσιον δὲ πῶς ἂν εἴη μᾶλλον ἢ εἴ τις, ὧν βουλὴν
ποιοῖτο, ταῦτα παραχρῆμα ἐξεργάζοιτο; καὶ μὴν τὴν
ἴσην γε δύναμιν ἔχει, ὅστις τε ἂν τῇ χειρὶ ἀποκτείνῃ
93 ἀδίκως καὶ ὅστις τῇ ψήφῳ. εὖ δ' ἴστε ὅτι οὐκ ἄν ποτ'
ἦλθον εἰς τὴν πόλιν, εἴ τι ξυνῄδειν ἐμαυτῷ τοιοῦτον· νῦν
δὲ πιστεύων τῷ δικαίῳ, οὗ πλέονος οὐδέν ἐστιν ἄξιον
ἀνδρὶ συναγωνίζεσθαι, μηδὲν αὑτῷ συνειδότι ἀνόσιον
εἰργασμένῳ μητ' εἰς τοὺς θεοὺς ἠσεβηκότι· ἐν γὰρ
τῷ τοιούτῳ ἤδη καὶ τὸ σῶμα ἀπειρηκὸς ἡ ψυχὴ
συνεξέσωσεν, ἐθέλουσα ταλαιπωρεῖν διὰ τὸ μὴ
ξυνειδέναι ἑαυτῇ· τῷ δὲ ξυνειδότι τοῦτο αὐτὸ πρῶτον

739 ἕτερον καὶ A[1]N : ἕτερον A[a] : ἀδίκως ἀποκτεῖναι Stob. 740 ἀνήκεστον Steph. : ἀνηκέστερον AN 741 ἀκεστῷ Steph. : ἑκάστῳ AN 742 πιθομένους Cobet[2] : πειθομένους AN ἔλαττόν A : ἔλαττον N : ἔλασσόν Blass γὰρ] γάρ <τις> Bohlmann : <τις> ante ὀρθῶς l. 743 add. Gernet 745 ἀπολωλεκόσι A : ἀπολελωκόσι N ὅπου Leo : οὔπω AN 746 ἦ Leo : εἰ AN 747 χρὴ AN : χρῆν Blass[2] ἀπολωλέναι N : ἀλωλωλέναι A 749 γὰρ A : om. N 750 γνώμης A : γνώμης ἐστίν N 752 ἐξεργάζοιτο N : ἐργάζοιτο A 755 ξυνῄδειν N : ξυνήδειν A : ξυνῄδη Jernstedt 756 ἐστιν A : ἐστι N 757 αὑτῷ N : αὐτῶ A 758 εἰργασμένῳ N : εἰργασμένον A μήτ' AN : μηδ' Franke 760 συνεξέσωσεν A[1] : συνεξείσωσεν ut vid. A[a] : συνεξέωσεν N

πολέμιόν ἐστιν· ἔτι γὰρ καὶ τοῦ σώματος ἰσχύοντος ἡ
ψυχὴ προαπολείπει, ἡγουμένη τὴν τιμωρίαν οἱ ἥκειν
ταύτην τῶν ἀσεβημάτων· ἐγὼ δ' ἐμαυτῷ τοιοῦτον
οὐδὲν ξυνειδὼς ἥκω εἰς ὑμᾶς. τὸ δὲ τοὺς κατηγόρους 94
διαβάλλειν οὐδέν ἐστι θαυμαστόν. τούτων γὰρ ἔργον
τοῦτο, ὑμῶν δὲ τὸ μὴ πείθεσθαι τὰ μὴ δίκαια. τοῦτο
μὲν γὰρ ἐμοὶ πειθομένοις ὑμῖν μεταμελῆσαι ἔστιν, καὶ
τούτου φάρμακον τὸ αὖθις κολάσαι, τοῦ δὲ τούτοις
πειθομένους ἐξεργάσασθαι ἃ οὗτοι βούλονται οὐκ ἔστιν
ἴασις. οὐδὲ χρόνος πολὺς ὁ διαφέρων, ἐν ᾧ ταῦτα νομίμως
πράξεθ' ἃ νῦν ὑμᾶς παρανόμως πείθουσιν οἱ κατήγοροι
ψηφίσασθαι. οὔ τοι τῶν ἐπειγομένων ἐστὶ τὰ πράγματα,
ἀλλὰ τῶν εὖ βουλευομένων. νῦν μὲν οὖν γνωρισταὶ
γίγνεσθε τῆς δίκης, τότε δὲ δικασταὶ τῶν μαρτύρων· νῦν
μὲν δοξασταί, τότε δὲ κριταὶ τῶν ἀληθῶν. ῥᾷστον δέ 95
τοί ἐστιν ἀνδρὸς περὶ θανάτου φεύγοντος τὰ ψευδῆ
καταμαρτυρῆσαι. ἐὰν γὰρ τὸ παραχρῆμα μόνον πείσωσιν
ὥστε ἀποκτεῖναι, ἅμα τῷ σώματι καὶ ἡ τιμωρία
ἀπόλωλεν. οὔτε γὰρ οἱ φίλοι ἔτι θελήσουσιν ὑπὲρ
ἀπολωλότος τιμωρεῖν. ἐὰν δὲ καὶ βουληθῶσιν, τί ἔσται
πλέον τῷ γε ἀποθανόντι; νῦν μὲν οὖν ἀποψηφίσασθέ
μου· ἐν δὲ τῇ τοῦ φόνου δίκῃ οὗτοί τε τὸν νομιζόμενον 96
ὅρκον διομοσάμενοι ἐμοῦ κατηγορήσουσι, καὶ ὑμεῖς περὶ
ἐμοῦ κατὰ τοὺς κειμένους νόμους διαγνώσεσθε, καὶ ἐμοὶ

762 *καὶ* A^{1}N : om. A^{a} 764 *ἀσεβημάτων* N : *ἀσεβηκότων* A 765 *τὸ δὲ* Ald. : *τῷ* N : *τῶ* A 766 *ἔργον* N : *ἔργω* A 768 *ἐμοὶ* A^{1}N : *ὑμῖν* A^{a} *ὑμῖν* N : *ἡμῖν* A *ἔστιν* Blass : *ἐστίν* N : *ἐστὶ* A 772 *πράξεθ'* A^{a} : *πράξεσθ'* A^{1}N *ἃ* A : *ἂν* N 773 *οὔ τοι* A^{1}N : *οὗτοι* A^{a} 775 *τῶν μαρτύρων* del. Jernstedt, post *δοξασταί* transp. Sauppe 776–7 *ῥᾷστον δέ τοί* Dobree : *ἀραῖς τῶνδε τοι* A : om. in vac. spat. N 781 *βουληθῶσιν* N : *βουληθῶσι* A^{1} : *δουληθῶσι* A^{a} 782 *ἀποψηφίσασθέ* AN^{1} : *ἀποψηφίσασθαι* ut vid. N^{a} 783 *μου* A^{1}N : *με* A^{a} *ἐν* A : *ἐὰν* N 784 *κατηγορήσουσι* AN^{a} : *κατηγορήσωσι* N^{1} 785 *διαγνώσεσθε* AN^{1} : *διαγνώσησθε* N^{a}

οὐδεὶς λόγος ἔσται ἔτι, ἐάν τι πάσχω, ὡς παρανόμως ἀπωλόμην. ταῦτά τοι δέομαι ὑμῶν, οὔτε τὸ ὑμέτερον εὐσεβὲς παρεὶς οὔτε ἐμαυτὸν ἀποστερῶν τὸ δίκαιον· ἐν δὲ τῷ ὑμετέρῳ ὅρκῳ καὶ ἡ ἐμὴ σωτηρία ἔνεστι. πειθόμενοι δὲ τούτων ὅτῳ βούλεσθε, ἀποψηφίσασθέ μου.

786 ἔσται A : ἐστὶ N   τι Bekker : τε AN   παρανόμως Reiske : παράνομος AN   788 παρεὶς AN : παριεὶς Fuhr[1]   suscriptio ὑπὲρ τοῦ ἡρώδου φόνου N

6

ΠΕΡΙ ΤΟΥ ΧΟΡΕΥΤΟΥ

ΥΠΟΘΕΣΙΣ

Πόσοι μέν εἰσιν Ἀθήνησι χορηγοί, καὶ τίνος προβάλλονται χάριν, καὶ πόσους τρέφειν ἀναγκάζονται παῖδας, ἐκ τῶν Δημοσθένους ἀκριβῶς ἔγνωμεν λόγων. ἐν τοίνυν τοῖς χρόνοις Ἀντιφῶντος τοῦ ῥήτορος χορηγός τις εἶναι λαχὼν τῆς αὑτοῦ φυλῆς Ἐρεχθηίδος, καὶ προσέτι Κεκροπίδος, τοὺς χορεύειν μέλλοντας ἐπὶ τῆς οἰκίας ἔτρεφε παῖδας. τούτων εἷς εὐφωνίας χάριν ἔπιε φάρμακον, καὶ πιὼν τέθνηκεν. ὁ οὖν πατὴρ τοῦ τεθνεῶτος παιδὸς κατηγορεῖ τοῦ χορηγοῦ ὡς αὐτοῦ πεποιηκότος τὸν φόνον. ἀπολογεῖται δὲ ὁ χορηγὸς ἀρνούμενος τὸν φόνον. Ἡ στάσις στοχασμός. ἀδήλου ⟨δὲ⟩ τοῦ ἐγκλήματος ὄντος, σημεῖον φανερὸν ὁ κατήγορος λαμβάνει τὸ ἐν τῇ οἰκίᾳ τοῦ χορηγοῦ γυμνάζεσθαι τοὺς παῖδας· ὅπερ ἐστὶν ἀνεύθυνον μέν, πιθανὸν δ' εἰς ὑποψίαν.

Ἥδιστον μέν, ὦ ἄνδρες δικασταί, ἀνθρώπῳ ὄντι μὴ 1
γενέσθαι μηδένα κίνδυνον περὶ τοῦ σώματος, καὶ εὐχόμενος ἄν τις ταῦτα εὔξαιτο· εἰ ⟨δ'⟩ ἄρα τις καὶ ἀναγκάζοιτο

Tit. *περὶ τοῦ χορευτοῦ* AN Harp. δ 54, δ 63 Arg. inscriptio *ὑπόθεσις τοῦ ἑξῆς* A : om. N 3 *ἐν τοίνυν* Jernstedt : *ὁ μέντοι νῦν ἐν* A : *ὁ μέντοι νῦν* N : *ὁ μὲν τοίνυν ἐν* Ald. : *τὸ μέντοι νῦν ἐν* Blass 5 *τῆς* N : *τοῖς* A *αὑτοῦ* Steph. : *αὐτου* AN *Ἐρεχθηίδος* Scaliger : *ἐρεχθίδος* AN 9 *χορηγοῦ* Spanheim apud Turr. : *χορευτοῦ* AN 9–10 *ἀπολογεῖται … φόνον* om. N 10 *χορηγὸς* Spanheim apud Turr. : *χορευτὴς* AN 11 add. Barigazzi (coll. 1 Arg. 14–15) : <*γὰρ*> Blass 12 *χορηγοῦ* Turr. : *χορευτοῦ* AN Inscriptio *Ἀντιφῶντος περὶ τοῦ χορευτοῦ* N : *περὶ τοῦ χορευτοῦ* A 15 *ὦ* A : om. N 17 add. Ald.

κινδυνεύειν, τοῦτο γοῦν ὑπάρχειν, ὅπερ μέγιστον ἐγὼ
νομίζω ἐν πράγματι τοιούτῳ, αὐτὸν ἑαυτῷ συνειδέναι
μηδὲν ἐξημαρτηκότι, ἀλλ᾽ εἴ τις καὶ συμφορὰ γίγνοιτο,
ἄνευ κακότητος καὶ αἰσχύνης γίγνεσθαι, καὶ τύχῃ
2 μᾶλλον ἢ ἀδικίᾳ. καὶ τοὺς μὲν νόμους οἳ κεῖνται περὶ τῶν
τοιούτων πάντες ἂν ἐπαινέσαιεν κάλλιστα νόμων κεῖσθαι
καὶ ὁσιώτατα. ὑπάρχει μὲν γὰρ αὐτοῖς ἀρχαιοτάτοις
εἶναι ἐν τῇ γῇ ταύτῃ, ἔπειτα τοὺς αὐτοὺς αἰεὶ περὶ τῶν
αὐτῶν, ὅπερ μέγιστον σημεῖον νόμων καλῶς κειμένων· ὁ
χρόνος γὰρ καὶ ἡ ἐμπειρία τὰ μὴ καλῶς ἔχοντα διδάσκει
τοὺς ἀνθρώπους. ὥστ᾽ οὐ δεῖ ὑμᾶς ἐκ τῶν λόγων τοῦ
κατηγοροῦντος τοὺς νόμους μαθεῖν εἰ καλῶς ἔχουσιν ἢ
μή, ἀλλ᾽ ἐκ τῶν νόμων τοὺς τούτων λόγους, εἰ ὀρθῶς
3 ὑμᾶς καὶ νομίμως διδάσκουσιν ἢ οὔ. ὁ μὲν οὖν ἀγὼν ἐμοὶ
μέγιστος τῷ κινδυνεύοντι καὶ διωκομένῳ· ἡγοῦμαι
μέντοι γε καὶ ὑμῖν τοῖς δικασταῖς περὶ πολλοῦ εἶναι τὰς
φονικὰς δίκας ὀρθῶς διαγιγνώσκειν, μάλιστα μὲν τῶν
θεῶν ἕνεκα καὶ τοῦ εὐσεβοῦς, ἔπειτα δὲ καὶ ὑμῶν αὐτῶν.
ἔστι μὲν γὰρ περὶ τοῦ τοιούτου {αὐτοῦ} μία δίκη· αὕτη δὲ
μὴ ὀρθῶς καταγνωσθεῖσα ἰσχυροτέρα ἐστὶ τοῦ δικαίου
4 καὶ τοῦ ἀληθοῦς. ἀνάγκη γάρ, ἐὰν ὑμεῖς καταψηφίσησθε,
καὶ μὴ ὄντα φονέα μηδὲ ἔνοχον τῷ ἔργῳ χρήσασθαι τῇ
δίκῃ, καὶ νόμῳ εἴργεσθαι πόλεως ἱερῶν ἀγώνων θυσιῶν,
ἅπερ μέγιστα καὶ παλαιότατα τοῖς ἀνθρώποις. τοσαύτην
γὰρ ἀνάγκην ὁ νόμος ἔχει, ὥστε καὶ ἄν τις κτείνῃ τινὰ ὧν
αὐτὸς κρατεῖ καὶ μὴ ἔστιν ὁ τιμωρήσων, τὸ νομιζόμενον

18 ὅπερ N : ὃ A   19 συνειδέναι A^{1}N : συνειδότι A^{a} §2 cfr. 5.14   23 ἐπαινέσαιεν Turr. : ἐπαινέσειεν A : ἐπαινέσειαν N   27 ἡ A : om. N   28 ὑμᾶς post κατηγοροῦντος l. 29 A   §§ 3–6 cfr. 5.87–89   36 del. Maetzner : <τοῦ> αὐτοῦ Scheibe   37 δικαίου A^{1}N : δικαίως A^{a} 38 γὰρ A^{1}N : δὲ A^{a} 40 εἴργεσθαι N : εἵργεσθαι A   41 παλαιότατα AN : σπουδαιότατα Jernstedt : alii aliter

καὶ τὸ θεῖον δεδιὼς ἁγνεύει τε ἑαυτὸν καὶ ἀφέξεται ὧν
εἴρηται ἐν τῷ νόμῳ, ἐλπίζων οὕτως ἂν ἄριστα πράξειν.
ἔστι μὲν γὰρ τὰ πλείω τοῖς ἀνθρώποις τοῦ βίου ἐν ταῖς 5
ἐλπίσιν· ἀσεβῶν δὲ καὶ παραβαίνων τὰ εἰς τοὺς θεοὺς καὶ
αὐτῆς ἂν τῆς ἐλπίδος, ὅπερ μέγιστόν ἐστι τοῖς ἀνθρώποις
ἀγαθόν, αὐτὸς αὑτὸν ἀποστεροίη. καὶ οὐδεὶς ἂν τολμήσειεν
οὔτε τὴν δίκην τὴν δεδικασμένην παραβαίνειν πιστεύσας
ὅτι οὐκ ἔνοχός ἐστι τῷ ἔργῳ, οὔτ' αὖ συνειδὼς αὑτὸς
αὑτῷ ἔργον εἰργασμένος τοιοῦτον μὴ οὐ χρῆσθαι τῷ
νόμῳ· ἀνάγκη δὲ τῆς τε δίκης νικᾶσθαι παρὰ τὸ ἀληθές,
αὐτοῦ τε τοῦ ἀληθοῦς, κἂν μὴ ὁ τιμωρήσων ᾖ. αὐτῶν δὲ 6
τούτων ἕνεκα οἵ τε νόμοι καὶ αἱ διωμοσίαι καὶ τὰ τόμια
καὶ αἱ προρρήσεις, καὶ τἆλλ' ὅσα γίγνεται τῶν δικῶν τοῦ
φόνου ἕνεκα, πολὺ διαφέροντά ἐστιν ἢ ἐπὶ τοῖς ἄλλοις, ὅτι
καὶ αὐτὰ τὰ πράγματα, περὶ ὧν οἱ κίνδυνοι, περὶ πλείστου
ἐστὶν ὀρθῶς γιγνώσκεσθαι· ὀρθῶς μὲν γὰρ γνωσθέντα
τιμωρία ἐστὶν ὑπὲρ τοῦ ἀδικηθέντος, φονέα δὲ τὸν μὴ
αἴτιον ψηφισθῆναι ἁμαρτία καὶ ἀσέβεια εἴς τε τοὺς θεοὺς
καὶ τοὺς νόμους. καὶ οὐκ ἴσον ἐστὶ τόν τε διώκοντα μὴ
ὀρθῶς ⟨αἰτιάσασθαι καὶ ὑμᾶς τοὺς δικαστὰς μὴ ὀρθῶς⟩
γνῶναι. ἡ μὲν γὰρ τούτου αἰτίασις οὐκ ἔχει {νῦν} τέλος,
ἀλλ' ἐν ὑμῖν ἐστι καὶ τῇ δίκῃ· ὅ τι δ' ἂν ὑμεῖς μὴ ὀρθῶς
γνῶτε, τοῦτο οὐκ ἔστιν ὅποι ἂν ἀνενεγκών τις τὴν αἰτίαν
ἀπολύσαιτο.

6 *αἰτίασις* stp Pollux 3.136 (item 5.26, 5.89)

---

44 *ἁγνεύει* AN : *ἁγνεύσει* Reiske *ἑαυτὸν* A : *αὑτὸν* N^c : *αὐτὸν* N^a 45 *πράξειν* AN : *πρᾶξαι* Dobree 48 *μέγιστον ἐστὶ τοῖς* N : *ἐστὶ μέγιστον* A 50 *οὔτε* Bekker: *οὔτ' ἂν* re vera A, N *δεδικασμένην* Steph. : *δεδοκιμασμένην* N : *δεδοκισμασμένην* A 52 *αὑτῷ* A^1N^1 : *αὐτῷ* A^aN^a 53 *νικᾶσθαι* A : *δικᾶσθαι* N 55 *διωμοσίαι* A : *δημοσίαι* N 56 *τἆλλ'* A : *τἄλλα* N 58 *τὰ* Ald. : *ταῦτα* AN 59 *γὰρ* A : om. N 62 *ἴσον* A : *ἶσον* N *τε* N : *γε* A 63 ex 5.89 add. Ald. 64 del. Reiske 66 *ἀνενεγκών* Reiske : *ἐνεγκών* N : *ἐνεγκὼν* A *τις* N : *τίς* A

7 Ἐγὼ δέ, ὦ ἄνδρες, οὐ τὴν αὐτὴν γνώμην ἔχω περὶ τῆς
ἀπολογίας, ἥνπερ οἱ κατήγοροι περὶ τῆς κατηγορίας.
οὗτοι γὰρ τὴν μὲν δίωξιν εὐσεβείας ἕνεκά φασι
ποιεῖσθαι καὶ τοῦ δικαίου, τὴν δὲ κατηγορίαν ἅπασαν
πεποίηνται διαβολῆς ἕνεκα καὶ ἀπάτης, ὅπερ
ἀδικώτατόν ἐστι τῶν ἐν ἀνθρώποις, καὶ οὐκ ἐλέγξαντες,
εἴ τι ἀδικῶ, δικαίως με βούλονται τιμωρεῖσθαι, ἀλλὰ
διαβάλλοντες, καὶ εἰ μηδὲν ἀδικῶ, ζημιῶσαι καὶ
8 ἐξελάσαι ἐκ τῆς γῆς ταύτης. ἐγὼ δὲ ἀξιῶ πρῶτον μὲν
περὶ αὐτοῦ τοῦ πράγματος κρίνεσθαι, καὶ διηγήσασθαι
ἐν ὑμῖν τὰ γενόμενα πάντα· ἔπειτα περὶ τῶν ἄλλων ὧν
οὗτοι κατηγοροῦσιν, ἐὰν ὑμῖν ἡδομένοις, βουλήσομαι
ἀπολογήσασθαι. ἡγοῦμαι γάρ μοι τιμὴν καὶ ὠφέλειαν
αὐτὰ οἴσειν, τοῖς δὲ κατηγόροις καὶ τοῖς ἐπηρεάζουσιν
9 αἰσχύνην· ἐπεί τοί γε καὶ δεινόν, ὦ ἄνδρες· ἵνα μὲν ἐξῆν
αὐτοῖς, εἴ τι ἠδίκουν ἐγὼ τὴν πόλιν ἢ ἐν χορηγίᾳ ἢ
ἐν ἄλλοις τισίν, ἀποφήνασι καὶ ἐξελέγξασιν ἄνδρα
τε ἐχθρὸν τιμωρήσασθαι καὶ τὴν πόλιν ὠφελῆσαι,
ἐνταῦθα μὲν οὐδεὶς πώποτε οἷός τε ἐγένετο αὐτῶν οὔτε
μικρὸν οὔτε μέγα ἐξελέγξαι ἀδικοῦντα τόνδε τὸν ἄνδρα
τὸ πλῆθος τὸ ὑμέτερον· ἐν δὲ τούτῳ τῷ ἀγῶνι, φόνου
διώκοντες καὶ τοῦ νόμου οὕτως ἔχοντος, εἰς αὐτὸ τὸ
πρᾶγμα κατηγορεῖν, μηχανῶνται ἐπ᾽ ἐμοὶ λόγους
ψευδεῖς συντιθέντες καὶ διαβάλλοντες τὰ εἰς τὴν πόλιν.
καὶ τῇ μὲν πόλει, εἴπερ ἀδικεῖται, κατηγορίαν ἀντὶ

73 ἐλέγξαντες A[1]N : ἐλέγξαντας A[a] 74 εἴ τι Bekker, Dobree : εἴ γ᾽ AN 75 διαβάλλοντες A[1]N : διαβαλλὸντες A[a] : διαβαλόντες Baiter 77 κρίνεσθαι AN : κρίνασθαι Barigazzi : ἀποκρίνεσθαι Reiske διηγήσασθαι AN : διηγήσομαι Wilamowitz[2] 79 ἡδομένοις <ἦ> Ald. 80 γάρ μοι A[1] N : γὰρ A : γὰρ ἐμοὶ Thalheim auctore Rosenthalio 82 δεινὸν A[c]N : δεινῶν A[a] ἐξῆν Ald. : ἐξῇ AN 83 εἴ τι A[1]N : ὅτι A[a] ἠδίκουν ἐγὼ N : ἐγὼ ἠδίκουν A 85 τιμωρήσασθαι Ald. : τιμωρήσεσθαι AN 87 ἐξελέγξαι N : ἐλέγξαι A 90 ἐπ᾽ ἐμοὶ Blass : ἐπ᾽ ἐμὲ AN 92 εἴπερ Blass : εἰ μὲν AN

τιμωρίας ἀπονέμουσιν, αὐτοὶ δὲ ὃ τὴν πόλιν φασὶν ἀδικεῖσθαι, τούτου ἰδίᾳ ἀξιοῦσι δίκην λαμβάνειν.

10 καίτοι αὗται αἱ κατηγορίαι οὔτε χάριτος ἄξιαι οὔτε πίστεως. οὔτε γὰρ δὴ οὗ ἡ πόλις ἐλάμβανεν ἂν δίκην εἴ τι ἠδίκητο, ἐνταῦθα τὴν κατηγορίαν ποιεῖται, ὥστε χάριτος ἄξιον εἶναι τῇ πόλει· οὔτε ὅστις {οὐκ} ἄλλα κατηγορεῖ ἢ ἃ διώκει ἐν πράγματι τοιούτῳ, πιστεῦσαι δήπου αὐτῷ ἀξιώτερόν ἐστιν ἢ ἀπιστῆσαι. ἐγὼ δὲ σχεδὸν ἐπίσταμαι τὴν ὑμετέραν γνώμην, ὅτι οὔτ᾽ ἂν καταψηφίσαισθε οὔτ᾽ ἂν ἀποψηφίσαισθε ἑτέρου τινὸς ἕνεκα μᾶλλον ἢ αὐτοῦ τοῦ πράγματος· ταῦτα γὰρ καὶ δίκαια καὶ ὅσια. ἄρξομαι δὲ ἐντεῦθεν.

11 Ἐπειδὴ χορηγὸς κατεστάθην εἰς Θαργήλια καὶ ἔλαχον Παντακλέα διδάσκαλον καὶ Κεκροπίδα φυλὴν πρὸς τῇ ἐμαυτοῦ, {τουτέστι τῇ Ἐρεχθηίδι,} ἐχορήγουν ὡς ἄριστα ἐδυνάμην καὶ δικαιότατα. καὶ πρῶτον μὲν διδασκαλεῖον ⟨ᾗ⟩ ἦν ἐπιτηδειότατον τῆς ἐμῆς οἰκίας κατεσκεύασα, ἐν ᾧπερ καὶ Διονυσίοις ὅτε ἐχορήγουν ἐδίδασκον· ἔπειτα τὸν χορὸν συνέλεξα ὡς ἐδυνάμην ἄριστα, οὔτε ζημιώσας οὐδένα οὔτε ἐνέχυρα βίᾳ φέρων οὔτ᾽ ἀπεχθανόμενος οὐδενί, ἀλλ᾽ ὥσπερ ἂν ἥδιστα καὶ ἐπιτηδειότατα ἀμφοτέροις ἐγίγνετο, ἐγὼ μὲν ἐκέλευον καὶ ᾐτούμην, οἱ δ᾽ ἑκόντες καὶ βουλόμενοι

11 ἔλαχον Παντακλέα διδάσκαλον Harp. δ 54 s.v. διδάσκαλος

93 ὃ Cobet^{3} : ᾧ N : ὦ A : ὧν Blass : οὗ Thalheim 94 τούτου ἰδίᾳ Bekker : τουτουὶ δὴ A^{1}N : τούτου εἰ δεῖ A^{a} ἀξιοῦσι N : ἀξιοῦσιν A 98 ὅστις {οὐκ} Sched. Eton., Taylor : ὅστις εἰς Leo : ὅστις αὖ Sykutris : ὁστισοῦν Dobson 101 οὔτ᾽ Turr. : οὐκ AN 102 καταψηφίσαισθε Bekker : καταψηφίσεσθε A^{a}N: καταψηφίσησθε A^{1} ἀποψηφίσαισθε Bekker : ἀποψηφίσησθε AN τινὸς A^{1}N : om. A^{a} 103 καὶ A^{1}N : om. A^{a} 104 ὅσια καὶ δίκαια N^{a}, corr. N^{1sv} 106 ἔλαχον A : ἔλεγχον N 107 post πρὸς τῇ ἐμαυτοῦ vac. spat., deinde πρὸς τῇ ἐμαυτοῦ iterat. punctis del. A^{c} del. Reiske 109 διδασκαλεῖον A^{1} : διδασκάλιον A^{a}N add. Bekker 115 ᾐτούμην Bekker : ἡγούμην AN

12 ἔπεμπον. ἐπεὶ δὲ ἧκον οἱ παῖδες, πρῶτον μέν μοι ἀσχολία
ἦν παρεῖναι καὶ ἐπιμελεῖσθαι· ἐτύγχανε γάρ μοι πράγματα
ὄντα πρὸς Ἀριστίωνα καὶ Φιλῖνον, ἃ ἐγὼ περί πολλοῦ
ἐποιούμην, ἐπειδήπερ εἰσήγγειλα, ὀρθῶς καὶ δικαίως
ἀποδεῖξαι τῇ βουλῇ καὶ τοῖς ἄλλοις Ἀθηναίοις. ἐγὼ
μὲν οὖν τούτοις προσεῖχον τὸν νοῦν, κατέστησα δὲ
ἐπιμελεῖσθαι, εἴ τι δέοι τῷ χορῷ, Φανόστρατον, δημότην
μὲν τουτωνὶ τῶν διωκόντων, κηδεστὴν δ' ἐμαυτοῦ, ᾧ
ἐγὼ δέδωκα τὴν θυγατέρα, καὶ ἠξίουν αὐτὸν ἄριστα
13 ἐπιμελεῖσθαι· ἔτι δὲ πρὸς τούτῳ δύο ἄνδρας, τὸν μὲν
Ἐρεχθῇδος Ἀμεινίαν, ὃν αὐτοὶ οἱ φυλέται ἐψηφίσαντο
συλλέγειν καὶ ἐπιμελεῖσθαι τῆς φυλῆς ἑκάστοτε,
δοκοῦντα χρηστὸν εἶναι, τὸν δ' ἕτερον τῆς Κεκροπίδος,
ὅσπερ ἑκάστοτε εἴωθεν ταύτην τὴν φυλὴν συλλέγειν· ἔτι
δὲ τέταρτον Φίλιππον, ᾧ προσετέτακτο ὠνεῖσθαι καὶ
ἀναλίσκειν εἴ τι φράζοι ὁ διδάσκαλος ἢ ἄλλος τις τούτων,
ὅπως ἄριστα χορηγοῖντο οἱ παῖδες καὶ μηδενὸς ἐνδεεῖς
εἶεν διὰ τὴν ἐμὴν ἀσχολίαν. καθειστήκει μὲν ἡ χορηγία
14 οὕτω. καὶ τούτων εἴ τι ψεύδομαι προφάσεως ἕνεκα,
ἔξεστι τῷ κατηγόρῳ ἐξελέγξαι ἐν τῷ ὑστέρῳ λόγῳ ὅ τι
ἂν βούληται {εἰπεῖν}· ἐπεί τοι οὕτως ἔχει, ὦ ἄνδρες·
πολλοὶ τῶν περιεστώτων τούτων τὰ μὲν πράγματα
ταῦτα πάντα ἀκριβῶς ἐπίστανται, καὶ τοῦ ὁρκωτοῦ
ἀκούουσι, καὶ ἐμοὶ προσέχουσι τὸν νοῦν ἅττα
ἐγὼ ἀποκρίνομαι, οἷς ἐγὼ βουλοίμην ἂν δοκεῖν αὐτός
τε εὔορκος εἶναι καὶ ὑμᾶς τἀληθῆ λέγων πεῖσαι
15 ἀποψηφίσασθαί μου. πρῶτον μὲν οὖν ἀποδείξω ὑμῖν

124 <ὡς> ἄριστα Blass 126 Ἐρεχθῇδος Blass[2] : ἐρεχθηίδος AN Ἀμεινίαν ὃν Jernstedt : ἀμηνιανὸν AN 128 post ἕτερον nomen excidisse aut in ἕτερον latere susp. Turr. 131 τούτων A[1]N : om. ut vid. A[a] 132 <ὡς> ἄριστα Blass 133 καθειστήκει A : καθεστήκει N 134 ἕνεκα, A[1im] N : om. A[a] 135 <καὶ> ὅ τι Thalheim, qui εἰπεῖν l. 136 servavit 136 del. Dobree 140 βουλοίμην Dobree : ἐβουλόμην AN

ὅτι οὔτε ἐκέλευσα πιεῖν τὸν παῖδα τὸ φάρμακον οὔτ' ἠνάγκασα οὔτ' ἔδωκα καὶ οὐδὲ παρῆν ὅτ' ἔπιεν. καὶ οὐ τούτου ἕνεκα ταῦτα σφόδρα λέγω, ὡς ἐμαυτὸν ἔξω αἰτίας καταστήσω, ἕτερον δέ τινα εἰς αἰτίαν ἀγάγω· οὐ δῆτα ἔγωγε, πλήν γε τῆς τύχης, ἥπερ οἶμαι καὶ ἄλλοις πολλοῖς ἀνθρώπων αἰτία ἐστὶν ἀποθανεῖν· ἣν οὔτ' ἂν ἐγὼ οὔτ' ἄλλος οὐδεὶς οἷός τ' ἂν εἴη ἀποστρέψαι μὴ οὐ γενέσθαι ἥντινα δεῖ ἑκάστῳ <. . .>

ΜΑΡΤΥΡΕΣ

Μεμαρτύρηται μὲν οὖν, ὦ ἄνδρες, περὶ τοῦ πράγματος ἃ 16
ἐγὼ ὑμῖν ὑπεσχόμην· ἐξ αὐτῶν δὲ τούτων χρὴ σκοπεῖν
ἅ τε οὗτοι διωμόσαντο καὶ ἃ ἐγώ, πότεροι ἀληθέστερα
καὶ εὐορκότερα. διωμόσαντο δὲ οὗτοι μὲν κτεῖναί με
Διόδοτον βουλεύσαντα τὸν θάνατον, ἐγὼ δὲ μὴ
ἀποκτεῖναι, μήτε χειρὶ ἀράμενος μήτε βουλεύσας.
αἰτιῶνται δὲ οὗτοι μὲν ἐκ τούτων, ὡς οὗτ⟨ος ἔνοχος⟩ ὃς 17
ἐκέλευσε πιεῖν τὸν παῖδα τὸ φάρμακον ἢ ἠνάγκασεν ἢ
ἔδωκεν· ἐγὼ δ' ἐξ αὐτῶν τούτων ὧν αἰτιῶνται οὗτοι
ἀποφανῶ ὅτι οὐκ ἔνοχός εἰμι· οὔτε γὰρ ἐκέλευσα οὔτ'
ἔδωκα οὔτ' ἠνάγκασα· καὶ ἐπιπροστίθημι αὐτοῖς ὅτι οὐ

143 πιεῖν τὸν παῖδα N : τὸν παῖδα πιεῖν A 144 οὐδὲ Reiske : οὔτε AN παρῆν AN : παρῇ Jernstedt ἔπιεν M : ἔπιε AN 146 ἀγάγω A^{sv} : ἀγαγεῖν A^{it} : ἀγάγω ἢ N 149 ἀποστρέψαι] ἀποτρέψαι Dobree 150 lacunam post ἑκάστῳ statuit Blass 154 ἀληθέστερα A^{1}N : ἀληθέστατα A^{a} 155 εὐορκότερα N^{1} : εὐορκώτατα A^{a} : εὐορκώτερα $A^{1}N^{a}$ κτεῖναι re vera AN (cfr. 5.57) : ἀποκτεῖναι L 157 ἀποκτεῖναι A : ἀποκτεῖναί με N ἀράμενος] ἐργασάμενος Dobree 158 ὡς in ras. A^{1} οὗτ<ος ἔνοχος> ὃς Barigazzi (οὗτος <ἔνοχος ὃς> $Fuhr^{1}$) : οὗτος AN : αἴτιος ὃς $Sauppe^{2}$ 159 ἐκέλευσε Baiter : κελεύσειε AN 160 δ' N : δὲ e compendio A 161 ἀποφανῶ A : ἀποφωνῶ N 162 ἔδωκα οὔτ' ἠνάγκασα AN : ἠνάγκασα οὔτ' ἔδωκα Dobree ἐπιπροστίθημι AN : ἔτι προστίθημι Ald. οὐ] οὐδὲ Blass

παρεγενόμην πίνοντι. καὶ εἴ φασιν ἀδικεῖν εἴ τις
ἐκέλευσεν, ἐγὼ οὐκ ἀδικῶ· οὐ γὰρ ἐκέλευσα. καὶ εἴ φασιν
ἀδικεῖν εἴ τις ἠνάγκασεν, ἐγὼ οὐκ ἀδικῶ· οὐ γὰρ
ἠνάγκασα. καὶ εἰ τὸν δόντα τὸ φάρμακόν φασιν αἴτιον
18 εἶναι, ἐγὼ οὐκ αἴτιος· οὐ γὰρ ἔδωκα. αἰτιάσασθαι μὲν οὖν
καὶ καταψεύσασθαι ἔξεστι τῷ βουλομένῳ· αὐτὸς γὰρ
ἕκαστος τούτου κρατεῖ· γενέσθαι μέντοι τὰ μὴ γενόμενα
καὶ ἀδικεῖν τὸν μὴ ἀδικοῦντα οὐκ ἐν τοῖς τούτων λόγοις
ἡγοῦμαι εἶναι, ἀλλ᾽ ἐν τῷ δικαίῳ καὶ τῷ ἀληθεῖ. ὁπόσα
μὲν γὰρ λάθρα πράττεται καὶ ἐπὶ θανάτῳ βουλευθέντα,
ὧν μή εἰσι μάρτυρες, ἀνάγκη περὶ τῶν τοιούτων ἐξ αὐτῶν
τῶν λόγων τῶν τε τοῦ κατηγόρου καὶ τοῦ ἀποκρινομένου
τὴν διάγνωσιν ποιεῖσθαι καὶ θηρεύειν καὶ ἐπὶ σμικρὸν
ὑπονοεῖν τὰ λεγόμενα, καὶ εἰκάζοντας μᾶλλον ἢ σάφα
19 εἰδότας ψηφίζεσθαι περὶ τῶν πραγμάτων· ὅπου δὲ
πρῶτον μὲν αὐτοὶ οἱ κατήγοροι ὁμολογοῦσι μὴ ἐκ προ-
νοίας μηδ᾽ ἐκ παρασκευῆς γενέσθαι τὸν θάνατον τῷ
παιδί, ἔπειτα τὰ πραχθέντα φανερῶς ἅπαντα πραχθῆναι
καὶ ἐναντίον μαρτύρων πολλῶν, καὶ ἀνδρῶν καὶ παίδων,
καὶ ἐλευθέρων καὶ δούλων, ἐξ ὧνπερ καὶ εἴ τίς τι ἠδίκηκε,
φανερώτατος ἂν εἴη, καὶ εἴ τις μὴ ἀδικοῦντα αἰτιῷτο,
μάλιστα ἐξελέγχοιτο.

20 Ἄξιον δ᾽ ἐνθυμηθῆναι, ὦ ἄνδρες, ἀμφότερα καὶ τῆς
γνώμης τῶν ἀντιδίκων καὶ οἵῳ τρόπῳ ἔρχονται ἐπὶ τὰ
πράγματα. ἐξ ἀρχῆς γάρ οὐδὲν ὁμοίως οὗτοί τε πρὸς
21 ἐμὲ πράττουσι καὶ ἐγὼ πρὸς τούτους. ἔλεξε μὲν γὰρ

163 παρεγενόμην] pr. ε in ras. N[1] 164–5 ἐκέλευσεν … τις om. N 171 lacunam post ἀλλ᾽ susp. nonnulli καὶ N : καὶ ἐν A 172 λάθρα AN : λάθρᾳ Blass 174 pr. τοῦ A[1]N : om. A[a] 175 σμικρὸν A, N[1] (ὸν in ras.) : σμικρῶν Dover[2] 176 ὑπονοεῖν A[1]N : νοεῖν A[a] 178 οἱ A[1]N : om. A[a] 182 δούλων A[1]N : παίδων A[a] 183 ἂν A : τ᾽ ἂν N μὴ A[1]N : om. A[a] 184 μάλιστα AN : μάλιστ᾽ ἂν Saupppe

*Φιλοκράτης οὑτοσὶ ἀναβὰς εἰς τὴν ἡλιαίαν τὴν τῶν
θεσμοθετῶν, τῇ ἡμέρᾳ ᾗ ὁ παῖς ἐξεφέρετο, ὅτι ἀδελφὸν
αὐτοῦ ἀποκτείναιμι ἐγὼ ἐν τῷ χορῷ, φάρμακον
ἀναγκάσας πιεῖν. ἐπειδὴ δὲ οὗτος ταῦτα ἔλεγεν, ἀναβὰς
ἐγὼ εἰς τὸ δικαστήριον τοῖς αὐτοῖς δικασταῖς ἔλεξα ὅτι
τὸν μὲν νόμον οὐ δίκαιον {οὐ} προκαθισταίη Φιλοκράτης
κατηγορῶν καὶ διαβάλλων εἰς τὸ δικαστήριον, μελλόντων
ἔσεσθαί μοι ἀγώνων πρὸς Ἀριστίωνα καὶ Φιλῖνον αὔριον
⟨καὶ⟩ τῇ ἕνῃ, ὧνπερ ἕνεκα τοὺς λόγους τούτους λέγοι· ἃ* 22
*μέντοι αἰτιῷτο καὶ διαβάλλοι, ῥᾳδίως ἐξελεγχθήσοιτο
ψευδόμενος. εἶεν γὰρ οἱ συνειδότες πολλοί, καὶ ἐλεύθεροι
καὶ δοῦλοι, καὶ νεώτεροι καὶ πρεσβύτεροι, σύμπαντες
πλείους ἢ πεντήκοντα, οἳ τούς τε λόγους τοὺς λεχθέντας
περὶ τῆς πόσεως τοῦ φαρμάκου καὶ τὰ πραχθέντα καὶ
τὰ λεγόμενα πάντα ἠπίσταντο. καὶ εἶπόν τε ταῦτα ἐν τῷ* 23
*δικαστηρίῳ, καὶ προὐκαλούμην αὐτὸν εὐθὺς τότε, καὶ
αὖθις τῇ ὑστεραίᾳ ἐν τοῖς αὐτοῖς δικασταῖς, καὶ ἰέναι
ἐκέλευον λαβόντα μάρτυρας ὁπόσους βούλοιτο ἐπὶ τοὺς
παραγενομένους, λέγων αὐτῷ ὀνόματι ἕκαστον, τούτους
ἐρωτᾶν καὶ ἐλέγχειν, τοὺς μὲν ἐλευθέρους ὡς χρὴ τοὺς
ἐλευθέρους, οἳ σφῶν ἕνεκα καὶ τοῦ δικαίου ἔφραζον ἂν
τἀληθῆ καὶ τὰ γενόμενα, τοὺς δὲ δούλους, εἰ μὲν αὐτῷ
ἐρωτῶντι τἀληθῆ δοκοῖεν λέγειν, εἰ δὲ μή, ἕτοιμος εἴην*

189 *ἡλιαίαν* Taylor : *ἡλιακὴν* AN   192 *πιεῖν* AN^{c} : *ποιεῖν* N^{a} *ταῦτα* N : *ταῦτ'* A   193 *ἔλεξα* AN^{c} : *ἔλεγξα* N^{a} 194 *δίκαιον* AN : *δικαίως* coni. Maetzner   *οὐ* om. A^{a}, del. Maetzner : habent A^{1}N^{a} : *οὗ* N^{1} : *μου* Thalheim   *προκαθισταίη* Maetzner : *προκαθῆσθαι, εἰ* A : *προκάθισται η* N (*σφάλμα*^{im})   196 *ἔσεσθαί* A et fort. N^{a} : *ἔσεσθέ* N^{1} 197 <*καὶ*> *τῇ* Reiske : *τῇ* AN : *καὶ* Maetzner   *ἕνῃ* Taylor : *ἔννη* A : *ἔνῃ* N   *λέγοι* N : *λέγει* A   199 *εἶεν* ut vid. A^{a} : *εἰσὶ* A^{1} : *εἰ ἓν* N   *οἱ* A^{1}N : *τοι* A^{a} 201 *τούς τε* A^{1}N : *τούτους* A^{a} 203 *λεγόμενα* AN : *λεγόμενα* <*στοιχεῖα*> Vollgraff : *γενόμενα* Reiske   *ἠπίσταντο* AN : *ἐπίσταιντο* vel *ἐπίστανται* Maetzner   209 *σφῶν* <*τ' αὐτῶν*> Sauppe^{1} 211 *ἐρωτῶντι* Ald. : *ἐρωτῶντι διδόναι* AN   *ἕτοιμος εἴην* Taylor : *ἕτοιμος εἶεν* A^{a} : *ἕτοιμός εἰμι* e ras N^{1} : *ἕτοιμοι εἶεν* e ras. A^{c}

διδόναι βασανίζειν τούς τε ἐμαυτοῦ πάντας, καὶ εἴ τινας τῶν ἀλλοτρίων κελεύοι, ὡμολόγουν πείσας τὸν δεσπότην παραδώσειν αὐτῷ βασανίζειν τρόπῳ ὁποίῳ βούλοιτο.
24 *καὶ ταῦτα ἐμοῦ προκαλουμένου καὶ λέγοντος ἐν τῷ δικαστηρίῳ, οὗ καὶ αὐτοὶ οἱ δικασταὶ καὶ ἕτεροι ἰδιῶται πολλοὶ μάρτυρες παρῆσαν, οὔτε τότε παραχρῆμα οὔτε ὕστερον ἐν παντὶ τῷ χρόνῳ οὐδεπώποτε ἠθέλησαν ἐλθεῖν ἐπὶ τοῦτο τὸ δίκαιον, εὖ εἰδότες ὅτι οὐκ ἂν τούτοις κατ' ἐμοῦ ἔλεγχος ἐγίγνετο οὗτος, ἀλλ' ἐμοὶ κατὰ τούτων, ὅτι*
25 *οὐδὲν δίκαιον οὐδ' ἀληθὲς ᾐτιῶντο. ἐπίστασθε δέ, ὦ ἄνδρες, ὅτι αἱ ἀνάγκαι αὗται ἰσχυρόταται καὶ μέγισταί εἰσι τῶν ἐν ἀνθρώποις, καὶ ἔλεγχοι ἐκ τούτων σαφέστατοι καὶ πιστότατοι περὶ τοῦ δικαίου, ὅπου εἶεν μὲν ἐλεύθεροι πολλοὶ οἱ συνειδότες, εἶεν δὲ δοῦλοι, καὶ ἐξείη μὲν τοὺς ἐλευθέρους ὅρκοις καὶ πίστεσιν ἀναγκάζειν, ἃ τοῖς ἐλευθέροις μέγιστα καὶ περὶ πλείστου ἐστίν, ἐξείη δὲ τοὺς δούλους ἑτέραις ἀνάγκαις, ὑφ' ὧν καὶ ἢν μέλλωσιν ἀποθανεῖσθαι κατειπόντες, ὅμως ἀναγκάζονται τἀληθῆ λέγειν· ἡ γὰρ παροῦσα ἀνάγκη ἑκάστῳ ἰσχυροτέρα ἐστὶ*
26 *τῆς μελλούσης ἔσεσθαι. εἰς πάντα τοίνυν ἐγὼ ταῦτα προὐκαλεσάμην τούτους, καὶ ἐξ ὧν γε χρὴ ἄνθρωπον ὄντα τἀληθῆ καὶ τὰ δίκαια πυνθάνεσθαι, ἐξῆν αὐτοῖς πυνθάνεσθαι, καὶ πρόφασις οὐδεμία ὑπελείπετο. καὶ ἐγὼ μὲν ὁ τὴν αἰτίαν ἔχων καὶ ἀδικῶν, ὡς οὗτοί φασιν, ἕτοιμος ἦν αὐτοῖς κατ' ἐμαυτοῦ παρέχειν ἔλεγχον τὸν δικαιότατον·*

213 *κελεύοι* Bekker : *κελεύει* AN 217 *παρῆσαν*] *παρ* in ras N[1] 218 *τῷ* AN[1] : om. N[a] 221 *ἐπίστασθε* A[1]N : *ἐπίστασθαι* A[a] 222 *ἰσχυρόταται* A : *ἰσχυρότατοι* N 224 *μὲν ἐλεύθεροι* N : *ἐλεύθεροι μὲν* A 225 *ἐξείη μὲν τοὺς* A[1] (qui primo *τοῖς* scripserat), N : *ἐξείη μέντοι* A[a] 226 *ἐλευθέρους* A[c]N : *ἐλευθέροις* A[a] 227 *ἐξείη δὲ* A[3]N[c] : *ἐξείημεν δὲ* A[a]N[a] 228 *ἢν* A[1]N : *ἣν* A[a] : *ἐὰν* Thalheim *μέλλωσιν* A[1]N : *μέλλουσιν* A[a] 231 *πάντα* Blass : *πᾶν* AN 232 *γε* Ald. : *σε* AN 233–4 *οἷς πυνθάνεσθαι καὶ προ* rescr. A[1] (*πυνθάνεσθαι* om. A[a]) 236 *ἦν*] *ᾗ* Jernstedt

οἱ δ᾽ αἰτιώμενοι καὶ φάσκοντες ἀδικεῖσθαι αὐτοὶ ἦσαν οἱ
οὐκ ἐθέλοντες ἐλέγχειν εἴ τι ἠδικοῦντο. καὶ εἰ μὲν ἐγὼ 27
τούτων προκαλουμένων μὴ ἠθέλησα τοὺς παραγενομέ-
νους ἀποφῆναι, ⟨ἢ⟩ θεράποντας ἐξαιτοῦσι μὴ ἤθελον
ἐκδιδόναι, ἢ ἄλλην τινὰ πρόκλησιν ἔφευγον, αὐτὰ ἂν
ταῦτα μέγιστα τεκμήρια κατ᾽ ἐμοῦ ἐποιοῦντο ὅτι ἀληθὴς
ἦν ἡ αἰτία· ἐπεὶ δ᾽ ἐμοῦ προκαλουμένου οὗτοι ἦσαν οἱ
φεύγοντες τὸν ἔλεγχον, ἐμοὶ δήπου δίκαιον κατὰ τούτων
τὸ αὐτὸ τοῦτο τεκμήριον γενέσθαι, ὅτι οὐκ ἀληθὴς ἦν
ἡ αἰτία ἣν αἰτιῶνται κατ᾽ ἐμοῦ. ἐπίσταμαι δὲ καὶ 28
τάδε, ὦ ἄνδρες, ὅτι εἰ μὲν τούτοις ἐμοῦ κατεμαρτύρουν
οἱ μάρτυρες οἱ παραγενόμενοι, αὐτοῖς ἂν τούτοις
ἰσχυροτάτοις ἐχρῶντο καὶ πίστιν ταύτην σαφεστάτην
ἀπέφαινον, τοὺς μάρτυρας τοὺς καταμαρτυροῦντας· τῶν
αὐτῶν δὲ τούτων μαρτυρούντων, ἃ μὲν ἐγὼ λέγω, ἀληθῆ
εἶναι, ἃ δὲ οὗτοι λέγουσιν, οὐκ ἀληθῆ, τοῖς μὲν μάρτυσι
τοῖς μαρτυροῦσιν ἀπιστεῖν ὑμᾶς διδάσκουσι, τοῖς δὲ
λόγοις οἷς αὐτοὶ λέγουσι πιστεύειν ὑμᾶς φασι χρῆναι, οὓς
ἐγὼ εἰ ἔλεγον ἄνευ μαρτύρων, ψευδεῖς ἂν κατηγόρουν
εἶναι. καίτοι δεινὸν εἰ οἱ αὐτοὶ μάρτυρες τούτοις μὲν ἂν 29
μαρτυροῦντες πιστοὶ ἦσαν, ἐμοὶ δὲ μαρτυροῦντες ἄπιστοι
ἔσονται. καὶ εἰ μὲν πάνυ μὴ παρεγένοντο μάρτυρες, ἐγὼ
δὲ παρειχόμην, ἢ τοὺς παραγενομένους μὴ παρειχόμην,
ἑτέρους δέ τινας, εἰκότως ἂν οἱ τούτων λόγοι πιστότεροι
ἦσαν τῶν ἐμῶν μαρτύρων· ὅπου δὲ μάρτυράς τε ὁμολογοῦσι
παραγενέσθαι, καὶ ἐγὼ τοὺς παραγενομένους παρέχομαι,

240 ἀποφῆναι A[1]N : ἀποφήνασθαι A[a] <ἢ> add. Bekker : post θεράποντας posuit N[1] 241 ἔφευγον A[1]N[2] : ἔφευγεν A[a]N 243 ἡ N : om. A 245 ἦν del. censuit Jernstedt[1] 246 ἣν A : ἢν N 246–8 ἐπίσταμαι ... μάρτυρες cfr. 5.84 251 μαρτυρούντων A[a] : καταμαρτυρούντων A[1]N 253 pr. τοῖς <ἐμοὶ> Reiske 256 μάρτυρες τούτοις μὲν N : μὲν μάρτυρες τούτοις A 259 alt. παρειχόμην Steph. : παρεσχόμην re vera A (cfr. παρεσχόμεθα Tetr. A.α.9, f. 101r), N

⟨καὶ⟩ εὐθὺς ἀπὸ τῆς πρώτης ἡμέρας καὶ αὐτὸς ἐγὼ καὶ οἱ
μάρτυρες ἅπαντες φανεροί ἐσμεν λέγοντες ἅπερ νυνὶ πρὸς
ὑμᾶς, πόθεν χρή, ὦ ἄνδρες, ἢ τἀληθῆ πιστὰ ἢ τὰ μὴ
30 ἀληθῆ ἄπιστα ποιεῖν ἄλλοθεν ἢ ἐκ τῶν τοιούτων; ὅπου
μὲν γὰρ λόγῳ τις διδάσκοι περὶ τῶν πραχθέντων,
μάρτυρας δὲ μὴ παρέχοιτο, μαρτύρων ἄν τις τοὺς λόγους
τούτους ἐνδεεῖς φαίη εἶναι· ὅπου δὲ μάρτυρας μὲν
παρέχοιτο, τεκμήρια δὲ αὖ τοῖς μαρτυροῦσιν ὅμοια μὴ
ἀποφαίνοιτο, ταὐτὰ ἄν τις ἔχοι εἰπεῖν, εἰ βούλοιτο.
31 ἐγὼ τοίνυν τούς τε λόγους ὑμῖν εἰκότας ἀποφαίνω, καὶ
τοῖς λόγοις τοὺς μάρτυρας ὁμολογοῦντας καὶ τοῖς
μάρτυσι τὰ ἔργα, καὶ τεκμήρια ἐξ αὐτῶν τῶν ἔργων, καὶ
ἔτι πρὸς τούτοις δύο τὼ μεγίστω καὶ ἰσχυροτάτω,
τούτους μὲν αὐτούς τε ὑπὸ σφῶν αὐτῶν ἐξελεγχομένους
καὶ ὑπ' ἐμοῦ, ἐμὲ δὲ ὑπό τε τούτων καὶ ὑπὸ ἐμαυτοῦ
32 ἀπολυόμενον· ὅπου γὰρ ἐμοῦ ἐθέλοντος ἐλέγχεσθαι περὶ
ὧν ᾐτιῶντο οὗτοι μὴ ἤθελον ἐλέγχειν, ἠδίκουν, καὶ ἐμὲ
μὲν δήπου ἀπέλυον, αὐτοὶ δὲ κατὰ σφῶν αὐτῶν μάρτυρες
ἐγένοντο, ὅτι οὐδὲν δίκαιον οὐδ' ἀληθὲς ᾐτιῶντο. καίτοι
εἰ πρὸς τοῖς ἐμαυτοῦ μάρτυσι τοὺς ἀντιδίκους αὐτοὺς
μάρτυρας παρέχομαι, ποῖ ἔτι ἐλθόντα δεῖ ἢ πόθεν
ἀποδείξαντα τῆς αἰτίας ἀπολελύσθαι;
33 Ἡγοῦμαι μὲν οὖν καὶ ἐκ τῶν εἰρημένων καὶ
ἀποδεδειγμένων, ὦ ἄνδρες, δικαίως ἄν μου
ἀποψηφίσασθαι ὑμᾶς, καὶ ἐπίστασθαι ἅπαντας ὅτι

263 add. Reiske τῆς A^{1}N : om. A^a 264 ἅπαντες N : πάντες A 267 διδάσκοι A^{a}N^1 (ο in ras.) : διδάσκει A^1, fort. N^a 268 παρέχοιτο N^c : παρέχοιντο AN^a 270 αὖ τοῖς Reiske : αὐτοῖς AN : αὐτοῖς τοῖς Redondo i Sànchez^1 271 ἀποφαίνοιτο N : ἀποφαίνοιντο A : ἀποφαίνοι Reiske (in indice graecitatis) ταὐτὰ Reiske : ταῦτα AN : τοιαῦτα Blass^2 275 δύο N : δύω A 278 ἐμοῦ ἐθέλοντος ἐλέγχεσθαι N : ἐθέλοντος ἐλέγχεσθαι ἐμοῦ A 279–81 οὗτοι ... ᾐτιῶντο om. N 279 ἠδίκουν καὶ A : <εἴ τι> ἠδικοῦντο Blass : <εἴ τι> ἀδικοῦνται Barigazzi

οὐδέν μοι προσήκει τῆς αἰτίας ταύτης. ἵνα δ' ἔτι καὶ
ἄμεινον μάθητε, τούτου ἕνεκα πλείω λέξω, καὶ ἀποδείξω
ὑμῖν τοὺς κατηγόρους τούτους ἐπιορκοτάτους ὄντας καὶ
ἀσεβεστάτους ἀνθρώπων, καὶ ἀξίους οὐ μόνον ὑπ' ἐμοῦ
μισεῖσθαι, ἀλλὰ καὶ ὑφ' ὑμῶν πάντων καὶ τῶν ἄλλων
πολιτῶν τῆς δίκης ἕνεκα ταυτησί. οὗτοι γὰρ τῇ μὲν 34
πρώτῃ ἡμέρᾳ ᾗ ἀπέθανεν ὁ παῖς, καὶ τῇ ὑστεραίᾳ ᾗ
προέκειτο, οὐδ' αὐτοὶ ἠξίουν αἰτιᾶσθαι ἐμὲ οὐδ' ἀδικεῖν
ἐν τῷ πράγματι τούτῳ οὐδέν, ἀλλὰ συνῆσαν ἐμοὶ καὶ
διελέγοντο· τῇ δὲ τρίτῃ ἡμέρᾳ ᾗ ἐξεφέρετο ὁ παῖς, ταύτῃ
δὴ πεπεισμένοι ἦσαν {τινες} ὑπὸ τῶν ἐχθρῶν τῶν
ἐμῶν, καὶ παρεσκευάζοντο αἰτιᾶσθαι καὶ προαγορεύειν
εἴργεσθαι τῶν νομίμων. τίνες οὖν ἦσαν οἱ πείσαντες
αὐτούς; καὶ τίνος ἕνεκα καὶ πρόθυμοι ἐγένοντο πεῖσαι
αὐτούς; δεῖ γάρ με καὶ ταῦτα ὑμᾶς διδάξαι. κατηγορήσειν 35
ἔμελλον Ἀριστίωνος καὶ Φιλίνου καὶ Ἀμπελίνου καὶ
τοῦ ὑπογραμματέως τῶν θεσμοθετῶν, μεθ' οὗπερ
συνέκλεπτον, περὶ ὧν εἰσήγγειλα εἰς τὴν βουλήν. καὶ
αὐτοῖς ἐκ μὲν τῶν πεπραγμένων οὐδεμία ἦν ἐλπὶς
ἀποφεύξεσθαι—τοιαῦτα ἄρ' ἦν τὰ ἠδικημένα· πείσαντες
δὲ τούτους ἀπογράφεσθαι καὶ προαγορεύειν ἐμοὶ
εἴργεσθαι τῶν νομίμων, ἡγήσαντο ταύτην σφίσιν ἔσεσθαι
σωτηρίαν καὶ ἀπαλλαγὴν τῶν πραγμάτων ἁπάντων.
ὁ γὰρ νόμος οὕτως ἔχει, ἐπειδάν τις ἀπογραφῇ φόνου 36
δίκην, εἴργεσθαι τῶν νομίμων· καὶ οὔτ' ἂν ἐγὼ οἷός τ'
ἦν ἐπεξελθεῖν εἰργόμενος τῶν νομίμων, ἐκεῖνοί τε ἐμοῦ

294 ὑστεραίᾳ A : ὑστέρᾳ N   295 οὐδ' del. Wilamowitz[2]   297 ταύτῃ N : ταυτὶ A   298 del. Dobree   300 εἴργεσθαι N : εἵργεσθαι A   302 αὐτούς del. Reiske   306 αὐτοῖς post ἦν punctis del. A[1]   307 ἄρ'] γὰρ maluit Baiter   309 εἴργεσθαι N : εἵργεσθαι A   311 ἐπειδάν A : ἐπειδ' ἂν N   312 εἴργεσθαι N : εἵργεσθαι A   313 ἦν] ᾖ Jernstedt   εἰργόμενος N : εἱργόμενος A   ἐκεῖνοί] οι in ras. N[2]   τε A[1]N : om. A[a]

τοῦ εἰσαγγείλαντος καὶ ἐπισταμένου τὰ πράγματα μὴ
ἐπεξιόντος ῥᾳδίως ἔμελλον ἀποφεύξεσθαι καὶ δίκην οὐ
δώσειν ὑμῖν ὧν ἠδίκησαν· καὶ τοῦτο οὐκ ἐπ' ἐμοὶ πρῶτον
ἐμηχανήσαντο Φιλῖνος καὶ οἱ ἕτεροι, ἀλλὰ καὶ ἐπὶ
37 Λυσιστράτῳ πρότερον, ὡς αὐτοὶ ὑμεῖς ἠκούσατε. καὶ
οὗτοι τότε μὲν πρόθυμοι ἦσαν ἀπογράφεσθαί με εὐθὺς
τῇ ὑστεραίᾳ ᾗ ὁ παῖς ἐθάπτετο, πρὶν τὴν οἰκίαν καθῆραι
καὶ τὰ νομιζόμενα ποιῆσαι, αὐτὴν ταύτην φυλάξαντες
τὴν ἡμέραν ἐν ᾗ ἔμελλεν ὁ πρῶτος ἐκείνων κριθήσεσθαι,
ὅπως μηδὲ καθ' ἑνὸς αὐτῶν οἷός τε γενοίμην ἐπεξελθεῖν
38 μηδ' ἐνδεῖξαι τῷ δικαστηρίῳ τἀδικήματα· ἐπειδὴ δὲ
αὐτοῖς ὁ βασιλεὺς τούς τε νόμους ἀνέγνω, καὶ χρόνους
ἐπέδειξεν ὅτι οὐκ ἐγχωροίη ἀπογράψασθαι καὶ τὰς
κλήσεις καλεῖσθαι ὅσας ἔδει, καὶ ἐγὼ τοὺς ταῦτα
μηχανωμένους εἰσάγων εἰς τὸ δικαστήριον εἷλον
ἅπαντας, καὶ ἐτιμήθη αὐτοῖς ὧν ὑμεῖς ἐπίστασθε, καὶ
οὗτοι ὧν ἕνεκα ἐλάμβανον χρήματα οὐδὲν αὐτοῖς οἷοί τε
ἦσαν ὠφελῆσαι, τότε δὴ προσιόντες αὐτῷ τ' ἐμοὶ καὶ
τοῖς φίλοις ἐδέοντο διαλλαγῆναι, καὶ δίκην ἕτοιμοι
39 ἦσαν διδόναι τῶν ἡμαρτημένων. καὶ ἐγὼ πεισθεὶς ὑπὸ
τῶν φίλων διηλλάγην τούτοις ἐν Διπολιείοις ἐναντίον
μαρτύρων, οἵπερ διήλλαττον ἡμᾶς πρὸς τῷ νεῴ τῆς
Ἀθηνᾶς· καὶ μετὰ τοῦτο συνῆσάν μοι καὶ διελέγοντο ἐν
τοῖς ἱεροῖς, ἐν τῇ ἀγορᾷ, ἐν τῇ ἐμῇ οἰκίᾳ, ἐν τῇ σφετέρᾳ

39 *Διιπολείοις* Harp. δ 63 s.v. *Διιπόλεια*

---

316 *ὑμῖν* A^1N : *ἐμοὶ* A^a *τοῦτο* A : *τοῦτ'* N *πρῶτον* A^1, N^1 (o in ras.) : *μόνον* A^a 319 *τότε μὲν πρόθυμοι* N : *μὲν πρόθυμοι τότε* A 320 *καθῆραι* Sauppe : *καθᾶραι* N : *καθάραι* A 323 *γενοίμην* A^1N : *ἐγενόμην* A^a 324 *τἀδικήματα* N : *τὰ ἀδικήματα* A 325 *αὐτοῖς* A^{1im} : om. A^a : *αὐτὸς* N^2 (quid N scripserit non liquet) *τούς τε* A^1N : *τούτους* A^a *χρόνους* AN : *χρόνον* Steph. : *τὸν χρόνον* mal. Maetzner 326 *ἐπέδειξεν ὅτι* Dobree : *ἐπέδειξε, τί* re vera A^1, N : *ἀπέδειξε, τί* A^a 334 *Διπολιείοις* scripsi auctore Scheibio (coll. Harp et cfr. 2.δ.8) : *τῇ πόλει* AN : *τῇ πόλει Διιπολείοις* Vollgraff 337 *οἰκίᾳ ἐν* A : *οἰκίᾳ καὶ ἐν* N

αὐτῶν καὶ ἑτέρωθι πανταχοῦ. τὸ τελευταῖον, ὦ Ζεῦ 40 καὶ θεοὶ πάντες, Φιλοκράτης αὐτὸς οὑτοσὶ ἐν τῷ βουλευτηρίῳ ἐναντίον τῆς βουλῆς, ἑστὼς μετ' ἐμοῦ ἐπὶ τοῦ βήματος, ἁπτόμενος ἐμοῦ διελέγετο, ὀνόματι οὗτος ἐμὲ προσαγορεύων, καὶ ἐγὼ τοῦτον, ὥστε δεινὸν δόξαι εἶναι τῇ βουλῇ, ἐπειδὴ ἐπύθετο προειρημένον μοι εἴργεσθαι τῶν νομίμων ὑπὸ τούτων, οὓς ἑώρων μοι τῇ προτεραίᾳ συνόντας καὶ διαλεγομένους. σκέψασθε δὲ 41 καί μοι μνήσθητε, ὦ ἄνδρες· ταῦτα γὰρ οὐ μόνον μάρτυσιν ὑμῖν ἀποδείξω, ἀλλὰ καὶ ἐξ αὐτῶν τῶν ἔργων ἃ τούτοις πέπρακται ῥᾳδίως γνώσεσθε ὅτι ἀληθῆ λέγω. καὶ πρῶτον ἃ τοῦ βασιλέως κατηγοροῦσι καὶ διὰ τὴν ἐμὴν σπουδὴν οὔ φασιν ἐθέλειν αὐτὸν ἀπογράφεσθαι τὴν δίκην, τοῦτο δὲ κατ' αὐτῶν τούτων ἔσται τεκμήριον ὅτι οὐκ ἀληθῆ λέγουσιν. ἔδει μὲν γὰρ τὸν βασιλέα, 42 ἐπειδὴ ἀπεγράψατο, τρεῖς προδικασίας ποιῆσαι ἐν τρισὶ μησί, τὴν δίκην δ' εἰσάγειν τετάρτῳ μηνί, ὥσπερ νυνί· τῆς δ' ἀρχῆς αὐτῷ λοιποὶ δύο μῆνες ἦσαν, Θαργηλιὼν καὶ Σκιροφοριών. καὶ οὔτ' εἰσάγειν δήπου οἷός τ' ἂν ἦν ἐφ' ἑαυτοῦ, οὔτε παραδοῦναι φόνου δίκην ἔξεστιν, οὐδὲ παρέδωκεν οὐδεὶς πώποτε βασιλεὺς ἐν τῇ γῇ ταύτῃ. ἥντινα οὖν μήτε εἰσάγειν μήτε παραδοῦναι ἐξῆν αὐτῷ, οὐδ' ἀπογράφεσθαι ἠξίου παρὰ τοὺς ὑμετέρους νόμους. καὶ ὅτι οὐκ ἀδικεῖ αὐτούς, μέγιστον σημεῖον· 43

42 προδικασίας stp Pollux 8.24

338 αὐτῶν A[a] : αὑτῶν A[1] : ἑαυτῶν N ἑτέρωθι N : ἑτέροθι A 341 οὗτος N : ὁ τοιοῦτος A 343–4 μοι εἴργεσθαι N : μοι post ἐπειδὴ A[a], post εἴργεσθαι (sic) A[1] 344 ἑώρων N : ἑώρα A 345 προτεραίᾳ Turr. : προτέρᾳ N : προτέρα A 349 πρῶτον <μὲν> Dobree 350 φασὶν A[1]N : φασὶ A[a] ἐθέλειν αὐτὸν N : αὐτον ἐθέλειν A 351 δὲ] δὴ maluit Baiter 352 λέγουσιν A : λέγουσι N 353 προδικασίας A[a] Pollux : προδιαδικασίας A[1]N 354 δ' AN[1] : δὲ N[a] 355 θαργηλιὼν N : γαρθηλιὼν A 356 ἦν A[1] N : om. A[a] 357 οὔτε Reiske : οὐδὲ AN δίκην N : om. A 361 ἀδικεῖ AN : ἠδίκει Reiske

Φιλοκράτης γὰρ οὑτοσὶ ἑτέρους τῶν ὑπευθύνων ἔσειε
καὶ ἐσυκοφάντει, τούτου δὲ τοῦ βασιλέως, ὅν φασι δεινὰ
καὶ σχέτλια εἰργάσθαι, οὐκ ἦλθε κατηγορήσων εἰς τὰς
εὐθύνας. καίτοι τί ἂν ὑμῖν τούτου μεῖζον τεκμήριον
ἀποδείξαιμι, ὅτι οὐκ ἠδικεῖτο οὔθ' ὑπ' ἐμοῦ οὔθ'
44 *ὑπ' ἐκείνου; ἐπειδὴ γὰρ οὑτοσὶ ὁ βασιλεὺς εἰσῆλθεν,*
ἐξὸν αὐτοῖς ἀπὸ τῆς πρώτης ἡμέρας ἀρξαμένοις
τοῦ Ἑκατομβαιῶνος μηνὸς τριάκονθ' ἡμέρας συνεχῶς
τούτων ᾗ τινι ἐβούλοντο ἀπογράφεσθαι, ἀπεγράφοντο
οὐδεμιᾷ· καὶ αὖθις τοῦ Μεταγειτνιῶνος μηνὸς ἀπὸ τῆς
πρώτης ἡμέρας ἀρξαμένοις ἐξὸν αὐτοῖς ἀπογράφεσθαι
ᾗ τινι ἐβούλοντο, οὐδ' αὖ πω ἐνταῦθα ἀπεγράψαντο,
ἀλλὰ παρεῖσαν καὶ τούτου τοῦ μηνὸς εἴκοσιν ἡμέρας·
ὥστε αἱ σύμπασαι ἡμέραι ἐγένοντο αὐτοῖς πλέον ἢ
πεντήκοντα ἐπὶ τούτου τοῦ βασιλέως, ἐν αἷς ἐξὸν αὐτοῖς
45 *ἀπογράψασθαι οὐκ ἀπεγράψαντο. καὶ οἱ μὲν ἄλλοι*
ἅπαντες ὅσοις ἐπὶ τοῦ αὐτοῦ βασιλέως ὁ χρόνος μὴ
ἐγχωρεῖ <. . .>, οὗτοι δ' ἐπιστάμενοι μὲν τοὺς νόμους
ἅπαντας, ὁρῶντες δ' ἐμὲ βουλεύοντα καὶ εἰσιόντ' εἰς τὸ
βουλευτήριον—καὶ ἐν αὐτῷ τῷ βουλευτηρίῳ Διὸς
βουλαίου καὶ Ἀθηνᾶς βουλαίας ἱερόν ἐστι, καὶ εἰσιόντες
οἱ βουλευταὶ προσεύχονται, ὧν κἀγὼ εἷς ἦν, ὁ ταῦτα
πράττων, καὶ εἰς τἆλλα ἱερὰ πάντα εἰσιὼν μετὰ τῆς

365 *τούτου μεῖζον* N : *μεῖζον τούτου* A 367 *γὰρ* AN : *δὲ* Gebauer^2 368 *ἀρξαμένοις* A^{1}N : *ἀρξαμένους* A^a 369 *ἡμέρας* B : *ἡμέραι* AN *συνεχῶς* L : *ὁ συνεχῶς* AN 373 *ᾗτινι* L : *τινι* AN *αὖ πω* Blass^2 : *αὐτῷ* AN : *αὖ* Bekker 374 *παρεῖσαν* N : *παρῆσαν* A *εἴκοσιν* (sc. *κ'*) in *κα'* vel sim. mutare voluit Vollgraff auctore Keilio : pro *πεντήκοντα*, l. 376, Maetzner *τριάκοντα* coniecerat (sc. *λ'* pro *ν'*) : aliter alii *ἡμέρας* Ald. : *ἡμέραι* A^a : *ἡμέραις* A^{1}N 375 *πλέον ἢ* AN : *πλέαι* ten Berge 378 *ὅσοις* A^1 (alt. *σ* e ras.) : *ὅσοι* N *ὁ χρόνος μὴ* in ras. A^1 379 *ἐγχωρεῖ* Dobree : *ἐνεχώρει* A : *ἐχώρει* N post *ἐγχωρεῖ* lacunam indicavit Dobree 380 *δ' ἐμὲ* Bekker : *δέ με* AN *εἰς* N : *ἐς* A 383 *ἦν*] *ᾖ* Jernstedt *ὁ* AN : *ὃς* Blass^2 : *καὶ* Sauppe 384 *τἆλλα* Bekker : *τἄλλα* AN *ἱερὰ πάντα* N : *πάντα ἱερὰ* A

*βουλῆς, καὶ θύων καὶ εὐχόμενος ὑπὲρ τῆς πόλεως
ταύτης, καὶ πρὸς τούτοις πρυτανεύσας τὴν πρώτην
πρυτανείαν ἅπασαν πλὴν δυοῖν ἡμέραιν, καὶ ἱεροποιῶν
καὶ θύων ὑπὲρ τῆς δημοκρατίας, καὶ ἐπιψηφίζων
καὶ λέγων γνώμας περὶ τῶν μεγίστων καὶ πλείστου
ἀξίων τῇ πόλει φανερὸς ἦν· καὶ οὗτοι παρόντες καὶ* 46
*ἐπιδημοῦντες, ἐξὸν αὐτοῖς ἀπογράφεσθαι καὶ εἴργειν ἐμὲ
τούτων ἁπάντων, οὐκ ἠξίουν ἀπογράφεσθαι· καὶ ἱκανά
γ' ἦν ὑπομνῆσαι καὶ ἐνθυμηθῆναι, εἴπερ ἠδικοῦντο,
ἀμφότερα καὶ σφῶν αὐτῶν ἕνεκα καὶ τῆς πόλεως. διὰ τί
οὖν οὐκ ἀπεγράφοντο; διὰ τί συνῆσαν καὶ διελέγοντο;
συνῆσάν τε γάρ μοι οὐκ ἀξιοῦντες φονέα εἶναι, καὶ οὐκ
ἀπεγράφοντο τούτου αὐτοῦ ἕνεκα, οὐχ ἡγούμενοί με
ἀποκτεῖναι τὸν παῖδα οὐδ' ἔνοχον εἶναι τοῦ φόνου οὐδὲ
προσήκειν μοι τούτου τοῦ πράγματος οὐδέν. καίτοι πῶς* 47
*ἂν ἄνθρωποι σχετλιώτεροι ἢ ἀνομώτεροι γένοιντο;
οἵτινες ἅπερ αὐτοὶ σφᾶς αὐτοὺς οὐκ ἔπεισαν, ταῦτα
ὑμᾶς ἀξιοῦσι πεῖσαι, καὶ ἃ αὐτοὶ ἔργῳ ἀπεδίκασαν,
ταῦτα ὑμᾶς κελεύουσι καταδικάσαι· καὶ οἱ μὲν ἄλλοι
ἄνθρωποι τοῖς ἔργοις τοὺς λόγους ἐξελέγχουσιν, οὗτοι
δὲ τοῖς λόγοις ζητοῦσι τὰ ἔργα ἄπιστα καταστῆσαι.
καίτοι εἰ μηδὲν ἄλλο μήτε εἶπον μήτε ἀπέφηνα μήτε* 48
μάρτυρας παρεσχόμην, ἀλλὰ ταῦτα ὑμῖν ἀπέδειξα,

386 *πρώτην*] *δευτέραν* ci. Vollgraff (sc. II) 390 *ἀξίων* A : *ἀξιῶν* N *ἦν*] *ᾖ* Jernstedt 391 *ἐξὸν* N : *ἐξ ὧν* A *φεσθαι* ... 392 *καὶ* in rasura spatio longiore N^{1} (haec verba geminasse vid. N^{a}) 391 *εἴργειν* N^{1} : *εἵργειν* A 392 *καὶ* AN^{1} : *καίτοι* Reiske 394 *αὐτῶν* A^{1im} N^{1} (*ν* e ras.) : om. A^{a} 394–5 *διὰ τί οὖν οὐκ ἀπεγράφοντο* Reiske : *διὰ τί; ὅπου κατεγράφοντο* AN 395 *διὰ τί* AN : *δι' ὅ τι* Dobree *συνῆσαν* Reiske : *συνήεσαν* AN 400 *γένοιντο;* sic distinxit N : *γένοιντο*, sic A 401 *αὐτοὺς* A^{1} N : om. A^{a} 403 *καταδικάσαι* A^{it} : *καταδικάσειν* A^{sv}N 405 *ἄπιστα* Reiske : *πιστὰ* AN 406 *εἰ* AN^{2} : *οἱ* N 407 *ταῦτα* AN : <*αὐτὰ*> *ταῦτα* Blass : *ταῦτα* <*μόνον*> Reiske

τούτους ὅπου μὲν χρήματα λαμβάνοιεν ἐπ᾽ ἐμοί, αἰτιωμένους καὶ προαγορεύοντας, ὅπου δὲ μὴ εἴη ὁ δώσων, συνόντας καὶ διαλεγομένους, ἱκανὰ ἦν καὶ αὐτὰ ταῦτα ἀκούσαντας ἀποψηφίσασθαι καὶ τούτους νομίζειν ἐπιορκοτάτους καὶ ἀνοσιωτάτους πάντων
49 ἀνθρώπων. οὗτοι γὰρ ποίαν δίκην οὐ δικάσαιντ᾽ ἂν ἢ ποῖον δικαστήριον οὐκ ἐξαπατήσειαν ἢ τίνας ὅρκους οὐκ ἂν τολμήσειαν παραβαίνειν; οἵτινες καὶ νῦν τριάκοντα μνᾶς ἐπ᾽ ἐμοὶ λαβόντες παρὰ τῶν ποριστῶν καὶ τῶν πωλητῶν καὶ τῶν πρακτόρων καὶ τῶν ὑπογραμματέων οἳ τούτοις ὑπεγραμμάτευον, ἐξελάσαντές με ἐκ τοῦ βουλευτηρίου, ὅρκους τοιούτους διωμόσαντο, ὅτι πρυτανεύων πυθόμενος αὐτοὺς δεινὰ καὶ σχέτλια ἐργάζεσθαι εἰσῆγον εἰς τὴν βουλήν, καὶ ἐδίδαξα ὡς χρὴ
50 ζητοῦντας ἐπεξελθεῖν τῷ πράγματι. καὶ νῦν δίκην διδόασιν ὧν ἠδικήκασιν αὐτοί τε καὶ οἱ μεσεγγυησάμενοι, καὶ παρ᾽ οἷς ἐτέθη τὰ χρήματα, καὶ τὰ πραχθέντα φανερὰ γεγένηται, ὥστ᾽ οὐδ᾽ ἂν οὗτοι βούλωνται ἀρνεῖσθαι ῥᾳδίως οἷοί τ᾽ ἔσονται· οὕτως αὐτοῖς πέπρακται
51 τὰ πράγματα. ποῖον οὖν δικαστήριον οὐκ ἂν ἔλθοιεν ἐξαπατήσοντες, ἢ τίνας ὅρκους οὐκ ἂν τολμήσαιεν παραβαίνειν οὗτοι οἱ ἀνοσιώτατοι; οἵτινες καὶ ὑμᾶς εἰδότες εὐσεβεστάτους τῶν Ἑλλήνων δικαστὰς καὶ δικαιοτάτους καὶ ἐφ᾽ ὑμᾶς ἥκουσιν ἐξαπατήσοντες εἰ δύναιντο, ὅρκους τοιούτους διομοσάμενοι.

408 τούτους Ald. : τούτοις AN 410 <ἂν> ἦν Dobree 412 ἐπιορκοτάτους A^{1}N : ἐπιορκωτάτους A^{a} 417 πωλητῶν Reiske : πολιτῶν AN 418 τούτοις ὑπεγραμμάτευον A^{1} N : τούτους ἐγραμμάτευον ut vid. A^{a} 419 διωμόσαντο Reiske : διομόσαντος AN^{1} : διωμόσαντος N^{a} : διομόσαντες N^{2} 422 πράγματι N : πράμματι A^{1} : γράμματι ut vid. A 423–4 μεσεγγυησάμενοι A^{1} N : μετεγγυησάμενοι A^{a} 428 τολμήσαιεν AN : τολμήσειαν Jernstedt 432 τοιούτους Maetzner : τοσούτους AN subscriptio φόνου ἀπολογία N

ΑΝΔΟΚΙΔΟΥ
ΛΟΓΟΙ

1

ΠΕΡΙ ΤΩΝ ΜΥΣΤΗΡΙΩΝ

Τὴν μὲν παρασκευήν, ὦ ἄνδρες, καὶ τὴν προθυμίαν τῶν 1
ἐχθρῶν τῶν ἐμῶν, ὥστ' ἐμὲ κακῶς ποιεῖν ἐκ παντὸς τρόπου καὶ δικαίως καὶ ἀδίκως, ἐξ ἀρχῆς ἐπειδὴ τάχιστα ἀφικόμην εἰς τὴν πόλιν ταυτηνί, σχεδόν τι πάντες ἐπίστασθε, καὶ οὐδὲν δεῖ περὶ τούτων πολλοὺς λόγους ποιεῖσθαι· ἐγὼ δέ, ὦ ἄνδρες, δεήσομαι ὑμῶν δίκαια καὶ ὑμῖν τε ῥᾴδια χαρίζεσθαι καὶ ἐμοὶ ἄξια
πολλοῦ τυχεῖν παρ' ὑμῶν. καὶ πρῶτον μὲν ἐνθυμηθῆναι 2
ὅτι νῦν ἐγὼ ἥκω οὐδεμιᾶς μοι ἀνάγκης οὔσης παραμεῖναι, οὔτ' ἐγγυητὰς καταστήσας οὔθ' ὑπὸ δεσμῶν ἀναγκασθείς, πιστεύσας δὲ μάλιστα μὲν τῷ δικαίῳ, ἔπειτα δὲ καὶ ὑμῖν, γνώσεσθαι τὰ δίκαια καὶ μὴ περιόψεσθαί με ἀδίκως ὑπὸ τῶν ἐχθρῶν τῶν ἐμῶν διαφθαρέντα, ἀλλὰ πολὺ μᾶλλον σώσειν δικαίως κατά τε τοὺς νόμους τοὺς ὑμετέρους καὶ τοὺς ὅρκους οὓς ὑμεῖς ὀμόσαντες μέλλετε
τὴν ψῆφον οἴσειν. εἰκότως δ' ἄν, ὦ ἄνδρες, τὴν αὐτὴν 3

1 *Τὴν μὲν—ἐμῶν, σχεδὸν—ἐπίστασθε* (*εἴσεσθε* Clem.) stp Clem. Al. *Strom.* 6.2.20.4 *Τὴν μὲν—τῶν ἐμῶν* et *πάντες—παρ' ὑμῶν* simillima nonnullis in Lysiae 19.2–4 et fr. 118.7–8 Carey, et in Aeschinis 3.1, cf. Isocratis 15.17

---

tit. *περὶ τῶν μυστηρίων* A una cum script. veteribus plerisque : *περὶ* (*περὶ τῆς* [Plut.]) *ἐνδείξεως* Harp. ζ 4 [Plut.] *Vita Andoc.* 14.835A 1 superscriptio *Ἀνδοκίδου περὶ τῶν μυστηρίων* 1 *ἄνδρες* A : *ἄνδρες δικασταί* Clem. 2–4 *ὥστ' … ταυτηνί* om. Clem. 4 *τι* A[a] Clem. : *τοι* A[1] 5 *ἐπίστασθε* A : *εἴσεσθε* Clem. *τούτων*] *των* in ras. A[1] 8 *καὶ* delendum cens. Baiter *ἐνθυμηθῆναι*] *ἐνθυμήθητε* Hirschig[1] 9 *παραμεῖναι*] *ὑπομεῖναι* Hirschig[1] 15 *ὁμόσαντες* Steph. : *ὀμόσαντες* A

γνώμην ἔχοιτε περὶ τῶν ἐθελόντων εἰς τοὺς κινδύνους
καθισταμένων, ἥνπερ αὐτοὶ περὶ αὑτῶν ἔχουσιν. ὁπόσοι
μὲν γὰρ μὴ ἠθέλησαν ὑπομεῖναι καταγνόντες αὑτῶν
ἀδικίαν, εἰκότως τοι καὶ ὑμεῖς τοιαῦτα περὶ αὐτῶν
γιγνώσκετε οἷά περ καὶ αὐτοὶ περὶ σφῶν αὐτῶν ἔγνωσαν·
ὁπόσοι δὲ πιστεύσαντες μηδὲν ἀδικεῖν ὑπέμειναν,
δίκαιοί ἐστε καὶ ὑμεῖς περὶ τούτων τοιαύτην ἔχειν τὴν
γνώμην οἵαν περ καὶ αὐτοὶ περὶ αὑτῶν ἔσχον, καὶ μὴ
4 προκαταγιγνώσκειν ἀδικεῖν. αὐτίκα ἐγὼ πολλῶν μοι
ἀπαγγελλόντων ὅτι λέγοιεν οἱ ἐχθροὶ ὡς ἄρα ἐγὼ οὔτ'
ἂν ὑπομείναιμι οἰχήσομαί τε φεύγων—"Τί γὰρ ἂν καὶ
βουλόμενος Ἀνδοκίδης ἀγῶνα τοσοῦτον ὑπομείνειεν,
ᾧ ἔξεστι μὲν ἀπελθόντι ἐντεῦθεν ἔχειν πάντα τὰ
ἐπιτήδεια, ἔστι δὲ πλεύσαντι εἰς Κύπρον, ὅθεν περ ἥκει,
γῆ πολλὴ καὶ ἀγαθὴ δεδομένη ἐν δωρειᾷ ὑπάρχουσα;
οὗτος ἄρα βουλήσεται περὶ τοῦ σώματος τοῦ ἑαυτοῦ
κινδυνεῦσαι; εἰς τί ἀποβλέψας; οὐχ ὁρᾷ τὴν πόλιν ἡμῶν
ὡς διάκειται;" ἐγὼ δέ, ὦ ἄνδρες, πολὺ τὴν ἐναντίαν
5 τούτοις γνώμην ἔχω. ἄλλοθί τε γὰρ ὢν πάντα τὰ
ἀγαθὰ ἔχειν στερόμενος τῆς πατρίδος οὐκ ἂν δεξαίμην,
τῆς πόλεως οὕτω διακειμένης ὥσπερ αὐτοὶ οἱ ἐχθροὶ
λέγουσι, πολὺ δ' ἂν αὐτῆς μᾶλλον ἐγὼ πολίτης δεξαίμην
εἶναι ἢ ἑτέρων πόλεων, αἳ ἴσως πάνυ μοι δοκοῦσιν ἐν τῷ
παρόντι εὐτυχεῖν. ἅπερ γιγνώσκων ἐπέτρεψα διαγνῶναι

17 ἐθελόντων A : ἐθελοντῶν Ald. 18 ἥνπερ Ald. : ἥπερ A αὑτῶν A[1] : αὐτῶν A[a] 19 αὑτῶν A[1] : αὐτῶν A[a] 21 γινώσκετε A[1] : γινώσκητε A[a] οἷά Markland : ὅσα A 24 αὑτῶν A[1] : αὐτῶν A[a] 28–9 ὑπομένειεν ᾧ Valckenaer : ὑπομένει ἐν ὧ A : ὑπομένοι ἐν ᾧ Reiske 30 ***πλεύσαντι (fort. καὶ vel ἀπο) A[c] : ἀποπλεύσαντι Blass[3] 31 γῆ Valckenaer : ἢ A δεδομένη ἐν δωρειᾷ Koepke : δεδομένη καὶ δωρειὰ A : δεδομένη δωρεὰ Dalmeyda 34 τὴν del. Dalmeyda 37 τῆς <τε> Sluiter 38 αὐτῆς del. Dalmeyda 40 εὐτυχεῖν] ευ in ras. A[1] γινώσκων L[c] : γινώσκω A[1] (alt. ω in ras.)

ὑμῖν περὶ τοῦ σώματος τοῦ ἐμαυτοῦ. αἰτοῦμαι οὖν 6 ὑμᾶς, ὦ ἄνδρες, εὔνοιαν πλείω παρασχέσθαι ἐμοὶ τῷ ἀπολογουμένῳ ἢ τοῖς κατηγόροις, εἰδότας ὅτι κἂν ἐξ ἴσου ἀκροᾶσθε, ἀνάγκη τὸν ἀπολογούμενον ἔλαττον ἔχειν. οἱ μὲν γὰρ ἐκ πολλοῦ χρόνου ἐπιβουλεύσαντες καὶ συνθέντες, αὐτοὶ ἄνευ κινδύνων ὄντες, τὴν κατηγορίαν ἐποιήσαντο· ἐγὼ δὲ μετὰ δέους καὶ κινδύνου καὶ διαβολῆς τῆς μεγίστης τὴν ἀπολογίαν ποιοῦμαι. εἰκὸς οὖν ὑμᾶς ἐστιν εὔνοιαν πλείω παρασχέσθαι ἐμοὶ ἢ τοῖς κατηγόροις. ἔτι δὲ καὶ τόδε ἐνθυμητέον, ὅτι πολλοὶ 7 ἤδη πολλὰ καὶ δεινὰ κατηγορήσαντες παραχρῆμα ἐξηλέγχθησαν ψευδόμενοι οὕτω φανερῶς, ὥστε ὑμᾶς πολὺ ἂν ἥδιον δίκην λαβεῖν παρὰ τῶν κατηγόρων ἢ παρὰ τῶν κατηγορουμένων· οἱ δὲ αὖ, μαρτυρήσαντες τὰ ψευδῆ ἀδίκως ἀνθρώπους ἀπολέσαντες, ἑάλωσαν παρ' ὑμῖν ψευδομαρτυριῶν, ἡνίκ' οὐδὲν ἦν ἔτι πλέον τοῖς πεπονθόσιν. ὁπότ' οὖν ἤδη πολλὰ τοιαῦτα γεγένηται, εἰκὸς ὑμᾶς ἐστι μήπω τοὺς τῶν κατηγόρων λόγους πιστοὺς ἡγεῖσθαι. εἰ μὲν γὰρ δεινὰ κατηγόρηται ἢ μή, οἷόν τε γνῶναι ἐκ τῶν τοῦ κατηγόρου λόγων· εἰ δὲ ἀληθῆ ταῦτά ἐστιν ἢ ψευδῆ, οὐχ οἷόν τε ὑμᾶς πρότερον εἰδέναι πρὶν ἂν καὶ ἐμοῦ ἀκούσητε ἀπολογουμένου.

Σκοπῶ μὲν οὖν ἔγωγε, ὦ ἄνδρες, πόθεν χρὴ ἄρξασθαι 8 τῆς ἀπολογίας, πότερον ἐκ τῶν τελευταίων λόγων, ὡς παρανόμως με ἐνέδειξαν, ἢ περὶ τοῦ ψηφίσματος τοῦ Ἰσοτιμίδου, ὡς ἄκυρόν ἐστιν, ἢ περὶ τῶν νόμων καὶ τῶν ὅρκων τῶν γεγενημένων, εἴτε καὶ ἐξ ἀρχῆς ὑμᾶς διδάξω

7 *ὅτι—ὥστε* et *οἱ δὲ—ἡγεῖσθαι* simillima nonnullis in Lysiae 19.4-5

42-3 *εὔνοιαν … κατηγόροις* del. Naber[1] coll. ll. 49-50 infra 52 *ἐξηλέγχθησαν* M : *ἐξειλέχθησαν* A 55 *ψευδῆ* A : *ψεύδη* Blass[3] <*καὶ*> *ἀδίκως* Blass 56 *ψευδομαρτυριῶν* A : *ψευδομαρτυρίων* Blass[3] *ἔτι* A : om. L 57 *γεγένηται* Dobree : *γεγένηνται* A 61 *ψευδῆ* A : *ψεύδη* Blass[3] 63 *οὖν* A[1] : om. A[a] 64 *λόγων* A : om. L τὰ γεγενημένα. ὃ δέ με ποιεῖ μάλιστ᾽ ἀπορεῖν, ἐγὼ ὑμῖν ἐρῶ, ὅτι οὐ πάντες ἴσως ἐπὶ πᾶσι τοῖς κατηγορουμένοις ὁμοίως ὀργίζεσθε, ἀλλ᾽ ἕκαστος τι ὑμῶν ἔχει πρὸς ὃ βούλοιτο ἄν με πρῶτον ἀπολογεῖσθαι· ἅμα δὲ περὶ πάντων εἰπεῖν ἀδύνατον. κράτιστον οὖν μοι εἶναι δοκεῖ ἐξ ἀρχῆς ὑμᾶς διδάσκειν πάντα τὰ γενόμενα καὶ παραλιπεῖν μηδέν. ἂν γὰρ ὀρθῶς μάθητε τὰ πραχθέντα, ῥᾳδίως γνώσεσθ᾽ ἅ μου κατεψεύσαντο οἱ κατήγοροι.

9 τὰ μὲν οὖν δίκαια γιγνώσκειν ὑμᾶς ἡγοῦμαι καὶ αὐτοὺς παρεσκευάσθαι, οἷσπερ ἐγὼ πιστεύσας ὑπέμεινα, ὁρῶν ὑμᾶς καὶ ἐν τοῖς ἰδίοις καὶ ἐν τοῖς δημοσίοις περὶ πλείστου τοῦτο ποιουμένους, ψηφίζεσθαι κατὰ τοὺς ὅρκους· ὅπερ καὶ συνέχει μόνον τὴν πόλιν, ἀκόντων τῶν οὐ βουλομένων ταῦτα οὕτως ἔχειν· τάδε δὲ ὑμῶν δέομαι, μετ᾽ εὐνοίας μου τὴν ἀκρόασιν τῆς ἀπολογίας ποιήσασθαι, καὶ μήτ᾽ ἐμοὶ ἀντιδίκους καταστῆναι μήτε ὑπονοεῖν τὰ λεγόμενα μήτε ῥήματα θηρεύειν, ἀκροασαμένους δὲ διὰ τέλους τῆς ἀπολογίας τότε ἤδη ψηφίζεσθαι τοῦτο ὅ τι ἂν ὑμῖν αὐτοῖς ἄριστον καὶ εὐορκότατον νομίζητε εἶναι.

10 ὥσπερ δὲ καὶ προεῖπον ὑμῖν, ὦ ἄνδρες, ἐξ ἀρχῆς περὶ πάντων ποιήσομαι τὴν ἀπολογίαν, πρῶτον μὲν περὶ αὐτῆς τῆς αἰτίας ὅθεν περ ἡ ἔνδειξις ἐγένετο, διόπερ εἰς τὸν ἀγῶνα τόνδε κατέστην, περὶ τῶν μυστηρίων ὡς οὔτ᾽ ἐμοὶ ἠσέβηται οὐδὲν οὔτε μεμήνυται οὔθ᾽ ὡμολόγηται, οὐδ᾽ οἶδα τοὺς μηνύσαντας ὑμῖν περὶ αὐτῶν οὔτ᾽ εἰ ψευδῆ οὔτ᾽ εἰ ἀληθῆ ἐμήνυσαν· ταῦθ᾽ ὑμᾶς διδάξω.

9 ὑμῶν—εἶναι simillima nonnullis in Lysiae 19.11

68–9 ἐγὼ ὑμῖν ἐρῶ del. Schoell[2] 74 παραλιπεῖν A[1] : παραλείπειν A[a] μάθητε] ε in ras. A[1] 76 αὐτοὺς Emperius[1] : λόγους A 83 μήτ᾽ ἐμοὶ A : μήτε μοι Blass[2] 85–6 ὅτι ἂν ὑμῖν in ras. A[1] (ἂν fort. om. A[a]) 90 τόνδε L : δὲ A 92 οὐδ᾽ Blass : οὔτ᾽ A ψευδῆ A : ψεύδη Blass[3]

Ἦν μὲν γὰρ ἐκκλησία τοῖς στρατηγοῖς τοῖς εἰς 11
Σικελίαν, Νικίᾳ καὶ Λαμάχῳ καὶ Ἀλκιβιάδῃ, καὶ τριήρης ἡ στρατηγὶς ἤδη ἐξώρμει ἡ Λαμάχου· ἀναστὰς δὲ Πυθόνικος ἐν τῷ δήμῳ εἶπεν· "Ὦ Ἀθηναῖοι, ὑμεῖς μὲν στρατιὰν ἐκπέμπετε καὶ παρασκευὴν τοσαύτην, καὶ κίνδυνον ἀρεῖσθαι μέλλετε· Ἀλκιβιάδην δὲ τὸν στρατηγὸν ἀποδείξω ὑμῖν τὰ μυστήρια ποιοῦντα ἐν οἰκίᾳ μεθ' ἑτέρων, καὶ ἐὰν ψηφίσησθε ἄδειαν ⟨ᾧ⟩ ἐγὼ κελεύω, θεράπων ὑμῖν ἑνὸς τῶν ἐνθάδε ἀνδρῶν ἀμύητος ὢν ἐρεῖ τὰ μυστήρια· εἰ δὲ μή, χρῆσθε ἐμοὶ ὅ τι ἂν ὑμῖν δοκῇ, ἐὰν μὴ τἀληθῆ λέγω." ἀντιλέγοντος δὲ Ἀλκιβιάδου 12
πολλὰ καὶ ἐξάρνου ὄντος ἔδοξε τοῖς πρυτάνεσι τοὺς μὲν ἀμυήτους μεταστήσασθαι, αὐτοὺς δ' ἰέναι ἐπὶ τὸ μειράκιον ὃ ὁ Πυθόνικος ἐκέλευε. καὶ ᾤχοντο, καὶ ἤγαγον θεράποντα Ἀλκιβιάδου {πολέμαρχον}· Ἀνδρόμαχος αὐτῷ ὄνομα ἦν. ἐπεὶ δὲ ἐψηφίσαντο αὐτῷ τὴν ἄδειαν, ἔλεγεν ὅτι ἐν τῇ οἰκίᾳ τῇ Πουλυτίωνος γίγνοιτο μυστήρια· Ἀλκιβιάδην μὲν οὖν καὶ Νικίδην καὶ Μέλητον, τούτους μὲν αὐτοὺς εἶναι τοὺς ποιοῦντας, συμπαρεῖναι δὲ καὶ ὁρᾶν τὰ γιγνόμενα καὶ ἄλλους, παρεῖναι δὲ καὶ δούλους, ἑαυτόν τε καὶ τὸν ἀδελφὸν καὶ Ἱκέσιον τὸν αὐλητὴν καὶ τὸν Μελήτου δοῦλον. πρῶτος μὲν οὗτος 13
ταῦτα ἐμήνυσε, καὶ ἀπέγραψε τούτους· ὧν Πολύστρατος μὲν συνελήφθη καὶ ἀπέθανεν, οἱ δὲ ἄλλοι φεύγοντες ᾤχοντο, καὶ αὐτῶν ὑμεῖς θάνατον κατέγνωτε. Καί μοι λαβὲ καὶ ἀνάγνωθι αὐτῶν τὰ ὀνόματα.

95 *λαμάχω* et mox *λαμάχου* A^{c} (*λαμμ-* A^{a}) 99 *ἀρεῖσθαι* Bekker : *αἱρεῖσθαι* A 101 add. Bekker 103 *χρῆσθε ἐμοὶ* A : *χρῆσθέ μοι* Hickie *ἂν ὑμῖν δο* in ras. A^{1} (*ἂν* fort. om. A^{a}) 108 *Ἀλκιβιάδου* A : *Ἀρχεβιάδου* dubitanter Lipsius del. MacDowell : *Πολεμάρχου* Reiske : <*τοῦ*> *πολεμάρχου* Lipsius : aliter alii 110 *πουλυτίωνος* A^{1} : *πολυτίωνος* A^{a} 111 *μὲν* A^{1} : om. A^{a} *Νικίδην* Meritt (coll. *IG* I^{3} 424, 426) : *νικιάδην* A 115 *πρῶτος* A^{1} : *πρῶτον* A^{a} *μὲν οὗτος* in ras. A^{1} (fort. *μὲν* om. A^{a})

ΟΝΟΜΑΤΑ. Τούσδε Ἀνδρόμαχος ἐμήνυσεν· Ἀλκιβιάδην, Νικίδην, Μέλητον, Ἀρχεβιάδην, Ἄρχιππον, Διογένην, Πολύστρατον, Ἀριστομένη, Οἰωνίαν, Παναίτιον.

14 Πρώτη μέν, ὦ ἄνδρες, μήνυσις ἐγένετο αὕτη ὑπὸ Ἀνδρομάχου κατὰ τούτων τῶν ἀνδρῶν. καί μοι κάλει Διόγνητον.

Ἦσθα ζητητής, ὦ Διόγνητε, ὅτε Πυθόνικος εἰσήγγειλεν ἐν τῷ δήμῳ περὶ Ἀλκιβιάδου; Ἦν. Οἶσθα οὖν μηνύσαντα Ἀνδρόμαχον τὰ ἐν τῇ οἰκίᾳ τῇ Πουλυτίωνος γιγνόμενα; Οἶδα. Τὰ ὀνόματα οὖν τῶν ἀνδρῶν ἐστι ταῦτα, καθ' ὧν ἐκεῖνος ἐμήνυσεν; ἔστι ταῦτα.

15 Δευτέρα τοίνυν μήνυσις ἐγένετο. Τεῦκρος ἦν ἐνθάδε μέτοικος, ὃς ᾤχετο Μέγαράδε ὑπεξελθών, ἐκεῖθεν δὲ ἐπαγγέλλεται τῇ βουλῇ, εἴ οἱ ἄδειαν δοῖεν, μηνύσειν περὶ τῶν μυστηρίων, συνεργὸς ὤν, καὶ τοὺς ἄλλους τοὺς ποιοῦντας μεθ' ἑαυτοῦ, καὶ περὶ τῶν Ἑρμῶν τῆς περικοπῆς ἃ ᾔδει. ψηφισαμένης δὲ τῆς βουλῆς (ἦν γὰρ αὐτοκράτωρ) ᾤχοντο ἐπ' αὐτὸν Μέγαράδε· καὶ κομισθείς, ἄδειαν εὑρόμενος, ἀπογράφει τοὺς μεθ' ἑαυτοῦ. καὶ οὗτοι κατὰ τὴν Τεύκρου μήνυσιν ᾤχοντο φεύγοντες. καί μοι λαβὲ καὶ ἀνάγνωθι τὰ ὀνόματα αὐτῶν.

ΟΝΟΜΑΤΑ. Τούσδε Τεῦκρος ἐμήνυσε· Φαῖδρον, Γνιφωνίδην, Ἰσόνομον, Ἡφαιστόδωρον, Κηφισόδωρον, ἑαυτόν, Διόγνητον, Σμινδυρίδην, Φιλοκράτην, Ἀντιφῶντα, Τείσαρχον, Παντακλέα.

Μέμνησθε δέ, ὦ ἄνδρες, ὅτι καὶ ταῦθ' ὑμῖν προσομολογεῖται ἅπαντα.

14 *ζητητής* Harp. ζ 4 s.v. (item 36, 65)

121 *Νικίδην* Meritt : *νικιάδην* A   *διογένην* A : *Διογένη* Schiller
122 *Οἰωνίαν* Kirchhoff (coll. *IG* I[3] 422) : *ἰωνίαν* A   127 *ἦν* A : *ἦ* Blass[3]
133 *περί* <*τε*> Blass : *καὶ* ante *περὶ* l. 135 huc transp. Lipsius
143 *φιλοκράτην* A : *Φιλοκράτη* Schiller   *Τείσαρχον* Blass[2] : *τίσαρχον* A
144 *δέ*] *δὲ* A[im]   *ὅτι* A[1] : om. A[a]

Τρίτη μήνυσις ἐγένετο. ἡ γυνὴ Ἀλκμεωνίδου, γενομένη 16
δὲ καὶ Δάμωνος (Ἀγαρίστη ὄνομα αὐτῇ), αὕτη ἐμήνυσεν
ἐν τῇ οἰκίᾳ τῇ Χαρμίδου τῇ παρὰ τὸ Ὀλυμπιεῖον
μυστήρια ποιεῖν Ἀλκιβιάδην καὶ Ἀξίοχον καὶ Ἀδείμαντον·
καὶ ἔφυγον οὗτοι πάντες ἐπὶ ταύτῃ τῇ μηνύσει.

Ἔτι μήνυσις ἐγένετο μία. Λυδὸς ὁ Φερεκλέους τοῦ 17
Θημακέως ἐμήνυσε μυστήρια γίγνεσθαι ἐν τῇ οἰκίᾳ
Φερεκλέους τοῦ δεσπότου τοῦ ἑαυτοῦ, ἐν Θημακῷ· καὶ
ἀπογράφει τούς τε ἄλλους, καὶ τὸν πατέρα ἔφη τὸν ἐμὸν
παρεῖναι μέν, καθεύδειν δὲ ἐγκεκαλυμμένον. Σπεύσιππος δὲ βουλεύων παραδίδωσιν αὐτοὺς τῷ δικαστηρίῳ.
κἄπειτα ὁ πατὴρ καταστήσας ἐγγυητὰς ἐγράψατο τὸν
Σπεύσιππον παρανόμων καὶ ἠγωνίσατο ἐν ἑξακισχιλίοις
Ἀθηναίων, καὶ μετέλαβε δικαστῶν τοσούτων οὐδὲ
διακοσίας ψήφους ὁ Σπεύσιππος. ὁ δὲ πείσας καὶ δεόμενος
μεῖναι τὸν πατέρα ἐγὼ ἦν μάλιστα, εἶτα δὲ καὶ οἱ ἄλλοι
συγγενεῖς. καί μοι κάλει Καλλίαν καὶ Στέφανον. 18

⟨ΜΑΡΤΥΡΕΣ⟩

Κάλει δὲ καὶ Φίλιππον καὶ Ἀλέξιππον· οὗτοι γάρ εἰσιν Ἀκουμενοῦ καὶ Αὐτοκράτορος συγγενεῖς, οἳ ἔφυγον ἐπὶ τῇ Λυδοῦ μηνύσει· τοῦ μὲν ἀδελφιδοῦς ἐστιν Αὐτοκράτωρ, τοῦ δὲ θεῖος Ἀκουμενός· οἷς προσήκει μισεῖν μὲν τὸν ἐξελάσαντα ἐκείνους, εἰδέναι δὲ μάλιστα δι' ὅντινα ἔφυγον. βλέπετε εἰς τούτους, καὶ μαρτυρεῖτε εἰ ἀληθῆ λέγω.

17 Θημακέως Harp. θ 21 s.v. θημακεύς

146 Ἀλκμεωνίδου Blass[2] : ἀλκμαιονίδου A 148 Ὀλυμπιεῖον Reiske : ὀλύμπιον A 149 Ἀδείμαντον Ald. : ἀδίμαντον A : postea lacunam susp. Makkink 150 ἔφυγον Blass : ἔφευγον A 153 θημακῶ A[1] (μ et κ in ras.) 154 ἀπογράφει sine rasura re vera A 163 tit. add. Radermacher 165 et 167 Ἀκουμενοῦ … Ἀκουμενός Ald. : ἀκουμένου … ἀκούμενος A 168 ἔφυγον Blass[2] : ἔφευγον A 169 μαρτυρεῖτε A[1] : μαρτυρεῖται A[a]

ΜΑΡΤΥΡΕΣ

19 Τὰ μὲν γενόμενα ἠκούσατε, ὦ ἄνδρες, καὶ ὑμῖν οἱ
μάρτυρες μεμαρτυρήκασιν· ἃ δὲ οἱ κατήγοροι ἐτόλμησαν
εἰπεῖν, ἀναμνήσθητε. οὕτω γὰρ καὶ δίκαιον ἀπολογεῖσθαι,
ἀναμιμνῄσκοντα τοὺς τῶν κατηγόρων λόγους ἐξελέγχειν.
ἔλεξαν γὰρ ὡς ἐγὼ μηνύσαιμι περὶ τῶν μυστηρίων,
ἀπογράψαιμί τε τὸν πατέρα τὸν ἐμαυτοῦ παρόντα, καὶ
γενοίμην μηνυτὴς κατὰ τοῦ πατρὸς τοῦ ἐμαυτοῦ, λόγον
οἶμαι πάντων δεινότατόν τε καὶ ἀνοσιώτατον λέγοντες.
ὁ μὲν γὰρ ἀπογράψας αὐτὸν Λυδὸς ἦν ὁ Φερεκλέους, ὁ δὲ
πείσας ὑπομεῖναι καὶ μὴ οἴχεσθαι φεύγοντα ἐγώ, πολλὰ
20 ἱκετεύσας καὶ λαμβανόμενος τῶν γονάτων. καίτοι τί
ἐβουλόμην, εἰ ἐμήνυσα μὲν κατὰ τοῦ πατρός, ὡς οὗτοί
φασιν, ἱκέτευον δὲ τὸν πατέρα μείναντά τι παθεῖν ὑπ᾿
ἐμοῦ; καὶ ὁ πατὴρ ἐπείσθη ἀγῶνα τοιοῦτον ἀγωνίσασθαι,
ἐν ᾧ δυοῖν τοῖν μεγίστοιν κακοῖν οὐκ ἦν αὐτῷ ἁμαρτεῖν;
ἢ γὰρ ἐμοῦ δόξαντος τὰ ὄντα μηνῦσαι κατ᾿ ἐκείνου ὑπ᾿
ἐμοῦ ἀποθανεῖν, ἢ αὐτῷ σωθέντι ἐμὲ ἀποκτεῖναι. ὁ γὰρ
νόμος οὕτως εἶχεν· εἰ μὲν τἀληθῆ μηνύσειέ τις, εἶναι
τὴν ἄδειαν, εἰ δὲ τὰ ψευδῆ, τεθνάναι. καὶ μὲν δὴ τοῦτό
γε ἐπίστασθε πάντες, ὅτι ἐσώθην καὶ ἐγὼ καὶ ὁ ἐμὸς
πατήρ· οἷόν τε δ᾿ οὐκ ἦν, εἴπερ ἐγὼ μηνυτὴς ἐγενόμην
περὶ τοῦ πατρός, ἀλλ᾿ ἢ ἐμὲ ἢ ἐκεῖνον ἔδει ἀποθανεῖν.
21 φέρε δὴ τοίνυν, εἰ καὶ ὁ πατὴρ ἐβούλετο ὑπομένειν,
τοὺς φίλους ἂν οἴεσθε ἢ ἐπιτρέπειν αὐτῷ μένειν ἢ
ἐγγυήσασθαι, ἀλλ᾿ οὐκ ἂν παραιτεῖσθαι καὶ δεῖσθαι

170 tit. habet M, punctum rubrum solum A 171 γενόμενα Sluiter : γινόμενα A ὑμῖν L : ἡμῖν A 173 οὕτω Reiske : οὐ A 174 ἀναμιμνῄσκοντα Reiske : ἀναμιμνήκοντας A 178 τε A[1] : om. A[a] : del. Fuhr[2] 182 ὡς L : ὧς A[1] : ὦ A 185 δυοῖν A[sv] : δυεῖν A[it] 186 ἢ in ras A[1] : εἰ A[a] γὰρ del. Dobree 189 τὰ A[1] : om. A[a] ψευδῆ A : ψεύδη Blass[3]

ἀπιέναι ὅπου ἂν ἔμελλεν αὐτὸς σωθήσεσθαι ἐμέ τε οὐκ
ἀπολεῖν; ἀλλὰ γὰρ καὶ ὅτε Σπεύσιππον ἐδίωκεν ὁ πατὴρ 22
τῶν παρανόμων, αὐτὰ ταῦτα ἔλεγεν, ὡς οὐδεπώποτε
ἔλθοι εἰς Θημακὸν ὡς Φερεκλέα· ἐκέλευε δὲ βασανίσαι
τὰ ἀνδράποδα, καὶ μὴ τοὺς μὲν παραδιδόντας μὴ ἐθέλειν
ἐλέγχειν, τοὺς δὲ μὴ θέλοντας ἀναγκάζειν. ταῦτα δὲ
λέγοντος τοῦ πατρὸς τοῦ ἐμοῦ, ὡς ἅπαντες ἴστε, τί
ὑπελείπετο τῷ Σπευσίππῳ λέγειν, εἰ ἀληθῆ οἵδε
λέγουσιν, ἄλλ' ἢ "Ὦ Λεωγόρα, τί βούλῃ περὶ θεραπόντων
λέγειν; οὐχ ὁ υἱὸς οὑτοσὶ μεμήνυκε κατὰ σοῦ, καὶ φησί
σε παρεῖναι ἐν Θημακῷ; ἔλεγχε σὺ τὸν πατέρα, ἢ οὐκ
ἔστι σοι ἄδεια." ταυτὶ ἔλεγεν ἂν ὁ Σπεύσιππος, ὦ
ἄνδρες, ἢ οὔ; ἐγὼ μὲν οἶμαι. εἰ τοίνυν ἀνέβην ἐπὶ 23
δικαστήριον, ἢ λόγος τις περὶ ἐμοῦ ἐγένετο, ἢ μήνυσίς
τις ἐμή ἐστιν ἢ ἀπογραφή, μὴ ὅτι ἐμὴ καθ' ἑτέρου, ἀλλ'
εἰ καὶ ἄλλου τινὸς κατ' ἐμοῦ, ἐλεγχέτω με ὁ βουλόμενος
ἐνταῦθα ἀναβάς. ἀλλὰ γὰρ λόγον ἀνοσιώτερον καὶ
ἀπιστότερον οὐδένας πώποτ' ἐγὼ εἰπόντας οἶδα, οἳ τοῦτο
μόνον ἡγήσαντο δεῖν, τολμῆσαι κατηγορῆσαι· εἰ δ'
ἐλεγχθήσονται ψευδόμενοι, οὐδὲν αὐτοῖς ἐμέλησεν.
ὥσπερ οὖν, εἰ ἀληθῆ ἦν ταῦτα ἅ μου κατηγόρησαν, ἐμοὶ 24
ἂν ὠργίζεσθε καὶ ἠξιοῦτε δίκην τὴν μεγίστην ἐπιτιθέναι,
οὕτως ἀξιῶ ὑμᾶς, γιγνώσκοντας ὅτι ψεύδονται, πονηρούς
τε αὐτοὺς νομίζειν, χρῆσθαί τε τεκμηρίῳ ὅτι εἰ τὰ
δεινότατα τῶν κατηγορηθέντων περιφανῶς ἐλέγχονται

196 ἂν A : δὴ Richards[1] : del. Dobree αὐτὸς A[1im] : om. A[a] 198 τῶν del. Valckenaer οὐδεπώποτε A[1] : οὐδέποτε A[a] 199 ἔλθοι L[sv] : ἔλθῃ A 200 μὴ τοὺς μὲν in ras. A[1] 201 θέλοντας] 'θέλοντας Baiter 204 Λεωγόρα Bekker : λεω[γρ'] A βούλῃ Fuhr : βούλει A 205 μεμήνυκε L : μεμύνηκε A (sed υ in ras.) 210 ἢ Reiske: ἥ A 212–13 ἀνοσιώτερον καὶ ἀπιστότερον Reiske : ἀνοσιώτατον καὶ ἀπιστότατον A 213 οὐδένας Reiske : οὐδένα A εἰπόντας A[1] : εἰπόντα A[a] 216 μου Dobree : με A

ψευδόμενοι, ᾗ που τά γε πολλῷ φαυλότερα ῥᾳδίως ὑμῖν ἀποδείξω ψευδομένους αὐτούς.

25 Αἱ μὲν μηνύσεις ὧδε περὶ τῶν μυστηρίων αὗται ἐγένοντο τέτταρες· οἳ δὲ ἔφυγον καθ' ἑκάστην μήνυσιν, ἀνέγνων ὑμῖν τὰ ὀνόματα αὐτῶν, καὶ οἱ μάρτυρες μεμαρτυρήκασιν. ἔτι δὲ πρὸς τούτοις ἐγὼ πιστότητος ὑμῶν ἕνεκα, ὦ ἄνδρες, τάδε ποιήσω. τῶν γὰρ φυγόντων ἐπὶ τοῖς μυστηρίοις οἱ μέν τινες ἀπέθανον φεύγοντες, οἱ δ' ἥκουσιν καὶ εἰσὶν ἐνθάδε καὶ πάρεισιν ὑπ' ἐμοῦ
26 κεκλημένοι. ἐγὼ οὖν ἐν τῷ ἐμῷ λόγῳ δίδωμι τῷ βουλομένῳ ἐμὲ ἐξελέγξαι ὅτι ἔφυγέ τις αὐτῶν δι' ἐμὲ ἢ ἐμήνυσα κατ' αὐτοῦ ἢ οὐχ ἕκαστοι ἔφυγον κατὰ τὰς μηνύσεις ταύτας ἃς ἐγὼ ὑμῖν ἀπέδειξα. καὶ ἐάν τις ἐλέγξῃ με ὅτι ψεύδομαι, χρήσασθέ μοι ὅ τι βούλεσθε. καὶ σιωπῶ, καὶ παραχωρῶ, εἴ τις ἀναβαίνειν βούλεται.

27 Φέρε δή, ὦ ἄνδρες, μετὰ ταῦτα τί ἐγένετο; ἐπειδὴ αἱ μηνύσεις ἐγένοντο, περὶ τῶν μηνύτρων—ἦσαν γὰρ κατὰ τὸ Κλεωνύμου ψήφισμα χίλιαι δραχμαί, κατὰ δὲ τὸ Πεισάνδρου μύριαι—περὶ δὲ τούτων ἠμφεσβήτουν οὗτοί τε οἱ μηνύσαντες καὶ Πυθόνικος, φάσκων πρῶτος
28 εἰσαγγεῖλαι, καὶ Ἀνδροκλῆς ὑπὲρ †τῆς βουλῆς†. ἔδοξεν οὖν τῷ δήμῳ ἐν τῷ τῶν θεσμοθετῶν δικαστηρίῳ

27 *περὶ—μηνύσαντες* Et.Gen. α 729.15 s.v. ἀμφισβητεῖν *EM* p. 94.39 Gaisford = α 729 Lasserre-Livadaras

---

221 τά γε Bekker : τάγα A (γ in ras.) : τἆλλα L   224 ἔφυγον Blass[2] : ἔφευγον A   227 ὑμῶν] ὑμῖν Richards[3]   φυγόντων Blass[2] : φευγόντων A   228 ἐπὶ τοῖς Reiske : ἐν τοῖς A   231 ἐμὲ A : με addubitanter Fuhr   ἐξελέγξαι A[1] : ἐλέγξαι A[a]   232 κατ' αὐτοῦ A : κατά του Sluiter   236 βούλεται Bekker : βούληται A   240 δὲ A : om. Et.Gen. *EM* : δὴ Reiske   ἠμφεσβήτουν Lipsius : ἠμφισβήτουν A Et.Gen. *EM*   241 τε A : γε Et.Gen. *EM*   242 τῆς βουλῆς A (obelis inclusi): <τῆς εἰσαγγελιᾶς εἰς> τὴν βουλήν vel <τῶν εἰρημένων ἐν> τῇ βουλῇ vel sim. Albini[1]

τοὺς μεμυημένους, ἀκούσαντας τὰς μηνύσεις ἃς ἕκαστος ἐμήνυσε, διαδικάσαι. καὶ ἐψηφίσαντο πρώτῳ μὲν Ἀνδρομάχῳ, δευτέρῳ δὲ Τεύκρῳ, καὶ ἔλαβον Παναθηναίων τῷ ἀγῶνι Ἀνδρόμαχος μὲν μυρίας δραχμάς, Τεῦκρος δὲ χιλίας. καί μοι κάλει τούτων τοὺς μάρτυρας.

ΜΑΡΤΥΡΕΣ

Περὶ μὲν τῶν μυστηρίων, ὦ ἄνδρες, ὧν ἕνεκα ἡ 29
ἔνδειξις ἐγένετο καὶ περὶ ὧν ὑμεῖς οἱ μεμυημένοι εἰσεληλύθατε, ἀποδέδεικταί μοι ὡς οὔτε ἠσέβηκα οὔτε μεμήνυκα περὶ οὐδενὸς οὔτε ὡμολόγηκα περὶ αὐτῶν, οὐδὲ ἔστι μοι ἁμάρτημα περὶ τὼ θεὼ οὔτε μεῖζον οὔτ' ἔλαττον οὐδέν. ὅπερ ἐμοὶ περὶ πλείστου ἐστὶν ὑμᾶς πεῖσαι. καὶ γὰρ οἱ λόγοι τῶν κατηγόρων—ταῦτα τὰ δεινὰ καὶ φρικώδη ἀνωρθίαζον, καὶ λόγους εἶπον ὡς πρότερον ἑτέρων ἁμαρτόντων καὶ ἀσεβησάντων περὶ τὼ θεώ, οἷα ἕκαστος αὐτῶν ἔπαθε καὶ ἐτιμωρήθη— τούτων οὖν ἐμοὶ τῶν λόγων ἢ τῶν ἔργων τί προσήκει; 30
ἐγὼ γὰρ πολὺ μᾶλλον ἐκείνων κατηγορῶ, καὶ δι' αὐτὸ τοῦτό φημι δεῖν ἐκείνους μὲν ἀπολέσθαι, ὅτι ἠσέβησαν, ἐμὲ δὲ σῴζεσθαι, ὅτι οὐδὲν ἡμάρτηκα. ἦ δεινόν γ' ἂν εἴη, εἰ ἐμοὶ ὀργίζοισθε ἐπὶ τοῖς ἑτέρων ἁμαρτήμασι, καὶ τὴν εἰς ἐμὲ διαβολὴν εἰδότες ὅτι ὑπὸ τῶν ἐχθρῶν τῶν ἐμῶν λέγεται, κρείττω τῆς ἀληθείας ἡγήσεσθε. δῆλον

29 ἀνωρθίαζον stp Harp. α 163 s.v. ἀνωρθίαζον, ac s.v. ἀνωρθρίαζον stp Photius α 2167 Suda α 2598 *Synagoge aucta* α I.107.3 Bachmann = Anec. Bekk. I.412.7 *Synagoge vers. B* α 1550 [Zonar.] α 223.25

244 μηνύσεις L : μυνήσεις A[1] : μυήσεις A 250 ἕνεκα Lipsius : εἵνεκα A 253 μεμήνυκα L : μεμύηκα A : μεμύνηκα A[1] 256 οἱ λόγοι τῶν κατηγόρων secl. Kayser[2], καὶ λόγους εἶπον l. 257 secl. Helbig <οἳ> ταῦτα Blass 257 ἀνωρθίαζον A Harp. : ἀνωρθρίαζον cett. lexica 261 ἐκείνων <ταῦτα> Blass 266 ἡγήσεσθε] ἡγήσαισθε Reiske 266–7 δῆλον γὰρ ὅτι Naber[1] : δῆλονότι γὰρ A

γὰρ ὅτι τοῖς μὲν ἡμαρτηκόσι τὰ τοιαῦτα ἁμαρτήματα
οὐκ ἔστιν ἀπολογία ὡς οὐκ ἐποίησαν· ἡ γὰρ βάσανος
δεινὴ παρὰ τοῖς εἰδόσιν· ἐμοὶ δὲ ὁ ἔλεγχος ἥδιστος, ἐν
οἷς ὑμῶν οὐδέν με δεῖ δεόμενον οὐδὲ παραιτούμενον
σωθῆναι ἐπὶ τοιαύτῃ αἰτίᾳ, ἀλλ' ἐλέγχοντα τοὺς
31 τῶν κατηγόρων λόγους. καὶ ὑμᾶς ἀναμιμνῄσκω τὰ
γεγενημένα, οἵτινες ὅρκους μεγάλους ὀμόσαντες οἴσετε
τὴν ψῆφον περὶ ἐμοῦ, καὶ ἀρασάμενοι τὰς μεγίστας
ἀρὰς ὑμῖν τε αὐτοῖς καὶ παισὶ τοῖς ὑμετέροις αὐτῶν, ἦ
μὴν ψηφιεῖσθαι περὶ ἐμοῦ τὰ δίκαια, πρὸς δὲ τούτοις
μεμύησθε καὶ ἑοράκατε τοῖν θεοῖν τὰ ἱερά, ἵνα
τιμωρήσητε μὲν τοὺς ἀσεβοῦντας, σῴζητε δὲ τοὺς
32 μηδὲν ἀδικοῦντας. νομίσατε τοίνυν ἀσέβημα οὐδὲν
ἔλαττον εἶναι τῶν μηδὲν ἠδικηκότων ἀσεβεῖν καταγνῶναι
ἢ τοὺς ἠσεβηκότας μὴ τιμωρεῖσθαι. ὥστ' ἐγὼ ὑμῖν
πολὺ μᾶλλον τῶν κατηγόρων πρὸς τοῖν θεοῖν ἐπισκήπτω,
ὑπέρ τε τῶν ἱερῶν ἃ εἴδετε, καὶ ὑπὲρ τῶν Ἑλλήνων οἳ
τῆς ἑορτῆς ἕνεκα ἔρχονται δεῦρο· εἰ μέν τι ἠσέβηκα ἢ
ὡμολόγηκα ἢ ἐμήνυσα κατά τινος ἀνθρώπων, ἢ ἄλλος
33 τις περὶ ἐμοῦ, ἀποκτείνατέ με· οὐ παραιτοῦμαι· εἰ δὲ
οὐδὲν ἡμάρτηταί μοι, καὶ τοῦτο ὑμῖν ἀποδείκνυμι σαφῶς,
δέομαι ὑμῶν αὐτὸ φανερὸν τοῖς Ἕλλησι πᾶσι ποιῆσαι,
ὡς ἀδίκως εἰς τόνδε τὸν ἀγῶνα κατέστην. ἐὰν γὰρ μὴ
μεταλάβῃ τὸ πέμπτον μέρος τῶν ψήφων καὶ ἀτιμωθῇ ὁ

32 ἐπισκήπτω Harp. ε 82.6 s.v. ἐπεσκήψατο, ac stp Phot. ε 1439.4 Suda ε 2083.4 *EM* 355.40 Gaisford *Anec. Oxon.* II.494.24

---

269 δεινὴ <ἡ> Blass[3] 271 τοιαύτῃ A[c] : τῇ τοιαύτῃ ut vid. A[a] 272 ἀναμιμνῄσκω A : ἀναμιμνῄσκοντα maluit Reiske 273 ὀμόσαντες M[1] : ὀμόσαντες A 274 ἀρασάμενοι A[1] : ἀράμενοι A 275–6 ἦ μὴν Klotz[1] : ἢ μην A[1] (ἢ in ras.) : εἰ (?) μὴν *** A[a] : εἰ μὴ L 276 ψηφιεῖσθαι A : ψηφιεῖσθε L 277 ἑοράκατε Lipsius : ἑωράκατε A 280 τῶν μηδὲν ἠδικηκότων Lipsius : τοὺς μηδὲν ἠδικηκότας A 284 ἕνεκα Blass[2] : ἕνεκεν A

ἐνδείξας ἐμὲ Κηφίσιος οὑτοσί, οὐκ ἔξεστιν αὐτῷ εἰς τὸ ἱερὸν τοῖν θεοῖν εἰσιέναι, ἢ ἀποθανεῖται. εἰ οὖν ὑμῖν δοκῶ ἱκανῶς περὶ τούτων ἀπολελογῆσθαι, δηλώσατέ μοι, ἵνα προθυμότερον περὶ τῶν ἄλλων ἀπολογῶμαι.

Περὶ δὲ τῶν ἀναθημάτων τῆς περικοπῆς καὶ τῆς 34
μηνύσεως, ὥσπερ καὶ ὑπεσχόμην ὑμῖν, οὕτω καὶ ποιήσω· ἐξ ἀρχῆς γὰρ ὑμᾶς διδάξω ἅπαντα τὰ γεγενημένα. ἐπειδὴ Τεῦκρος ἦλθε Μεγαρόθεν, ἄδειαν εὑρόμενος μηνύει περί τε τῶν μυστηρίων ἃ ᾔδει καὶ τῶν περικοψάντων τὰ ἀναθήματα, καὶ ἀπογράφει δυοῖν δέοντας εἴκοσιν ἄνδρας. ἐπειδὴ δὲ οὗτοι ἀπεγράφησαν, οἱ μὲν αὐτῶν φεύγοντες ᾤχοντο, οἱ δὲ συλληφθέντες ἀπέθανον κατὰ τὴν Τεύκρου μήνυσιν. καί μοι ἀνάγνωθι αὐτῶν τὰ ὀνόματα.

ΟΝΟΜΑΤΑ. Τεῦκρος ἐπὶ τοῖς Ἑρμαῖς ἐμήνυσεν Εὐκτήμονα, 35
Γλαύκιππον, Εὐρύμαχον, Πολύευκτον, Πλάτωνα, Ἀντίδωρον, Χάριππον, Θεόδωρον, Ἀλκισθένην, Μενέστρατον, Ἐρυξίμαχον, Εὐφίλητον, Εὐρυδάμαντα, Φερεκλέα, Μέλητον, Τιμάνθην, Ἀρχίδαμον, Τελένικον.

Τούτων τοίνυν τῶν ἀνδρῶν οἱ μὲν ἥκουσι καὶ εἰσὶν ἐνθάδε, τῶν δὲ ἀποθανόντων εἰσὶ πολλοὶ προσήκοντες· ὧν ὅστις βούλεται, ἐν τῷ ἐμῷ λόγῳ ἀναβάς με ἐλεγξάτω ἢ ὡς ἔφυγέ τις δι᾽ ἐμὲ τούτων τῶν ἀνδρῶν ἢ ὡς ἀπέθανεν.

Ἐπειδὴ δὲ ταῦτα ἐγένετο, Πείσανδρος καὶ Χαρικλῆς, 36
ὄντες μὲν τῶν ζητητῶν, δοκοῦντες δ᾽ ἐν ἐκείνῳ τῷ χρόνῳ εὐνούστατοι εἶναι τῷ δήμῳ, ἔλεγον ὡς εἴη τὰ ἔργα τὰ γεγενημένα οὐχ ὀλίγων ἀνδρῶν ἀλλ᾽ ἐπὶ τῇ τοῦ

36 *ζητητῶν* Harp. ζ 4.3 s.v. (item 14, 65)

---

291 *Κηφίσιος* Steph. : *κηφήσιος* A 299 *ἃ ᾔδει καὶ* Ald. : *ἃ ᾔδει ἐκ* A : *ἃ ᾔδει* <*καὶ*> *ἐκ* Rosenberg[1], qui *καὶ* l. 300 delevit : <*καὶ*> *ἃ ᾔδει ἐκ* Blass[2] 300 *εἴκοσιν* A[1]: *εἴκοσι* A[a] 306 *ἀλκισθένην* A : *Ἀλκισθένη* Schiller *Ἐρυξίμαχον* Steph. : *εὐρυξίμαχον* A 307 *εὐρυδάμαντα* L : *εὐρυμάδαντα* A : *Εὐρυμέδοντα* Lipsius *τιμάνθην* A : *Τιμάνθη* Schiller 316 *ἀλλ᾽ ἐπὶ*] *ἀλλὰ* <*πολλῶν*> *ἐπὶ* Dalmeyda

δήμου καταλύσει, καὶ χρῆναι ἔτι ζητεῖν καὶ μὴ παύσασθαι.
καὶ ἡ πόλις οὕτως διέκειτο, ὥστ' ἐπειδὴ τὴν βουλὴν εἰς
τὸ βουλευτήριον ὁ κῆρυξ ἀνείποι ἰέναι καὶ τὸ σημεῖον
καθέλοι, τῷ αὐτῷ σημείῳ ἡ μὲν βουλὴ εἰς τὸ
βουλευτήριον ᾔει, οἱ δ' ἐκ τῆς ἀγορᾶς ἔφευγον, δεδιότες
37 εἷς ἕκαστος μὴ συλληφθείη. ἐπαρθεὶς οὖν τοῖς τῆς
πόλεως κακοῖς εἰσαγγέλλει Διοκλείδης εἰς τὴν βουλήν,
φάσκων εἰδέναι τοὺς περικόψαντας τοὺς Ἑρμᾶς, καὶ
εἶναι αὐτοὺς εἰς τριακοσίους· ὡς δ' ἴδοι καὶ περιτύχοι
τῷ πράγματι, ἔλεγε. καὶ τούτοις, ὦ ἄνδρες, δέομαι
ὑμῶν προσέχοντας τὸν νοῦν ἀναμιμνῄσκεσθαι, ἐὰν
ἀληθῆ λέγω, καὶ διδάσκειν ἀλλήλους· ἐν ὑμῖν γὰρ ἦσαν
38 οἱ λόγοι, καί μοι ὑμεῖς τούτων μάρτυρές ἐστε. ἔφη γὰρ
εἶναι μὲν ἀνδράποδόν οἱ ἐπὶ Λαυρείῳ, δεῖν δὲ κομίσασθαι
ἀποφοράν. ἀναστὰς δὲ πρῴ ψευσθεὶς τῆς ὥρας βαδίζειν·
εἶναι δὲ πανσέληνον. ἐπεὶ δὲ παρὰ τὸ προπύλαιον τοῦ
Διονύσου ἦν, ὁρᾶν ἀνθρώπους πολλοὺς ἀπὸ τοῦ ᾠδείου
καταβαίνοντας εἰς τὴν ὀρχήστραν· δείσας δὲ αὐτούς,
εἰσελθὼν ὑπὸ τὴν σκιὰν καθέζεσθαι μεταξύ του κίονος
καί τῆς στήλης ἐφ' ᾗ ὁ στρατηγός ἐστιν ὁ χαλκοῦς. ὁρᾶν
δὲ ἀνθρώπους τὸν μὲν ἀριθμὸν μάλιστα τριακοσίους,
ἑστάναι δὲ κύκλῳ ἀνὰ πέντε καὶ δέκα ἄνδρας, τοὺς δὲ
ἀνὰ εἴκοσιν· ὁρῶν δὲ αὐτῶν πρὸς τὴν σελήνην τὰ
39 πρόσωπα τῶν πλείστων γιγνώσκειν. καὶ πρῶτον μέν, ὦ

38 ὁρᾶν (ἄδων Gal. : ἰδεῖν Sluiter) δ'—τριακοσίους Galenus *In Hippocr. de articulis* XVIII.1.450 Kuehn

---

317 ἔτι ζητεῖν A[c] : ἐπιζητεῖν A 319 ἀνείποι Schömann[1] : ἀνείπῃ A 321 ἔφευγον Baiter : ἔφυγον A 323 Διοκλείδης Ald. : διὸ καὶ δὶς A 324 τοὺς ἑρμᾶς A[1] : τὰς ἑρμᾶς A[a] 330 λαυρείῳ Ald. : λαυρίῳ A 331 πρῴ Reiske : πρωὶ A 332 τοῦ A : τὸ M 335 σκιὰν A[1] : οἰκίαν A[a] του Lipsius : τοῦ A 336 ὁρᾶν A : ἄδων Galenus 337 δὲ A : δ' Galenus μὲν Galenus : deest in A μάλιστα Galenus : deest in A 340 τῶν πλείστων A[1] : τὰ πλεῖστα A[a]

ἄνδρες, τοῦθ᾽ ὑπέθετο—δεινότατον πρᾶγμα, οἶμαι—ὅπως ἐν ἐκείνῳ εἴη ὅντινα βούλοιτο Ἀθηναίων φάναι τῶν ἀνδρῶν τούτων εἶναι, ὅντινα δὲ μὴ βούλοιτο, λέγειν ὅτι οὐκ ἦν. ἰδὼν δὲ ταῦτ᾽ ἔφη ἐπὶ Λαύρειον ἰέναι, καὶ τῇ ὑστεραίᾳ ἀκούειν ὅτι οἱ Ἑρμαῖ εἶεν περικεκομμένοι· γνῶναι οὖν εὐθὺς ὅτι τούτων εἴη τῶν ἀνδρῶν τὸ ἔργον. ἥκων δὲ εἰς ἄστυ ζητητάς τε ἤδη ᾑρημένους 40
καταλαμβάνειν καὶ μήνυτρα κεκηρυγμένα ἑκατὸν μνᾶς. ἰδὼν δὲ Εὔφημον τὸν Καλλίου τοῦ Τηλοκλέους ἀδελφὸν ἐν τῷ χαλκείῳ καθήμενον, ἀναγαγὼν αὐτὸν εἰς τὸ Ἡφαιστεῖον λέγειν ἅπερ ὑμῖν ἐγὼ εἴρηκα, ὡς ἴδοι ἡμᾶς ἐν ἐκείνῃ τῇ νυκτί· οὔκουν δέοιτο παρὰ τῆς πόλεως χρήματα λαβεῖν μᾶλλον ἢ παρ᾽ ἡμῶν, ὥσθ᾽ ἡμᾶς ἔχειν φίλους. εἰπεῖν οὖν τὸν Εὔφημον ὅτι καλῶς ποιήσειεν εἰπών, καὶ νῦν ἥκειν κελεῦσαί οἱ εἰς τὴν Λεωγόρου οἰκίαν, "Ἵνα ἐκεῖ συγγένῃ μετ᾽ ἐμοῦ Ἀνδοκίδῃ καὶ ἑτέροις οἷς δεῖ." ἥκειν ἔφη τῇ ὑστεραίᾳ, καὶ δὴ κόπτειν 41
τὴν θύραν· τὸν δὲ πατέρα τὸν ἐμὸν τυχεῖν ἐξιόντα, καὶ εἰπεῖν αὐτόν "Ἆρά γε σὲ οἵδε περιμένουσι; χρὴ μέντοι μὴ ἀπωθεῖσθαι τοιούτους φίλους." εἰπόντα δὲ αὐτὸν ταῦτα οἴχεσθαι. καὶ τούτῳ μὲν τῷ τρόπῳ τὸν πατέρα μου ἀπώλλυε, συνειδότα ἀποφαίνων. εἰπεῖν δὲ ἡμᾶς ὅτι δεδογμένον ἡμῖν εἴη δύο μὲν τάλαντα ἀργυρίου διδόναι οἱ ἀντὶ τῶν ἑκατὸν μνῶν τῶν ἐκ τοῦ δημοσίου, ἐὰν δὲ κατάσχωμεν ἡμεῖς ἃ βουλόμεθα, ἕνα αὐτὸν ἡμῶν εἶναι, πίστιν δὲ τούτων δοῦναί τε καὶ δέξασθαι. ἀποκρίνασθαι 42

344 *Λαύρειον* Lipsius : *λαυρίαν* A 349 *Τηλοκλέους* Kirchner : *τηλεκλέους* A 350 *τῷ* A : *τῳ* Valckenaer 351 *ἡμᾶς* Ald. : *ὑμᾶς* A 352 *δέοιτο*] *ἕλοιτο* Dalmeyda 355 *νῦν ἥκειν*] *συνήκειν* Emperius[1] *τὴν* et *οἰκίαν*, l. 356, del. Hirschig[1] 356 *συγγένῃ* A^c (*ται* s.v. add. deinde eras.) 359 *αὐτὸν* A : *αὐτῷ* Lipsius : *πρὸς αὐτόν* Reiske *ἆρά γε σὲ* sic accent. pos. Dobree : *ἆρα γέ σε* A 365 *βουλόμεθα* B : *βουλώμεθα* A *αὐτὸν* Reiske : *αὐτῶν* A

δὲ αὐτὸς πρὸς ταῦτα ὅτι βουλεύσοιτο· ἡμᾶς δὲ κελεύειν αὐτὸν ἥκειν εἰς Καλλίου τοῦ Τηλοκλέους ἵνα κἀκεῖνος παρείη. τὸν δ' αὖ κηδεστήν μου οὕτως ἀπώλλυεν. ἥκειν ἔφη εἰς Καλλίου, καὶ καθομολογήσας ἡμῖν πίστιν δοῦναι ἐν ἀκροπόλει, καὶ ἡμᾶς συνθεμένους οἱ τὸ ἀργύριον εἰς τὸν εἰσιόντα μῆνα δώσειν διαψεύδεσθαι καὶ οὐ διδόναι· ἥκειν οὖν μηνύσων τὰ γενόμενα.

43 Ἡ μὲν εἰσαγγελία αὐτῷ, ὦ ἄνδρες, τοιαύτη· ἀπογράφει δὲ τὰ ὀνόματα τῶν ἀνδρῶν ὧν ἔφη γνῶναι, δύο καὶ τετταράκοντα, πρώτους μὲν Μαντίθεον καὶ Ἀψεφίωνα, βουλευτὰς ὄντας καὶ καθημένους ἔνδον, εἶτα δὲ καὶ τοὺς ἄλλους. ἀναστὰς δὲ Πείσανδρος ἔφη χρῆναι λύειν τὸ ἐπὶ Σκαμανδρίου ψήφισμα καὶ ἀναβιβάζειν ἐπὶ τὸν τροχὸν τοὺς ἀπογραφέντας, ὅπως μὴ πρότερον νὺξ ἔσται πρὶν πυθέσθαι τοὺς ἄνδρας ἅπαντας. ἀνέκραγεν ἡ βουλὴ ὡς
44 εὖ λέγει. ἀκούσαντες δὲ ταῦτα Μαντίθεος καὶ Ἀψεφίων ἐπὶ τὴν ἑστίαν ἐκαθέζοντο, ἱκετεύοντες μὴ στρεβλωθῆναι ἀλλ' ἐξεγγυηθέντες κριθῆναι. μόλις δὲ τούτων τυχόντες, ἐπειδὴ τοὺς ἐγγυητὰς κατέστησαν, ἐπὶ τοὺς ἵππους ἀναβάντες ᾤχοντο εἰς τοὺς πολεμίους αὐτομολήσαντες, καταλιπόντες τοὺς ἐγγυητάς, οὓς ἔδει ⟨ἐν⟩ τοῖς αὐτοῖς
45 ἐνέχεσθαι ἐν οἷσπερ οὓς ἠγγυήσαντο. ἡ δὲ βουλὴ ἐξελθοῦσα ἐν ἀπορρήτῳ συνέλαβεν ἡμᾶς καὶ ἔδησεν ἐν τοῖς ξύλοις. ἀνακαλέσαντες δὲ τοὺς στρατηγοὺς ἀνειπεῖν ἐκέλευσαν Ἀθηναίων τοὺς μὲν ἐν ἄστει οἰκοῦντας ἰέναι εἰς τὴν ἀγορὰν τὰ ὅπλα λαβόντας, τοὺς δ' ἐν μακρῷ τείχει εἰς τὸ Θησεῖον, τοὺς δ' ἐν Πειραιεῖ εἰς τὴν

368 Τηλοκλέους Kirchner : τηλεκλέους A 369 παρείη A[1] : παρήει A[a] ἀπώλλυεν A[1] : ἀπώλλυε A[a] 372 εἰσιόντα A : ἐπιόντα Emperius[1] 374 αὐτῷ Reiske : αὐτῶν A 376 ἀψεφίωνα A : Ἀψηφίονα Lipsius 383 ἱκετεύοντες A[1] : ἡκετεύοντες A[a] 384 ἐξεγγυηθέντες Sluiter : ἐξεγγυηθέντας A μόλις A : μόγις Fuhr 387 add. Weidner 393 εἰς τὸ Reiske : εἴς τε A

Ἱπποδαμείαν ἀγοράν, τούς δὲ ἱππέας ἔτι ⟨πρὸ⟩ νυκτὸς σημῆναι τῇ σάλπιγγι ἥκειν εἰς τὸ Ἀνάκιον, τὴν δὲ βουλὴν εἰς ἀκρόπολιν ἰέναι κἀκεῖ καθεύδειν, τοὺς δὲ πρυτάνεις ἐν τῇ θόλῳ. Βοιωτοὶ δὲ πεπυσμένοι τὰ πράγματα ἐπὶ τοῖς ὁρίοις ἦσαν ἐξεστρατευμένοι. τὸν δὲ τῶν κακῶν τούτων αἴτιον Διοκλείδην ὡς σωτῆρα ὄντα τῆς πόλεως ἐπὶ ζεύγους ἦγον εἰς τὸ πρυτανεῖον στεφανώσαντες, καὶ ἐδείπνει ἐκεῖ.

Πρῶτον μὲν οὖν ταῦτα, ὦ ἄνδρες, ὁπόσοι ὑμῶν παρῆσαν, 46
ἀναμιμνῄσκεσθε καί τοὺς ἄλλους διδάσκετε· εἶτα δέ μοι τοὺς πρυτάνεις κάλει τοὺς τότε πρυτανεύσαντας, Φιλοκράτη καὶ τοὺς ἄλλους. διδάσκετε.

ΜΑΡΤΥΡΕΣ

Φέρε δή, καὶ τὰ ὀνόματα ὑμῖν ἀναγνώσομαι τῶν ἀνδρῶν 47
ὧν ἀπέγραψεν, ἵν᾽ εἰδῆτε ὅσους μοι τῶν συγγενῶν ἀπώλλυεν, πρῶτον μὲν τὸν πατέρα, εἶτα δὲ τὸν κηδεστήν, τὸν μὲν συνειδότα ἀποδεικνύς, τοῦ δ᾽ ἐν τῇ οἰκίᾳ φάσκων τὴν σύνοδον γενέσθαι. τῶν δ᾽ ἄλλων ἀκούσεσθε τὰ ὀνόματα. καὶ αὐτοῖς ἀναγίγνωσκε.

Χαρμίδης Ἀριστοτέλους·
οὗτος ἀνεψιὸς ἐμός· ἡ μήτηρ ἐκείνου καὶ ὁ πατὴρ ὁ ἐμὸς ἀδελφοί.

Ταυρέας·
οὑτοσὶ ἀνεψιὸς τοῦ πατρός.

394 Ἱπποδαμείαν Turr. auctore Lobeckio (ad S. *Aj.* 108) : ἱπποδαμίαν A ἱππέας Jebb : ἱππεῖς A add. Blass 395 Ἀνάκιον Blass^3 : ἀνάκειον A 398 ἐξεστρατευμένοι A^1 : ἐστρατευμένοι A^a 399 τῶν add. A^{1sv} 400 ζεύγους A^1 : ζεῦγος A^a 401 στεφανώσαντες Bekker, Dobree : στεφανώσοντες A 405 διδάσκετε del. Muret 407 ὑμῖν A^{1im} : om. A^a 412 ἀναγίνωσκε A^1 : ἀναγινώσκετε A^a 414 <ἥ> ἐκείνου Bekker

Νισαῖος·
υἱὸς Ταυρέου.
Καλλίας ὁ Ἀλκμέωνος·
ἀνεψιὸς τοῦ πατρός.
Εὔφημος·
Καλλίου τοῦ Τηλοκλέους ἀδελφός.
Φρύνιχος ὁ ὀρχησάμενος·
ἀνεψιός.
Εὐκράτης ὁ Νικίου ἀδελφός·
κηδεστὴς οὗτος Καλλίου.
Κριτίας·
ἀνεψιὸς {Εὐκρατίας ὁ Νικίου ἀδελφὸς} καὶ οὗτος τοῦ πατρός· αἱ μητέρες ἀδελφαί.

Τούτους πάντας ἐν τοῖς τετταράκοντα ἀνδράσιν ἀπέγραψεν.

48 Ἐπειδὴ δὲ ἐδεδέμεθα πάντες ἐν τῷ αὐτῷ καὶ νύξ τε ἦν καὶ τὸ δεσμωτήριον συνεκέκλῃτο, ἧκον δὲ τῷ μὲν μήτηρ τῷ δὲ ἀδελφὴ τῷ δὲ γυνὴ καὶ παῖδες, ἦν δὲ βοὴ καὶ οἶκτος κλαόντων καὶ ὀδυρομένων τὰ παρόντα κακά, λέγει πρός με Χαρμίδης, ὢν μὲν ἀνεψιός, ἡλικιώτης δὲ καὶ συνεκτραφεὶς ἐν τῇ οἰκίᾳ τῇ ἡμετέρᾳ ἐκ παιδός, ὅτι 49 "Ἀνδοκίδη, τῶν μὲν παρόντων κακῶν ὁρᾷς τὸ μέγεθος, ἐγὼ δ' ἐν μὲν τῷ παρελθόντι χρόνῳ οὐδὲν ἐδεόμην λέγειν οὐδέ σε λυπεῖν, νῦν δὲ ἀναγκάζομαι διὰ τὴν παροῦσαν ἡμῖν συμφοράν. οἷς γὰρ ἐχρῶ καὶ οἷς συνῆσθα ἄνευ ἡμῶν τῶν συγγενῶν, οὗτοι ἐπὶ ταῖς αἰτίαις δι' ἃς

48 *ἐδεδέμεθα* stp Poll. 8.72.2, qui tamen Aeschini attribuit

420 *Ἀλκμέωνος* Blass[2] : *ἀλκμαίονος* A 423 *Τηλοκλέους* Kirchner : *τηλεκλέους* A 424 *Φρύνιχος* Ald. : *φρίνικος* A *ὀρχησάμενος* A : *Ὀρχησαμενοῦ* Wilhelm (cfr. Rosenberg[1] 341) 429 del. Reiske 432 *ἀπέγραψεν* Steph. : *ἐπέγραψεν* A 434 *συνεκέκλῃτο* Sauppe : *συνεκέκλειστο* A 436 *κλαόντων* Schiller : *κλαιόντων* A

ἡμεῖς ἀπολλύμεθα οἱ μὲν αὐτῶν τεθνᾶσιν, οἱ δὲ οἴχονται
φεύγοντες, σφῶν αὐτῶν καταγνόντες ἀδικεῖν <. . .> εἰ 50
ἤκουσάς τι τούτου τοῦ πράγματος τοῦ γενομένου, εἰπέ,
καὶ πρῶτον μὲν σεαυτὸν σῷσον, εἶτα δὲ τὸν πατέρα, ὃν
εἰκός ἐστί σε μάλιστα φιλεῖν, εἶτα δὲ τὸν κηδεστήν, ὃς
ἔχει σου τὴν ἀδελφὴν ἥπερ σοι μόνη ἐστίν, ἔπειτα δὲ
τοὺς ἄλλους συγγενεῖς καὶ ἀναγκαίους τοσούτους
ὄντας, ἔτι δὲ ἐμέ, ὃς ἐν ἅπαντι τῷ βίῳ ἠνίασα μέν σε
οὐδὲν πώποτε, προθυμότατος δὲ εἰς σὲ καὶ τὰ σὰ
πράγματά εἰμι, ὅ τι ἂν δέῃ ποιεῖν.” λέγοντος δέ, ὦ 51
ἄνδρες, Χαρμίδου ταῦτα, ἀντιβολούντων δὲ τῶν ἄλλων
καὶ ἱκετεύοντος ἑνὸς ἑκάστου, ἐνεθυμήθην πρὸς ἐμαυτόν·
“Ὦ πάντων ἐγὼ δεινοτάτῃ συμφορᾷ περιπεσών, πότερα
περιίδω τοὺς ἐμαυτοῦ συγγενεῖς ἀπολλυμένους ἀδίκως,
καὶ αὐτούς τε ἀποθανόντας καὶ τὰ χρήματα αὐτῶν
δημευθέντα, πρὸς δὲ τούτοις ἀναγραφέντας ἐν στήλαις
ὡς ὄντας ἀλιτηρίους τῶν θεῶν τοὺς οὐδενὸς αἰτίους τῶν
γεγενημένων, ἔτι δὲ τριακοσίους Ἀθηναίων μέλλοντας
ἀδίκως ἀπολεῖσθαι, τὴν δὲ πόλιν ἐν κακοῖς οὖσαν τοῖς
μεγίστοις καὶ ὑποψίαν εἰς ἀλλήλους ἔχοντας, ἢ εἴπω Ἀθη-
ναίοις ἅπερ ἤκουσα Εὐφιλήτου αὐτοῦ τοῦ ποιήσαντος;”
ἔτι δὲ ἐπὶ τούτοις καὶ τόδε ἐνεθυμήθην, ὦ ἄνδρες, καὶ 52
ἐλογιζόμην πρὸς ἐμαυτὸν τοὺς ἐξημαρτηκότας καὶ τὸ
ἔργον εἰργασμένους, ὅτι οἱ μὲν αὐτῶν ἤδη ἐτεθνήκεσαν
ὑπὸ Τεύκρου μηνυθέντες, οἱ δὲ φεύγοντες ᾤχοντο καὶ
αὐτῶν θάνατος κατέγνωστο, τέτταρες δὲ ἦσαν ὑπόλοιποι
οἳ οὐκ ἐμηνύθησαν ὑπὸ Τεύκρου τῶν πεποιηκότων,
Παναίτιος Χαιρέδημος Διάκριτος Λυσίστρατος· οὓς 53

445 post *ἀδικεῖν* vac. spat. xi–xii litt. in A : <*τούτων τοίνυν*> Sauppe : <*ἀλλὰ δέομαί σου*> Schoell[2] : alia alii 453 *δέῃ* Bekker, Dobree : *δέοι* A 457 *ἀπολλυμένους* A : *ἀπολομένους* Lipsius 460 *ἀλιτηρίους* L[1] (*ηρίου* in ras.) : *ἀλιτρίους* re vera A 462 *ἀπολεῖσθαι* Steph. : *ἀπολέσθαι* A : *ἀπολῆσθαι* Ald 467 *ἐτεθνήκεσαν* A : *ἐτέθνασαν* Fuhr[3]

εἰκὸς ἦν ἁπάντων μάλιστα δοκεῖν εἶναι τούτων τῶν ἀνδρῶν οὓς ἐμήνυσε Διοκλείδης, φίλους ὄντας τῶν ἀπολωλότων ἤδη. καὶ τοῖς μὲν οὐδέπω βέβαιος ἦν ἡ σωτηρία, τοῖς δὲ ἐμοῖς οἰκείοις φανερὸς ⟨ὁ⟩ ὄλεθρος, εἰ μή τις ἐρεῖ Ἀθηναίοις τὰ γενόμενα. ἐδόκει οὖν μοι κρεῖττον εἶναι τέτταρας ἄνδρας ἀποστερῆσαι τῆς πατρίδος δικαίως, οἳ νῦν ζῶσι καὶ κατεληλύθασι καὶ ἔχουσι τὰ σφέτερα αὐτῶν, ἢ ἐκείνους ἀποθανόντας
54 *ἀδίκως περιιδεῖν. εἰ οὖν τινι ὑμῶν, ὦ ἄνδρες, τῶν ἄλλων πολιτῶν γνώμη τοιαύτη παρειστήκει πρότερον περὶ ἐμοῦ, ὡς ἄρα ἐγὼ ἐμήνυσα κατὰ τῶν ἑταίρων τῶν ἐμαυτοῦ, ὅπως ἐκεῖνοι μὲν ἀπόλοιντο, ἐγὼ δὲ σωθείην (ἃ ἐλογοποίουν οἱ ἐχθροὶ περὶ ἐμοῦ, βουλόμενοι διαβάλλειν με), σκοπεῖσθε ἐξ αὐτῶν τῶν γεγενημένων.*
55 *νῦν γὰρ ἐμὲ μὲν λόγον ⟨δεῖ⟩ δοῦναι τῶν ἐμοὶ πεπραγμένων μετὰ τῆς ἀληθείας, αὐτῶν παρόντων οἵπερ ἥμαρτον καὶ ἔφυγον ταῦτα ποιήσαντες, ἴσασι δὲ ἄριστα εἴτε ψεύδομαι εἴτε ἀληθῆ λέγω, ἔξεστι δὲ αὐτοῖς ἐλέγχειν με ἐν τῷ*
56 *ἐμῷ λόγῳ· ἐγὼ γὰρ ἐφίημι· ὑμᾶς δὲ δεῖ μαθεῖν τὰ γενόμενα (ἐμοὶ γάρ, ὦ ἄνδρες, τοῦδε τοῦ ἀγῶνος τοῦτ᾽ ἔστι μέγιστον, σωθέντι μὴ δοκεῖν κακῷ εἶναι), εἶτα δὲ καὶ τοὺς ἄλλους ἅπαντας μαθεῖν ὅτι οὔτε μετὰ κακίας οὔτε μετ᾽ ἀνανδρίας οὐδεμιᾶς τῶν γεγενημένων πέπρακται ὑπ᾽ ἐμοῦ οὐδέν, ἀλλὰ διὰ συμφορὰν γεγενημένην μάλιστα μὲν τῇ πόλει, εἶτα ⟨δὲ⟩ καὶ ἡμῖν, εἶπον δὲ ἃ ἤκουσα Εὐφιλήτου προνοίᾳ μὲν τῶν συγγενῶν καὶ τῶν φίλων, προνοίᾳ δὲ τῆς πόλεως ἁπάσης, μετ᾽ ἀρετῆς ἀλλ᾽ οὐ μετὰ κακίας, ὡς ἐγὼ νομίζω. εἰ οὖν οὕτως ἔχει ταῦτα,*

473 *φίλους* <*γ’*> Hirschig[1] 475 add. Reiske 480 *ὑμῶν* A[1] (*ῶν* in ras.) <*ἢ*> *τῶν* Sched. Eton., Sluiter 486 add. Reiske *δοῦναι* Dobree : *διδόναι* A 491–2 parentheses posui auctore MacDowellio : alii lacunam statuerunt, varie emend. conati 496 add. Reiske : 2 litt. eras. in A *δὲ* A[1] : om. ut vid. A[a], del. Reiske

σῴζεσθαί τε ἀξιῶ καὶ δοκεῖν ὑμῖν εἶναι μὴ κακός. φέρε δὴ (χρὴ γάρ, ὦ ἄνδρες, ἀνθρωπίνως περὶ τῶν 57 *πραγμάτων ἐκλογίζεσθαι, ὥσπερ ἂν αὐτὸν ὄντα ἐν τῇ συμφορᾷ), τί ἂν ὑμῶν ἕκαστος ἐποίησεν; εἰ μὲν γὰρ ἦν δυοῖν τὸ ἕτερον ἑλέσθαι, ἢ καλῶς ἀπολέσθαι ἢ αἰσχρῶς σωθῆναι, ἔχοι ἄν τις εἰπεῖν κακίαν εἶναι τὰ γενόμενα· καίτοι πολλοὶ ἂν καὶ τοῦτο εἵλοντο, τὸ ζῆν περὶ πλείονος ποιησάμενοι τοῦ καλῶς ἀποθανεῖν· ὅπου δὲ τούτων τὸ* 58 *ἐναντιώτατον ἦν, σιωπήσαντι μὲν αὐτῷ τε αἴσχιστα ἀπολέσθαι μηδὲν ἀσεβήσαντι, ἔτι δὲ τὸν πατέρα περιιδεῖν ἀπολόμενον καὶ τὸν κηδεστὴν καὶ τοὺς συγγενεῖς καὶ ἀνεψιοὺς τοσούτους, οὓς οὐδεὶς ἄλλος ἀπώλλυεν ἢ ἐγὼ μὴ εἰπὼν ὡς ἕτεροι ἥμαρτον· Διοκλείδης μὲν γὰρ ψευσάμενος ἔδησεν αὐτούς, σωτηρία δὲ αὐτῶν ἄλλη οὐδεμία ἦν ἢ πυθέσθαι Ἀθηναίους πάντα τὰ πραχθέντα· φονεὺς οὖν αὐτῶν ἐγιγνόμην ἐγὼ μὴ εἰπὼν ὑμῖν ἃ ἤκουσα. ἔτι δὲ τριακοσίους Ἀθηναίων ἀπώλλυον, καί ἡ πόλις ἐν κακοῖς τοῖς μεγίστοις ἐγίγνετο. ταῦτα* 59 *μὲν οὖν ἦν ἐμοῦ μὴ εἰπόντος· εἰπὼν δὲ τὰ ὄντα αὐτός τε ἐσῳζόμην καὶ τὸν πατέρα ἔσῳζον καὶ τοὺς ἄλλους συγγενεῖς, καὶ τὴν πόλιν ἐκ φόβου καὶ κακῶν τῶν μεγίστων ἀπήλλαττον. φυγάδες δὲ δι' ἐμὲ τέτταρες ἄνδρες ἐγίγνοντο, οἵπερ καὶ ἥμαρτον· τῶν δ' ἄλλων, οἳ {λοιποὶ} πρότερον ὑπὸ Τεύκρου ἐμηνύθησαν, οὔτε δήπου οἱ τεθνεῶτες δι' ἐμὲ μᾶλλον ἐτέθνασαν οὔτε οἱ φεύγοντες μᾶλλον ἔφευγον. ταῦτα δὲ πάντα σκοπῶν ηὕρισκον, ὦ* 60

504 *δυοῖν* Bekker : *δυσὶ* A, quod obelis inclusit MacDowell   505 *ἔχοι* A^1 : *ἔχει* A^a *γενόμενα* Reiske : *λεγόμενα* A   510 aut *τοὺς* <*ἄλλους*> *συγγενεῖς καὶ ἀναγκαίους τοσούτους* <*ὄντας*> aut *συγγενεῖς καὶ ἀναγκαίους τοσούτους* legendum esse censuit Blass[3]   511 *ἄλλος* A : om. B et cett.   512 *μὲν* A^1 : om. A^a 517 post *ἐγίνετο* 2 litt. eras. in A   522 *οἳ* Dobree : *οἱ* A   523 del. Dobree   *πρότερον* A^{1im} : om. A^a 525 *ηὕρισκον* Lipsius : *εὕρισκον* A

ἄνδρες, τῶν παρόντων κακῶν ταῦτα ἐλάχιστα εἶναι, εἰπεῖν τὰ γενόμενα ὡς τάχιστα καὶ ἐλέγξαι Διοκλείδην ψευσάμενον, καὶ τιμωρήσασθαι ἐκεῖνον, ὃς ἡμᾶς μὲν ἀπώλλυεν ἀδίκως, τὴν δὲ πόλιν ἐξηπάτα, ταῦτα δὲ ποιῶν μέγιστος εὐεργέτης ἐδόκει εἶναι καὶ χρήματα

61 ἐλάμβανε. διὰ ταῦτα εἶπον τῇ βουλῇ ὅτι εἰδείην τοὺς ποιήσαντας, καὶ ἐξήλεγξα τὰ γενόμενα, ὅτι εἰσηγήσατο μὲν πινόντων ἡμῶν ταύτην τὴν βουλὴν {γενέσθαι} Εὐφίλητος, ἀντεῖπον δὲ ἐγώ, καὶ τότε μὲν οὐ γένοιτο δι' ἐμέ, ὕστερον δ' ἐγὼ μὲν ἐν Κυνοσάργει ἐπὶ πωλίον ὅ μοι ἦν ἀναβὰς ἔπεσον καὶ τὴν κλεῖν συνετρίβην καὶ τὴν κεφαλὴν κατεάγην, φερόμενός τε ἐπὶ κλίνης ἀπεκομίσθην

62 οἴκαδε· αἰσθόμενος δ' Εὐφίλητος ὡς ἔχοιμι, λέγει πρὸς αὐτοὺς ὅτι πέπεισμαι ταῦτα συμποιεῖν καὶ ὡμολόγηκα αὐτῷ μεθέξειν τοῦ ἔργου καὶ περικόψειν τὸν Ἑρμῆν τὸν παρὰ τὸ Φορβαντεῖον. ταῦτα δ' ἔλεγεν ἐξαπατῶν ἐκείνους· καὶ διὰ ταῦτα ὁ Ἑρμῆς ὃν ὁρᾶτε πάντες, ὁ παρὰ τὴν πατρῴαν οἰκίαν τὴν ἡμετέραν, ὃν ἡ Αἰγῂς ἀνέθηκεν, οὐ περιεκόπη μόνος τῶν Ἑρμῶν τῶν Ἀθήνησιν, ὡς ἐμοῦ

63 τοῦτο ποιήσοντος, ὡς ἔφη πρὸς αὐτοὺς Εὐφίλητος. οἱ δ' αἰσθόμενοι δεινὰ ἐποίουν, ὅτι εἰδείην μὲν τὸ πρᾶγμα, πεποιηκὼς δὲ οὐκ εἴην. προσελθόντες δέ μοι τῇ ὑστεραίᾳ Μέλητος καὶ Εὐφίλητος ἔλεγον ὅτι "Γεγένηται, ὦ Ἀνδοκίδη, καὶ πέπρακται ἡμῖν ταῦτα. σὺ μέντοι, εἰ μὲν ἀξιοῖς ἡσυχίαν ἔχειν καὶ σιωπᾶν, ἕξεις ἡμᾶς ἐπιτηδείους ὥσπερ καὶ πρότερον· εἰ δὲ μή, χαλεπώτεροί σοι ἡμεῖς

62 Αἰγῂς Harp. α 128.3–4 s.v. *Ἀνδοκίδου Ἑρμῆς*, ac stp Phot. α 1737

532 *ἐξήλεγξα* A : *ἐπέδειξα* MacDowell 533 del. Bekker 534 *τότε* A[c] : *τόπε* A[a] *οὐ γένοιτο*] *οὐκ ἐγένετο* Schoell[2] 535 *πωλίον* Muret : *πωλεῖον* A 540 *αὐτῷ* A[c] : *αὐτῶν* A[a] 541 *Φορβαντεῖον* de Valois : *φορβάντιον* A 543 Αἰγῂς Lipsius : *αἰγηὶς* A 545 *ποιήσοντος* Valckenaer : *ποιήσαντος* A 549 *ἡμῖν* A[1] : *ὑμῖν* A[a] 551 *σοι* in ras. A[1]

ἐχθροὶ ἐσόμεθα ἢ ἄλλοι τινὲς δι᾽ ἡμᾶς φίλοι." εἶπον 64
αὐτοῖς ὅτι νομίζοιμι μὲν διὰ τὸ πρᾶγμα Εὐφίλητον
πονηρὸν εἶναι, ἐκείνοις δὲ οὐκ ἐμὲ δεινὸν εἶναι, ὅτι οἶδα,
ἀλλὰ μᾶλλον αὐτὸ τὸ ἔργον πολλῷ, ὅτι πεποίηται. ὡς
οὖν ἦν ταῦτ᾽ ἀληθῆ, τόν τε παῖδα τὸν ἐμὸν παρέδωκα
βασανίσαι, ὅτι ἔκαμνον καὶ οὐδ᾽ ἀνιστάμην ἐκ τῆς
κλίνης, καὶ τὰς θεραπαίνας ἔλαβον οἱ πρυτάνεις, ὅθεν
ὁρμώμενοι ταῦτ᾽ ἐποίουν ἐκεῖνοι. ἐξελέγχοντες δὲ τὸ 65
πρᾶγμα ἥ τε βουλὴ καὶ οἱ ζητηταί, ἐπειδὴ ἦν ἣ ἐγὼ
ἔλεγον καὶ ὡμολογεῖτο πανταχόθεν, τότε δὴ καλοῦσι
τὸν Διοκλείδην· καὶ οὐ πολλῶν λόγων ἐδέησεν, ἀλλ᾽
εὐθὺς ὡμολόγει ψεύδεσθαι, καὶ ἐδεῖτο σῴζεσθαι
φράσας τοὺς πείσαντας αὐτὸν λέγειν ταῦτα· εἶναι δὲ
Ἀλκιβιάδην τὸν Φηγούσιον καὶ Ἀμίαντον τὸν ἐξ Αἰγίνης.
καὶ οὗτοι μὲν δείσαντες ᾤχοντο φεύγοντες· ὑμεῖς δὲ 66
ἀκούσαντες ταῦτα Διοκλείδην μὲν τῷ δικαστηρίῳ
παραδόντες ἀπεκτείνατε, τοὺς δὲ δεδεμένους καὶ
μέλλοντας ἀπολεῖσθαι ἐλύσατε, τοὺς ἐμοὺς συγγενεῖς,
δι᾽ ἐμέ, καὶ τοὺς φεύγοντας κατεδέξασθε, αὐτοὶ δὲ
λαβόντες τὰ ὅπλα ἀπῇτε, πολλῶν κακῶν καὶ κινδύνων
ἀπαλλαγέντες. ἐν οἷς ἐγώ, ὦ ἄνδρες, τῆς μὲν τύχης ᾗ 67
ἐχρησάμην δικαίως ἂν ὑπὸ πάντων ἐλεηθείην, τῶν δὲ
γενομένων ἕνεκα εἰκότως ἀνὴρ ἄριστος δοκοίην εἶναι,
ὅστις εἰσηγησαμένῳ μὲν Εὐφιλήτῳ πίστιν τῶν ἐν
ἀνθρώποις ἀπιστοτάτην ἠναντιώθην καὶ ἀντεῖπον καὶ
ἐλοιδόρησα ἐκεῖνον ὧν ἦν ἄξιος, ἁμαρτόντων δ᾽ ἐκείνων

65 ζητηταί Harp. ζ 4 s.v. (item 14, 36) **67** τῆς μὲν—ἐλεηθείην Priscian. 18.211 p. 311 Hertz

556 οὖν A[1] : δ᾽ ut vid. A[a] ταῦτ᾽ L : ταῦθ᾽ A 571 ἀπῇτε Weidner : ἀπίητε A 573 ὑπὸ πάντων A : ὑφ᾽ ὑμῶν Priscian δὲ <δι᾽ ἐμὲ> Blass 574 γενομένων Baiter : γινομένων A ἕνεκα Blass[2] : ἕνεκεν A εἰκότως <ἂν> Reiske 577 ἐκεῖνον Lipsius : ἐκείνω A[c]: ἐκείνων A[a] : del. Weidner

τὴν ἁμαρτίαν αὐτοῖς συνέκρυψα, καὶ μηνύσαντος κατ'
αὐτῶν Τεύκρου οἱ μὲν αὐτῶν ἀπέθανον οἱ δὲ ἔφυγον,
πρὶν ἡμᾶς ὑπὸ Διοκλείδου δεθῆναι καὶ μέλλειν
ἀπολεῖσθαι. τότε δὲ ἀπέγραψα τέτταρας ἄνδρας,
68 Παναίτιον Διάκριτον Λυσίτρατον Χαιρέδημον· οὗτοι
μὲν ἔφυγον δι' ἐμέ, ὁμολογῶ· ἐσώθη δέ γε ὁ πατήρ,
ὁ κηδεστής, ἀνεψιοὶ τρεῖς, τῶν ἄλλων συγγενῶν ἑπτά,
μέλλοντες ἀποθανεῖσθαι ἀδίκως· οἳ νῦν ὁρῶσι τοῦ ἡλίου
τὸ φῶς δι' ἐμέ, καὶ αὐτοὶ ὁμολογοῦσιν· ὁ δὲ τὴν πόλιν
ὅλην συνταράξας καὶ εἰς τοὺς ἐσχάτους κινδύνους
καταστήσας ἐξηλέγχθη, ὑμεῖς δὲ ἀπηλλάγητε μεγάλων
69 φόβων καὶ τῶν εἰς ἀλλήλους ὑποψιῶν. καὶ ταῦτ' εἰ
ἀληθῆ λέγω, ὦ ἄνδρες, ἀναμιμνῄσκεσθε, καὶ οἱ εἰδότες
διδάσκετε τοὺς ἄλλους. σὺ δέ μοι αὐτοὺς κάλει τοὺς
λυθέντας δι' ἐμέ· ἄριστα γὰρ ἂν εἰδότες τὰ γενόμενα
λέγοιεν εἰς τούτους. οὑτωσὶ δὲ ἔχει, ὦ ἄνδρες· μέχρι
τούτου ἀναβήσονται καὶ λέξουσιν ὑμῖν, ἕως ἂν ἀκροᾶσθαι
βούλησθε, ἔπειτα δ' ἐγὼ περὶ τῶν ἄλλων ἀπολογήσομαι.

⟨ΜΑΡΤΥΡΕΣ⟩

70 Περὶ μὲν οὖν τῶν τότε γενομένων ἀκηκόατε πάντα καὶ
ἀπολελόγηταί μοι ἱκανῶς, ὥς γ' ἐμαυτὸν πείθω· εἰ δέ τίς
τι ὑμῶν ποθεῖ ἢ νομίζει τι μὴ ἱκανῶς εἰρῆσθαι ἢ
παραλέλοιπά τι, ἀναστὰς ὑπομνησάτω, καὶ ἀπολογήσομαι
καὶ πρὸς τοῦτο· περὶ δὲ τῶν νόμων ἤδη ὑμᾶς διδάξω.
71 Κηφίσιος γὰρ οὑτοσὶ ἐνέδειξε μέν με κατὰ τὸν νόμον τὸν
κείμενον, τὴν δὲ κατηγορίαν ποιεῖται κατὰ ψήφισμα

579 δὲ A : δ' L 584 ἀνεψιοὶ τρεῖς ... ἑπτά A : ἀνεψιοὶ τρεῖς ... πέντε Sluiter : ἀνεψιὸς εἷς ... ἑπτά Elter 588 ἐξηλέγχθη L : ἐξηλέγχη A 590 οἱ A[1] : om. A[a] εἰδότες Reiske : ἰδόντες A 592 εἰδότες A[1] : ἰδόντες A[a] 596 tit. add . Markland : vac. spat. 3 litt. in A 599 pr. τι A[1sv] : om. A[a]

πρότερον γενόμενον, ὃ εἶπεν Ἰσοτιμίδης, οὗ ἐμοὶ προσήκει
οὐδέν. ὁ μὲν γὰρ εἶπεν εἴργεσθαι τῶν ἱερῶν τοὺς
ἀσεβήσαντας καὶ ὁμολογήσαντας, ἐμοὶ δὲ τούτων
οὐδέτερα πεποίηται· οὔτε ἠσέβηται οὔτε ὡμολόγηται. ὡς 72
δὲ καὶ τοῦτο τὸ ψήφισμα λέλυται καὶ ἄκυρόν ἐστιν, ἐγὼ
ὑμᾶς διδάξω. καίτοι γε τοιαύτην ἀπολογίαν περὶ αὐτοῦ
ποιήσομαι, ὅπου μὴ πείθων μὲν ὑμᾶς αὐτὸς ζημιώσομαι,
πείσας δὲ ὑπὲρ τῶν ἐχθρῶν ἀπολελογημένος ἔσομαι. ἀλλὰ
γὰρ τἀληθῆ εἰρήσεται. ἐπεὶ γὰρ αἱ νῆες διεφθάρησαν καὶ 73
ἡ πολιορκία ἐγένετο, ἐβουλεύσασθε περὶ ὁμονοίας, καὶ
ἔδοξεν ὑμῖν τοὺς ἀτίμους ἐπιτίμους ποιῆσαι, καὶ εἶπε τὴν
γνώμην Πατροκλείδης. οἱ δὲ ἄτιμοι τίνες ἦσαν, καὶ τίνα
τρόπον ἕκαστοι; ἐγὼ ὑμᾶς διδάξω. οἱ μὲν ἀργύριον
ὀφείλοντες τῷ δημοσίῳ, ὁπόσοι εὐθύνας ὦφλον ἄρξαντες
ἀρχάς, ἢ ἐξούλας ἢ γραφὰς ἢ ἐπιβολὰς ὦφλον, ἢ ὠνὰς
πριάμενοι ἐκ τοῦ δημοσίου μὴ κατέβαλον τὰ χρήματα,
ἢ ἐγγύας ἠγγυήσαντο πρὸς τὸ δημόσιον· τούτοις ἡ
μὲν ἔκτεισις ἦν ἐπὶ τῆς ἐνάτης πρυτανείας, εἰ δὲ μή,
διπλάσιον ὀφείλειν καὶ τὰ κτήματα αὐτῶν πεπρᾶσθαι.
εἷς μὲν τρόπος οὗτος ἀτιμίας ἦν, ἕτερος δὲ ὧν τὰ μὲν 74
σώματα ἄτιμα ἦν, τὴν δ' οὐσίαν εἶχον καὶ ἐκέκτηντο.
οὗτοι δ' αὖ ἦσαν ὁπόσοι κλοπῆς ἢ δώρων ὄφλοιεν·
τούτους ἔδει καὶ αὐτοὺς καὶ τοὺς ἐκ τούτων ἀτίμους εἶναι·

74 τούτους ἔδει (οὕτω δὲ δεῖ Suda)—εἶναι stp Suda α 2115 s.v. ἀναυμαχίου

---

604 Ἰσοτιμίδης, οὗ Reiske : εἰς ὅτι μὴδ' ἴσου A 605 εἴργεσθαι B : εἴργευθαι A 613 ἐβουλεύσασθε A[1] : ἐβουλεύσασθαι A[a] 617 ὦφλον Reiske : ὤφειλον A ἄρξαντες Ald. : ἄρξαντας A 618 ἐπιβολὰς Steph. : ἐπιβουλὰς A 620 ἠγγυήσαντο Steph. : ἐγγυήσαντο A : ἐγγυησάμενοι Reiske 621 ἔκτεισις Blass[2] : ἔκτισις A ἐνάτης A[c] : ἐννάτης A[a] 623 τὰ μὲν Ald. : μὲν τὰ codd. 624 εἶχον Bekker : ἔσχον A 625 δ' αὖ hinc ante κλοπῆς transtulit MacDowell 625–6 ὁπόσοι ... εἶναι hinc ante εἷς μὲν l. 623 transtulit Paoli 626 τούτους ἔδει A : οὕτω δὲ δεῖ Suda ἐκ τούτων A : ἐξ αὐτῶν Suda

καὶ ὁπόσοι λίποιεν τὴν τάξιν ἢ ἀστρατείας ἢ δειλίας ἢ ἀναυμαχίου ὄφλοιεν ἢ τὴν ἀσπίδα ἀποβάλοιεν, ἢ τρὶς ψευδομαρτυριῶν ἢ τρὶς ψευδοκλητείας ὄφλοιεν, ἢ τοὺς γονέας κακῶς ποιοῖεν· οὗτοι πάντες ἄτιμοι ἦσαν τὰ
75 *σώματα, τὰ δὲ χρήματα εἶχον. ἄλλοι αὖ κατὰ προστάξεις, οἵτινες οὐ παντάπασιν ἄτιμοι ἦσαν, ἀλλὰ μέρος τι αὑτῶν, οἷον οἱ στρατιῶται, οἷς, ὅτι ἐπέμειναν ἐπὶ τῶν τυράννων ἐν τῇ πόλει, τὰ μὲν ἄλλα ἦν ἅπερ τοῖς ἄλλοις πολίταις, εἰπεῖν δ' ἐν τῷ δήμῳ οὐκ ἐξῆν αὐτοῖς οὐδὲ βουλεῦσαι. τούτων ἦσαν οὗτοι ἄτιμοι· αὕτη γὰρ ἦν*
76 *τούτοις πρόσταξις. ἑτέροις οὐκ ἦν γράψασθαι, τοῖς δὲ ἐνδεῖξαι· τοῖς δὲ μὴ ἀναπλεῦσαι εἰς Ἑλλήσποντον, ἄλλοις δ' εἰς Ἰωνίαν, τοῖς δ' εἰς τὴν ἀγορὰν μὴ εἰσιέναι πρόσταξις ἦν. ταῦτ' οὖν ἐψηφίσασθε ἐξαλεῖψαι πάντα τὰ ψηφίσματα, καὶ αὐτὰ καὶ εἴ πού τι ἀντίγραφον ἦν, καὶ πίστιν ἀλλήλοις περὶ ὁμονοίας δοῦναι ἐν ἀκροπόλει. Καί μοι ἀνάγνωθι τὸ ψήφισμα τὸ Πατροκλείδου, καθ' ὃ ταῦτα ἐγένετο.*

77 *ΨΗΦΙΣΜΑ. {Πατροκλείδης εἶπεν· ἐπειδὴ ἐψηφίσαντο Ἀθηναῖοι τὴν ἄδειαν περὶ τῶν ὀφειλόντων, ὥστε λέγειν ἐξεῖναι καὶ ἐπιψηφίζειν, ψηφίσασθαι τὸν δῆμον ταὐτὰ ἅπερ ὅτε ἦν τὰ Μηδικά, καὶ συνήνεγκεν Ἀθηναίοις ἐπὶ τὸ ἄμεινον. περὶ δὲ τῶν ἐπιγεγραμμένων εἰς τοὺς πράκτορας ἢ τοὺς ταμίας τῆς θεοῦ καὶ τῶν ἄλλων θεῶν ἢ τὸν βασιλέα, ἢ εἴ τις μὴ ἐξεγράφη, μέχρι τῆς ἐξελθούσης*

627 *καὶ* del. MacDowell, transpositionem Paolii secutus 628 *ἀναυμαχίου* Suda: *ναυμαχίου* A 629 *ψευδομαρτυριῶν* A : *ψευδομαρτυρίων* Blass[3] *ψευδοκλητείας* Sauppe : *ψευδοκλητίας* A 633 *αὑτῶν* Lipsius : *αὐτῶν* A 634 *τυράννων* A : *τετρακοσίων* Dobree 635 *δ' ἐν* Ald. : *δὲ* A 645–74 spuria esse statuerunt Canevaro et Harris 646 *περὶ* A : *περὶ <τῶν ἀτίμων καὶ>* Sauppe 647 *ταὐτὰ* Boeckh[1] : *ταῦτα* A 649 *ἐπιγεγραμμένων* A : *ἐγγεγραμμένων* Emperius[1] 651 *ἢ* susp. Emperius[1] *ἐξεγράφη* A : *ἐνεγράφη* Droysen : *ἐπεγράφη* Sauppe

βουλῆς ἐφ’ ἧς Καλλίας ἦρχεν, ὅσοι ἄτιμοι ἦσαν ἢ 78
ὀφείλοντες, καὶ ὅσων εὔθυναί τινές εἰσι κατεγνωσμέναι ἐν τοῖς λογιστηρίοις ὑπὸ τῶν εὐθύνων ἢ τῶν παρέδρων, ἢ μήπω εἰσηγμέναι εἰς τὸ δικαστήριον γραφαί τινές εἰσι περὶ τῶν εὐθυνῶν, ἢ προστάξεις, ἢ ἐγγύαι τινές εἰσι κατεγνωσμέναι, εἰς τὸν αὐτὸν τοῦτον χρόνον· καὶ ὅσα ὀνόματα τῶν τετρακοσίων τινὸς ἐγγέγραπται, ἢ ἄλλο τι περὶ τῶν ἐν τῇ ὀλιγαρχίᾳ πραχθέντων ἐστί που γεγραμμένον· πλὴν ὁπόσα ἐν στήλαις γέγραπται τῶν μὴ ἐνθάδε μεινάντων, ἢ ἐξ Ἀρείου πάγου ἢ τῶν ἐφετῶν ἢ ἐκ πρυτανείου ἢ Δελφινίου ἐδικάσθη· ἢ ὑπὸ τῶν βασιλέων, ἢ ἐπὶ φόνῳ τίς ἐστι φυγή, ἢ θάνατος κατεγνώσθη, ἢ σφαγεῦσιν ἢ τυράννοις· τὰ δὲ ἄλλα 79
πάντα ἐξαλεῖψαι τοὺς πράκτορας καὶ τὴν βουλὴν καὶ τὰ εἰρημένα πανταχόθεν, ὅπου τι ἔστιν ἐν τῷ δημοσίῳ, καὶ εἴ ἀντίγραφόν που ἔστι, παρέχειν τοὺς θεσμοθέτας καὶ τὰς ἄλλας ἀρχάς. ποιεῖν δὲ ταῦτα τριῶν ἡμερῶν, ἐπειδὰν δόξῃ τῷ δήμῳ. ἃ δ’ εἴρηται ἐξαλεῖψαι, μὴ κεκτῆσθαι ἰδίᾳ μηδενὶ ἐξεῖναι μηδὲ μνησικακῆσαι μηδέποτε· εἰ δὲ μή, ἔνοχον εἶναι τὸν παραβαίνοντα ταῦτα ἐν τοῖς αὐτοῖς ἐν οἷσπερ οἱ ἐξ Ἀρείου πάγου φεύγοντες, ὅπως ἂν ὡς πιστότατα ἔχῃ ‘Αθηναίοις καὶ νῦν καὶ εἰς τὸν λοιπὸν χρόνον.}

Κατὰ μὲν τὸ ψήφισμα τουτὶ τοὺς ἀτίμους ἐπιτίμους 80
ἐποιήσατε· τοὺς δὲ φεύγοντας οὔτε Πατροκλείδης εἶπε

78 λογιστηρίοις Harp. λ 24.10 s.v. λογισταὶ καὶ λογιστήρια, ac stp Phot. λ 376.5 Suda λ 651.4

652 ἢ del. Reiske 653 ὅσων L : ὅσον A 654 ἢ A : καὶ Boeckh[1] 655 παρέδρων A[1] : προέδρων A[a] ἢ del. Dalmeyda, transp. post δικαστήριον Reiske 658 τινὸς del. Reiske 660 ἐστί Turr. : ἔστι A 661 pr. ἢ A : ἢ <οἷς ἢ> MacDowell : ἢ <οἷς> Lipsius 662 ἐδικάσθη· ἢ A : δικασθεῖσιν Lipsius 663 pr. ἢ del. Sauppe[2] φόνῳ A[c] : φθόνῳ A[a] 665 alt. καὶ A : κατὰ Sluiter 666 εἰρημένα A : εὑρημένα Reiske 673 ἔχῃ Hermann : ἔχει A : ἔχοι e ras. L[1]

κατιέναι οὔθ' ὑμεῖς ἐψηφίσασθε. ἐπεὶ δ' αἱ σπονδαὶ πρὸς Λακεδαιμονίους ἐγένοντο, καὶ τὰ τείχη καθείλετε, καὶ τοὺς φεύγοντας κατεδέξασθε, καὶ κατέστησαν οἱ τριάκοντα, καὶ μετὰ ταῦτα Φυλή τε κατελήφθη Μουνιχίαν τε κατέλαβον, ἐγένετο ὑμῖν ὧν ἐγὼ οὐδὲν δέομαι μεμνῆσθαι οὐδ' ἀναμιμνῄσκειν ὑμᾶς τῶν γεγενημένων
81 *κακῶν. ἐπειδὴ δ' ἐπανήλθετε ἐκ Πειραιέως, γενόμενον ἐφ' ὑμῖν τιμωρεῖσθαι ἔγνωτε ἐᾶν τὰ γεγενημένα, καὶ περὶ πλείονος ἐποιήσασθε σῴζειν τὴν πόλιν ἢ τὰς ἰδίας τιμωρίας, καὶ ἔδοξε μὴ μνησικακεῖν ἀλλήλοις τῶν γεγενημένων. δόξαντα δὲ ὑμῖν ταῦτα εἵλεσθε ἄνδρας εἴκοσι· τούτους δὲ ἐπιμελεῖσθαι τῆς πόλεως, ἕως ἄλλοι νόμοι τεθεῖεν· τέως δὲ χρῆσθαι τοῖς Σόλωνος νόμοις*
82 *καὶ τοῖς Δράκοντος θεσμοῖς. ἐπειδὴ δὲ βουλήν τε ἀπεκληρώσατε νομοθέτας τε εἵλεσθε, ηὕρισκον τῶν νόμων τῶν τε Σόλωνος καὶ τῶν Δράκοντος πολλοὺς ὄντας οἷς πολλοὶ τῶν πολιτῶν ἔνοχοι ἦσαν τῶν πρότερον ἕνεκα γενομένων. ἐκκλησίαν ποιήσαντες ἐβουλεύσασθε περὶ αὐτῶν, καὶ ἐψηφίσασθε, δοκιμάσαντες πάντας τοὺς νόμους, εἶτ' ἀναγράψαι ἐν τῇ στοᾷ τούτους τῶν νόμων οἳ ἂν δοκιμασθῶσι. καί μοι ἀνάγνωθι τὸ ψήφισμα.*

83 *⟨ΨΗΦΙΣΜΑ.⟩ {Ἔδοξε τῷ δήμῳ, Τεισαμενὸς εἶπε· πολιτεύεσθαι Ἀθηναίους κατὰ τὰ πάτρια, νόμοις δὲ χρῆσθαι τοῖς Σόλωνος, καὶ μέτροις καὶ σταθμοῖς, χρῆσθαι δὲ καὶ τοῖς Δράκοντος θεσμοῖς, οἷσπερ ἐχρώμεθα ἐν τῷ*

677 *ἐπεί δ' αἱ* A[1] : *ἐπειδὴ* A[a] 680 *Μουνιχίαν* Lipsius : *μουνυχίαν* A 681 <*θ'*> *ὑμῖν* Reiske 684 *τιμωρεῖσθαι* A[1] : *τιμωρεῖσθε* A[a] 688 *ἄλλοι* Stahl : *ἂν οἱ* A (*ἂν* del. Dobree) : *αὖ οἱ* Weidner : *δὴ οἱ* Richards[2] 691 *ηὕρισκον* Blass[3] : *εὕρισκον* A : *εὕρισκόν τε* Sched. Eton. : *εὑρίσκοντες* Reiske 692 *καὶ τῶν* Bekker : *καὶ τοῦ* A 693 pr. *τῶν* L : *τῶν τῶν* A 694 *γενομένων* Reiske : *γινομένων* A 696 *νόμους* L : *ἀνόμους* A 699–715 spuria statuerunt Canevaro et Harris 699 tit. add. Ald. *Τεισαμενὸς* Blass[2] : *τισάμενος* A

*πρόσθεν χρόνῳ. ὁπόσων δ' ἂν προσδέῃ, †οἵδε† ᾑρημένοι
νομοθέται ὑπὸ τῆς βουλῆς ἀναγραφέντας ἐν σανίσιν
ἐκτιθέντων πρὸς τοὺς ἐπωνύμους σκοπεῖν τῷ βουλομένῳ,
καὶ παραδιδόντων ταῖς ἀρχαῖς ἐν τῷδε τῷ μηνί. τοὺς δὲ* **84**
*παραδιδομένους νόμους δοκιμασάτω πρότερον ἡ βουλὴ
καὶ οἱ νομοθέται οἱ πεντακόσιοι, οὓς οἱ δημόται εἵλοντο,
ἐπειδὰν ὀμωμόκωσιν. ἐξεῖναι δὲ καὶ ἰδιώτῃ τῷ βουλομένῳ
εἰσιόντι εἰς τὴν βουλὴν συμβουλεύειν ὅ τι ἂν ἀγαθὸν ἔχῃ περὶ
τῶν νόμων. ἐπειδὰν δὲ τεθῶσιν οἱ νόμοι, ἐπιμελείσθω ἡ
βουλὴ ἡ ἐξ Ἀρείου πάγου τῶν νόμων, ὅπως ἂν αἱ ἀρχαὶ τοῖς
κειμένοις νόμοις χρῶνται. τοὺς δὲ κυρουμένους τῶν νόμων
ἀναγράφειν εἰς τὸν τοῖχον, ἵνα περ πρότερον ἀνεγράφησαν,
σκοπεῖν τῷ βουλομένῳ.}*

Ἐδοκιμάσθησαν μὲν οὖν οἱ νόμοι, ὦ ἄνδρες, κατὰ τὸ **85**
*ψήφισμα τουτί, τοὺς δὲ κυρωθέντας ἀνέγραψαν εἰς τὴν
στοάν. ἐπειδὴ ⟨δ'⟩ ἀνεγράφησαν, ἐθέμεθα νόμον, ᾧ
πάντες χρῆσθε. καί μοι ἀνάγνωθι τὸν νόμον.*

*ΝΟΜΟΣ. {Ἀγράφῳ δὲ νόμῳ τὰς ἀρχὰς μὴ χρῆσθαι μηδὲ
περὶ ἑνός.}*

Ἆρά γε ἔστιν οὕτως ὅ τι περιελείπετο περὶ ὅτου οἷόν **86**
τε ἢ ἀρχὴν εἰσάγειν ἢ ὑμῶν πρᾶξαί τινι, ἀλλ' ἢ κατὰ

703 *προσδέῃ* Bekker : *προσδέοι* A *οἵδε* A, quod obelis inclusit MacDowell : *οἱ* vel *οἱ ΔΕ* (sc. decies quinque) Reiske : *οἱ ἤδη* Dobree : *οἱ* N (sc. quinquaginta) vel *οἱ δέκα* Sluiter : *οἱ δὲ* Blass, qui etiam lacunam praeced. susp. 704 *ἀναγραφέντας* Naber[1] (coll. §85) : *ἀναγράφοντας* A : *ἀναγράφοντες* Bekker 705 *πρὸς τοὺς ἐπωνύμους*] *πρὸ τῶν ἐπωνύμων* aut *πρὸς τοῖς ἐπωνύμοις* Reiske : *πρόσθε τῶν ἐπωνύμων* Lipsius : *παρὰ τοὺς ἐπωνύμους* dubitanter Fuhr 708 *καὶ οἱ νομοθέται οἱ πεντακόσιοι*] *οἱ πεντακόσιοι καὶ οἱ νομοθέται* ci. Petit *δημόται* L : *δημῶται* A 709 *ἐπειδὰν ὀμωμόκωσιν* Dobree : *ἐπειδὴ ὀμωμόκασιν* A 710 *ἀγαθὸν*] *ἀγαθῶς* Redondo i Sànchez[2] 718 add. Sauppe 719 *πάντες* A[1] : *πάντως* A[a] 720–1 spur. stat. Canevaro et Harris 722 *ἔστιν οὕτως* MacDowell : *ἔστι τοῦτο* A : *ἔστιν ἐνταυθοῖ* Blass *περιελείπετο* Reiske : *περιέλειπτο* A : *περιελέλειπτο* etiam Reiske 723 *ἀρχὴν … τινι* A : *ἀρχὴν … τινα* Sluiter : *ἀρχῇ … τινι* aut *ἀρχὴν … ὑμᾶς πρᾶξαί τι* Dobree

τοὺς ἀναγεγραμμένους νόμους; ὅπου οὖν {ἂν} ἀγράφῳ νόμῳ οὐκ ἔξεστι χρήσασθαι, ἦ που {ἂν} ἀγράφῳ γε ψηφίσματι παντάπασιν οὐ δεῖ γε χρήσασθαι. ἐπειδὴ τοίνυν ἑωρῶμεν ὅτι πολλοῖς τῶν πολιτῶν εἶεν συμφοραί, τοῖς μὲν κατὰ νόμους, τοῖς δὲ κατὰ ψηφίσματα τὰ πρότερον γενόμενα, τουτουσὶ τοὺς νόμους ἐθέμεθα, αὐτῶν ἕνεκα τῶν νυνὶ ποιουμένων, ἵνα τούτων μηδὲν γίγνηται μηδὲ ἐξῇ συκοφαντεῖν μηδενί. καί μοι ἀνάγνωθι τοὺς νόμους.

87 *ΝΟΜΟΙ. {Ἀγράφῳ δὲ νόμῳ τὰς ἀρχὰς μὴ χρῆσθαι μηδὲ περὶ ἑνός. ψήφισμα δὲ μηδὲν μήτε βουλῆς μήτε δήμου νόμου κυριώτερον εἶναι. μηδὲ ἐπ᾽ ἀνδρὶ νόμον ἐξεῖναι θεῖναι, ἐὰν μὴ τὸν αὐτὸν ἐπὶ πᾶσιν Ἀθηναίοις, ἐὰν μὴ ἑξακισχιλίοις δόξῃ κρύβδην ψηφιζομένοις.}*

Τί οὖν ἦν ἐπίλοιπον; οὑτοσὶ ὁ νόμος. καί μοι ἀνάγνωθι τοῦτον.

⟨ΝΟΜΟΣ.⟩ {Τὰς δὲ δίκας καὶ τὰς διαίτας κυρίας εἶναι, ὁπόσαι ἐν δημοκρατουμένῃ τῇ πόλει ἐγένοντο. τοῖς δὲ νόμοις χρῆσθαι ἀπ᾽ Εὐκλείδου ἄρχοντος.}

88 *Τὰς μὲν δίκας, ὦ ἄνδρες, καὶ τὰς διαίτας ἐποιήσατε κυρίας εἶναι, ὁπόσαι ἐν δημοκρατουμένῃ ⟨τῇ⟩ πόλει*

87 *ψήφισμα—εἶναι* eadem in D. 23.87   *μηδὲ—ψηφιζομένοις* simillima in D. 24.59, 23.86, [D.] 46.12   **88** *Τὰς δὲ—ἐγένοντο* similia in D. 24.56

---

724 *ἀγράφῳ* Ald. : *ἂν ἀγράφω* A : *δὴ ἀγράφῳ* MacDowell   725 *ἀγράφῳ* Bekker : *ἂν ἀγράφω* A   726 *γε* post *παντάπασιν* transp. maluit Gebauer[2] : *γε χρήσασθαι* del. Blass auct. Hirschigio, qui etiam *δεῖ* deleverat   728 *τὰ* del. Naber[1]   730 *ἕνεκα* L : *εἵνεκα* A   733–7 spur. esse stat. Canevaro et Harris   tit. *νόμοι* M : *νόμος* A   735 *ἐπ᾽ ἀνδρὶ νόμον ἐξεῖναι*] cfr. *νόμον ἐξεῖναι ἐπ᾽ ἀνδρὶ* Demosth.   736 *ἐὰν μὴ*] *τιθῇ* Demosth. *ἑξακισχιλίοις δόξῃ*] cfr. *ψηφισαμένων μὴ ἔλαττον ἑξακισχιλίων οἷς ἂν δόξῃ* Demosth.   740–2 spur. esse stat. Canevaro et Harris   740 tit. add. Ald.   740–1 *κυρίας … ἐγένοντο*] cfr. *ὅσαι ἐγένοντο ἐπὶ τοῖς νόμοις ἐν δημοκρατουμένῃ τῇ πόλει, κυρίας εἶναι* Demosth.   744 add. Bekker

ἐγένοντο, ὅπως μήτε χρεῶν ἀποκοπαὶ εἶεν μήτε δίκαι ἀνάδικοι γίγνοιντο, ἀλλὰ τῶν ἰδίων συμβολαίων αἱ πράξεις εἶεν· τῶν δὲ δημοσίων ⟨ἐφ'⟩ ὁπόσοις ἢ γραφαί εἰσιν ἢ φάσεις ἢ ἐνδείξεις ἢ ἀπαγωγαί, τούτων ἕνεκα τοῖς νόμοις ἐψηφίσασθε χρῆσθαι ἀπ' Εὐκλείδου ἄρχοντος. ὅπου οὖν ἔδοξεν ὑμῖν δοκιμάσαι μὲν τοὺς νόμους, **89** δοκιμάσαντας δὲ ἀναγράψαι, ἀγράφῳ δὲ νόμῳ τὰς ἀρχὰς μὴ χρῆσθαι μηδὲ περὶ ἑνός, ψήφισμα δὲ ⟨μηδὲν⟩ μήτε βουλῆς μήτε δήμου ⟨νόμου⟩ κυριώτερον εἶναι, μηδ' ἐπ' ἀνδρὶ νόμον τιθέναι ἐὰν μὴ τὸν αὐτὸν ἐπὶ πᾶσιν Ἀθηναίοις, τοῖς δὲ νόμοις τοῖς κειμένοις χρῆσθαι ἀπ' Εὐκλείδου ἄρχοντος, ἐνταυθοῖ ἔστιν ὅ τι ὑπολείπεται ἢ μεῖζον ἢ ἔλαττον τῶν γενομένων πρότερον ψηφισμάτων, πρὶν Εὐκλείδην ἄρξαι, ὅπως κύριον ἔσται; οὐκ οἶμαι ἔγωγε, ⟨ὦ⟩ ἄνδρες. σκοπεῖτε δὲ καὶ αὐτοί.

Φέρε δὴ τοίνυν, οἱ ὅρκοι ὑμῖν πῶς ἔχουσιν; ὁ μὲν **90** κοινὸς τῇ πόλει ἁπάσῃ, ὃν ὀμωμόκατε πάντες μετὰ τὰς διαλλαγάς, "Καὶ οὐ μνησικακήσω τῶν πολιτῶν οὐδενὶ πλὴν τῶν τριάκοντα καὶ τῶν ἕνδεκα· οὐδὲ τούτων ὃς ἂν ἐθέλῃ εὐθύνας διδόναι τῆς ἀρχῆς ἧς ἦρξεν." ὅπου τοίνυν αὐτοῖς τοῖς τριάκοντα ὤμνυτε μὴ μνησικακήσειν, τοῖς μεγίστων κακῶν αἰτίοις, εἰ διδοῖεν εὐθύνας, ἦ που σχολῇ τῶν γε ἄλλων πολιτῶν τινι ἠξιοῦτε μνησικακεῖν. ἡ δὲ βουλὴ αὖ ἡ ἀεὶ βουλεύουσα τί ὄμνυσι; "Καὶ οὐ **91** δέξομαι ἔνδειξιν οὐδὲ ἀπαγωγὴν ἕνεκα τῶν πρότερον

747 add. Blass 750 ὅπου Lipsius : ὁπότ' A 752 add. Blass 753 add. Reiske 754 νόμον <ἐξεῖναι> Sluiter 757 γενομένων Turr. : γινομένων A 759 add. Blass[3] 763 πλὴν A[1] : πρὶν A[a] ἕνδεκα <καὶ τῶν δέκα> de Valois (coll. Arist. Ath. 39.6) : ἕνδεκα <καὶ τῶν ἐν Πειραιεῖ δέκα> Lipsius 764 ὅπου L : ὅποι A 765 ὤμνυτε Ald. : ὤμνυται A 766 μεγίστων Reiske : μεγίστοις A 767 σχολῇ M : σχολὴ A 768 αὖ ἡ Reiske : αὕτη A 769 πρότερον Steph. : προτέρων A

γεγενημένων, πλὴν τῶν φυγόντων.” ὑμεῖς δ’ αὖ, ὦ Ἀθηναῖοι, τί ὀμόσαντες δικάζετε; “Καὶ οὐ μνησικακήσω, οὐδὲ ἄλλῳ πείσομαι, ψηφιοῦμαι δὲ κατὰ τοὺς κειμένους νόμους.” ἃ χρὴ σκοπεῖν, εἰ δοκῶ ὀρθῶς ὑμῖν λέγειν ὡς ὑπὲρ ὑμῶν λέγω καὶ τῶν νόμων.

92 *Σκέψασθε τοίνυν, ὦ ἄνδρες, καὶ τοὺς νόμους καὶ τοὺς κατηγόρους, τί αὐτοῖς ὑπάρχον ἑτέρων κατηγοροῦσι. Κηφίσιος μὲν οὑτοσὶ πριάμενος ὠνὴν ἐκ τοῦ δημοσίου, τὰς ἐκ ταύτης ἐπικαρπίας τῶν ἐν τῇ γῇ γεωργούντων ἐνενήκοντα μνᾶς ἐκλέξας, οὐ κατέβαλε τῇ πόλει καὶ*
93 *ἔφυγεν· εἰ γὰρ ἦλθεν, ἐδέδετ’ ἂν ἐν τῷ ξύλῳ. ὁ γὰρ νόμος οὕτως εἶχε, κυρίαν εἶναι τὴν βουλήν, ὃς ἂν πριάμενος τέλος μὴ καταβάλῃ, δεῖν εἰς τὸ ξύλον. οὗτος τοίνυν, ὅτι τοῖς νόμοις ἐψηφίσασθε ἀπ’ Εὐκλείδου ἄρχοντος χρῆσθαι, ἀξιοῖ ἃ ἔχει ὑμῶν ἐκλέξας μὴ ἀποδοῦναι, καὶ νῦν γεγένηται ἀντὶ μὲν φυγάδος πολίτης, ἀντὶ δὲ ἀτίμου συκοφάντης, ὅτι τοῖς νόμοις τοῖς νῦν κειμένοις χρῆσθε.*
94 *Μέλητος δ’ αὖ οὑτοσὶ ἀπήγαγεν ἐπὶ τῶν τριάκοντα Λέοντα, ὡς ὑμεῖς ἅπαντες ἴστε, καὶ ἀπέθανεν ἐκεῖνος ἄκριτος· καὶ οὗτος ὁ νόμος καὶ πρότερον ἦν ⟨καὶ⟩ ὡς καλῶς ἔχων καὶ νῦν ἔστι, καὶ χρῆσθε αὐτῷ, τὸν βουλεύσαντα ἐν τῷ αὐτῷ ἐνέχεσθαι καὶ τὸν τῇ χειρὶ ἐργασάμενον. Μέλητον τοίνυν τοῖς παισὶ τοῖς τοῦ Λέοντος οὐκ ἔστι φόνου διώκειν, ὅτι τοῖς νόμοις δεῖ χρῆσθαι ἀπ’ Εὐκλείδου ἄρχοντος, ἐπεὶ ὥς γε οὐκ*

770 *φυγόντων* Sauppe : *φευγόντων* A   771 *τί* Steph. : *ὅτι* A : *τὶ* Ald.   *ὀμόσαντες* Ald. : *ὁμόσαντες* A   774 *ὑμῶν* M : *ἡμῶν* A   775 pr. *καὶ* A : *κατὰ* Luzac : *καὶ τοὺς νόμους* del. Reiske   776 *ὑπάρχον* Emperius[1] : *ὑπαρχόντων* A   *ἑτέρων*] *ω* in ras. A[1]   778 *ἐν τῇ γῇ* del. Reiske : *τὴν γῆν* maluit Dobree : *ἐν Αἰγίνῃ* (sc. *ΕΝΕΓΙΝΗΙ*) Wilamowitz[3]   779 *ἐνενήκοντα* L : *ἐννενήκοντα* A   781 *τὴν* Steph. : *τήν τε* A   782 *καταβάλῃ* A[1] : *καταλάβῃ* A[a]   783 *ἐψηφίσασθε* Reiske : *ἀπεψηφίσασθε* A   786 *χρῆσθε* A[1] : *χρῆσθαι* A[a]   789 pr. *καὶ* A : *καίτοι* Sluiter   add. Baiter

ἀπήγαγεν, οὐδ᾽ αὐτὸς ἀντιλέγει. Ἐπιχάρης δ᾽ οὑτοσί, ὁ 95
πάντων πονηρότατος καὶ βουλόμενος εἶναι τοιοῦτος, ὁ μνησικακῶν αὐτὸς αὑτῷ—οὗτος γὰρ ἐβούλευεν ἐπὶ τῶν τριάκοντα· ὁ δὲ νόμος τί κελεύει, ὃς ἐν τῇ στήλῃ ἔμπροσθέν ἐστι τοῦ βουλευτηρίου; "Ὃς ἂν ἄρξῃ ἐν τῇ πόλει τῆς δημοκρατίας καταλυθείσης, νηποινεὶ τεθνάναι, καὶ τὸν ἀποκτείναντα ὅσιον εἶναι καὶ τὰ χρήματα ἔχειν τοῦ ἀποθανόντος." ἄλλο τι οὖν, ὦ Ἐπίχαρες, ἢ νῦν ὁ ἀποκτείνας σε καθαρὸς τὰς χεῖρας ἔσται, κατά γε τὸν Σόλωνος νόμον; καί μοι ἀνάγνωθι τὸν νόμον τὸν ἐκ τῆς 96
στήλης.

ΝΟΜΟΣ. {Ἔδοξε τῇ βουλῇ καὶ τῷ δήμῳ. Αἰαντὶς ἐπρυτάνευε, Κλεογένης ἐγραμμάτευε, Βοηθὸς ἐπεστάτει. τάδε Δημόφαντος συνέγραψεν. ἄρχει χρόνος τοῦδε τοῦ ψηφίσματος ἡ βουλὴ οἱ πεντακόσιοι λαχόντες τῷ κυάμῳ, ὅτε Κλεογένης πρῶτος ἐγραμμάτευεν. ἐάν τις δημοκρατίαν καταλύῃ τὴν Ἀθήνησιν, ἢ ἀρχήν τινα ἄρχῃ καταλελυμένης τῆς δημοκρατίας, πολέμιος ἔσται Ἀθηναίων καὶ νηποινεὶ τεθνάτω, καὶ τὰ χρήματα αὐτοῦ δημόσια ἔστω, καὶ τῆς θεοῦ τὸ ἐπιδέκατον· ὁ δὲ ἀποκτείνας τὸν ταῦτα ποιήσαντα καὶ ὁ συμβουλεύσας ὅσιος ἔστω καὶ εὐαγής.
ὀμόσαι δ᾽ Ἀθηναίους ἅπαντας καθ᾽ ἱερῶν τελείων, κατὰ 97
φυλὰς καὶ κατὰ δήμους, ἀποκτενεῖν τὸν ταῦτα ποιήσαντα. ὁ δὲ ὅρκος ἔστω ὅδε· "Κτενῶ τῇ ἐμαυτοῦ χειρί, ἂν δυνατὸς

795 οὑτοσί Blass[3] : οὗτος A 800 νηποινεὶ Blass : νηποινὶ A 802 ἄλλο τι Canter : ἀλλ᾽ ὅτι A Ἐπίχαρες Valckenaer : ἐπιχάρης A ἢ Ald. : εἰ A 806–36 spuria stat. Canevaro et Harris 807 Κλεογένης A hic et mox : Κλειγένης Boeckh[2] hic et mox 809 <οἱ> λαχόντες Bekker 810 ὅτε A : οἷς Droysen 811 καταλύῃ ... ἄρχῃ Ald. : καταλύει ... ἄρχει A καταλελυμένης A[c] : καταλελυμμένης A 812 ἔσται A : ἔστω Steph. νηποινεὶ Blass : νηποινὶ A 816 ὀμόσαι Steph. : ὁμόσαι A 817 ἀποκτενεῖν Droysen : ἀποκτείνειν A 818 ἂν A[1] : ἐὰν A[a]

ὦ, ὃς ἂν καταλύσῃ τὴν δημοκρατίαν τὴν Ἀθήνησι, καὶ ἐάν τις ἄρξῃ τιν' ἀρχὴν καταλελυμένης τῆς δημοκρατίας τὸ λοιπόν, καὶ ἐάν τις τυραννεῖν ἐπαναστῇ ἢ τὸν τύραννον συγκαταστήσῃ. καὶ ἐάν τις ἄλλος ἀποκτείνῃ, ὅσιον αὐτὸν νομιῶ εἶναι καὶ πρὸς θεῶν καὶ δαιμόνων, ὡς πολέμιον κτείναντα τὸν Ἀθηναίων, καὶ τὰ κτήματα τοῦ ἀποθανόντος πάντα ἀποδόμενος ἀποδώσω τὰ ἡμίσεα τῷ ἀποκτείναντι καὶ λόγῳ καὶ ἔργῳ καὶ ψήφῳ, καὶ οὐκ
98 *ἀποστερήσω οὐδέν. ἐὰν δέ τις κτείνων τινὰ τούτων ἀποθάνῃ ἢ ἐπιχειρῶν, εὖ ποιήσω αὐτόν τε καὶ τοὺς παῖδας τοὺς ἐκείνου καθάπερ Ἁρμόδιόν τε καὶ Ἀριστογείτονα καὶ τοὺς ἀπογόνους αὐτῶν. ὁπόσοι δὲ ὅρκοι ὀμώμονται Ἀθήνησιν ἢ ἐν τῷ στρατοπέδῳ ἢ ἄλλοθί που ἐναντίοι τῷ δήμῳ τῷ Ἀθηναίων, λύω καὶ ἀφίημι." ταῦτα δὲ ὀμοσάντων Ἀθηναῖοι πάντες καθ' ἱερῶν τελείων, τὸν νόμιμον ὅρκον, πρὸ Διονυσίων· καὶ ἐπεύχεσθαι εὐορκοῦντι μὲν εἶναι πολλὰ καὶ ἀγαθά, ἐπιορκοῦντι δ' ἐξώλη αὐτὸν εἶναι καὶ γένος.}*

99 *Πότερον, ὦ συκοφάντα καὶ ἐπίτριπτον κίναδος, κύριος ὁ νόμος ὅδε ἐστὶν ἢ οὐ κύριος; διὰ τοῦτο δ' οἶμαι γεγένηται ἄκυρος, ὅτι τοῖς νόμοις δεῖ χρῆσθαι ἀπ' Εὐκλείδου ἄρχοντος. καὶ σὺ ζῇς καὶ περιέρχῃ τὴν πόλιν ταύτην, οὐκ ἄξιος ὤν· ὃς ἐν δημοκρατίᾳ μὲν*

97 *καὶ λόγῳ—ψήφῳ* simillima in Lycurg. 127

820 *τιν'* Reiske : *τὴν* A   821 *<ἐπὶ τῷ> τυραννεῖν* Dobree   822 *συγκαταστήσῃ* Ald. : *συγκαταστή*^{ση} L : *συγκαταστήσει* A *ἀποκτείνῃ* A^1 : *ἀποκτείνει* A^a 824 *τὸν* M : *τῶν* A   826 *καὶ λόγῳ καὶ ἔργῳ καὶ ψήφῳ*] hinc post *κτενῶ* l. 818 transp. Valckenaer (coll. Lycurg., qui tamen *χειρὶ καὶ ψήφῳ* habet), *καὶ* post *ψήφῳ* add. Sauppe   828 *ἀποθάνῃ* Ald. : *ἀποθάνοι* A   830 *ὀμώμονται* Steph. : *ὁμώμονται* A   832 *τῷ Ἀθηναίων* Osann : *τῶν Ἀθηναίων* A   833 *ὀμοσάντων* Bekker : *ὁμοσάντων* A : *ὠμόσατε* Ald.   834 *διονυσίων* A^1 : *διονύσων* A^a 838 *οὐ κύριος;* sic interpunxit Reiske : *οὐ κύριος·* codd.

συκοφαντῶν ἔζης, ἐν ὀλιγαρχίᾳ δέ, ὡς μὴ ἀναγκασθείης τὰ χρήματα ἀποδοῦναι ὅσα συκοφαντῶν ἔλαβες, ἐδούλευες τοῖς τριάκοντα. εἶτα σὺ περὶ ἑταιρείας ἐμοὶ 100
μνείαν ποιῇ καὶ κακῶς τινας λέγεις; ὃς ἑνὶ μὲν οὐχ ἡταίρησας (καλῶς γὰρ ἄν σοι εἶχε), πραττόμενος δ' οὐ πολὺ ἀργύριον τὸν βουλόμενον ἀνθρώπων, ὡς οὗτοι ἴσασιν, ἐπὶ τοῖς αἰσχίστοις ἔργοις ἔζης, καὶ ταῦτα οὕτως μοχθηρὸς ὢν τὴν ἰδέαν. ἀλλ' ὅμως οὗτος ἑτέρων ἐτόλμα κατηγορεῖν, ᾧ κατὰ τοὺς νόμους τοὺς ὑμετέρους οὐδ' αὐτῷ ὑπὲρ αὑτοῦ ἔστιν ἀπολογεῖσθαι.
ἀλλὰ γάρ, ὦ ἄνδρες, καθήμενος ἡνίκα μου κατηγόρει, 101
βλέπων εἰς αὐτὸν οὐδὲν ἄλλο ἢ ὑπὸ τῶν τριάκοντα συνειλημμένος ἔδοξα κρίνεσθαι. εἰ γὰρ τότε ἠγωνιζόμην, τίς ἄν μου κατηγόρει; οὐχ οὗτος ὑπῆρχεν, εἰ μὴ ἐδίδουν ἀργύριον; καὶ γὰρ νῦν. ἀνέκρινε δ' ἄν με τίς ἄλλος ἢ Χαρικλῆς, ἐρωτῶν, Εἰπέ μοι, ὦ Ἀνδοκίδη, ἦλθες εἰς Δεκέλειαν, καὶ ἐπετείχισας τῇ πατρίδι τῇ σεαυτοῦ; Οὐκ ἔγωγε. Τί δέ; ἔτεμες τὴν χώραν, καὶ ἐλῄσω ἢ κατὰ γῆν ἢ κατὰ θάλατταν τοὺς πολίτας τοὺς σεαυτοῦ; Οὐ δῆτα. Οὐδ' ἐναυμάχησας ἐναντία τῇ πόλει, οὐδὲ συγκατέσκαψας τὰ τείχη, οὐδὲ συγκατέλυσας τὸν δῆμον, οὐδὲ βίᾳ κατῆλθες εἰς τὴν πόλιν; Οὐδὲν τούτων πεποίηκα. Οὐδέν; δοκεῖς οὖν χαιρήσειν ἢ οὐκ ἀποθανεῖσθαι, ὡς ἕτεροι πολλοί; ἆρ' 102
⟨ἂν⟩ οἴεσθε, ὦ ἄνδρες, ἄλλων τινῶν τυχεῖν με δι' ὑμᾶς, εἰ ἐλήφθην ὑπ' αὐτῶν; οὐκ οὖν δεινόν, εἰ ὑπὸ μὲν τούτων διὰ τοῦτ' ἂν ἀπωλόμην, ὅτι εἰς τὴν πόλιν οὐδὲν ἥμαρτον,

100 ἑταιρείας Harp. ε 147 s.v., ac stp s.v. ἑταιρία Phot. ε 2068 Suda ε 3270

850 ἑτέρων Reiske : ἑταιρῶν A   ἐτόλμα A : τολμᾷ Blass[3]   858 ἐπετείχισας Steph. : ἐπετείχισες A   860 ἐλῄσω Naber[1] : ἐληίσω A   861 σεαυτοῦ L : ἑαυτοῦ A   864 οὐδὲν A : οὐδὲ Muret   865 ἢ A : καὶ Dobree   866 add. Dobree   ὑμᾶς Sched. Eton., Reiske : ἡμᾶς A

ὥσπερ καὶ ἑτέρους ἀπέκτειναν, ἐν ὑμῖν δὲ κρινόμενος,
οὓς οὐδὲν κακὸν πεποίηκα, οὐ σωθήσομαι; πάντως
103 *δήπου· ἢ σχολῇ γέ τις ἄλλος ἀνθρώπων. ἀλλὰ γάρ, ὦ*
ἄνδρες, τὴν μὲν ἔνδειξιν ἐποιήσαντό μου κατὰ νόμον
κείμενον, τὴν δὲ κατηγορίαν κατὰ τὸ ψήφισμα τὸ
πρότερον γεγενημένον περὶ ἑτέρων. εἰ οὖν ἐμοῦ
καταψηφιεῖσθε, ὁρᾶτε μὴ οὐκ ἐμοὶ μάλιστα τῶν πολιτῶν
προσήκει λόγον δοῦναι τῶν γεγενημένων, ἀλλὰ πολλοῖς
ἑτέροις μᾶλλον, τοῦτο μὲν οἷς ὑμεῖς ἐναντία μαχεσάμενοι
διηλλάγητε καὶ ὅρκους ὠμόσατε, τοῦτο δὲ οὓς φεύγοντας
κατηγάγετε, τοῦτο δὲ οὓς ἀτίμους ὄντας ἐπιτίμους
ἐποιήσατε· ὧν ἕνεκα καὶ στήλας ἀνείλετε καὶ νόμους
ἀκύρους ἐποιήσατε καὶ τὰ ψηφίσματα ἐξηλείψατε· οἳ
νυνὶ μένουσιν ἐν τῇ πόλει πιστεύοντες ὑμῖν, ὦ ἄνδρες.
104 *εἰ οὖν γνώσονται ὑμᾶς ἀποδεχομένους τὰς κατηγορίας*
τῶν πρότερον γεγενημένων, τίνα αὐτοὺς οἴεσθε γνώμην
ἕξειν περὶ σφῶν αὐτῶν; ἢ τίνα αὐτῶν ἐθελήσειν εἰς
ἀγῶνα καθίστασθαι ἕνεκα τῶν πρότερον γεγενημένων;
φανήσονται γὰρ πολλοὶ μὲν ἐχθροὶ πολλοὶ δὲ συκοφάνται,
105 *οἳ καταστήσουσιν αὐτῶν ἕκαστον εἰς ἀγῶνα. ἥκουσι δὲ*
νυνὶ ἀκροασόμενοι ἀμφότεροι, οὐ τὴν αὐτὴν γνώμην
ἔχοντες ἀλλήλοις, ἀλλ' οἱ μὲν εἰσόμενοι εἰ χρὴ πιστεύειν
τοῖς νόμοις τοῖς κειμένοις καὶ τοῖς ὅρκοις οὓς ὠμόσατε
ἀλλήλοις, οἱ δὲ ἀποπειρώμενοι τῆς ὑμετέρας γνώμης, εἰ
αὐτοῖς ἐξέσται ἀδεῶς συκοφαντεῖν καὶ γράφεσθαι, τοὺς
δὲ ἐνδεικνύναι, τοὺς δὲ ἀπάγειν. οὕτως οὖν ἔχει, ὦ
ἄνδρες· ὁ μὲν ἀγὼν ἐν τῷ σώματι τῷ ἐμῷ καθέστηκεν,

869 *ὑμῖν* L : *ἡμῖν* A   877 *μαχεσάμενοι* A : *μαχεσαμένοις* maluit Reiske   878 *ὠμόσατε* Ald. : *ὡμόσατε* L[c] : *ὀμόσατε* A   879 *ἀτίμους* L : *ἀτίμως* A   880 *ἕνεκα* B : *εἵνεκα* A   881 *τὰ ψηφίσματα* A[1sv] : *ψηφίσματα* A[a] : *τὰ* reiecit Bekker   884 et 886 *πρότερον* Steph. : *προτέρων* A   886 *ἀγῶνα* A : *ἀγῶνας* B   889 *ἀκροασόμενοι* A[1] : *ἀκροασάμενοι* A[a]   891 *ὠμόσατε* Steph. : *ὡμόσατε* L[c] : *ὀμόσατε* A

ἡ δὲ ψῆφος ἡ ὑμετέρα δημοσίᾳ κρινεῖ, πότερον χρὴ τοῖς νόμοις τοῖς ὑμετέροις πιστεύειν, ἢ τοὺς συκοφάντας παρασκευάζεσθαι, ἢ φεύγειν αὐτοὺς ἐκ τῆς πόλεως καὶ ἀπιέναι ὡς τάχιστα.

Ἵνα δὲ εἰδῆτε, ὦ ἄνδρες, ὅτι τὰ πεποιημένα ὑμῖν εἰς 106
ὁμόνοιαν οὐ κακῶς ἔχει, ἀλλὰ τὰ προσήκοντα καὶ τὰ συμφέροντα ὑμῖν αὐτοῖς ἐποιήσατε, βραχέα βούλομαι καὶ περὶ τούτων εἰπεῖν. οἱ γὰρ πατέρες οἱ ὑμέτεροι γενομένων τῇ πόλει κακῶν μεγάλων, ὅτε οἱ τύραννοι μὲν εἶχον τὴν πόλιν, ὁ δὲ δῆμος ἔφευγε, νικήσαντες μαχόμενοι τοὺς τυράννους ἐπὶ Παλληνίῳ, στρατηγοῦντος Λεωγόρου τοῦ προπάππου τοῦ ἐμοῦ καὶ Χαρίου οὗ ἐκεῖνος τὴν θυγατέρα εἶχεν, ἐξ ἧς ὁ ἡμέτερος ἦν πάππος, κατελθόντες εἰς τὴν πατρίδα τοὺς μὲν ἀπέκτειναν, τῶν δὲ φυγὴν κατέγνωσαν, τοὺς δὲ μένειν ἐν τῇ πόλει ἐάσαντες
ἠτίμωσαν. ὕστερον δὲ ἡνίκα βασιλεὺς ἐπεστράτευσεν 107
ἐπὶ τὴν Ἑλλάδα, γνόντες τῶν συμφορῶν τῶν ἐπιουσῶν τὸ μέγεθος καὶ τὴν παρασκευὴν τὴν βασιλέως, ἔγνωσαν τούς τε φεύγοντας καταδέξασθαι καὶ τοὺς ἀτίμους ἐπιτίμους ποιῆσαι καὶ κοινὴν τήν τε σωτηρίαν καὶ τοὺς κινδύνους ποιήσασθαι. πράξαντες δὲ ταῦτα, καὶ δόντες ἀλλήλοις πίστεις καὶ ὅρκους μεγάλους, ἠξίουν σφᾶς αὐτοὺς προτάξαντες πρὸ τῶν Ἑλλήνων ἁπάντων ἀπαντῆσαι τοῖς βαρβάροις Μαραθῶνάδε, νομίσαντες τὴν σφετέραν αὐτῶν ἀρετὴν ἱκανὴν εἶναι τῷ πλήθει τῷ ἐκείνων ἀντιτάξασθαι· μαχεσάμενοί τε ἐνίκων, καὶ τήν τε Ἑλλάδα ἠλευθέρωσαν καὶ τὴν πατρίδα ἔσῳσαν.

896 *ἡ ὑμετέρα* A^1 : om. ut vid. A^a *κρινεῖ* Steph. : *κρίνει* A
902 *βραχέα* L : *βραχεῖα* A 905 *ἔφευγε* Sauppe : *ἔφυγε* A
907 *Χαρίου* A : *Καλλίου* Sluiter (coll. Hdt. 6.121) 909 *τῶν* L^{sv} : *τοὺς* A
913 alt. *τὴν* Bekker : *τοῦ* A 914 *φεύγοντας* Turr. : *φυγόντας* A
916 *πράξαντες* L^cM^{1sv} : *πράξαντας* A *δόντες* Z Ald. : *διδόντες* A
918 *προτάξαντες* A^c : *προστάξαντες* A^a *πρὸ* del. Dalmeyda

108 *ἔργον δὲ τοιοῦτον ἐργασάμενοι, οὐκ ἠξίωσάν τινι τῶν
πρότερον γενομένων μνησικακῆσαι. τοιγάρτοι διὰ
ταῦτα, τὴν πόλιν ἀνάστατον παραλαβόντες ἱερά τε
κατακεκαυμένα τείχη τε καὶ οἰκίας καταπεπτωκυίας,
ἀφορμήν τε οὐδεμίαν ἔχοντες, διὰ τὸ ἀλλήλοις ὁμονοεῖν
τὴν ἀρχὴν τῶν Ἑλλήνων κατηργάσαντο καὶ τὴν πόλιν*
109 *ὑμῖν τοιαύτην καὶ τοσαύτην παρέδοσαν. ὑμεῖς οὖν
καὶ αὐτοὶ ὕστερον, κακῶν οὐκ ἐλαττόνων ἢ ἐκείνοις
γεγενημένων, ἀγαθοὶ ἐξ ἀγαθῶν ὄντες ἀπέδοτε τὴν
ὑπάρχουσαν ἀρετήν· ἠξιώσατε γὰρ τούς τε φεύγοντας
καταδέξασθαι καὶ τοὺς ἀτίμους ἐπιτίμους ποιῆσαι. τί
οὖν ὑμῖν ὑπόλοιπόν ἐστι τῆς ἐκείνων ἀρετῆς; μὴ
μνησικακῆσαι, εἰδότας, ὦ ἄνδρες, ὅτι ἡ πόλις ἐκ πολὺ
ἐλάττονος ἀφορμῆς ἐν τῷ ἔμπροσθεν χρόνῳ μεγάλη καὶ
εὐδαίμων ἐγένετο· ἃ νῦν αὐτῇ ὑπάρχει, εἰ ἐθέλοιμεν οἱ
πολῖται σωφρονεῖν τε καὶ ὁμονοεῖν ἀλλήλοις.*
110 *Κατηγόρησαν δέ μου καὶ περὶ τῆς ἱκετηρίας, ὡς
καταθείην ἐγὼ ἐν τῷ Ἐλευσινίῳ, νόμος δ' εἴη πάτριος,
ὃς ἂν θῇ ἱκετηρίαν μυστηρίοις, τεθνάναι. καὶ οὕτως εἰσὶ
τολμηροί, ὥσθ' ἃ αὐτοὶ κατεσκεύασαν, οὐκ ἀρκεῖ αὐτοῖς
ὅτι οὐ κατέσχον ἃ ἐπεβούλευσαν, ἀλλὰ καὶ κατηγορίαν*
111 *ἐμοῦ ποιοῦνται ὡς ἀδικοῦντος. ἐπειδὴ γὰρ ἤλθομεν
Ἐλευσινόθεν καὶ ἡ ἔνδειξις ἐγεγένητο, προσῄει ⟨τοῖς
πρυτάνεσιν⟩ ὁ βασιλεὺς περὶ τῶν γεγενημένων Ἐλευσῖνι
κατὰ τὴν τελετήν, ὥσπερ ἔθος ἐστίν, οἱ δὲ πρυτάνεις*

923 *τινι* A^{1} : *τι* A^{a} 924 *διὰ* A : *μετὰ* Bake 928 *κατηργάσαντο* B : *κατειργάσαντο* A 930 *οὐκ* A^{1} : om. A^{a} 937 *ἃ* <*καὶ*> Blass^{3} 940 *ελευσειινιωι* sic PFlor *δ' εἴη* Bekker : *δὲ εἴη* Dobree : *δει|η* PFlor : *δὲ ἦν* A 941 *ἂν θῇ* A : *εαν θη* PFlor^{2sv} : *αν επι* PFlor 942 *ἃ αὐτοὶ κατεσκεύασαν* del. vel transposuit post *ἀδικοῦντος* l. 944 Sluiter 943 *ἃ ἐπεβούλευσαν* secl. Albini^{3} ut glossema ad *ἃ … κατεσκεύασαν* 945–6 add. Blass^{3} auct. Koepkio, qui haec verba post *ἔθος ἐστίν*, l. 947 inseruerat

προσάξειν ἔφασαν αὐτὸν πρὸς τὴν βουλήν, ἐπαγγεῖλαί
τ' ἐκέλευον ἐμοί τε καὶ Κηφισίῳ παρεῖναι εἰς τὸ
Ἐλευσίνιον· ἡ γὰρ βουλὴ ἐκεῖ καθεδεῖσθαι ἔμελλε κατὰ
τὸν Σόλωνος νόμον, ὃς κελεύει τῇ ὑστεραίᾳ τῶν
μυστηρίων ἕδραν ποιεῖν ἐν τῷ Ἐλευσινίῳ. καὶ παρῆμεν 112
κατὰ τὰ προειρημένα. καὶ ἡ βουλὴ ἐπειδὴ ἦν πλήρης,
ἀναστὰς Καλλίας ὁ Ἱππονίκου τὴν σκευὴν ἔχων λέγει
ὅτι ἱκετηρία κεῖται ἐπὶ τοῦ βωμοῦ, καὶ ἔδειξεν αὐτοῖς.
κᾆθ' ὁ κῆρυξ ἐκήρυττε τίς τὴν ἱκετηρίαν καταθείη, καὶ
οὐδεὶς ὑπήκουεν. ἡμεῖς δὲ παρέσταμεν, καὶ οὗτος ἡμᾶς
ἑώρα. ἐπειδὴ δὲ οὐδεὶς ὑπήκουεν καὶ ᾤχετο εἰσιών,
ἐπεξελθὼν Εὐκλῆς οὑτοσί—καί μοι κάλει αὐτόν. πρῶτα
μὲν οὖν ταῦτα εἰ ἀληθῆ λέγω, μαρτύρησον, Εὔκλεις.

⟨ΜΑΡΤΥΡΙΑ⟩

Ὡς μὲν ἀληθῆ λέγω, μεμαρτύρηται· πολὺ δέ μοι δοκεῖ 113
τὸ ἐναντίον εἶναι ἢ οἱ κατήγοροι εἶπον. ἔλεξαν γάρ, εἰ
μέμνησθε, ὅτι αὐτώ με τὼ θεὼ παραγάγοιεν ὥστε
θεῖναι τὴν ἱκετηρίαν μὴ εἰδότα τὸν νόμον, ἵνα δῶ δίκην.
ἐγὼ δέ, ὦ ἄνδρες, εἰ ὡς μάλιστα ἀληθῆ λέγουσιν οἱ
κατήγοροι, ὑπ' αὐτοῖν μὲν φημὶ τοῖν θεοῖν σεσῶσθαι.
εἰ γὰρ ἔθηκα μὲν τὴν ἱκετηρίαν, ὑπήκουσα δὲ μή, ἄλλο 114
τι ἢ αὐτὸς μὲν αὑτὸν ἀπώλλυον τιθεὶς τὴν ἱκετηρίαν,
ἐσῳζόμην δὲ τῇ τύχῃ διὰ τὸ μὴ ὑπακοῦσαι, δῆλον ὅτι
διὰ τὼ θεώ; εἰ γὰρ ἐβουλέσθην με ἀπολλύναι τὼ θεώ,

948 ἐπαγγεῖλαί Bekker : ἀπαγγεῖλαι A 949 Κηφισίω B : Κηφησίω A 953 προειρημένα L : προηρημένα A 956 κᾆθ' Bekker : καθὰ A 957 παρέσταμεν Bekker : παρέστημεν A 958 καὶ A$^{\text{1im}}$: om. A^{a} : ante ἐπεξελθὼν transp. Lipsius 961 tit. add. Ald. : vac. spat. in A 963 ἢ <ὃ> MacDowell 964 παραγάγοιεν Dobree : περιαγάγοιεν A 967 μὲν A : με Reiske 969 αὑτὸν A$^{\text{1}}$: αὐτὸν A^{a} 971 εἰ γὰρ ... τὼ θεώ A$^{\text{1im}}$

ἐχρῆν δήπου καὶ μὴ θέντα με τὴν ἱκετηρίαν ὁμολογῆσαι.
115 ἀλλ᾽ οὔτε ὑπήκουσα οὔτ᾽ ἔθηκα. ἐπειδὴ δ᾽ ἔλεγε τῇ
βουλῇ Εὐκλῆς ὅτι οὐδεὶς ὑπακούοι, πάλιν ὁ Καλλίας
⟨ἀνα⟩στὰς ἔλεγεν ὅτι εἴη νόμος πάτριος, εἴ τις ἱκετηρίαν
θείη ἐν τῷ Ἐλευσινίῳ, ἄκριτον ἀποθανεῖν, καὶ ὁ πατήρ
ποτ᾽ αὐτοῦ Ἱππόνικος ἐξηγήσατο ταῦτα Ἀθηναίοις,
ἀκούσειε δὲ ὅτι ἐγὼ θείην τὴν ἱκετηρίαν. ἐντεῦθεν
116 ἀναπηδᾷ Κέφαλος οὑτοσὶ καὶ λέγει· "Ὦ Καλλία, πάντων
ἀνθρώπων ἀνοσιώτατε, πρῶτον μὲν ἐξηγῇ Κηρύκων
ὤν, οὐχ ὅσιον ⟨ὄν⟩ σοι ἐξηγεῖσθαι· ἔπειτα δὲ νόμον
πάτριον λέγεις, ἡ δὲ στήλη παρ᾽ ᾗ ἕστηκας χιλίας
δραχμὰς κελεύει ὀφείλειν, ἐάν τις ἱκετηρίαν θῇ ἐν τῷ
Ἐλευσινίῳ. ἔπειτα δὲ τίνος ἤκουσας ὅτι Ἀνδοκίδης θείη
τὴν ἱκετηρίαν; κάλεσον αὐτὸν τῇ βουλῇ, ἵνα καὶ ἡμεῖς
ἀκούσωμεν." ἐπειδὴ δὲ ἀνεγνώσθη ἡ στήλη κἀκεῖνος
οὐκ εἶχεν εἰπεῖν ὅτου ἤκουσεν, καταφανὴς ἦν τῇ βουλῇ
αὐτὸς θεὶς τὴν ἱκετηρίαν.

117 Φέρε δὴ τοίνυν, ὦ ἄνδρες (τάχα γὰρ ἂν αὐτὸ βούλοισθε
πυθέσθαι), ὁ δὲ Καλλίας τί βουλόμενος ἐτίθει τὴν
ἱκετηρίαν; ἐγὼ δὲ ὑμῖν διηγήσομαι ὧν ὑπ᾽ αὐτοῦ ἕνεκα
ἐπεβουλεύθην. Ἐπίλυκος ἦν ὁ Τεισάνδρου θεῖός μοι,
ἀδελφὸς τῆς μητρὸς τῆς ἐμῆς· ἀπέθανε δὲ ἐν Σικελίᾳ
ἄπαις ἀρρένων παίδων, θυγατέρας δὲ δύο καταλιπών,
118 αἳ ἐγίγνοντο εἴς τε ἐμὲ καὶ Λέαγρον. τὰ δὲ πράγματα τὰ
οἴκοι πονήρως εἶχε· τὴν μὲν γὰρ φανερὰν οὐσίαν οὐδὲ
δυοῖν ταλάντοιν κατέλιπε, τὰ δὲ ὀφειλόμενα πλέον ἦν ἢ
πέντε τάλαντα. ὅμως δ᾽ ἐγὼ καλέσας Λέαγρον ἐναντίον
τῶν φίλων ἔλεγον, ὅτι ταῦτ᾽ εἴη ἀνδρῶν ἀγαθῶν, ἐν τοῖς

975 add. Baiter 976 ἐν] <μυστηρίοις> ἐν Dalmeyda 977 ἐξηγήσατο A : ἐξηγήσαιτο Dobree 981 ὤν Reiske : ὧν A add. Frohberger[2] 984 ελευσεινιωι sic PFlor 989 βούλοισθε Dobree : βούλεσθε A 991 ἕνεκα Lipsius : εἵνεκα A 992 Τεισάνδρου Blass[2] : τισάνδρου A

τοιούτοις δεικνύναι τὰς οἰκειότητας ἀλλήλοις. "Ἡμᾶς 119
γὰρ οὐ δίκαιόν ἐστιν οὔτε χρήματα ἕτερα οὔτ' εὐτυχίαν
ἀνδρὸς ἑλέσθαι, ὥστε καταφρονῆσαι τῶν Ἐπιλύκου
θυγατέρων. καὶ γὰρ εἰ ἔζη Ἐπίλυκος ἢ τεθνεὼς πολλὰ
κατέλιπε χρήματα, ἠξιοῦμεν ἂν γένει ὄντες ἐγγυτάτω
ἔχειν τὰς παῖδας. τοιγάρτοι ἐκεῖνα μὲν δι' Ἐπίλυκον ἂν
ἦν ἢ διὰ τὰ χρήματα· νῦν δὲ διὰ τὴν ἡμετέραν ἀρετὴν
τάδε ἔσται. τῆς μὲν οὖν σὺ ἐπιδικάζου, τῆς δὲ ἐγώ."
ὡμολόγησέ μοι, ὦ ἄνδρες. ἐπεδικασάμεθα ἄμφω 120
κατὰ τὴν πρὸς ἡμᾶς ὁμολογίαν. καὶ ἧς μὲν ἐγὼ
ἐπεδικασάμην, ἡ παῖς τύχῃ χρησαμένη καμοῦσα
ἀπέθανεν· ἡ δ' ἑτέρα ἔστιν ἔτι. ταύτην Καλλίας
ἔπειθε Λέαγρον, χρήματα ὑπισχνούμενος, ἐὰν αὑτὸν
λαβεῖν· αἰσθόμενος δ' ἐγὼ εὐθὺς ἔθηκα παράστασιν,
καὶ ἔλαχον πρότερον μὲν ⟨λέγων⟩ Λεάγρῳ, ὅτι "Εἰ
μὲν σὺ βούλῃ ἐπιδικάζεσθαι, ἔχε τύχῃ ἀγαθῇ, εἰ δὲ μή,
ἐγὼ ἐπιδικάσομαι." γνοὺς ταῦτα Καλλίας λαγχάνει 121
τῷ υἱεῖ τῷ ἑαυτοῦ τῆς ἐπικλήρου, τῇ δεκάτῃ ἱσταμένου,
ἵνα μὴ ἐπιδικάσωμαι ἐγώ. ταῖς δ' εἰκάσι, μυστηρίοις
τούτοις, δοὺς Κηφισίῳ χιλίας δραχμὰς ἐνδείκνυσί με
καὶ εἰς τὸν ἀγῶνα τοῦτον καθίστησιν. ἐπειδή δ' ἑώρα
με ὑπομένοντα, τίθησι τὴν ἱκετηρίαν, ὡς ἐμὲ μὲν
ἀποκτενῶν ἄκριτον ἢ ἐξελῶν, αὐτὸς δὲ πείσας Λέαγρον
χρήμασι συνοικήσων τῇ Ἐπιλύκου θυγατρί. ἐπειδὴ δ' 122
⟨οὐδ'⟩ οὕτως ἄνευ ἀγῶνος ἑώρα ἐσόμενα τὰ πράγματα,
τότε δὴ προσιὼν Λυσίστρατον, Ἡγήμονα, Ἐπιχάρην,

1001 ἕτερα] ἑτέρου Richards[1] 1004 ἠξιοῦμεν A[1] : ἀξιοῦμεν A[a] 1012 αὑτὸν Blass[3] : αὐτὸν A 1014 πρότερον μὲν <λέγων> MacDowell : προτέρω μὲν A : fort. προτείνων μὲν Albini[2] 1015 βούλῃ Blass[3] : βούλει A 1018 ἵνα … δ'] ἵνα <δὲ> … {δ'} MacDowell 1022 ἐξελῶν Valckenaer : ἐξελὼν A πείσας Scaliger : πείσων A 1024 add. Reiske : οὐδ' ὡς Bekker : οὕτως A 1025 Ἡγήμονα Valcknaer : ἡγεμόνα A ἐπιχάρην A : Ἐπιχάρη Schiller

ὁρῶν φίλους ὄντας ἐμοὶ καὶ χρωμένους, εἰς τοῦτο βδελυρίας ἦλθε καὶ παρανομίας, ὥστ' ἔλεγε πρὸς τούτους, ὡς εἰ ἔτι καὶ νῦν βουλοίμην ἀποστῆναι τῆς Ἐπιλύκου θυγατρός, ἕτοιμος εἴη παύσασθαί με κακῶς ποιῶν, ἀπαλλάξαι δὲ Κηφίσιον, δίκην δ' ἐν τοῖς φίλοις
123 δοῦναί μοι τῶν πεποιημένων. εἶπον αὐτῷ καὶ κατηγορεῖν καὶ παρασκευάζειν ἄλλους· εἰ δ' ἐγὼ αὐτὸν ἀποφεύξομαι καὶ γνώσονται Ἀθηναῖοι περὶ ἐμοῦ τὰ δίκαια, ἐγὼ αὐτὸν οἴομαι περὶ τοῦ σώματος τοῦ ἑαυτοῦ ἐν τῷ μέρει κινδυνεύσειν. ἅπερ αὐτὸν οὐ ψεύσομαι, ἐὰν ὑμῖν, ὦ ἄνδρες, δοκῇ. ὡς δ' ἀληθῆ λέγω, κάλει μοι τοὺς μάρτυρας.

ΜΑΡΤΥΡΕΣ

124 Ἀλλὰ γὰρ τὸν υἱὸν αὐτοῦ τοῦτον, ᾧ λαχεῖν ἠξίωσε τῆς Ἐπιλύκου θυγατρός, σκέψασθε πῶς γέγονε, καὶ πῶς ἐποιήσατ' αὐτόν· ταῦτα γὰρ καὶ ἄξιον ἀκοῦσαι, ὦ ἄνδρες. γαμεῖ μὲν Ἰσχομάχου θυγατέρα· ταύτῃ δὲ συνοικήσας οὐδ' ἐνιαυτὸν τὴν μητέρα αὐτῆς ἔλαβε, καὶ συνῴκει ὁ πάντων σχετλιώτατος ἀνθρώπων τῇ μητρὶ καὶ τῇ θυγατρί, ἱερεὺς ὢν τῆς Μητρὸς καὶ τῆς Θυγατρός,
125 καὶ εἶχεν ἐν τῇ οἰκίᾳ ἀμφοτέρας. καὶ οὗτος μὲν οὐκ ἠσχύνθη οὐδ' ἔδεισε τὼ θεώ· ἡ δὲ τοῦ Ἰσχομάχου θυγάτηρ τεθνάναι νομίσασα λυσιτελεῖν ἢ ζῆν ὁρῶσα τὰ γιγνόμενα, ἀπαγχομένη μεταξὺ κατεκλίθη, καὶ ἐπειδὴ ἀνεβίω, ἀποδρᾶσα ἐκ τῆς οἰκίας ᾤχετο, καὶ ἐξήλασεν ἡ μήτηρ τὴν θυγατέρα. ταύτης δ' αὖ διαπεπλησμένος ἐξέβαλε καὶ ταύτην. ἡ δ' ἔφη κυεῖν ἐξ αὐτοῦ· καὶ ἐπειδὴ

1030 ἀπαλλάξαι] διαλλάξαι dubitanter Cominis 1031 μοι A[1] : om A[a] 1032 ἀποφεύξομαι Valckenaer : ἀποφεύξαιμι A 1034 οἴομαι A : οἶμαι Marchant 1048 κατεκλίθη A : κατεκωλύθη Sluiter : κατελήφθη Dobree : κατελύθη Baiter 1049 ἀποδρᾶσα Bekker : ἀποδράσασα A 1051 κυεῖν Klotz[2] : κύειν A

ἔτεκεν υἱόν, ἔξαρνος ἦν μὴ εἶναι ἐξ αὑτοῦ τὸ παιδίον. λαβόντες δὲ οἱ προσήκοντες τῇ γυναικὶ τὸ παιδίον ἧκον 126
ἐπὶ τὸν βωμὸν Ἀπατουρίοις, ἔχοντες ἱερεῖον, καὶ ἐκέλευον κατάρξασθαι τὸν Καλλίαν. ὁ δ' ἠρώτα τίνος εἴη τὸ παιδίον· ἔλεγον "Καλλίου τοῦ Ἱππονίκου." "Ἐγώ εἰμι οὗτος." "Καὶ ἔστι γε σὸν τὸ παιδίον." λαβόμενος τοῦ βωμοῦ ὤμοσεν ἦ μὴν μὴ εἶναί ⟨οἱ⟩ υἱὸν ἄλλον μηδὲ γενέσθαι πώποτε, εἰ μὴ Ἱππόνικον ἐκ τῆς Γλαύκωνος θυγατρός· ἢ ἐξώλη εἶναι καὶ αὐτὸν καὶ τὴν οἰκίαν— ὥσπερ ἔσται. μετὰ ταῦτα τοίνυν, ὦ ἄνδρες, ὑστέρῳ 127
πάλιν χρόνῳ τῆς γραὸς τολμηροτάτης γυναικὸς ἀνηράσθη, καὶ κομίζεται αὐτὴν εἰς τὴν οἰκίαν, καὶ τὸν παῖδα ἤδη μέγαν ὄντα εἰσάγει εἰς Κήρυκας, φάσκων εἶναι υἱὸν αὑτοῦ. ἀντεῖπε μὲν Καλλιάδης μὴ εἰσδέξασθαι, ἐψηφίσαντο δὲ οἱ Κήρυκες κατὰ τὸν νόμον ὅς ἐστιν αὑτοῖς, τὸν πατέρα ὀμόσαντα εἰσάγειν ἦ μὴν υἱὸν ὄντα ἑαυτοῦ εἰσάγειν. λαβόμενος τοῦ βωμοῦ ὤμοσεν ἦ μὴν τὸν παῖδα ἑαυτοῦ εἶναι γνήσιον, ἐκ Χρυσίλλης γεγονότα· ὃν ἀπώμοσε. καί μοι τούτων ἁπάντων τοὺς μάρτυρας κάλει.

⟨ΜΑΡΤΥΡΕΣ⟩

Φέρε δὴ τοίνυν, ὦ ἄνδρες, σκεψώμεθα εἰ πώποτε ἐν τοῖς 128
Ἕλλησι πρᾶγμα τοιοῦτον ἐγένετο, ὅπου γυναῖκά τις γήμας ἐπέγημε τῇ θυγατρὶ τὴν μητέρα καὶ ἐξήλασεν ἡ μήτηρ τὴν θυγατέρα· ταύτῃ δὲ συνοικῶν βούλεται τὴν

1052 αὑτοῦ Steph. : αὐτοῦ A 1053 ἧκον] ἦγον Steph. 1054 ἱερεῖον] ῖο in ras. A^{1} 1058 add. Muret 1065 αὑτοῦ Baiter : αὐτοῦ A μὲν A^{1} : om. A^{a} Καλλιάδης Valckenaer : Καλλικλῆς MacDowell : καλλίδης A^{1} : καλίδης A^{a} 1066 ὅς Steph. : ὃς Ald. : ὅ A αὑτοῖς Bekker : αὐτός A : αὐτὸν Reiske 1067 ὀμόσαντα Steph. : ὁμόσαντα A 1069 Χρυσίλλης Dindorf : χρυσιάδης A ὃν <πρότερον> MacDowell 1071 tit. add. Ald. 1074–5 καὶ … θυγατέρα A^{1im}

Ἐπιλύκου θυγατέρα λαβεῖν, ἵν᾽ ἐξελάσῃ τὴν τήθην ἡ
θυγατριδῆ. ἀλλὰ γὰρ τῷ παιδὶ αὐτοῦ τί χρὴ τοὔνομα
129 *θέσθαι; οἶμαι γὰρ ἔγωγε οὐδένα οὕτως ἀγαθὸν εἶναι*
λογίζεσθαι, ὅστις ἐξευρήσει τοὔνομα αὐτοῦ. τριῶν γὰρ
οὐσῶν γυναικῶν αἷς συνῳκηκὼς ἔσται ὁ πατὴρ αὐτοῦ,
τῆς μὲν υἱός ἐστιν, ὥς φησι, τῆς δὲ ἀδελφὸς, τῆς δὲ
θεῖος. τίς ἂν εἴη οὗτος; Οἰδίπους, ἢ Αἴγισθος; ἢ τί χρὴ
αὐτὸν ὀνομάσαι;

130 *Ἀλλὰ γάρ, ὦ ἄνδρες, βραχύ τι ὑμᾶς ἀναμνῆσαι περὶ*
Καλλίου βούλομαι. εἰ γὰρ μέμνησθε, ὅτε ἡ πόλις ἦρχε
τῶν Ἑλλήνων καὶ ηὐδαιμόνει μάλιστα, Ἱππόνικος δὲ
ἦν πλουσιώτατος τῶν Ἑλλήνων, τότε μέντοι πάντες
ἴστε ὅτι παρὰ τοῖς παιδαρίοις τοῖς μικροτάτοις καὶ
τοῖς γυναίοις κληδὼν ἐν ἁπάσῃ τῇ πόλει κατεῖχεν, ὅτι
Ἱππόνικος ἐν τῇ οἰκίᾳ ἀλιτήριον τρέφει, ὃς αὐτοῦ τὴν
131 *τράπεζαν ἀνατρέπει. μέμνησθε ταῦτα, ὦ ἄνδρες. πῶς*
οὖν ἡ φήμη ἡ τότε οὖσα δοκεῖ ὑμῖν ἀποβῆναι; οἰόμενος
γὰρ Ἱππόνικος υἱὸν τρέφειν ἀλιτήριον αὑτῷ ἔτρεφεν, ὃς
ἀνατέτροφεν ἐκείνου τὸν πλοῦτον, τὴν σωφροσύνην,
τὸν ἄλλον βίον ἅπαντα. οὕτως οὖν χρὴ περὶ τούτου
γιγνώσκειν, ὡς ὄντος Ἱππονίκου ἀλιτηρίου.

132 *Ἀλλὰ γάρ, ὦ ἄνδρες, διὰ τί ποτε τοῖς ἐμοὶ νυνὶ*
ἐπιτιθεμένοις μετὰ Καλλίου καὶ συμπαρασκευάσασι
τὸν ἀγῶνα καὶ χρήματα εἰσενεγκοῦσιν ἐπ᾽ ἐμοὶ τρία
μὲν ἔτη ἐπιδημῶν καὶ ἥκων ἐκ Κύπρου οὐκ ἀσεβεῖν
ἐδόκουν αὐτοῖς, μυῶν μὲν <. . .>α Δελφόν, ἔτι δὲ ἄλλους
ξένους ἐμαυτοῦ, καὶ εἰσιὼν εἰς τὸ Ἐλευσίνιον καὶ θύων,

1077 *παιδὶ* A[a] : *παιδίῳ* A[1]   1082 *οὗτος* A[1] : om. A[a]   1086 *ηὐδαιμόνει* Lipsius : *εὐδαιμόνει* A   1089 *ἁπάσῃ* L[2] : *ἅπασι* A   *κατεῖχεν* Blass : *κατέσχεν* A   1090 *ἀλιτήριον* B : *ἁλιτήριον* A   1093 *ἀλιτήριον* B : *ἁλιτήριον* A   *αὑτῷ* M : *αὐτῷ* A   *ἔτρεφεν* A[1] : *ἔτροφεν* A[a]   1096 *ἀλιτηρίου* B : *ἁλιτηρίου* A   1101 < . . . >*α Δελφόν* Thompson : *ἀδελφὸν* A : *Ἀ*< . . . > *Δελφόν* Bekker

ὥσπερ ἐμαυτὸν ἄξιον νομίζω εἶναι· ἀλλὰ τοὐναντίον
λῃτουργεῖν οὗτοι προὐβάλλοντο, πρῶτον μὲν γυμνασί-
αρχον Ἡφαιστίοις, ἔπειτα ἀρχεθέωρον εἰς Ἰσθμὸν καὶ
Ὀλυμπίαζε, εἶτα δὲ ταμίαν ἐν πόλει τῶν ἱερῶν
χρημάτων· νῦν δὲ ἀσεβῶ καὶ ἀδικῶ εἰσιὼν εἰς τὰ ἱερά;
ἐγὼ ὑμῖν ἐρῶ, διότι οὗτοι ταῦτα νῦν γιγνώσκουσιν. 133
Ἀγύρριος γὰρ οὑτοσί, ὁ καλὸς κἀγαθός, ἀρχώνης
ἐγένετο τῆς πεντηκοστῆς τρίτον ἔτος, καὶ ἐπρίατο
τριάκοντα ταλάντων. μετέσχον δ' αὐτῷ οὗτοι πάντες οἱ
παρασυλλεγέντες ὑπὸ τὴν λεύκην, οὓς ὑμεῖς ἴστε οἷοί
εἰσιν· οἳ διὰ τοῦτο ἔμοιγε δοκοῦσι συλλεγῆναι ἐκεῖσε, ἵν'
αὐτοῖς ἀμφότερα ᾖ, καὶ μὴ ὑπερβάλλουσι λαβεῖν
ἀργύριον καὶ ὀλίγου πραθείσης μετασχεῖν. κερδάναντες 134
δὲ τριά τάλαντα, γνόντες τὸ πρᾶγμα οἷον εἴη, ὡς πολλοῦ
ἄξιον, συνέστησαν πάντες, καὶ μεταδόντες τοῖς ἄλλοις
ἐωνοῦντο πάλιν τριάκοντα ταλάντων. ἐπεὶ δ' οὐκ
ἀντεωνεῖτο οὐδείς, παρελθὼν ἐγὼ εἰς τὴν βουλὴν
ὑπερέβαλλον, ἕως ἐπριάμην ἓξ καὶ τριάκοντα ταλάντων.
ἀπελάσας δὲ τούτους καὶ καταστήσας ὑμῖν ἐγγυητὰς
ἐξέλεξα τὰ χρήματα καὶ κατέβαλον τῇ πόλει καὶ αὐτὸς
οὐκ ἐζημιώθην, ἀλλὰ καὶ βραχέα ἀπεκερδαίνομεν οἱ
μετασχόντες· τούτους δ' ἐποίησα τῶν ὑμετέρων μὴ
διανείμασθαι ἓξ τάλαντα ἀργυρίου. ἃ οὗτοι γνόντες 135

1104 λῃτουργεῖν Blass[2] : λειτουργεῖν A 1105 ἀρχεθέωρον Lipsius : ἀρχιθεωρὸν 1106 ταμίαν A : ταμίας <ἦν> MacDowell 1109 ἀγύρριος A[c] : ἀργύρριος A[a] ἀρχώνης Valckenaer : ἄρχων εἷς A 1111 αὐτῷ Reiske : αὐτοὶ A 1112 λεύκην, οὓς Muret : λευκὴν τὸ, πόσους A 1114 ὑπερβάλλουσι Steph. : ὑπερβάλλωσι A 1115 πραθείσης A[1] : πειραθείσης A[a] κερδάναντες A : κερδήναντες Blass[3] 1116 τρία A : ἓξ Reiske 1116–17 ὡς πολλοῦ ἄξιον del. Sluiter 1117 τοῖς ἄλλοις] ἀλλήλοις Bake 1118–20 δ' οὐκ ... ἕω in ras. A[1] 1119 ἀντεωνεῖτο Lipsius : ἀντωνεῖτο A[1] 1120 ὑπερέβαλλον Ald. : ὑπερέβαλον A[1] 1123 καὶ A[1] : om. A[a] βραχέα A[c] : βραχεῖα A[a] 1124 ἐποίησα A[c] : ἐποίησαν A[a]

ἔδοσαν σφίσιν αὐτοῖς λόγον, ὅτι "Ἄνθρωπος οὑτοσὶ οὔτε
αὐτὸς λήψεται τῶν κοινῶν χρημάτων οὔθ' ἡμᾶς ἐάσει,
φυλάξει δὲ καὶ ἐμποδὼν ἔσται διανείμασθαι τὰ κοινά·
πρὸς δὲ τούτοις, ὃν ἂν ἡμῶν ἀδικοῦντα λάβῃ, εἰσάξει εἰς
τὸ πλῆθος τὸ Ἀθηναίων καὶ ἀπολεῖ. δεῖ οὖν τοῦτον
136 *ἐκποδὼν ἡμῖν εἶναι καὶ δικαίως καὶ ἀδίκως." ταῦτα*
μὲν οὖν, ὦ ἄνδρες δικασταί, τούτοις ποιητέα ἦν, ὑμῖν δέ
γε ⟨τὸ⟩ ἐναντίον τούτων· ὡς γὰρ πλείστους εἶναι ὑμῖν
ἤθελον ἂν τοιούσδε οἷόσπερ ἐγώ, τούτους δὲ μάλιστα
⟨μὲν⟩ ἀπολωλέναι, εἰ δὲ μή, εἶναι τοὺς μὴ ἐπιτρέψοντας
αὐτοῖς, οἷς καὶ προσήκει ἀνδράσιν εἶναι καὶ ἀγαθοῖς καὶ
δικαίοις περὶ τὸ πλῆθος τὸ ὑμέτερον, καὶ βουλόμενοι
δυνήσονται εὖ ποιεῖν ὑμᾶς. ἐγὼ οὖν ὑμῖν ὑπισχνοῦμαι ἢ
παύσειν τούτους ταῦτα ποιοῦντας καὶ βελτίους παρέξειν,
ἢ εἰς ὑμᾶς εἰσαγαγὼν κολάσειν τοὺς ἀδικοῦντας αὐτῶν.
137 *Κατηγόρησαν δέ μου καὶ περὶ τῶν ναυκληριῶν καὶ*
περὶ τῆς ἐμπορίας, ὡς ἄρα οἱ θεοὶ διὰ τοῦτό με ἐκ τῶν
κινδύνων σῴσαιεν, ἵνα ἐλθὼν δεῦρο, ὡς ἔοικεν, ὑπὸ
Κηφισίου ἀπολοίμην. ἐγὼ δέ, ὦ Ἀθηναῖοι, οὐκ ἀξιῶ
τοὺς θεοὺς τοιαύτην γνώμην ἔχειν, ὥστ' εἰ ἐνόμιζον ὑπ'
ἐμοῦ ἀδικεῖσθαι, λαμβάνοντάς με ἐν τοῖς μεγίστοις
κινδύνοις μὴ τιμωρεῖσθαι· τίς γὰρ κίνδυνος μείζων
ἀνθρώποις ἢ χειμῶνος ὥρᾳ πλεῖν τὴν θάλατταν; ἐν οἷς
ἔχοντες μὲν τὸ σῶμα τοὐμόν, κρατοῦντες δὲ τοῦ βίου
138 *καὶ τῆς οὐσίας τῆς ἐμῆς, εἶτα ἔσῳζον; οὐκ ἐξῆν αὐτοῖς*
ποιῆσαι μηδὲ ταφῆς τὸ σῶμα ἀξιωθῆναι; ἔτι δὲ πολέμου
γενομένου καὶ τριήρων ἀεὶ κατὰ θάλατταν οὐσῶν καὶ

1126 *ἄνθρωπος* Blass : *ἄνθρωπος* A 1128 *καὶ* A[1] : om. A[a] 1130 *τὸ Ἀθηναίων* Fuhr[1] : *τῶν Ἀθηναίων* A 1131 *ἡμῖν* Reiske : *ὑμῖν* A 1133 add. Valckenaer *ὡς* Blass : *τοὺς* A *ὑμῖν* Reiske : *ἡμῖν* A 1134 *τοιούσδε*] *υσ* in ras. A[1] 1135 add. Reiske 1138 *ποιεῖν* B : *ποιὲν* sic A 1150 *οὐκ ἐξῆν* Ald. : *οὐ πεζὴν* A *αὐτοῖς* A[1] : *αὐτῆς* ut vid. A[a]

ληστῶν, ὑφ᾽ ὧν πολλοὶ ληφθέντες, ἀπολέσαντες τὰ ὄντα, δουλεύοντες τὸν βίον διετέλεσαν, οὔσης δὲ χώρας βαρβάρου, εἰς ἣν πολλοὶ ἤδη ἐκπεσόντες αἰκίαις ταῖς μεγίσταις περιέπεσον καὶ τὰ σφέτερα αὐτῶν σώματα αἰκισθέντες ἀπέθανον—εἶτα οἱ μὲν θεοὶ ἐκ τοσούτων 139
κινδύνων ἔσῳζόν με, σφῶν δὲ αὐτῶν προὐστήσαντο τιμωρὸν γενέσθαι Κηφίσιον τὸν πονηρότατον Ἀθηναίων, ὧν οὗτός φησι πολίτης εἶναι οὐκ ὤν, ᾧ οὐδ᾽ ὑμῶν τῶν καθημένων οὐδεὶς ἂν ἐπιτρέψειεν οὐδὲν τῶν ἰδίων, εἰδὼς τοῦτον οἷός ἐστιν; ἐγὼ μὲν οὖν, ὦ ἄνδρες, ἡγοῦμαι χρῆναι νομίζειν τοὺς τοιούτους κινδύνους ἀνθρωπίνους, τοὺς δὲ κατὰ θάλατταν θείους. εἴπερ οὖν δεῖ τὰ τῶν θεῶν ὑπονοεῖν, πάνυ ἂν αὐτοὺς οἶμαι ἐγὼ ὀργίζεσθαι καὶ ἀγανακτεῖν, εἰ τοὺς ὑφ᾽ ἑαυτῶν σῳζομένους ὑπ᾽ ἄλλων ἀπολλυμένους ὁρῷεν.

Καὶ μὲν δὴ καὶ τάδε ὑμῖν ἄξιον, ὦ ἄνδρες, ἐνθυμηθῆναι, 140
ὅτι νυνὶ πᾶσι τοῖς Ἕλλησιν ἄνδρες ἄριστοι καὶ εὐβουλότατοι δοκεῖτε γεγενῆσθαι, οὐκ ἐπὶ τιμωρίαν τραπόμενοι τῶν γεγενημένων, ἀλλ᾽ ἐπὶ σωτηρίαν τῆς πόλεως καὶ ὁμόνοιαν τῶν πολιτῶν. συμφοραὶ μὲν γὰρ ἤδη καὶ ἄλλοις πολλοῖς ἐγένοντο οὐκ ἐλάττους ἢ καὶ ἡμῖν· τὸ δὲ τὰς γενομένας διαφορὰς πρὸς ἀλλήλους θέσθαι καλῶς, τοῦτ᾽ εἰκότως ἤδη δοκεῖ ἀνδρῶν ἀγαθῶν καὶ σωφρόνων ἔργον εἶναι. ἐπειδὴ τοίνυν παρὰ πάντων ὁμολογουμένως ταῦθ᾽ ὑμῖν ὑπάρχει, καὶ εἴ τις φίλος ὢν τυγχάνει καὶ εἴ τις ἐχθρός, μὴ μεταγνῶτε, μηδὲ βούλεσθε τὴν πόλιν ἀποστερῆσαι ταύτης τῆς δόξης,

1153 *ληφθέντες* L : *ληφθ᾽ἐν* in fine vers. A 1155 *αἰκίαις* A : *αἰκείαις* Blass[3] : *ἀτυχίαις* Sluiter 1157 *αἰκισθέντες* Steph. : *αἰκισθέν᾽* in fine vers. A 1160 *ὑμῶν*] *υ* in ras. A[1] 1165 *πάνυ* Reiske : *πολὺ* A 1166 *ἄλλων*] *ἀνθρώπων* Hertlein[2] 1168 *ὑμῖν*] *υ* in ras. A[1] 1177 *ταῦθ᾽* Steph. : *τάθ᾽* A 1179 *βούλεσθε* Taylor : *βουλεύεσθε* A

μηδὲ αὐτοὶ δοκεῖν τύχῃ ταῦτα μᾶλλον ἢ γνώμῃ ψηφίσασθαι.
141 Δέομαι οὖν ἁπάντων ⟨ὑμῶν⟩ περὶ ἐμοῦ τὴν αὐτὴν γνώμην ἔχειν ἥνπερ καὶ περὶ τῶν ἐμῶν προγόνων, ἵνα κἀμοὶ ἐγγένηται ἐκείνους μιμήσασθαι, ἀναμνησθέντας αὐτῶν ὅτι ὅμοιοι τοῖς πλείστων καὶ μεγίστων ἀγαθῶν αἰτίοις τῇ πόλει γεγένηνται, πολλῶν ἕνεκα σφᾶς αὐτοὺς παρέχοντες τοιούτους, μάλιστα δὲ τῆς εἰς ὑμᾶς εὐνοίας, καὶ ὅπως, εἴ ποτέ τις αὐτοῖς ἢ τῶν ἐξ ἐκείνων τινὶ κίνδυνος γένοιτο ἢ συμφορά, σῴζοιντο συγγνώμης παρ'
142 ὑμῶν τυγχάνοντες. εἰκότως δ' ἂν αὐτῶν μεμνῇσθε· καὶ γὰρ τῇ πόλει ἁπάσῃ αἱ τῶν ὑμετέρων προγόνων ἀρεταὶ πλείστου ἄξιαι ἐγένοντο. ἐπειδὴ γάρ, ὦ ἄνδρες, αἱ νῆες διεφθάρησαν, πολλῶν βουλομένων τὴν πόλιν ἀνηκέστοις συμφοραῖς περιβαλεῖν, Λακεδαιμόνιοι ἔγνωσαν ὅμως τότε ἐχθροὶ ὄντες σῴζειν τὴν πόλιν διὰ τὰς ἐκείνων τῶν ἀνδρῶν ἀρετάς, οἳ ὑπῆρξαν τῆς ἐλευθερίας ἁπάσῃ τῇ
143 Ἑλλάδι. ἐπειδὴ τοίνυν καὶ ἡ πόλις ἐσώθη δημοσίᾳ διὰ τὰς τῶν προγόνων τῶν ὑμετέρων ἀρετάς, ἀξιῶ κἀμοὶ διὰ τὰς τῶν προγόνων τῶν ἐμῶν ἀρετὰς σωτηρίαν γενέσθαι. καὶ γὰρ αὐτῶν τῶν ἔργων, δι' ἅπερ ἡ πόλις ἐσώθη, οὐκ ἐλάχιστον μέρος οἱ ἐμοὶ πρόγονοι συνεβάλοντο· ὧν ἕνεκα καὶ ἐμοὶ δίκαιον ὑμᾶς μεταδοῦναι τῆς σωτηρίας, ἧσπερ καὶ αὐτοὶ παρὰ τῶν Ἑλλήνων ἐτύχετε.
144 Σκέψασθε τοίνυν καὶ τάδε, ἄν με σῴσητε, οἷον ἕξετε πολίτην· ὃς πρῶτον μὲν ἐκ πολλοῦ πλούτου, ὅσον ὑμεῖς ἴστε, οὐ δι' ἐμαυτὸν ἀλλὰ διὰ τὰς τῆς πόλεως συμφορὰς

1182 add. Reiske 1184 *ἐγγένηται* A[1] : *γένηται* A[a] 1186 *ἕνεκα* Blass[2] : *ἕκενεν* A 1187 *εἰς* A[1] : om. A[a] 1189 *γένοιτο* Dobree : *γένηται* A : *γενήσεται* Madvig[2] 1190 *μεμνῇσθε* Schneider : *μεμνῆσθαι* A 1191 *ὑμετέρων* Reiske : *ἡμετέρων* A 1193 *τὴν πόλιν* A[1] : *τῇ πόλει* A[a] 1198 *ὑμετέρων* Reiske : *ἡμετέρων* A *κἀμοὶ* Ald. : *καί μοι* A : *καὶ ἐμοὶ* L 1205 *μὲν* A[1] : om. A[a] εἰς πενίαν πολλὴν καὶ ἀπορίαν κατέστην, ἔπειτα δὲ καινὸν βίον ἠργασάμην ἐκ τοῦ δικαίου, τῇ γνώμῃ καὶ τοῖν χεροῖν τοῖν ἐμαυτοῦ· ἔτι δὲ εἰδότα μὲν οἷόν ἐστι πόλεως τοιαύτης πολίτην εἶναι, εἰδότα δὲ οἷόν ἐστι ξένον εἶναι καὶ μέτοικον ἐν τῇ τῶν πλησίον, ἐπιστάμενον 145 δὲ οἷον τὸ σωφρονεῖν καὶ ὀρθῶς βουλεύεσθαι, ἐπιστάμενον δ᾽ οἷον τὸ ἁμαρτόντα πρᾶξαι κακῶς <. . .> πολλοῖς συγγενόμενος καὶ πλείστων πειραθείς, ἀφ᾽ ὧν ἐμοὶ ξενίαι καὶ φιλότητες πρὸς πολλοὺς καὶ βασιλέας καὶ πόλεις καὶ ἄλλους ἰδίᾳ ξένους γεγένηνται, ὧν ἐμὲ σῴσαντες μεθέξετε, καὶ ἔστιν ὑμῖν χρῆσθαι τούτοις, ὅπου ἂν ἐν καιρῷ τι ὑμῖν γίγνηται.

Ἔχει δὲ καὶ ὑμῖν, ὦ ἄνδρες, οὕτως· ἐάν με νυνὶ 146 διαφθείρητε, οὐκ ἔστιν ὑμῖν ἔτι λοιπὸς τοῦ γένους τοῦ ἡμετέρου οὐδείς, ἀλλ᾽ οἴχεται πᾶν πρόρριζον. καίτοι οὐκ ὄνειδος ὑμῖν ἐστιν ἡ Ἀνδοκίδου καὶ Λεωγόρου οἰκία οὖσα, ἀλλὰ πολὺ μᾶλλον τότ᾽ ἦν ὄνειδος, ὅτ᾽ ἐμοῦ φεύγοντος Κλεοφῶν αὐτὴν ὁ λυροποιὸς ᾤκει. οὐ γὰρ ἔστιν ὅστις πώποτε ὑμῶν παριὼν τὴν οἰκίαν τὴν ἡμετέραν ἀνεμνήσθη ἢ ἰδίᾳ τι ἢ δημοσίᾳ κακὸν παθὼν ὑπ᾽ ἐκείνων, οἳ πλείστας μὲν στρατηγήσαντες στρατηγίας 147 πολλὰ τρόπαια τῶν πολεμίων καὶ κατὰ γῆν καὶ κατὰ θάλατταν ὑμῖν ἀπέδειξαν, πλείστας δὲ ἄλλας ἀρχὰς ἄρξαντες καὶ χρήματα διαχειρίσαντες τὰ ὑμέτερα οὐδένα πώποτε ὦφλον, οὐδ᾽ ἡμάρτηται οὐδὲν οὔτε ἡμῖν εἰς ὑμᾶς οὔτε ὑμῖν εἰς ἡμᾶς, οἰκία δὲ πασῶν ἀρχαιοτάτη

1208 καινὸν Emperius[1] : καὶ A   ἠργασάμην Blass[3] : εἰργασάμην A   1209 τοῖν ... τοῖν Marchant : ταῖν ... τοῖν A[a] : ταῖν ... ταῖν A[1]   1211 πλησίον A[1] : πλησίων ut vid. A[a]   1213 ante πολλοῖς lacunam posuit Reiske   1217 ἔστιν A : ἔσται Steph.   1221 ἡμετέρου A[1] : ὑμετέρου A[a]   1222 ὑμῖν L[c] (υ in ras.) M[1sv] : ἡμῖν A   1225–6 οἰκίαν τὴν ἡμετέραν] αν τὴν ἡ e ras. A[1]   1231 οὐδένα Blass : οὐδὲν ἂν A : ἂν del. Sluiter   ἡμάρτηται] ηται e ras. A[1]

καὶ κοινοτάτη ἀεὶ τῷ δεομένῳ. οὐδ᾽ ἔστιν ὅπου ἐκείνων
τις τῶν ἀνδρῶν καταστὰς εἰς ἀγῶνα ἀπῄτησεν ὑμᾶς
148 χάριν τούτων τῶν ἔργων. μὴ τοίνυν, εἰ αὐτοὶ τεθνᾶσι,
καὶ περὶ τῶν πεπραγμένων αὐτοῖς ἐπιλάθησθε, ἀλλ᾽
ἀναμνησθέντες τῶν ἔργων νομίσατε τὰ σώματα αὐτῶν
ὁρᾶν αἰτουμένων ἐμὲ παρ᾽ ὑμῶν σῷσαι. τίνα γὰρ καὶ
ἀναβιβάσομαι δεησόμενον ὑπὲρ ἐμαυτοῦ; τὸν πατέρα;
ἀλλὰ τέθνηκεν. ἀλλὰ τοὺς ἀδελφούς; ἀλλ᾽ οὐκ εἰσί. ἀλλὰ
149 τοὺς παῖδας; ἀλλ᾽ οὔπω γεγένηνται. ὑμεῖς τοίνυν καὶ
ἀντὶ πατρὸς ἐμοὶ καὶ ἀντὶ ἀδελφῶν καὶ ἀντὶ παίδων
γένεσθε· εἰς ὑμᾶς καταφεύγω καὶ ἀντιβολῶ καὶ ἱκετεύω·
ὑμεῖς με παρ᾽ ὑμῶν αὐτῶν αἰτησάμενοι σῴσατε, καὶ μὴ
βούλεσθε Θετταλοὺς καὶ Ἀνδρίους πολίτας ποιεῖσθαι δι᾽
ἀπορίαν ἀνδρῶν, τοὺς δὲ ὄντας πολίτας ὁμολογουμένως,
οἷς προσήκει ἀνδράσιν ἀγαθοῖς εἶναι καὶ βουλόμενοι
δυνήσονται, τούτους δὲ ἀπόλλυτε. μὴ δῆτα. ἔπειτα καὶ
ταῦθ᾽ ὑμῶν δέομαι, εὖ ποιῶν ὑμᾶς ὑφ᾽ ὑμῶν τιμᾶσθαι.
ὥστ᾽ ἐμοὶ μὲν πειθόμενοι οὐκ ἀποστερεῖσθε εἴ τι ἐγὼ
δυνήσομαι ὑμᾶς εὖ ποιεῖν· ἐὰν δὲ τοῖς ἐχθροῖς τοῖς ἐμοῖς
πεισθῆτε, οὐδ᾽ ἂν ὑστέρῳ χρόνῳ ὑμῖν μεταμελήσῃ,
150 οὐδὲν ἔτι πλέον ποιήσετε. μὴ τοίνυν μήθ᾽ ὑμᾶς αὐτοὺς
τῶν ἀπ᾽ ἐμοῦ ἐλπίδων ἀποστερήσητε μήτ᾽ ἐμὲ τῶν εἰς
ὑμᾶς. ἀξιῶ δ᾽ ἔγωγε τούτους οἵτινες ὑμῖν ἀρετῆς ἤδη
τῆς μεγίστης εἰς τὸ πλῆθος τὸ ὑμέτερον ἔλεγχον ἔδοσαν,
ἀναβάντας ἐνταυθοῖ συμβουλεύειν ὑμῖν ἃ γιγνώσκουσι
περὶ ἐμοῦ. Δεῦρο Ἄνυτε, Κέφαλε, ἔτι δὲ καὶ οἱ φυλέται οἱ
ᾑρημένοι μοι συνδικεῖν, Θράσυλλος καὶ οἱ ἄλλοι.

1236 *περὶ* del. maluerunt Turr. *αὐτοῖς*] *οι* in ras. A^1 1239 *ἀναβιβάσομαι* A : *ἀναβιβάσωμαι* Blass^3 *δεησόμενον*] *δεησ* in ras. A^1 1242 *ἐμοὶ* add. A^1 : om. A^a 1244 *ὑμῶν* L : *ὑμῖν* A 1245 *ἀνδρίους* A^c : *ἀνδρείους* A^a 1248 *ἀπόλλυτε* A : *ἀπολλύναι* Reiske 1250 *ἀποστερεῖσθε* M : *ἀποστερεῖσθαι* A 1252 *χρόνῳ* A^1 : om. A^a 1259 *ᾑρημένοι* Valkenaer : *εἰρήμενοι* A

2

ΠΕΡΙ ΤΗΣ ΕΑΥΤΟΥ ΚΑΘΟΔΟΥ

Εἰ μέν, ὦ ἄνδρες, ἐν ἑτέρῳ τῳ πράγματι οἱ παριόντες 1
μὴ τὴν αὐτὴν γνώμην ἔχοντες πάντες ἐφαίνοντο, οὐδὲν ἂν θαυμαστὸν ἐνόμιζον· ὅπου μέντοι δεῖ τὴν πόλιν ἐμέ τι ποιῆσαι ἀγαθόν, ἢ εἴ τις ἕτερος βούλοιτο ἐμοῦ κακίων, δεινότατον ἁπάντων χρημάτων ἡγοῦμαι, εἰ τῷ μὲν δοκεῖ ταῦτα τῷ δὲ μή, ἀλλὰ μὴ πᾶσιν ὁμοίως. εἴπερ γὰρ ἡ πόλις ἁπάντων τῶν πολιτευομένων κοινή ἐστι, καὶ τὰ γιγνόμενα δήπου ἀγαθὰ τῇ πόλει κοινά ἐστι.
τουτὶ τοίνυν τὸ μέγα καὶ δεινὸν πάρεστιν ὑμῖν ὁρᾶν 2
τοὺς μὲν ἤδη πράττοντας, τοὺς δὲ τάχα μέλλοντας· καί μοι μέγιστον θαῦμα παρέστηκε, τί ποτε οὗτοι οἱ ἄνδρες δεινῶς οὕτως περικαίονται, εἴ τι ὑμᾶς χρὴ ἀγαθὸν ἐμοῦ ἐπαυρέσθαι. δεῖ γὰρ αὐτοὺς ἤτοι ἀμαθεστάτους εἶναι πάντων ἀνθρώπων, ἢ τῇ πόλει ταύτῃ δυσμενεστάτους. εἰ μέν γε νομίζουσι τῆς πόλεως εὖ πραττούσης καὶ τὰ ἴδια σφῶν αὐτῶν ἄμεινον ἂν φέρεσθαι, ἀμαθέστατοί
εἰσι τὰ ἐναντία νῦν τῇ ἑαυτῶν ὠφελείᾳ σπεύδοντες· εἰ 3
δὲ μὴ ταὐτὰ ἡγοῦνται σφίσι τε αὐτοῖς συμφέρειν καὶ τῷ ὑμετέρῳ κοινῷ, δυσμενεῖς ἂν τῇ πόλει εἶεν· οἵτινες εἰσαγγείλαντός μου ἀπόρρητα εἰς τὴν βουλὴν περὶ τῶν πραγμάτων, ὧν ἀποτελεσθέντων οὐκ εἰσὶ τῇ πόλει

tit. *περὶ τῆς ἑαυτου καθόδου* A, Phot. *Bibl.* cod. 261 488a.16 : *περὶ τῆς ἀδείας* Harp. o 36 subiecit *ἀνδοκίδου* A 1 *τῳ* Ald : *τω* L : *τῶ* A 4 *ποιῆσαι*] *οι* in ras. A[1] *ἕτερος* Reiske : *ἑτέρως* A 11 *παρέστηκε* Reiske : *περέστηκε* A : *περιέστηκε* B 12 *περικαίονται* A : *περικάονται* Schiller 15 *γε*] *γὰρ* Valckenaer 16 *ἀμαθέστατοι* L : *ἀμεθέστατοι* A 20 *τῶν* del. Dobree

ταύτῃ μείζους ὠφέλειαι, καὶ τούτων ἀποδεικνύντος μου
τοῖς βουλευταῖς σαφεῖς τε καὶ βεβαίους τὰς ἀποδείξεις,
ἐκεῖ μὲν οὔτε τούτων τῶν ἀνδρῶν οἱ παραγενόμενοι
ἐλέγχοντες οἷοί τ᾽ ἦσαν ἀποδεῖξαι εἴ τι μὴ ὀρθῶς ἐλέγετο,
οὔτ᾽ ἄλλος οὐδείς, ἐνθάδε δὲ νῦν πειρῶνται διαβάλλειν.
4 σημεῖον οὖν τοῦτο ὅτι οὗτοι οὐκ ἀφ᾽ αὑτῶν ταῦτα
πράττουσιν (εὐθὺς γὰρ ἂν τότε ἠναντιοῦντο) ἀλλ᾽ ἀπὸ
ἀνδρῶν ἑτέρων, οἷοί εἰσιν ἐν τῇ πόλει ταύτῃ, οὐδενὸς ἂν
χρήματος δεξάμενοι ὑμᾶς τι ἀγαθὸν ἐξ ἐμοῦ πρᾶξαι.
καὶ αὐτοὶ μὲν οὗτοι οἱ ἄνδρες οὐ τολμῶσι σφᾶς αὐτοὺς εἰς
τὸ μέσον καταστήσαντες διισχυρίζεσθαι περὶ τούτων,
φοβούμενοι ἔλεγχον διδόναι εἴ τι εἰς ὑμᾶς τυγχάνουσι
μὴ εὖ φρονοῦντες· ἑτέρους δὲ εἰσπέμπουσι, τοιούτους
ἀνθρώπους οἷς εἰθισμένοις ἤδη ἀναισχυντεῖν οὐδὲν
διαφέρει εἰπεῖν τε καὶ ἀκοῦσαι τὰ μέγιστα τῶν κακῶν.
5 τὸ δ᾽ ἰσχυρὸν τοῦτο μόνον εὕροι τις ἂν αὐτῶν ἐν τοῖς
λόγοις, τὰς ἐμὰς συμφορὰς ἐπὶ παντὶ ὀνειδίζειν, καὶ
ταῦτα ἐν εἰδόσι δήπου κάλλιον ὑμῖν, ὥστε μηδὲν ἂν
τούτων δικαίως τιμὴν αὐτοῖς τινα φέρειν. ἐμοὶ δέ, ὦ
ἄνδρες, καὶ τῷ πρώτῳ τοῦτο εἰπόντι ὀρθῶς δοκεῖ
εἰρῆσθαι, ὅτι πάντες ἄνθρωποι γίγνονται ἐπὶ τῷ εὖ καὶ
κακῶς πράττειν, μεγάλη δὲ δήπου καὶ τὸ ἐξαμαρτεῖν
6 δυσπραξία ἐστί, καὶ εἰσὶν εὐτυχέστατοι μὲν οἱ ἐλάχιστα
ἐξαμαρτάνοντες, σωφρονέστατοι δὲ οἳ ἂν τάχιστα
μεταγιγνώσκωσι. καὶ ταῦτα οὐ διακέκριται τοῖς μὲν
γίγνεσθαι τοῖς δὲ μή, ἀλλ᾽ ἔστιν ἐν τῷ κοινῷ πᾶσιν
ἀνθρώποις καὶ ἐξαμαρτεῖν τι καὶ κακῶς πρᾶξαι. ὧν ἕνεκα,
ὦ Ἀθηναῖοι, εἰ ἀνθρωπίνως περὶ ἐμοῦ γιγνώσκοιτε, εἴητε

22 *μείζους* Lipsius : *μείζονες* A   25 *ἐλέγχοντες* Emperius[1] : *ἐλέγξοντες* A : *ἐλέγξαντες* Taylor   27 *οὖν* A[1] : om. A[a]   *αὑτῶν* L : *αὐτῶν* A   36 *τῶν* A[1] : om. A[a]   38 <*τὸ*> *τὰς* mal. Reiske   44 *καὶ* del. Emperius[3]   46 *μεταγινώσκωσι* Ald. : *μεταγινώσκουσι* A   48 alt. *καὶ* A[1sv] : om. A[a]   49 *εἴητε* A : *εἶτε* Lipsius

ἂν ἄνδρες εὐγνωμονέστεροι. οὐ γὰρ φθόνου μᾶλλον ἢ
οἴκτου ἄξιά μοί ἐστι τὰ γεγενημένα· ὃς εἰς τοσοῦτον 7
ἦλθον τῆς ἐμαυτοῦ δυσδαιμονίας, εἴτε χρὴ εἰπεῖν
νεότητί τε καὶ ἀνοίᾳ, εἴτε καὶ δυνάμει τῶν πεισάντων
με ἐλθεῖν εἰς τοιαύτην συμφορὰν τῶν φρενῶν, ὥστ᾽
ἀνάγκην μοι γενέσθαι δυοῖν κακοῖν τοῖν μεγίστοιν
θάτερον ἑλέσθαι, ἢ μὴ βουληθέντι κατειπεῖν τοὺς
ταῦτα ποιήσαντας οὐ περὶ ἐμοῦ μόνου ὀρρωδεῖν, εἴ τι
ἔδει παθεῖν, ἀλλὰ καὶ τὸν πατέρα οὐδὲν ἀδικοῦντα σὺν
ἐμαυτῷ ἀποκτεῖναι (ὅπερ ἀνάγκη παθεῖν ἦν αὐτῷ, εἰ
ἐγὼ μὴ ἐβουλόμην ταῦτα ποιῆσαι), ἢ κατειπόντι τὰ
γεγενημένα αὐτὸν μὲν ἀφεθέντα μὴ τεθνάναι, τοῦ δὲ
ἐμαυτοῦ πατρὸς μὴ φονέα γενέσθαι. τί δ᾽ ἂν οὐ πρό γε
τούτου τολμήσειεν ἄνθρωπος ποιῆσαι; ἐγὼ τοίνυν ἐκ 8
τῶν παρόντων εἱλόμην ταῦτα, ἃ ἐμοὶ μὲν λύπας ἐπὶ
χρόνον πλεῖστον οἴσειν ἔμελλεν, ὑμῖν δὲ ταχίστην τοῦ
παρόντος τότε κακοῦ μετάστασιν. ἀναμνήσθητε δὲ ἐν
οἵῳ κινδύνῳ τε καὶ ἀμηχανίᾳ καθέστατε, καὶ ὅτι οὕτως
σφόδρα σφᾶς αὐτοὺς ἐπεφόβησθε, ὥστ᾽ οὐδ᾽ εἰς τὴν ἀγορὰν
ἔτι ἐξῇτε, ἕκαστος ὑμῶν οἰόμενος συλληφθήσεσθαι.
ταῦτα τοίνυν ὥστε μὲν γενέσθαι τοιαῦτα, πολλοστὸν δή
τι ἐγὼ μέρος τῆς αἰτίας ηὑρέθην ἔχων, ὥστε μέντοι
παυθῆναι, ἐγὼ εἷς ὢν μόνος αἴτιος. καὶ ὅμως τό γε 9
δυστυχέστατος εἶναι ἀνθρώπων οὐδαμῇ ἐκφεύγω, ὅτε
δὴ προαγομένης μὲν τῆς πόλεως ἐπὶ ταύτας τὰς συμφορὰς
οὐδεὶς ἐμοῦ ἤρχετο γίγνεσθαι δυσδαιμονέστερος,
μεθισταμένης δὲ πάλιν εἰς τὸ ἀσφαλὲς ἁπάντων ἐγὼ
ἀθλιώτατος. ὄντων γὰρ κακῶν τοσούτων τῇ πόλει

7 ὀρρωδεῖν Harp. ο 36 s.v.

52 τῆς ἐμαυτοῦ post ἀνοίᾳ l. 53 transp. Frohberger[2], τῆς in τῇ mutans 56 βουληθέντι Ald. : βουληθέντα A 69 ἐξῇτε Lipsius : ἐξήειτε A 71 ηὑρέθην Lipsius : εὑρέθην A

ἀδύνατον ἦν ταῦτα ἰαθῆναι ἄλλως ἢ τῷ ἐμῷ αἰσχρῷ, ὥστ᾽ ἐν αὐτῷ ᾧ ἐγὼ κακῶς ἔπραττον, ἐν τούτῳ ὑμᾶς σῴζεσθαι. χάριν οὖν εἰκός με, οὐ μῖσος τῷ δυστυχήματι τούτῳ φέρεσθαι παρ᾽ ὑμῶν.

10 Καίτοι ἐγὼ τότ᾽ αὐτὸς γνοὺς τὰς ἐμαυτοῦ συμφοράς, ᾧ τινι κακῶν τε καὶ αἰσχρῶν οὐκ οἶδ᾽ εἴ τι ἀπεγένετο, τὰ μὲν παρανοίᾳ τῇ ἐμαυτοῦ, τὰ δ᾽ ἀνάγκῃ τῶν παρόντων πραγμάτων, ἔγνων ἥδιστον εἶναι πράττειν τε τοιαῦτα καὶ διαιτᾶσθαι ἐκεῖ, ὅπου ἥκιστα μέλλοιμι ὀφθήσεσθαι ὑφ᾽ ὑμῶν. ἐπειδὴ δὲ χρόνῳ ὕστερον εἰσῆλθέ μοι, ὥσπερ εἰκός, ἐπιθυμία τῆς τε μεθ᾽ ὑμῶν πολιτείας ἐκείνης καὶ διαίτης, ἐξ ἧς δευρὶ μετέστην, ἔγνων λυσιτελεῖν μοι ἢ τοῦ βίου ἀπηλλάχθαι, ἢ τὴν πόλιν ταύτην ἀγαθόν τι τοσοῦτον ἐργάσασθαι, ὥστε ὑμῶν ἑκόντων εἶναί ποτέ

11 μοι πολιτεύσασθαι μεθ᾽ ὑμῶν. ἐκ δὲ τούτου οὐ πώποτε οὔτε τοῦ σώματος οὔτε τῶν ὄντων ἐμοὶ ἐφεισάμην, ὅπου ἔδει παρακινδυνεύειν· ἀλλ᾽ αὐτίκα μὲν τότε εἰσήγαγον εἰς στρατιὰν ὑμῶν οὖσαν ἐν Σάμῳ κωπέας, τῶν τετρακοσίων ἤδη τὰ πράγματα ἐνθάδε κατειληφότων, ὄντος μοι Ἀρχελάου ξένου πατρικοῦ καὶ διδόντος τέμνεσθαί τε καὶ ἐξάγεσθαι ὁπόσους ἐβουλόμην. τούτους τε εἰσήγαγον τοὺς κωπέας, καὶ παρόν μοι πέντε δραχμῶν τὴν τιμὴν αὐτῶν δέξασθαι οὐκ ἠθέλησα πράξασθαι πλέον ἢ ὅσου ἐμοὶ κατέστησαν, εἰσήγαγον δὲ σῖτόν

12 τε καὶ χαλκόν· καὶ οἱ ἄνδρες ἐκεῖνοι ἐκ τούτων παρεσκευασμένοι ἐνίκησαν μετὰ ταῦτα Πελοποννησίους ναυμαχοῦντες, καὶ τὴν πόλιν ταύτην μόνοι ἀνθρώπων ἔσῳσαν ἐν τῷ τότε χρόνῳ. εἰ τοίνυν μεγάλων ἀγαθῶν

79 αὐτῷ ante τούτῳ transp. Sluiter 87 ὕστερον A[1im] : om. A[a] : secl. Fuhr[1] 88–9 ἐκείνης καὶ διαίτης A : καὶ τῆς ἐκεῖ διαίτης <κόρος> Kayser[2] : aliter alii, haud necessarie 89 ἔγνων L : ἔγνω A 98 τέμνεσθαί Dobree : γενέσθαί A 101 ὅσου A[1] : ὅσον A 103 πελοποννησίους L[1] : πελοπονησίους A

αἴτια ὑμᾶς ἠργάσαντο ἐκεῖνοι, μέρος ἐγὼ οὐκ ἂν ἐλάχιστον δικαίως ταύτης τῆς αἰτίας ἔχοιμι. εἰ γὰρ τοῖς ἀνδράσιν ἐκείνοις τότε τὰ ἐπιτήδεια μὴ εἰσήχθη, οὐ περὶ τοῦ σῷσαι τὰς Ἀθήνας ὁ κίνδυνος ἦν αὐτοῖς μᾶλλον ἢ περὶ τοῦ μηδὲ αὐτοὺς σωθῆναι.

Τούτων τοίνυν οὕτως ἐχόντων οὐκ ὀλίγῳ μοι παρὰ 13
γνώμην ηὑρέθη τὰ ἐνταῦθα πράγματα ἔχοντα. κατέπλευσα μὲν γὰρ ὡς ἐπαινεθησόμενος ὑπὸ τῶν ἐνθάδε προθυμίας τε ἕνεκα καὶ ἐπιμελείας τῶν ὑμετέρων πραγμάτων· πυθόμενοι δέ τινές με ἥκοντα τῶν τετρακοσίων ἐζήτουν τε παραχρῆμα, καὶ λαβόντες ἤγαγον
εἰς τὴν βουλήν. εὐθὺς δὲ παραστάς μοι Πείσανδρος 14
"Ἄνδρες" ἔφη "βουλευταί, ἐγὼ τὸν ἄνδρα τοῦτον ἐνδεικνύω ὑμῖν σῖτόν τε εἰς τοὺς πολεμίους εἰσαγαγόντα καὶ κωπέας." καὶ τὸ πρᾶγμα ἤδη πᾶν διηγεῖτο ὡς ἐπέπρακτο. ἐν δὲ τῷ τότε τὰ ἐναντία φρονοῦντες δῆλοι ἦσαν ἤδη οἱ
ἐπὶ στρατιᾶς ὄντες τοῖς τετρακοσίοις. κἀγώ (θόρυβος 15
γὰρ δὴ τοιοῦτος ἐγίγνετο τῶν βουλευτῶν {καὶ}) ἐπειδὴ ἐγίγνωσκον ἀπολούμενος, εὐθὺς προσπηδῶ πρὸς τὴν ἑστίαν καὶ λαμβάνομαι τῶν ἱερῶν. ὅπερ μοι καὶ πλείστου ἄξιον ἐγένετο ἐν τῷ τότε· εἰς γὰρ τοὺς θεούς ἔχοντα ὀνείδη οὗτοί με μᾶλλον τῶν ἀνθρώπων ἐοίκασι κατελεῆσαι, βουληθέντων τε αὐτῶν ἀποκτεῖναί με οὗτοι ἦσαν οἱ διασῴσαντες. δεσμά τε ὕστερον καὶ κακὰ ὅσα τε καὶ
οἷα τῷ σώματι ἠνεσχόμην, μακρὸν ἂν εἴη μοι λέγειν. οὗ 16
δὴ καὶ μάλιστ' ἐμαυτὸν ἀπωλοφυράμην· ὅστις τοῦτο μὲν ἐν ᾧ ἐδόκει ὁ δῆμος κακοῦσθαι, ἐγὼ ἀντὶ τούτου κακὰ

106 αἴτια Blass : ἄξια A   ἠργάσαντο Blass[3] : εἰργάσαντο A   107 τῆς αἰτίας A : ἀξίας Ald.   112 ηὑρέθη Lipsius : εὑρέθη A   114 ἕνεκα Lipsius : εἵνεκα A   119–20 <καὶ χαλκὸν> καὶ κωπέας Meier   121 ἤδη A[1] : om. A[a]   123 del. Reiske : verbum postea excidisse susp. Fuhr   126–7 ἐγένετο Emperius[3] : ἐγίνετο A   126–7 ἔχοντα ὀνείδη οὗτοί Sauppe : εἶχον τὰ ὀνείδη οὗτοι· οἵ A   131 τοῦτο μὲν M[1] : τούτω μὲν A

εἶχον, τοῦτο δὲ ἐπειδὴ ἐφαίνετο ⟨εὖ⟩ ὑπ' ἐμοῦ πεπονθώς, πάλιν αὖ καὶ διὰ τοῦτ' ἐγὼ ἀπωλλύμην· ὥστε ὁδόν τε καὶ πόρον μηδαμῇ ἔτι εἶναί μοι εὐθαρσεῖν· ὅποι γὰρ τραποίμην, πάντοθεν κακόν τί μοι ἐφαίνετο ἑτοιμαζόμενον. ἀλλ' ὅμως καὶ ἐκ τούτων τοιούτων ὄντων ἀπαλλαγεὶς οὐκ ἔστιν ὅ τι ἕτερον ἔργον περὶ πλείονος ἐποιούμην ἢ τὴν πόλιν ταύτην ἀγαθόν τι ἐργάσασθαι.

17 Ὁρᾶν δὲ χρή, ὦ Ἀθηναῖοι, ὅσῳ τὰ τοιαῦτα τῶν ὑπουργημάτων διαφέρει. τοῦτο μὲν γὰρ ὅσοι τῶν πολιτῶν τὰ ὑμέτερα πράγματα διαχειρίζοντες ἀργύριον ὑμῖν ἐκπορίζουσιν, ἄλλο τι ἢ τὰ ὑμέτερα ὑμῖν διδόασι; τοῦτο δὲ ὅσοι στρατηγοὶ γενόμενοι καλόν τι τὴν πόλιν κατεργάζονται, τί ἄλλο ἢ μετὰ τῆς τῶν ὑμετέρων σωμάτων ταλαιπωρίας τε καὶ κινδύνων, καὶ ἔτι τῶν κοινῶν χρημάτων δαπάνης, ποιοῦσιν ὑμᾶς εἴ τι τυγχάνουσιν ἀγαθόν; ἐν ᾧ καὶ ἄν τι ἐξαμάρτωσιν, οὐκ αὐτοὶ τῆς σφετέρας αὐτῶν ἁμαρτίας δίκην διδόασιν,
18 ἀλλ' ὑμεῖς ὑπὲρ τῶν ἐκείνοις ἡμαρτημένων. ἀλλ' ὅμως οὗτοι στεφανοῦνταί γε ὑφ' ὑμῶν καὶ ἀνακηρύττονται ὡς ὄντες ἄνδρες ἀγαθοί. καὶ οὐκ ἐρῶ ὡς οὐ δικαίως· μεγάλη γάρ ἐστιν ἀρετή, ὅστις τὴν ἑαυτοῦ πόλιν ὁτῳοῦν δύναται τρόπῳ ἀγαθόν τι ἐργάζεσθαι. ἀλλ' οὖν {τι} γιγνώσκειν γε χρή, ὅτι ἐκεῖνος ἂν εἴη πολὺ πλείστου ἄξιος ἀνήρ, ὅστις τοὺς ἑαυτοῦ παρακινδυνεύων χρήμασί τε καὶ σώματι τολμῴη ἀγαθόν τι ποιεῖν τοὺς ἑαυτοῦ πολίτας.

133 add. Ald. : post *ἐμοῦ* posuit Edwards 134 *ἀπωλλύμην* Dobree : *ἀπολοίμην* A 135 *ὅποι* Reiske : *ὅπου* A 138 *ἕτερον ἔργον* A^1 : *ἔργον* A^a : del. Sauppe^2 : aliter alii 154 del. Reiske 155 *γινώσκειν*] *γι* ex *γε* A^1 *πολὺ* e ras A^c : *πολλοῦ* A : *πολλῷ* Rosenberg^1 157–8 *τοὺς* ... *πολίτας* A^1 : *τοῖς* ... *πολίταις* A^a

Ἐμοὶ τοίνυν τὰ μὲν ἤδη εἰς ὑμᾶς πεπραγμένα σχεδόν 19
τι ἅπαντες ἂν εἰδεῖτε, τὰ δὲ μέλλοντά τε καὶ ἤδη
πραττόμενα ἄνδρες ὑμῶν πεντακόσιοι ἐν ἀπορρήτῳ
ἴσασιν, ἡ βουλή· οὓς πολλῷ δήπου εἰκὸς ἧττον ἄν τι
ἐξαμαρτεῖν, ἢ εἰ ὑμᾶς δέοι ἀκούσαντάς τι ἐν τῷ
παραχρῆμα νῦν διαβουλεύσασθαι. οἱ μέν γε σχολῇ περὶ
τῶν εἰσαγγελλομένων σκοποῦνται, ὑπάρχει τε αὐτοῖς,
ἐάν τι ἐξαμαρτάνωσιν, αἰτίαν ἔχειν καὶ λόγον αἰσχρὸν
ἐκ τῶν ἄλλων πολιτῶν· ὑμῖν δὲ οὐκ εἰσὶν ἕτεροι ὑφ' ὧν
αἰτίαν ἔχοιτε· τὰ γὰρ ὑμέτερα αὐτῶν ἐφ' ὑμῖν δικαίως
ἐστὶ καὶ εὖ καὶ κακῶς, ἐὰν βούλησθε, διαθέσθαι. ἅ 20
γε μέντοι ἔξω τῶν ἀπορρήτων οἷόν τέ μοί ἐστιν εἰπεῖν
εἰς ὑμᾶς ἤδη πεπραγμένα, ἀκούσεσθε. ἐπίστασθε γάρ
που ὡς ἠγγέλθη ὑμῖν ὅτι οὐ μέλλει ἐκ Κύπρου σῖτος
ἥξειν ἐνταῦθα· ἐγὼ τοίνυν τοιοῦτός τε καὶ τοσοῦτος
ἐγενόμην, ὥστε τοὺς ἄνδρας τοὺς ταῦτα βουλεύσαντας
ἐφ' ὑμῖν καὶ πράξαντας ψευσθῆναι τῆς αὑτῶν γνώμης.
καὶ ὡς μὲν ταῦτα διεπράχθη, οὐδὲν προὔργου ἀκοῦσαι 21
ὑμῖν· τάδε δὲ νυνὶ βούλομαι ὑμᾶς εἰδέναι, ὅτι αἱ
μέλλουσαι νῆες ἤδη σιταγωγοὶ καταπλεῖν εἰς τὸν
Πειραιᾶ εἰσιν ὑμῖν τέτταρες καὶ δέκα, αἱ δὲ λοιπαὶ τῶν
ἐκ Κύπρου ἀναχθεισῶν ἥξουσιν ἁθρόαι οὐ πολὺ
ὕστερον. ἐδεξάμην δ' ⟨ἂν⟩ ἀντὶ πάντων χρημάτων εἶναι
ἐν ἀσφαλεῖ φράσαι πρὸς ὑμᾶς ἃ καὶ τῇ βουλῇ ἐν
ἀπορρήτῳ εἰσήγγειλα, ὅπως αὐτόθεν προειδῆτε. νῦν 22
δὲ ἐκεῖνα μὲν τότε ὅταν ἀποτελεσθῇ γνώσεσθε ἅμα καὶ
ὠφεληθήσεσθε· νῦν δέ, ὦ Ἀθηναῖοι, εἴ μοι βουληθεῖτε

160 εἰδεῖτε Lipsius : εἰδείητε A 162 ἡ βουλή del. Valckenaer εἰκὸς Ald. : εἰς A 168 <ἂν> αἰτίαν Lipsius : αἰτίαν <ἂν> Dobree 170 τέ Steph. : γέ A 172 ὑμῖν Valckenaer : ἡμῖν A 175 αὑτῶν Turr. : αὐτῶν A 177 τάδε Gebauer[1] : τὰ A 180 ἁθρόαι Lipsius : ἀθρόαι A 181 add. Dobree 183 προειδῆτε A : προῄδετε Blass[3] : προῄδειτε Bekker 185 ὠφεληθήσεσθε A : ὠφελήσεσθε Fuhr βουληθεῖτε Lipsius : βουληθείητε A

δοῦναι χάριν μικράν τε καὶ ἄπονον ὑμῖν καὶ ἅμα δικαίαν, πάνυ ἄν μοι τοῦτο ἐν μεγάλῃ ἡδονῇ γένοιτο. ὡς δὲ καὶ δικαία ἐστίν, εἴσεσθε. ἃ γάρ μοι αὐτοὶ γνόντες τε καὶ ὑποσχόμενοι ἔδοτε, ὕστερον δὲ ἑτέροις πειθόμενοι ἀφείλεσθε, ταῦθ' ὑμᾶς, εἰ μὲν βούλεσθε, αἰτῶ, εἰ δὲ μὴ
23 βούλεσθε, ἀπαιτῶ. ὁρῶ δὲ ὑμᾶς πολλάκις καὶ δούλοις ἀνθρώποις καὶ ξένοις παντοδαποῖς πολιτείαν διδόντας τε καὶ εἰς χρήματα μεγάλας δωρεάς, οἳ ἂν ὑμᾶς φαίνωνται ποιοῦντές τι ἀγαθόν. καὶ ταῦτα μέντοι ὀρθῶς ὑμεῖς φρονοῦντες δίδοτε· οὕτω γὰρ ἂν ὑπὸ πλείστων ἀνθρώπων εὖ πάσχοιτε. ἐγὼ τοίνυν τοσοῦτον ὑμῶν μόνον δέομαι· τὸ ψήφισμα ὃ Μενίππου εἰπόντος ἐψηφίσασθε, εἶναί μοι ἄδειαν, πάλιν ἀπόδοτε. ἀναγνώσεται δὲ ὑμῖν αὐτό· ἔτι γὰρ καὶ νῦν ἐγγέγραπται ἐν τῷ βουλευτηρίῳ.

ΨΗΦΙΣΜΑ

24 Τουτὶ τὸ ψήφισμα ὃ ἠκούσατε ψηφισάμενοί μοι, ὦ Ἀθηναῖοι, ὕστερον ἀφείλεσθε χάριν ἑτέρῳ φέροντες. πείθεσθε οὖν μοι, καὶ ἤδη παύσασθε εἴ τῳ ὑμῶν διάβολόν τι ἐν τῇ γνώμῃ περὶ ἐμοῦ παρέστηκεν. εἰ γὰρ ὅσα οἱ ἄνθρωποι γνώμῃ ἁμαρτάνουσι, τὸ σῶμα αὐτῶν μὴ αἴτιόν ἐστιν, ἐμοῦ τὸ μὲν σῶμα τυγχάνει ταὐτὸν ἔτι ὄν, ὅπερ τῆς αἰτίας ἀπήλλακται, ἡ δὲ γνώμη ἀντὶ τῆς προτέρας ἑτέρα νυνὶ παρέστηκεν. οὐδὲν οὖν ἔτι
25 ὑπολείπεται ὅτῳ ἄν μοι δικαίως διαβεβλῆσθε. ὥσπερ δὲ τῆς τότε ἁμαρτίας τὰ ἀπὸ τῶν ἔργων σημεῖα ἔφατε

190 μὴ del. Reiske   192 παντοδαποῖς Steph. : παντοδαπῆς A   πολιτείαν Reiske : πολιτείας A   193 τε] ante διδόντας l. 192 ponere maluit Reiske   δωρεὰς A : δωρειάς Lipsius   205 γνώμη e ras. A[1] : τῇ γνώμῃ fort. A[a]   206 ἐμοῦ Sched. Eton., Reiske : ὁμοῦ A   206–7 ταὐτὸν ἔτι ὄν Bekker : τοῦτ' ἀναίτιον A   209 διαβεβλῆσθε Ald. (-ῇσθε Dobree) : διαβεβλῆσθαι A

χρῆναι πιστότατα ποιούμενοι κακόν με ἄνδρα ἡγεῖσθαι,
οὕτω καὶ ἐπὶ τῇ νῦν εὐνοίᾳ μὴ ζητεῖτε ἑτέραν βάσανον ἢ
τὰ ἀπὸ τῶν νυνὶ ἔργων σημεῖα ὑμῖν γιγνόμενα. πολὺ 26
δέ μοι προσήκει ταῦτα μᾶλλον ἐκείνων καὶ τῷ γένει
συνηθέστερά ἐστι. τάδε γὰρ οὐ ψευσαμένῳ μοι λαθεῖν
οἷόν τ' ἐστι τούς γε πρεσβυτέρους ὑμῶν, ὅτι ὁ τοῦ ἐμοῦ
πατρὸς πρόπαππος Λεωγόρας στασιάσας πρὸς τοὺς
τυράννους ὑπὲρ τοῦ δήμου, ἐξὸν αὐτῷ διαλλαχθέντι τῆς
ἔχθρας καὶ γενομένῳ κηδεστῇ ἄρξαι μετ' ἐκείνων τῶν
ἀνδρῶν τῆς πόλεως, εἵλετο μᾶλλον ἐκπεσεῖν μετὰ τοῦ
δήμου καὶ φεύγων κακοπαθεῖν μᾶλλον ἢ προδότης
αὐτῶν καταστῆναι. ὥστ' ἔμοιγε καὶ διὰ τὰ τῶν
προγόνων ἔργα εἰκότως ὑπάρχει δημοτικῷ εἶναι, εἴπερ
τι ἀλλὰ νῦν γε φρονῶν τυγχάνω. ὧν καὶ ἕνεκα εἰκὸς
ὑμᾶς, ἐὰν χρηστὸς ὢν ἀνὴρ εἰς ὑμᾶς φαίνωμαι,
προθυμότερόν μου ἀποδέχεσθαι τὰ πραττόμενα. τὸ δὲ 27
δόντας ἐμοὶ τὴν ἄδειαν ἀφελέσθαι ὑμᾶς, εὖ ἴστε ὅτι
οὐδεπώποτε ἠγανάκτησα· ὅπου γὰρ ὑπὸ τῶν ἀνδρῶν
τούτων αὐτοὶ εἰς ὑμᾶς αὐτοὺς ἐπείσθητε τὰ μέγιστα
ἐξαμαρτεῖν, ὥστε ἀντὶ τῆς ἀρχῆς δουλείαν ἀλλάξασθαι,
ἐκ δημοκρατίας δυναστείαν καταστήσαντες, τί ἄν τις
ὑμῶν θαυμάζοι καὶ εἰς ἐμὲ εἴ τι ἐπείσθητε ἐξαμαρτεῖν;
βουλοίμην μέντ' ἄν, ὥσπερ ἐν τοῖς ὑμετέροις αὐτῶν 28
πράγμασιν, ἐπειδὴ ἐξουσίαν ἐλάβετε, τὰς τῶν ἐξα-
πατησάντων ὑμᾶς ἀκύρους ἔθετε βουλάς, οὕτω καὶ ἐν
ᾧ περὶ ἐμοῦ ἐπείσθητε γνῶναί τι ἀνεπιτήδειον, ἀτελῆ
τήν γνώμην αὐτῶν ποιῆσαι, καὶ μήτε ἐν τούτῳ μήτε ἐν
ἑτέρῳ τῳ τοῖς ὑμῶν αὐτῶν ἐχθίστοις ὁμόψηφοί ποτε
γένησθε.

211 ἡγεῖσθαι Ald. : ἡγεῖσθε A 212 ζητεῖτε L : ζητῆτε A 217 πρόπαππος A : πάππος Valckenaer 222 αὐτῶν A : αὐτοῦ Rosenberg[1] 224 ἀλλὰ Reiske : ἄλλο A 232 θαυμάζοι L[csv] : θαυμάζει A 238 τω A[1] : *τῶ A[a]

3

ΠΕΡΙ ΤΗΣ ΠΡΟΣ ΛΑΚΕΔΑΙΜΟΝΙΟΥΣ ΕΙΡΗΝΗΣ

ΥΠΟΘΕΣΙΣ

Τοῦ Ἑλληνικοῦ μηκυνομένου πολέμου, καὶ πολλὰ μὲν Ἀθηναίων κακὰ πολλὰ δὲ Λακεδαιμονίων ὑπομεινάντων καὶ τῶν ἑκατέρων συμμάχων, Ἀθηναῖοι πρέσβεις ἀπέστειλαν πρὸς Λακεδαιμονίους αὐτοκράτορας· ὧν ἐστι καὶ Ἀνδοκίδης. τινῶν δὲ προταθέντων παρὰ Λακεδαιμονίων, καὶ ἀποστειλάντων κἀκείνων ἰδίους πρέσβεις, ἔδοξεν ὥστε εἴσω τεσσαράκοντα ἡμερῶν ἐπιβουλεύσασθαι τὸν δῆμον περὶ τῆς εἰρήνης. καὶ ἐπὶ τούτοις Ἀνδοκίδης συμβουλεύει τοῖς Ἀθηναίοις καταδέξασθαι τὴν εἰρήνην. Ἔστι μὲν οὖν συμβουλῆς τὸ εἶδος· κεφάλαιον τὸ συμφέρον. Φιλόχορος μὲν οὖν λέγει καὶ ἐλθεῖν τοὺς πρέσβεις ἐκ Λακεδαιμονίας, καὶ ἀπράκτους ἀνελθεῖν μὴ πείσαντος τοῦ Ἀνδοκίδου· ὁ δὲ Διονύσιος νόθον εἶναι λέγει τὸν λόγον.

Ὅτι μὲν εἰρήνην ποιεῖσθαι δικαίαν ἄμεινόν ἐστιν ἢ 1
πολεμεῖν, δοκεῖτέ μοι, ὦ Ἀθηναῖοι, πάντες γιγνώσκειν·
ὅτι δὲ οἱ ῥήτορες τῷ μὲν ὀνόματι τῆς εἰρήνης
συγχωροῦσι, τοῖς δ' ἔργοις ἀφ' ὧν ἂν ἡ εἰρήνη γένοιτο
ἐναντιοῦνται, τοῦτο δὲ οὐ πάντες αἰσθάνεσθε. λέγουσι
γὰρ ὡς ἔστι δεινότατον τῷ δήμῳ, γενομένης εἰρήνης, ἡ
νῦν οὖσα πολιτεία μὴ καταλυθῇ. εἰ μὲν οὖν μηδεπώποτε 2

Tit. *περὶ τῆς πρὸς λακεδαιμονίους εἰρήνης* AQ, Phot. *Bibl.* cod. 261 488a.17 : *περὶ τῆς εἰρήνης* Harp. *ε* 40, *ν* 13, *π* 65, [Plut.] *Vita Andoc.* 14.835A arg. tit. *ὑπόθεσις τοῦ ἑξῆς* A : arg. om. Q 12 *ἀνελθεῖν* A : *ἐπανελθεῖν* Reiske 13 *διονύσιος* L : *διόνυσος* A subscriptio *περὶ τῆς πρὸς λακεδαιμονίους εἰρήνης* AQ 17 *ἂν ἡ* Lipsius : *ἂν* Q : *ἡ* A 18 *ἐναντιοῦνται* Q : *ἐναντιοοῦνται* A

*πρότερον ὁ δῆμος ὁ {τῶν} Ἀθηναίων εἰρήνην ἐποιήσατο
πρὸς Λακεδαιμονίους, εἰκότως ἂν ἐφοβούμεθα αὐτὸ διά
τε τὴν ἀπειρίαν τοῦ ἔργου διά τε τὴν ἐκείνων ἀπιστίαν·
ὅπου δὲ πολλάκις ἤδη πρότερον εἰρήνην ἐποιήσασθε
δημοκρατούμενοι, πῶς οὐκ εἰκὸς ὑμᾶς πρῶτον ἐκεῖνα
σκέψασθαι τὰ τότε γενόμενα; χρὴ γάρ, ὦ Ἀθηναῖοι,
τεκμηρίοις χρῆσθαι τοῖς πρότερον γενομένοις περὶ τῶν
3 μελλόντων ἔσεσθαι. ἡνίκα τοίνυν ἦν μὲν ὁ πόλεμος ἡμῖν
ἐν Εὐβοίᾳ, Μέγαρα δὲ εἴχομεν καὶ Πηγὰς καὶ Τροζῆνα,
εἰρήνης ἐπεθυμήσαμεν, καὶ Μιλτιάδην τὸν Κίμωνος
ὠστρακισμένον καὶ ὄντα ἐν Χερρονήσῳ κατεδεξάμεθα δι᾽
αὐτὸ τοῦτο, πρόξενον ὄντα Λακεδαιμονίων, ὅπως πέμψαι-
μεν εἰς Λακεδαίμονα προκηρυκευσόμενον περὶ σπονδῶν.
4 καὶ τότε ἡμῖν εἰρήνη ἐγένετο πρὸς Λακεδαιμονίους ἔτη
πέντε, καὶ ἐνεμείναμεν ἀμφότεροι ταύταις ταῖς σπονδαῖς
ἔτη τριακαίδεκα. ἓν δὴ τοῦτο, ὦ Ἀθηναῖοι, πρῶτον
σκεψώμεθα. ἐν ταύτῃ τῇ εἰρήνῃ ὁ δῆμος ὁ {τῶν}
Ἀθηναίων ἔσθ᾽ ὅπου κατελύθη; οὐδεὶς ἀποδείξει. ἀγαθὰ
δὲ ὅσα ἐγένετο διὰ ταύτην τὴν εἰρήνην, ἐγὼ ὑμῖν
5 φράσω. πρῶτον μὲν τὸν Πειραιᾶ ἐτειχίσαμεν ἐν τούτῳ
τῷ χρόνῳ, εἶτα τὸ μακρὸν τεῖχος τὸ βόρειον· ἀντὶ δὲ*

2 *χρὴ—ἔσεσθαι* stp Clem. Al. *Strom.* 6.2.18.5, quem locum usurpavit mutavitque Theodoretus *Graec. affect. curatio* 6.91 **3—9** similia in Aeschin. 2.172–176 **3** *Πηγὰς* Harp. *π* 65 s.v.

---

21 del. Spengel[1] 22 *ἐφοβούμεθα* A : *ἐφοβώμεθα* Q 24 *ἤδη* om. Q *ἐποιήσασθε* Reiske : *ἐποιήσατε* AQ 26 *ὦ Ἀθηναῖοι* AQ : om. Clem. 29 *πηγὰς* A : *παγασὰς* Q *Τροζῆνα* Lipsius : *τροιζῆνα* AQ 30 *Μιλτιάδην τὸν Κίμωνος*] *Κίμωνα τὸν Μιλτιάδου* Mitford 32–3 *πέμψαιμεν* M : *πέμψαιεν* A : *πέμψωμεν* Q 33 *εἰς* Q : *ἐς* A *περὶ* A : *τῶν* Q 35 *πέντε* AQ : *πεντήκοντα* ex Aeschin. 2.172 v. Meurs 35–6 *καὶ … τριακαίδεκα* transp. post l. 56 *ἔτη τριάκοντα* Dobree 36 *ὦ ἀθηναῖοι πρῶτον* A : *πρῶτον ὦ ἀθηναῖοι* Q 37 alt. *ὁ* A : om. Q del. Spengel[1] 39 *ἐγένετο* post *εἰρήνην* Q *ἐγὼ ὑμῖν* L[isv] : *ἐγὼ ἡμῖν* A : *ἡμῖν ἐγὼ* Q 40 *πειραιᾶ* A : *πειραῖα* Q *ἐτειχίσαμεν* Q : *ἐτειχίσαμεν τότε* A

τῶν τριήρων αἳ τότε ἡμῖν ἦσαν παλαιαὶ καὶ ἄπλοι, αἷς
βασιλέα καὶ τοὺς βαρβάρους καταναυμαχήσαντες
ἠλευθερώσαμεν τοὺς Ἕλληνας, ἀντὶ τούτων τῶν νεῶν
ἑκατὸν τριήρεις ἐναυπηγησάμεθα, καὶ πρῶτον τότε
τριακοσίους ἱππέας κατεστησάμεθα, καὶ τοξότας
τριακοσίους Σκύθας ἐπριάμεθα. καὶ ταῦτα ἐκ τῆς
εἰρήνης τῆς πρὸς Λακεδαιμονίους ἀγαθὰ τῇ πόλει καὶ
δύναμις τῷ δήμῳ τῷ Ἀθηναίων ἐγένετο. μετὰ δὲ ταῦτα 6
δι' Αἰγινήτας εἰς πόλεμον κατέστημεν, καὶ πολλὰ κακὰ
παθόντες πολλὰ δὲ ποιήσαντες ἐπεθυμήσαμεν πάλιν
τῆς εἰρήνης, καὶ ᾑρέθησαν δέκα ἄνδρες ἐξ Ἀθηναίων
ἁπάντων πρέσβεις εἰς Λακεδαίμονα περὶ εἰρήνης
αὐτοκράτορες, ὧν ἦν καὶ Ἀνδοκίδης ὁ πάππος ὁ ἡμέτερος.
οὗτοι ἡμῖν εἰρήνην ἐποίησαν πρὸς Λακεδαιμονίους
ἔτη τριάκοντα. καὶ ἐν τοσούτῳ χρόνῳ ἔστιν ὅπου, ὦ
Ἀθηναῖοι, ὁ δῆμος κατελύθη; τί δέ; πράττοντές τινες
δήμου κατάλυσιν ἐλήφθησαν; οὐκ ἔστιν ὅστις ἀποδείξει.
ἀλλ' αὐτὸ τὸ ἐναντιώτατον· αὕτη γάρ ἡ εἰρήνη τὸν 7
δῆμον τὸν Ἀθηναίων ὑψηλὸν ἦρε καὶ κατέστησεν
ἰσχυρὸν οὕτως, ὥστε πρῶτον μὲν ἐν τούτοις τοῖς ἔτεσιν
εἰρήνην λαβόντες ἀνηνέγκαμεν χίλια τάλαντα εἰς
τὴν ἀκρόπολιν, καὶ νόμῳ κατεκλῄσαμεν ἐξαίρετα
εἶναι τῷ δήμῳ, τοῦτο δὲ τριήρεις ἄλλας ἑκατὸν
ἐναυπηγησάμεθα, καὶ ταύτας ἐξαιρέτους ἐψηφισάμεθα

42 τριήρων Bekker : τριηρῶν AQ 43 τοὺς Q : om. A 44 ἠλευθερώσαμεν QL[1] : ἐλευθερώσαμεν A 46 ἱππέας Lipsius : ἱππεῖς AQ τοξότας del. maluit Sauppe 47 καὶ del. Blass[2] ταῦτα <τότε> Weidner 49 τῷ δήμῳ A[1] : om. A[a] alt. τῷ Spengel[1] : τῶν AQ 50 αἰγινήτας Q : αἰγηνίτας A κατέστημεν A[c]Q : κατεστήσαμεν A[a] 52 ᾑρέθησαν Q : εὑρέθησαν A 55 ἡμῖν Q : ὑμῖν A ἐποίησαν Bekker : ἐποιήσαντο AQ 59 ἡ A : om. Q 60 τὸν Bekker : τῶν AQ ἦρε A : ἦρεν Q 62 λαβόντες] ἄγοντες Reiske : εἰρήνην λαβόντες del. Kayser[2] ἀνηνέγκαμεν χίλια τάλαντα A : χίλια τάλαντα ἀνηνέγκαμεν Q 63 κατεκλῄσαμεν Blass[2] : κατεκλείσαμεν AQ

εἶναι, νεωσοίκους τε ᾠκοδομησάμεθα, χιλίους τε καὶ διακοσίους ἱππέας καὶ τοξότας τοσούτους ἑτέρους κατεστήσαμεν, καὶ τὸ τεῖχος τὸ μακρὸν τὸ νότιον ἐτειχίσθη. ταῦτα ἐκ τῆς εἰρήνης τῆς πρὸς Λακεδαιμονίους ἀγαθὰ τῇ πόλει καὶ δύναμις τῷ δήμῳ τῷ Ἀθηναίων
8 ἐγένετο. πάλιν δὲ διὰ Μεγαρέας πολεμήσαντες καὶ τὴν χώραν τμηθῆναι προέμενοι, πολλῶν ἀγαθῶν στερηθέντες αὖθις τὴν εἰρήνην ἐποιησάμεθα, ἣν ἡμῖν Νικίας ὁ Νικηράτου κατηργάσατο. οἶμαι δ' ὑμᾶς ἅπαντας εἰδέναι τοῦτο, ὅτι διὰ ταύτην τὴν εἰρήνην ἑπτακισχίλια μὲν τάλαντα νομίσματος εἰς τὴν ἀκρόπολιν ἀνηνέγκαμεν,
9 ναῦς δὲ πλείους ἢ τετρακοσίας ἐκτησάμεθα, καὶ φόρος προσῄει κατ' ἐνιαυτὸν πλέον ἢ διακόσια καὶ χίλια τάλαντα, καὶ Χερρόνησόν τε εἴχομεν καὶ Νάξον καὶ Εὐβοίας πλέον ἢ τὰ δύο μέρη· τάς τε ἄλλας ἀποικίας καθ' ἕκαστον διηγεῖσθαι μακρὸς ἂν εἴη λόγος. ταῦτα δ' ἔχοντες τὰ ἀγαθὰ πάλιν κατέστημεν εἰς πόλεμον πρὸς Λακεδαιμονίους, πεισθέντες καὶ τότε ὑπ' Ἀργείων.

10 Πρῶτον μὲν οὖν, ὦ Ἀθηναῖοι, τούτου ἀναμνήσθητε, τί ὑμῖν ἐξ ἀρχῆς ὑπεθέμην τῷ λόγῳ. ἄλλο τι ἢ τοῦτο, ὅτι διὰ τὴν εἰρήνην οὐδεπώποτε ὁ δῆμος ὁ {τῶν} Ἀθηναίων κατελύθη; οὐκοῦν ἀποδέδεικται. καὶ οὐδεὶς ἐξελέγξει με ὡς οὐκ ἔστι ταῦτα ἀληθῆ. ἤδη δέ τινων ἤκουσα λεγόντων ὡς ἐκ τῆς τελευταίας εἰρήνης τῆς πρὸς Λακεδαιμονίους οἵ τε τριάκοντα κατέστησαν,

7 νεωσοίκους Harp. ν 13 s.vv. νεώρια καὶ νεώσοικοι, ac stp Phot. ν 162.3 Suda ν 235

---

67 τοσούτους ἑτέρους A : ἑτέρους τοσούτους Q 69 pr. τῆς A : ταύτης τῆς Q 70 alt. τῷ Spengel[1] : τῶν AQ 73 αὖθις vel τὴν del. maluit Ydén ἐποιησάμεθα A : ἐστερησάμεθα Q 74 κατηργάσατο Blass[3] : κατειργάσατο AQ 76 νομίσματος post ἀκρόπολιν Q 77 τετρακοσίας AQ : τριακοσίας Markland ex Aeschin. 2.175 81 δ' A : δὲ Q 86 del. Spengel[1] 88 ἐξελέγξει Taylor : ἐξελέγχει AQ ταῦτα A : ταῦτ' Q

πολλοί τε Ἀθηναίων κώνειον πιόντες ἀπέθανον, οἱ δὲ
φεύγοντες ᾤχοντο. ὁπόσοι οὖν ταῦτα λέγουσιν, οὐκ 11
ὀρθῶς γιγνώσκουσιν· εἰρήνη γὰρ καὶ σπονδαὶ πολὺ
διαφέρουσι σφῶν αὐτῶν· εἰρήνην μὲν γὰρ ἐξ ἴσου
ποιοῦνται πρὸς ἀλλήλους ὁμολογήσαντες περὶ ὧν ἂν
διαφέρωνται· σπονδὰς δέ, ὅταν κρατήσωσιν κατὰ τὸν
πόλεμον, οἱ κρείττους τοῖς ἥττοσιν ἐξ ἐπιταγμάτων
ποιοῦνται, ὥσπερ ἡμῶν κρατήσαντες Λακεδαιμόνιοι
τῷ πολέμῳ ἐπέταξαν ἡμῖν καὶ ⟨τὰ⟩ τείχη καθαιρεῖν καὶ
τὰς ναῦς παραδιδόναι καὶ τοὺς φεύγοντας καταδέχεσθαι.
τότε μὲν οὖν σπονδαὶ κατ᾽ ἀνάγκην ἐξ ἐπιταγμάτων 12
ἐγένοντο, νῦν δὲ περὶ εἰρήνης βουλεύεσθε. σκέψασθε
δὲ ἐξ αὐτῶν τῶν γραμμάτων, ἅ τε ἡμῖν ἐν τῇ στήλῃ
γέγραπται, ἐφ᾽ οἷς τε νῦν ἔξεστι τὴν εἰρήνην ποιεῖσθαι.
ἐκεῖ μὲν γὰρ γέγραπται τὰ τείχη καθαιρεῖν, ἐν δὲ τοῖσδε
ἔξεστιν οἰκοδομεῖν· ναῦς ἐκεῖ μὲν δώδεκα κεκτῆσθαι, νῦν
δ᾽ ὁπόσας ἂν βουλώμεθα· Λῆμνον δὲ καὶ Ἴμβρον καὶ
Σκῦρον τότε μὲν ἔχειν τοὺς ἔχοντας, νῦν δὲ ἡμετέρας εἶναι·
καὶ φεύγοντας νῦν μὲν οὐκ ἐπάναγκες οὐδένα καταδέχεσθαι,
τότε δ᾽ ἐπάναγκες, ἐξ ὧν ὁ δῆμος κατελύθη. τί ταῦτα
ἐκείνοις ὁμολογεῖ; τοσοῦτον οὖν ἔγωγε, ὦ Ἀθηναῖοι,
διορίζομαι περὶ τούτων, τὴν μὲν εἰρήνην σωτηρίαν εἶναι
τῷ δήμῳ καὶ δύναμιν, τὸν δὲ πόλεμον δήμου κατάλυσιν
γίγνεσθαι. περὶ μὲν οὖν τούτων ταῦτα λέγω.

Φασὶ δέ τινες ἀναγκαίως νῦν ἡμῖν ἔχειν πολεμεῖν· 13
σκεψώμεθα οὖν πρῶτον, ὦ ἄνδρες Ἀθηναῖοι, διὰ τί
καὶ πολεμήσωμεν. οἶμαι γὰρ ἂν πάντας ἀνθρώπους

96 κρατήσωσιν A : κρατήσωσι Q 99 add. Reiske 104–5 ἐφ᾽ οἷς … γέγραπται A^{1im} 105 γὰρ A^{1im} : om. Q 108 Σκῦρον Bekker : σκύρον Q Steph. : σκί*ρον A^{c} : σκίρρον A^{a} 111 ἐκείνοις Ald. : ἐκεῖνος AQ 113 δὲ A : om. Q δήμου Canter : δήπου AQ 116 ὦ Q : om. A ἄνδρες habent AQ 117 γὰρ et πάντας ἀνθρώπους in ras. A^{1}

*ὁμολογῆσαι διὰ τάδε δεῖν πολεμεῖν, ἢ ἀδικουμένους ἢ
βοηθοῦντας ἠδικημένοις. ἡμεῖς τοίνυν αὐτοί τε
ἠδικούμεθα, Βοιωτοῖς τε ἀδικουμένοις ἐβοηθοῦμεν. εἰ
τοίνυν ἡμῖν τέ ἐστι τοῦτο παρὰ Λακεδαιμονίων, τὸ
μηκέτι ἀδικεῖσθαι, Βοιωτοῖς τε δέδοκται ποιεῖσθαι τὴν
εἰρήνην ἀφεῖσιν Ὀρχομενὸν αὐτόνομον, τίνος ἕνεκα*
14 *πολεμήσωμεν; ἵνα ἡ πόλις ἡμῶν ἐλευθέρα ᾖ; ἀλλὰ
τοῦτό γε αὐτῇ ὑπάρχει. ἀλλ' ὅπως ἡμῖν τείχη γένηται;
ἔστι καὶ ταῦτα ἐκ τῆς εἰρήνης. ἀλλ' ἵνα τριήρεις ἐξῇ
ναυπηγεῖσθαι καὶ τὰς οὔσας ἐπισκευάζειν καὶ
κεκτῆσθαι; καὶ τοῦτο ὑπάρχει· τὰς γὰρ πόλεις
αὐτονόμους αἱ συνθῆκαι ποιοῦσιν. ἀλλ' ὅπως τὰς νήσους
κομισώμεθα, Λῆμνον καὶ Σκῦρον καὶ Ἴμβρον; οὐκοῦν*
15 *διαρρήδην γέγραπται ταύτας Ἀθηναίων εἶναι. φέρε,
ἀλλὰ Χερρόνησον καὶ τὰς ἀποικίας καὶ τὰ ἐγκτήματα
καὶ τὰ χρέα ἵνα ἀπολάβωμεν; ἀλλ' οὔτε βασιλεὺς οὔτε οἱ
σύμμαχοι συγχωροῦσιν ἡμῖν, μεθ' ὧν αὐτὰ δεῖ
πολεμοῦντας κτήσασθαι. ἀλλὰ νὴ Δία ἕως ἂν Λακε-
δαιμονίους καταπολεμήσωμεν καὶ τοὺς συμμάχους
αὐτῶν, μέχρι τούτου δεῖ πόλεμεῖν; ἀλλ' οὔ μοι δοκοῦμεν
οὕτω παρεσκευάσθαι. ἐὰν δὲ ἄρα κατεργασώμεθα,
τί ποτε αὐτοὶ πείσεσθαι δοκοῦμεν ὑπὸ τῶν*
16 *βαρβάρων, ὅταν ταῦτα πράξωμεν; εἰ τοίνυν περὶ τούτου
μὲν ἔδει πολεμεῖν, χρήματα δὲ ὑπῆρχεν ἡμῖν ἱκανά,
τοῖς δὲ σώμασιν ἦμεν δυνατοί, οὐδὲ οὕτως ἔδει
πολεμεῖν. εἰ δὲ μήτε δι' ὅ τι μήτε ὅτοισι μήτε ἀφ' ὅτου*

118 *ἀδικουμένους* A^1: *ἠδικημένους* A^a : *ἀδικοῦντας* Q 119 *ἠδικημένοις* A : *ἀδικουμένοις* Q 123 *ἀφεῖσιν* Reiske : *ἀφήσειν* AQ : *ἀφιεῖσιν* Blass^3 125 *ἡμῖν* om. Q 130 *Σκῦρον* Steph. : *σκύρον* Q : *σκί*ρον* A^c : *σκίρρον* A^a 132 *ἐγκτήματα* Valckenaer : *ἐγκλήματα* AQ 133 *ἀπολάβωμεν* Q : *ἀπολαύωμεν* A 134 *δεῖ* AQ^{1im} : *δὴ* Q^1, quod postea del. : *δὲ* ut vid. Q^a 137 *δεῖ* AQ^{1im} : *δὲ* Q^a *δοκοῦμεν* Q : *δοκεῖ* A 138 *παρεσκευάσθαι* A^1Q : *παρασκευάσθαι* A^a *δὲ ἄρα* in ras. A^1, re vera Q : *δ' ἄρα* Lipsius 141 *ὑπῆρχεν ἡμῖν* A : *ὑπῆρχε μὲν* Q 143 *ὅτοισι* A : *ὅτοις* Q

πολεμήσωμεν ἔστι, πῶς οὐκ ἐκ παντὸς τρόπου τὴν εἰρήνην ποιητέον ἡμῖν;

Σκέψασθε δέ, ὦ Ἀθηναῖοι, καὶ τόδε, ὅτι νυνὶ πᾶσι 17
τοῖς Ἕλλησι κοινὴν εἰρήνην καὶ ἐλευθερίαν πράττετε, καὶ μετέχειν ἅπασι πάντων ἐξουσίαν ποιεῖτε. ἐνθυμήθητε οὖν τῶν πόλεων τὰς μεγίστας, τίνι τρόπῳ τὸν πόλεμον καταλύονται. πρῶτον μὲν Λακεδαιμονίους, οἵτινες ἀρχόμενοι μὲν ἡμῖν καὶ τοῖς συμμάχοις πολεμεῖν ἦρχον καὶ κατὰ γῆν καὶ κατὰ θάλατταν, νῦν δ' αὐτοῖς ἐκ τῆς εἰρήνης οὐδέτερον τούτων ὑπάρχει. καὶ οὐχ ὑφ' ἡμῶν 18
ἀναγκαζόμενοι ταῦτ' ἀφιᾶσιν, ἀλλ' ἐπ' ἐλευθερίᾳ πάσης τῆς Ἑλλάδος. νενικήκασι γὰρ τρὶς ἤδη μαχόμενοι, τοτὲ μὲν ἐν Κορίνθῳ πάντας πανδημεὶ τοὺς συμμάχους παρόντας, οὐχ ὑπολιπόντες πρόφασιν οὐδεμίαν, ἀλλ' ἐν τῷ κρατιστεύειν μόνοι πάντων, αὖθις δ' ἐν Βοιωτοῖς, ὅτ' αὐτῶν Ἀγησίλαος ἡγεῖτο, τὸν αὐτὸν τρόπον καὶ τότε τὴν νίκην ἐποιήσαντο, τρίτον δ' ἡνίκα Λέχαιον ἔλαβον, Ἀργείους μὲν ἅπαντας καὶ Κορινθίους, ἡμῶν δὲ καὶ Βοιωτῶν τοὺς παρόντας. τοιαῦτα δ' ἔργα ἐπιδειξάμενοι, 19
τὴν εἰρήνην εἰσὶν ἕτοιμοι ποιεῖσθαι τὴν ἑαυτῶν ἔχοντες, οἳ ἐνίκων μαχόμενοι, καὶ τὰς πόλεις αὐτονόμους εἶναι καὶ τὴν θάλατταν κοινὴν ἐῶντες τοῖς ἡττημένοις. καίτοι ποίας τινὸς ἂν ἐκεῖνοι παρ' ἡμῶν εἰρήνης ἔτυχον, εἰ μίαν μόνον μάχην ἡττήθησαν; Βοιωτοὶ δ' αὖ πῶς τὴν εἰρήνην ποιοῦνται; οἵτινες τὸν 20
μὲν πόλεμον ἐποιήσαντο ἕνεκα Ὀρχομενοῦ, ὡς οὐκ

144 *πολεμήσωμεν ἔστι* Bekker : *πολεμήσωμέν ἐστι* AQ 146 *δὲ ὦ* A : *δ' ὦ* Q 149 *τῶν* A : om. Q 153 *τούτων* A : *τούτω* e ras. Q[1] (fort. *τούτων* Q[a]) *ἡμῶν* Q : *ὑμῶν* A 154 *ἀφιᾶσιν* Bekker : *ἀφίασιν* AQ 155 *τῆς* om. Q 157–8 *ἀλλ' ἐν τῷ* AQ : *ἀλλ' ἢ τῷ* Linder : aliter alii 158 *δ' ἐν* Sauppe : *δὲ* AQ 159 *τότε* Sluiter : *ὅτε* AQ 162 *δ' ἔργα* A : *δὲ ἔργα* Q 162–3 *ἐπιδειξάμενοι* A : *ἐπιδειξάμενοι τοῖς Ἕλλησι* Q 163 *εἰσὶν* A : om. Q 167 *μίαν μόνον* in ras. A[1] 169 *μὲν* A : om. Q

ἐπιτρέψοντες αὐτόνομον εἶναι, νῦν δὲ τεθνεώτων μὲν
αὐτοῖς ἀνδρῶν τοσούτων τὸ πλῆθος, τῆς δὲ γῆς ἐκ
μέρους τινὸς τετμημένης, χρήματα δ᾽ εἰσενηνοχότες
πολλὰ καὶ ἰδίᾳ καὶ δημοσίᾳ, ὧν στέρονται, πολεμήσαντες
δὲ ἔτη τέτταρα, ὅμως Ὀρχομενὸν ἀφέντες αὐτόνομον
τὴν εἰρήνην ποιοῦνται καὶ ταῦτα μάτην πεπόνθασιν·
ἐξῆν γὰρ αὐτοῖς καὶ τὴν ἀρχὴν ἐῶσιν Ὀρχομενίους
αὐτονόμους εἰρήνην ἄγειν. οὗτοι δ᾽ αὖ τούτῳ τῷ τρόπῳ
21 τὸν πόλεμον καταλύονται. ἡμῖν δέ, ὦ Ἀθηναῖοι,
πῶς ἔξεστι τὴν εἰρήνην ποιήσασθαι; ποίων τινῶν
Λακεδαιμονίων τυγχάνοντας; καὶ γὰρ εἴ τις ὑμῶν
ἀχθεσθήσεται παραιτοῦμαι· ⟨τὰ⟩ γὰρ ὄντα λέξω.
πρῶτον μὲν γὰρ ἡνίκα ἀπωλέσαμεν τὰς ναῦς ἐν
Ἑλλησπόντῳ καὶ τειχήρεις ἐγενόμεθα, τίνα γνώμην
ἔθεντο περὶ ἡμῶν οἱ νῦν μὲν ἡμέτεροι τότε δὲ
Λακεδαιμονίων ὄντες σύμμαχοι; οὐ τὴν πόλιν ἡμῶν
ἀνδραποδίζεσθαι καὶ τὴν χώραν ἐρημοῦν; οἱ δὲ
διακωλύσαντες ταῦτα μὴ γενέσθαι τίνες ἦσαν; οὐ
Λακεδαιμόνιοι, τοὺς μὲν συμμάχους ἀποτρέψαντες τῆς
γνώμης, αὐτοὶ δ᾽ οὐδ᾽ ἐπιχειρήσαντες διαβουλεύσασθαι
22 περὶ τοιούτων ἔργων; μετὰ δὲ τοῦτο ὅρκους ὀμόσαντες
αὐτοῖς καὶ τὴν στήλην εὑρόμενοι ⟨παρ᾽⟩ αὐτῶν στῆσαι,
κακὸν ἀγαπητὸν ἐν ἐκείνῳ τῷ χρόνῳ, σπονδὰς ἤγομεν
ἐπὶ ῥητοῖς. εἶτα δὲ συμμαχίαν ποιησάμενοι Βοιωτοὺς
καὶ Κορινθίους ἀποστήσαντες αὐτῶν, Ἀργείους δὲ
ἀγαγόντες εἰς τὴν ποτὲ φιλίαν, αἴτιοι τῆς ἐν Κορίνθῳ

172 *τετμημένης*] alt. *η* in ras. A[1] 174 *δὲ* AQ : *δ᾽* Blass[3] *ἀφέντες* AQ : *ἀφιέντες* Blass[3] 175 *ταῦτα* A : om. Q 177 *τῷ* L : deest in AQ 179 *τινῶν* A : *τίνων* Q 181 add. Ald. : deest in codd. 183 *τειχήρεις* A, Q[1] (quid fuit non liquet) 187 *γενέσθαι* Q : *γεγέσθαι* A 190 *ὀμόσαντες* Steph. : *ὁμόσαντες* AQ 191 add. Ald. 193 *βοιωτοὺς* AQ : *Βοιωτοῖς* Blass[3] 195 *ἀγαγόντες* A : om. Q *ποτὲ* AQ : *τότε* Luzac : *πρότερον* Osann

μάχης ἐγενόμεθα αὐτοῖς. τίνες δὲ βασιλέα πολέμιον
αὐτοῖς ἐποίησαν, καὶ Κόνωνι τὴν ναυμαχίαν παρεσκεύασαν,
δι' ἣν ἀπώλεσαν τὴν ἀρχὴν τῆς θαλάττης; ὅμως τοίνυν 23
ταῦτα πεπονθότες ὑφ' ἡμῶν συγχωροῦσι ταὐτὰ ἅπερ οἱ
σύμμαχοι, καὶ διδόασιν ἡμῖν τὰ τείχη καὶ τὰς ναῦς καὶ
τὰς νήσους ἡμῶν εἶναι, ποίαν τιν' οὖν χρὴ εἰρήνην
πρεσβεύοντας ἥκειν; οὐ ταὐτὰ παρὰ τῶν πολεμίων
εὑρομένους, ἅπερ οἱ φίλοι διδόασι, καὶ δι' ἅπερ ἠρξάμεθα
πολεμεῖν, ἵνα ἡμῶν γένηται τῇ πόλει, ταῦτα; οἱ μὲν
τοίνυν ἄλλοι τὴν εἰρήνην ποιοῦνται τῶν ὑπαρχόντων
ἀφιέντες, ἡμεῖς δὲ προσλαμβάνοντες αὐτὰ ὧν μάλιστα
δεόμεθα.

Τί οὖν ἐστιν ὑπόλοιπον περὶ ὅτου δεῖ βουλεύεσθαι; 24
περὶ Κορίνθου καὶ περὶ ὧν {ἂν} ἡμᾶς Ἀργεῖοι
προκαλοῦνται. πρῶτον μὲν περὶ Κορίνθου διδαξάτω μέ
τις, Βοιωτῶν μὴ συμπολεμούντων, εἰρήνην δὲ
ποιουμένων πρὸς Λακεδαιμονίους, τίνος ἐστὶν ἡμῖν ἀξία
Κόρινθος. ἀναμνήσθητε γάρ, ὦ Ἀθηναῖοι, τῆς ἡμέρας 25
ἐκείνης, ὅτε Βοιωτοῖς τὴν συμμαχίαν ἐποιούμεθα, τίνα
γνώμην ἔχοντες ταῦτα ἐπράττομεν. οὐχ ὡς ἱκανὴν
οὖσαν τὴν Βοιωτῶν δύναμιν μεθ' ἡμῶν γενομένην κοινῇ
πάντας ἀνθρώπους ἀμύνασθαι; νῦν δὲ βουλευόμεθα,
Βοιωτῶν εἰρήνην ποιουμένων πῶς δυνατοὶ Λακεδαιμο-
νίοις πολεμεῖν ἐσμεν ἄνευ Βοιωτῶν. ναί, φασί τινες, 26
ἂν Κόρινθόν τε φυλάττωμεν καὶ συμμάχους ἔχωμεν

196 *τίνες* Ald. : *τινὲς* AQ 196–7 *πολέμιον αὐτοῖς* A : *πολέμιον ἑαυτοῖς* Q[1] : *ἑαυτοῖς πολέμιον* Q[a] 199 *ταὐτὰ* Osann : *ταῦτα* AQ 202 *πρεσβεύοντας* AQ[2im] : *πρεσβεύοντες* Q *ταὐτὰ* Osann : *ταῦτα* AQ 204 *πόλει, ταῦτα;* sic interpunxit Sauppe 205 *ὑπαρχόντων* Q : *ὑπαρχότων* A 206 *αὐτὰ* A[1]Q[2im] : *αὐτῶν* A[a] : *αὐτὸν* Q 209 *περὶ Κορίνθου* Q : om. A del. Dobree 210 *προκαλοῦνται* M : *προσκαλοῦνται* AQ 213 *Κόρινθος* A : *ἡ Κόρινθος* Q 217 *βουλευόμεθα* Q : *βουλευώμεθα* A 218–19 *Λακεδαιμονίοις πολεμεῖν ἐσμεν* A : *πολεμεῖν ἐσμεν Λακεδαιμονίοις* Q

Ἀργείους. ἰόντων δὲ Λακεδαιμονίων εἰς Ἄργος πότερον βοηθήσομεν αὐτοῖς ἢ οὔ; πολλὴ γὰρ ἀνάγκη ὁπότερον τούτων ἑλέσθαι. μὴ βοηθούντων μὲν οὖν ἡμῶν οὐδὲ λόγος ὑπολείπεται μὴ οὐκ ἀδικεῖν καὶ ποιεῖν Ἀργείους ὁποῖον ἄν τι βούλωνται δικαίως· βοηθούντων δὲ ἡμῶν εἰς Ἄργος οὐχ ἕτοιμον μάχεσθαι Λακεδαιμονίοις; ἵνα ἡμῖν τί γένηται; ἵνα ἡττώμενοι μὲν καὶ τὴν οἰκείαν χώραν ἀπολέσωμεν πρὸς τῇ Κορινθίων, νικήσαντες δὲ τὴν Κορινθίων Ἀργείων ποιήσωμεν. οὐχ ἕνεκα τούτων πολεμήσομεν;

27 σκεψώμεθα δὴ καὶ τοὺς Ἀργείων λόγους. κελεύουσι γὰρ ἡμᾶς κοινῇ μετὰ σφῶν καὶ μετὰ Κορινθίων πολεμεῖν, αὐτοὶ δ᾽ ἰδίᾳ εἰρήνην ποιησάμενοι τὴν χώραν οὐ παρέχουσιν ἐμπολεμεῖν. καὶ μετὰ μὲν πάντων τῶν συμμάχων τὴν εἰρήνην ποιουμένους οὐκ ἐῶσιν ἡμᾶς οὐδὲν πιστεύειν Λακεδαιμονίοις· ἃ δὲ πρὸς τούτους μόνους ἐκεῖνοι συνέθεντο, ταῦτα δ᾽ οὐδεπώποτ᾽ αὐτούς φασι παραβῆναι. πατρίαν τε εἰρήνην ὀνομάζοντες ᾗ χρῶνται, τοῖς δὲ ἄλλοις Ἕλλησιν οὐκ ἐῶσι πατρίαν γενέσθαι τὴν εἰρήνην· ἐκ γὰρ τοῦ πολέμου χρονισθέντος Κόρινθον ἑλεῖν προσδοκῶσι, κρατήσαντες δὲ τούτων ὑφ᾽ ὧν ἀεὶ κρατοῦνται, καὶ τοὺς συννικῶντας ἐλπίζουσι παραστήσεσθαι.

221 ἰόντων Ald. : ὄντων AQ 222 βοηθήσομεν A : βοηθήσωμεν Q 223 τούτων A : τοῦτον Q 224 καὶ ποιεῖν Ἀργείους Sluiter : ἀργείους καὶ ποιεῖν AQ 225 ὁποῖον ἄν τι AQ : ὁποῖα ἂν οὗτοι Q[2im] 228 ἀπολέσωμεν Q : ἀπωλέσομεν A 229 ποιήσωμεν M : ποιήσομεν AQ 230 πολεμήσομεν Ald. : πολεμήσωμεν AQ 233 οὐ παρέχουσιν A : οὐχ ὑπαρέχουσιν Q ἐμπολεμεῖν A[1] : ἐνπολεμεῖν A[a] : ἐν*πολεμεῖν re vera Q 234 ποιουμένους Reiske (qui viii. 461 ποιούμενοι etiam proposuit) : ποιουμένοις AQ 235 λακεδαιμονίοις AQ[1] : λακεδαιμονίους Q 236 ταῦτα δ᾽ Q : ταῦτ᾽ A οὐδεπώποτ᾽ A : οὐδὲ πώποτ᾽ Q 237 φασὶ Q : φησὶ A τε Q : δὲ A 238 δὲ del. Reiske 240 ἑλεῖν <ἂν> Stahl 241 κρατοῦνται A : κρατῶνται Q συννικῶντας A : συνικῶντας Q ἐλπίζουσι A : ἐλπίζουσιν Q 242 παραστήσεσθαι Reiske : ἀποστήσεσθαι AQ : ἀπώσεσθαι maluerit Albini

Τοιούτων δ᾽ ἐλπίδων μετασχόντας ἡμᾶς δεῖ δυοῖν θά- 28
τερον ἑλέσθαι, ἢ πολεμεῖν μετὰ Ἀργείων Λακεδαιμονίοις,
ἢ μετὰ Βοιωτῶν κοινῇ τὴν εἰρήνην ποιεῖσθαι. ἐγὼ μὲν
οὖν ἐκεῖνο δέδοικα μάλιστα, ὦ Ἀθηναῖοι, τὸ εἰθισμένον
κακόν, ὅτι τοὺς κρείττους φίλους ἀφιέντες ἀεὶ τοὺς
ἥττους αἱρούμεθα, καὶ πόλεμον ποιούμεθα δι᾽ ἑτέρους,
ἐξὸν δι᾽ ἡμᾶς αὐτοὺς εἰρήνην ἄγειν· οἵτινες πρῶτον μὲν 29
βασιλεῖ τῷ μεγάλῳ (χρὴ γὰρ ἀναμνησθέντας τὰ
γεγενημένα καλῶς βουλεύσασθαι) σπονδὰς ποιησάμενοι
καὶ συνθέμενοι φιλίαν εἰς τὸν ἅπαντα χρόνον, ἃ ἡμῖν
ἐπρέσβευσεν Ἐπίλυκος Τεισάνδρου, τῆς μητρὸς τῆς
ἡμετέρας ἀδελφός, ⟨μετὰ⟩ ταῦτα Ἀμόργῃ πειθόμενοι
τῷ δούλῳ τῷ βασιλέως καὶ φυγάδι τὴν μὲν βασιλέως
δύναμιν ἀπεβαλόμεθα ὡς οὐδενὸς οὖσαν ἀξίαν, τὴν δὲ
Ἀμόργου φιλίαν εἱλόμεθα, κρείττω νομίσαντες εἶναι·
ἀνθ᾽ ὧν βασιλεὺς ὀργισθεὶς ἡμῖν, σύμμαχος γενόμενος
Λακεδαιμονίοις, παρέσχεν αὐτοῖς εἰς τὸν πόλεμον
πεντακισχίλια τάλαντα, ἕως κατέλυσεν ἡμῶν τὴν
δύναμιν. ἓν μὲν βούλευμα τοιοῦτον ἐβουλευσάμεθα·
Συρακόσιοι δ᾽ ὅτε ἦλθον ἡμῶν δεόμενοι, φιλότητα μὲν 30
ἀντὶ διαφορᾶς ἐθέλοντες εἰρήνην δ᾽ ἀντὶ πολέμου
ποιεῖσθαι, τήν τε συμμαχίαν ἀποδεικνύντες ὅσῳ
κρείττων ἡ σφετέρα εἴη τῆς Ἐγεσταίων καὶ Καταναίων,
εἰ βουλόμεθα πρὸς αὐτοὺς ποιεῖσθαι, ἡμεῖς τοίνυν

246 *μάλιστα* A : om. Q 248 *αἱρούμεθα* A : *ἡρούμεθα* Q^{1} (quid primo scripserit non liquet) 250 *γὰρ* bis Q 253 *Ἐπίλυκος* <*ὑ*> maluit Baiter *Τεισάνδρου* Blass^{2} : *τισάνδρου* AQ 254 *ἡμετέρας* A^{1}Q : *ὑμετέρας* A add. Reiske 255 alt. *τῷ* Q : *τοῦ* A 256 *ἀπεβαλόμεθα* A : *ἀπεβαλλόμμεθα* Q *οὐδενὸς* Reiske : *οὐδὲν* AQ 258 *ὧν* A : *ᾧ* Q 260 *κατέλυσεν*] *κατέλυσαν* Reiske 262 *Συρακόσιοι* Lipsius (et mox ll. 268, 269) : *Συρακούσιοι* A^{c}Q : *Συρρακούσιοι* A^{a} et mox 265 *τῆς Ἐγεσταίων καὶ Καταναίων* Francke : *τῶν ἐγεσταίων* (*ἐγεστέων* A^{a}) *καὶ τῶν καταναίων* A^{1}Q 266 *εἰ βουλόμεθα* AQ : *εἰ βουλοίμεθα* Reiske : *ἢν βουλώμεθα* Ald.

εἱλόμεθα καὶ τότε πόλεμον μὲν ἀντὶ εἰρήνης, Ἐγεσταίους
δὲ ἀντὶ Συρακοσίων, στρατεύεσθαι δ' εἰς Σικελίαν ἀντὶ
τοῦ μένοντες οἴκοι συμμάχους ἔχειν Συρακοσίους· ἐξ
ὧν πολλοὺς μὲν Ἀθηναίων ἀπολέσαντες ἀριστίνδην
καὶ τῶν συμμάχων, πολλὰς δὲ ναῦς καὶ χρήματα
καὶ δύναμιν ἀποβαλόντες, αἰσχρῶς διεκομίσθησαν οἱ
31 σωθέντες αὐτῶν. ὕστερον δὲ ὑπ' Ἀργείων ἐπείσθημεν,
οἵπερ νῦν ἥκουσι πείθοντες πολεμεῖν, πλεύσαντες ἐπὶ
τὴν Λακωνικὴν εἰρήνης ἡμῖν οὔσης πρὸς Λακεδαιμονίους
ἐκτεῖναι τὸν θυμόν, ἀρχὴν πολλῶν κακῶν· ἐξ οὗ
πολεμήσαντες ἠναγκάσθημεν τὰ τείχη κατασκάπτειν
καὶ τὰς ναῦς παραδιδόναι καὶ τοὺς φεύγοντας
καταδέχεσθαι. ταῦτα δὲ πασχόντων ἡμῶν οἱ πείσαντες
ἡμᾶς πολεμεῖν Ἀργεῖοι τίνα ὠφέλειαν παρέσχον ἡμῖν;
τίνα δὲ κίνδυνον ὑπὲρ {τῶν} Ἀθηναίων ἐποιήσαντο;
32 νῦν οὖν τοῦτο ὑπόλοιπόν ἐστιν ἡμῖν, πόλεμον μὲν
ἑλέσθαι καὶ νῦν ἀντ' εἰρήνης, τὴν δὲ συμμαχίαν τὴν
Ἀργείων ἀντὶ τῆς Βοιωτῶν, Κορινθίων δὲ τοὺς
νῦν ἔχοντας τὴν πόλιν ἀντὶ Λακεδαιμονίων. μὴ δῆτα,
ὦ Ἀθηναῖοι, μηδεὶς ἡμᾶς ταῦτα πείσῃ· τὰ γὰρ
παραδείγματα τὰ γεγενημένα τῶν ἁμαρτημάτων ἱκανὰ
τοῖς σώφροσι τῶν ἀνθρώπων ὥστε μηκέτι ἁμαρτάνειν.
33 Εἰσὶ δέ τινες ὑμῶν οἳ τοσαύτην ὑπερβολὴν τῆς
ἐπιθυμίας ἔχουσιν εἰρήνην ὡς τάχιστα γενέσθαι· φασὶ
γὰρ καὶ τὰς τετταράκονθ' ἡμέρας ἐν αἷς ὑμῖν ἔξεστι
βουλεύεσθαι περίεργον εἶναι, καὶ τοῦτο ἀδικεῖν ἡμᾶς·

267 μὲν A : om. Q 269 μένοντες Blass : μένοντας AQ 274 ἥκουσι πείθοντες A : ἥκοντες πείθουσι Q 275 ἡμῖν οὔσης A : οὔσης ἡμῖν Q 276 ἐκτεῖναι <αὐτῶν> Lipsius : ἐντεῖναι <ἐκείνων> Maidment 280 ἡμᾶς Q : ὑμᾶς A^1 : om. A^a 281 del. Pertz 282 ἡμῖν A : om. Q μὲν A^1 : om. A^aQ 283 alt. τὴν Q : om. A 286 πείσῃ Q : πείσει A τὰ A : ταὶ Q 289 ὑμῶν A : ἡμῶν Q 291 τετταράκονθ' Blass : τεταρακονθ' Q : τεσσαράκονθ' A ὑμῖν Bekker : ἡμῖν AQ 292 βουλεύεσθαι A : βουλεύσασθαι Q

αὐτοκράτορας γὰρ πεμφθῆναι εἰς Λακεδαίμονα διὰ
ταῦθ', ἵνα μὴ πάλιν ἐπαναφέρωμεν. τήν τε ἀσφάλειαν
ἡμῶν τῆς ἐπαναφορᾶς δέος ὀνομάζουσι, λέγοντες ὡς
οὐδεὶς πώποτε τὸν δῆμον τὸν Ἀθηναίων ἐκ τοῦ φανεροῦ
πείσας ἔσῳσεν, ἀλλὰ δεῖ λαθόντας ἢ ἐξαπατήσαντας
αὐτὸν εὖ ποιῆσαι. τὸν λόγον οὖν τοῦτον οὐκ ἐπαινῶ.
φημὶ γάρ, ὦ Ἀθηναῖοι, πολέμου μὲν ὄντος ἄνδρα 34
στρατηγὸν τῇ πόλει τε εὔνουν εἰδότα τε ὅ τι πράττει,
λανθάνοντα δεῖν τοὺς πολλοὺς τῶν ἀνθρώπων καὶ
ἐξαπατῶντα ἄγειν ἐπὶ τοὺς κινδύνους, εἰρήνης δὲ πέρι
πρεσβεύοντας κοινῆς τοῖς Ἕλλησιν, ἐφ' οἷς ὅρκοι τε
ὀμοσθήσονται στῆλαί τε σταθήσονται γεγραμμέναι,
ταῦτα δὲ οὔτε λαθεῖν οὔτε ἐξαπατῆσαι δεῖν, ἀλλὰ πολὺ
μᾶλλον ἐπαινεῖν ἢ ψέγειν, εἰ πεμφθέντες αὐτοκράτορες
ἔτι ἀποδώσομεν ὑμῖν περὶ αὐτῶν σκέψασθαι.
βουλεύσασθαι μὲν οὖν ἀσφαλῶς χρὴ κατὰ δύναμιν, οἷς
δ' ἂν ὁμόσωμεν καὶ συνθώμεθα, τούτοις ἐμμένειν. οὐ 35
γὰρ μόνον, ὦ Ἀθηναῖοι, πρὸς γράμματα {τὰ} γεγραμμένα
δεῖ βλέποντας πρεσβεύειν ἡμᾶς, ἀλλὰ καὶ πρὸς τοὺς
τρόπους τοὺς ὑμετέρους. ὑμεῖς γὰρ περὶ μὲν τῶν ἑτοίμων
ὑμῖν ὑπονοεῖν εἰώθατε καὶ δυσχεραίνειν, τὰ δ' οὐκ ὄντα
λογοποιεῖν ὡς ἔστιν ὑμῖν ἕτοιμα· κἂν μὲν πολεμεῖν δέῃ,

293 *αὐτοκράτορας* AQ[1] : *αὐτοκράτορες* Q[a]   294 *ταῦθ'* Reiske : *ταύτην* AQ   296 *τὸν δῆμον* A : *τοῦ δήμου* Q   *τὸν* Spengel[1] : *τῶν* AQ   297 *δεῖ* AQ : *δεῖν* Valckenaer   300 *ὅ τι* A : *ὅττι* Q   *πράττει* Richards[1] : *πράττοι* AQ : *πράττῃ* Ydén   302 *ἐπὶ* A : *παρὰ* Q   *τοὺς* A[1]Q : om. A[a]   303 *πρεσβεύοντας* A : *πρεσβεύοντα* Q   305 *δὲ* A[1]Q : om. A[a]   *δεῖν* A[1]Q : *δεῖ* A[a]   307 *ἔτι* Reiske : *τι* A : deest in Q (approb. Lipsius)   *ἀποδώσομεν* AQ : *ἀπεδώκαμεν* Blass, postea *ἀπέδομεν* Blass[3] : *ἀποδίδομεν* Lipsius   *ὑμῖν* Ald. : *ἡμῖν* AQ   *αὐτῶν* A : *τῶν αὐτῶν* Q   308 *ἀσφαλῶς* A : om. Q   309 *ὀμόσωμεν* Steph. : *ὁμόσωμεν* A : *ὁμώσομεν* Q   310 delevi auctore Albinio : habent AQBLMZ   312 *ὑμετέρους* A : *ἡμετέρους* Q   *ὑμεῖς* A : *ἡμεῖς* Q   *μὲν* A : om. Q   313 *ὑμῖν* A : *ἡμῖν* Q

τῆς εἰρήνης ἐπιθυμεῖτε, ἐὰν δέ τις ὑμῖν τὴν εἰρήνην
πράττῃ, λογίζεσθε τὸν πόλεμον ὅσα ἀγαθὰ ὑμῖν
36 κατηργάσατο. ὅπου καὶ νῦν ἤδη τινὲς λέγουσιν οὐ
γιγνώσκειν τὰς διαλλαγὰς αἵτινές εἰσι, τείχη καὶ νῆες εἰ
γενήσονται τῇ πόλει· τὰ γὰρ ἴδια τὰ σφέτερ' αὐτῶν ἐκ
τῆς ὑπερορίας οὐκ ἀπολαμβάνειν, ἀπὸ δὲ τῶν τειχῶν
οὐκ εἶναι σφίσι τροφήν. ἀναγκαίως οὖν ἔχει καὶ πρὸς
ταῦτ' ἀντειπεῖν.
37 Ἦν γάρ ποτε χρόνος, ὦ Ἀθηναῖοι, ὅτε τείχη καὶ ναῦς
οὐκ ἐκεκτήμεθα· γενομένων δὲ τούτων τὴν ἀρχὴν
ἐποιησάμεθα τῶν ἀγαθῶν. ὧν εἰ καὶ νῦν ἐπιθυμεῖτε,
ταῦτα κατεργάσασθε. ταύτην δὲ λαβόντες ἀφορμὴν
οἱ πατέρες ἡμῶν κατηργάσαντο τῇ πόλει δύναμιν
τοσαύτην ὅσην οὔπω τις ἄλλη πόλις ἐκτήσατο, τὰ μὲν
πείσαντες τοὺς Ἕλληνας, τὰ δὲ λαθόντες, τὰ δὲ
38 πριάμενοι, τὰ δὲ βιασάμενοι· πείσαντες μὲν οὖν Ἀθήνησι
ποιήσασθαι τῶν κοινῶν χρημάτων Ἑλληνοταμίας, καὶ
τὸν σύλλογον τῶν νεῶν παρ' ἡμῖν γενέσθαι, ὅσαι δὲ τῶν
πόλεων τριήρεις μὴ κέκτηνται, ταύταις ἡμᾶς παρέχειν·
λαθόντες δὲ Πελοποννησίους τειχισάμενοι τὰ τείχη·
πριάμενοι δὲ παρὰ Λακεδαιμονίων μὴ δοῦναι τούτων
δίκην· βιασάμενοι δὲ τοὺς ἐναντίους τὴν ἀρχὴν τῶν
Ἑλλήνων κατηργασάμεθα. καὶ ταῦτα τὰ ἀγαθὰ ἐν
39 ὀγδοήκοντα καὶ πέντε ἡμῖν ἔτεσιν ἐγένετο. κρατηθέντες

38 Ἑλληνοταμίας Harp. ε 40 s.v.

315 ὑμῖν Q : ἡμῖν A 316 λογίζεσθε Q[2] : λογίζεσθαι AQ ὑμῖν Q : ἡμῖν A 317 κατηργάσατο Blass[3] : κατειργάσατο AQ 318 εἰσί, τεῖχη A : εἰς τείχη Q 322 ταῦτ' A : ταῦτα Q 324 οὐκ ἐκεκτήμεθα Hirschig[1] : οὐ κεκτήμεθα AQ : οὐκ ἐκτήμεθα Bekker δὲ τούτων τὴν AQ : δέ, ταύτην Hirschig[1] 326 κατεργάσασθε AQ[1] : κατεργάσασθαι Q[a] 327 κατηργάσαντο Blass[3] : κατειργάσαντο AQ 333 μὴ A : μὲν Q 334 λαθόντες A[1]Q : λαθόντας A[a] πελοποννησίους A[1]Q : πελοπονησίους A[a] τειχισάμενοι Emperius[3] : ἐτειχίσαμεν AQ 337 κατηργασάμεθα Blass[3] : κατειργασάμεθα AQ 338 ἐγένετο A : ἐγένοντο Q

*δὲ τῷ πολέμῳ τά τε ἄλλα ἀπωλέσαμεν καὶ τὰ τείχη καὶ
τὰς ναῦς ἔλαβον ἡμῶν ἐνέχυρα Λακεδαιμόνιοι, τὰς μὲν
παραλαβόντες, τὰ δὲ καθελόντες, ὅπως μὴ πάλιν ταῦτ᾽
ἔχοντες ἀφορμὴν δύναμιν τῇ πόλει κατασκευάσαιμεν.
πεισθέντες τοίνυν ὑφ᾽ ἡμῶν Λακεδαιμόνιοι πάρεισι
νυνὶ πρέσβεις αὐτοκράτορες, τά τε ἐνέχυρα ἡμῖν
ἀποδιδόντες, καὶ τὰ τείχη καὶ ⟨τὰς⟩ ναῦς ἐῶντες
κεκτῆσθαι, τάς τε νήσους ἡμετέρας εἶναι. τὴν αὐτὴν* 40
*τοίνυν ἀρχὴν ἀγαθῶν λαμβάνοντας, ἥνπερ ἡμῶν
ἐλάμβανον οἱ πρόγονοι, ταύτην οὐ πρακτέον φασὶ τὴν
εἰρήνην τινὲς εἶναι. παριόντες οὖν αὐτοὶ διδασκόντων
ὑμᾶς (ἐξουσίαν δ᾽ αὐτοῖς ἡμεῖς ἐποιήσαμεν, προσθέντες
τετταράκοντα ἡμέρας βουλεύσασθαι) τοῦτο μὲν τῶν
γεγραμμένων εἴ τι τυγχάνει μὴ καλῶς ἔχον (ἔξεστι γὰρ
ἀφελεῖν) τοῦτο δ᾽ εἴ τίς ⟨τι⟩ προσθεῖναι βούλεται,
πείσας ὑμᾶς προσγραψάτω. πᾶσί τε τοῖς γεγραμμένοις
χρωμένοις ἔστιν εἰρήνην ἄγειν. εἰ δὲ μηδὲν ἀρέσκει
τούτων, πολεμεῖν ἕτοιμον. καὶ ταῦτ᾽ ἐφ᾽ ὑμῖν πάντ᾽* 41
*ἐστίν, ὦ Ἀθηναῖοι· τούτων ὅ τι ἂν βούλησθε ἕλεσθε.
πάρεισι μὲν γὰρ Ἀργεῖοι καὶ Κορίνθιοι διδάξοντες ὡς
ἄμεινόν ἐστι πολεμεῖν, ἥκουσι δὲ Λακεδαιμόνιοι
πείσοντες ὑμᾶς εἰρήνην ποιήσασθαι. τούτων δ᾽ ἐστὶ τὸ
τέλος παρ᾽ ὑμῖν, ἀλλ᾽ οὐκ ἐν Λακεδαιμονίοις, δι᾽ ἡμᾶς.*

339 *ἄλλα* A : *ἄλλα πάντα* Q 340 alt. *τὰς* Reiske : *τὰ* AQ 341 *παραλαβόντες … καθελόντες* A : *καθελόντες … παραλαβόντες* Q *ταῦτ᾽* AQ : *ταύτην* Hirschig[1] 344 *νυνὶ* A : *νῦν* Q 345 add. Fuhr[3] 348 *οὐ πρακτέον* mal. Albini : *οὐκ ἀκτέον* AQ : *οὐ δεκτέον* Naber[3] 350 *ὑμᾶς* Q : *ἡμᾶς* A 352 *γεγραμμένων* Q : *γεγραμένων* A *εἴ τι* Ald. : *ἔτι* AQ 353 *τίς <τι>* Blass : *τις* AQ : *<τί> τις* Turr. : *<τι>* post *προσθεῖναι* inseruit Sluiter 354 *ὑμᾶς* B : *ἡμᾶς* AQ 355 *δὲ* A : *δὴ* Q 356 *ὑμῖν* Q : *ἡμῖν* A 357 *βούλησθε* A : *βούλοισθε* Q *ἕλεσθε* Bekker : *ἑλέσθε* Ald. : *ἑλέσθαι* AQ 360 *ὑμᾶς* A : *ἡμᾶς* Q *ποιήσασθαι* Q : *ποιήσεσθαι* A 361 *ἡμᾶς* Q : *ὑμᾶς* A

πρεσβευτὰς οὖν πάντας ὑμᾶς ἡμεῖς οἱ πρέσβεις ποιοῦμεν· ὁ γὰρ τὴν χεῖρα μέλλων ὑμῶν αἴρειν, οὗτος ὁ πρεσβεύων ἐστίν, ὁπότερ᾽ ἂν αὐτῷ δοκῇ, καὶ τὴν εἰρήνην καὶ τὸν πόλεμον {ποιεῖν}. μέμνησθε μὲν οὖν, ὦ Ἀθηναῖοι, τοὺς ἡμετέρους λόγους, ψηφίσασθε δὲ τοιαῦτα, ἐξ ὧν ὑμῖν μηδέποτε μεταμελήσει.

362 ὑμᾶς ἡμεῖς A : ἡμᾶς οἱμεῖς Q 363 ὑμῶν A : ἡμῶν Q οὗτος A : οὕτως Q 364 ἐστίν] ἔσται Dobree δοκῇ Q : δοκεῖ A 365 del. Reiske 367 ὑμῖν A : ἡμῖν Q

4

[*ΑΝΔΟΚΙΔΟΥ*]
ΚΑΤΑ ΑΛΚΙΒΙΑΔΟΥ

ΥΠΟΘΕΣΙΣ

Ἀνδοκίδης Ἀλκιβιάδου κατηγορεῖ τοῦ Κλεινίου ὡς καὶ τὰ τῆς πόλεως καὶ τὰ τῶν συμμάχων διαφθείραντος καὶ κατὰ τὸν ἴδιον βίον πλεῖστα ἡμαρτηκότος· τοῦ δὲ δήμου βουλευομένου καὶ αὐτὸν ἐξοστρακίσαι τὸν Ἀνδοκίδην πρῶτον παραγράφεται, λέγων ἤδη ἀπολελογῆσθαι καὶ ἀνεύθυνος εἶναι. εἰρήκαμεν γὰρ πολλάκις, ὅτι δεῖ τὸν τοῖς αὐτοῖς ἐγκλήμασι δοκοῦντα ἐνέχεσθαι πρῶτον ἑαυτὸν ἐλευθεροῦν, εἶτα διαβάλλειν. τὴν δὲ στάσιν οἱ μέν φασιν ὁρικὴν εἶναι, οἱ δὲ πραγματικήν. ἠκριβωμένως δὲ ἡ στάσις κατὰ μὲν τὴν ἀρχὴν μετάληψίς ἐστι (παραγράφεται γάρ), ἐν δὲ τοῖς ὑστέροις πραγματική· δίκαιον γάρ φησι καὶ συμφέρον ἐξοστρακισθῆναι Ἀλκιβιάδην.

Οὐκ ἐν τῷ παρόντι μόνον γιγνώσκω τῶν πολιτικῶν 1
πραγμάτων ὡς σφαλερόν ἐστιν ἅπτεσθαι, ἀλλὰ καὶ πρότερον χαλεπὸν ἡγούμην, πρὶν τῶν κοινῶν ἐπιμελεῖσθαί

tit. *κατὰ Ἀλκιβιάδου* A, Phot. *Bibl.* cod. 261 488a.17 : *κατ' Ἀλκιβιάδου* Harp. ε 45 s.v. *ἐμποδών*, ε 152 s.v. *εὐανδρία*. Commemorat ut Andocidis etiam *ἀπολογία πρὸς Φαίακα* [Plut.] *Vita Andoc.* 14.835A. Hanc vero orationem non Andocidis esse iudicaverunt docti plerique; cfr. praef. p. vi. Arg. tit. *ὑπόθεσις τοῦ ἑξῆς* A : om. Q 1 *ἀλκιβιάδου* A : *ἀλκιβιάδην* Q 4 *βουλευομένου* A : *βουλομένου* Q 5 *ἀπολελογῆσθαι* A : *ἀπολελειγῆσθαι* Q 6 *εἰρήκαμεν* Reiske : *εἴρηκε μὲν* A : *εἴρηκεν μὲν* Q *γὰρ* A : om. Q 7 *ἐνέχεσθαι* A : *ἀνέχεσθαι* Q 9 *ἠκριβωμένως* re vera A, Q subscriptio: *κατὰ ἀλκιβιάδου* A : om. Q

τινος. πολίτου δὲ ἀγαθοῦ νομίζω προκινδυνεύειν ἐθέλειν τοῦ πλήθους, καὶ μὴ καταδείσαντα τὰς ἔχθρας τὰς ἰδίας ὑπὲρ τῶν δημοσίων ἔχειν ἡσυχίαν· διὰ μὲν γὰρ τοὺς τῶν ἰδίων ἐπιμελουμένους οὐδὲν αἱ πόλεις μείζους καθίστανται, διὰ δὲ τοὺς τῶν κοινῶν μεγάλαι καὶ
2 ἐλεύθεραι γίγνονται. ὧν {τῶν ἀγαθῶν} εἷς ἐγὼ βουληθεὶς ἐξετάζεσθαι μεγίστοις περιπέπτωκα κινδύνοις, προθύμων μὲν καὶ ἀγαθῶν ἀνδρῶν ὑμῶν τυγχάνων, δι᾿ ὅπερ σῴζομαι, πλείστοις δὲ καὶ δεινοτάτοις ἐχθροῖς χρώμενος, ὑφ᾿ ὧν διαβάλλομαι. ὁ μὲν οὖν ἀγὼν ὁ παρὼν οὐ στεφανηφόρος, ἀλλ᾿ εἰ χρὴ μηδὲν ἀδικήσαντα τὴν πόλιν δέκα ἔτη φεύγειν· οἱ δ᾿ ἀνταγωνιζόμενοι περὶ τῶν ἄθλων τούτων ἐσμὲν ἐγὼ καὶ Ἀλκιβιάδης καὶ Νικίας, ὧν ἀναγκαῖον ἕνα τῇ συμφορᾷ περιπεσεῖν.

3 Ἄξιον δὲ μέμψασθαι τὸν θέντα τὸν νόμον, ὃς ἐναντία τῷ ὅρκῳ τοῦ δήμου καὶ τῆς βουλῆς ἐνομοθέτησεν· ἐκεῖ μὲν γὰρ ὄμνυτε μηδένα μήτ᾿ ἐξελᾶν μήτε δήσειν μήτε ἀποκτενεῖν ἄκριτον, ἐν δὲ τῷδε τῷ καιρῷ οὔτε κατηγορίας γενομένης οὔτε ἀπολογίας ἀποδοθείσης {οὔτε} διαψηφισαμένων κρύβδην τὸν ὀστρακισθέντα
4 τοσοῦτον χρόνον δεῖ στερηθῆναι τῆς πόλεως. εἶτα ἐν τοῖς τοιούτοις οἱ τοὺς ἑταίρους καὶ συνωμότας κεκτημένοι πλέον φέρονται τῶν ἄλλων· οὐ γὰρ ὥσπερ ἐν τοῖς δικαστηρίοις οἱ λαχόντες κρίνουσιν, ἀλλὰ τούτου τοῦ πράγματος ἅπασιν Ἀθηναίοις μέτεστι. πρὸς δὲ τούτοις τῷ μὲν ἐλλείπειν τῷ δ᾿ ὑπερβάλλειν ὁ νόμος μοι

16 νομίζω A : om. Q 21 del. Valckenaer 22 περιπέπτωκα A : περιπίπτω Q 23 ὅπερ AQ : ὧνπερ Markland 24 καὶ A[1]Q : om. A[a] 30 ὃς AQ : ὡς Dobree 31 ἐνομοθέτησεν A : ἐνομοθέτησε Q 33 ἀποκτενεῖν Steph. : ἀποκτείνειν AQ 34 ἀποδοθείσης A[1] (ἀπο in ras.), Q 35 del. Schleiermacher apud Bekkerum 37 τοὺς AQ : <πολλοὺς> τοὺς Röhl : delend. vel cum πολλοὺς mutand. censuit Meier 41 μοι A : om. Q

δοκεῖ· τῶν μὲν γὰρ ἰδίων ἀδικημάτων μεγάλην τιμωρίαν
ταύτην νομίζω, τῶν δὲ δημοσίων μικρὰν καὶ οὐδενὸς
ἀξίαν ἡγοῦμαι ζημίαν, ἐξὸν κολάζειν χρήμασι καὶ
δεσμῷ καὶ θανάτῳ. ἔτι δ' εἴ τις διὰ τοῦτο μεθίσταται 5
ὅτι ⟨πονηρὸς⟩ πολίτης ἐστίν, οὗτος οὐδ' ἀπελθὼν
ἐνθένδε παύσεται, ἀλλ' ὅπου ἂν οἰκῇ, ταύτην τὴν πόλιν
διαφθερεῖ, καὶ τῇδε οὐδὲν ἧττον ἐπιβουλεύσει, ἀλλὰ καὶ
μᾶλλον δικαιότερον ἢ πρὶν ἐκβληθῆναι. οἶμαι δὲ καὶ
τοὺς φίλους ὑμῶν ἐν ταύτῃ μάλιστα τῇ ἡμέρᾳ λυπεῖσθαι
καὶ τοὺς ἐχθροὺς ἥδεσθαι, συνειδότας ὡς ἂν ἀγνοήσαντες
ἐξελάσητε τὸν βέλτιστον, δέκα ἐτῶν ἡ πόλις οὐδὲν
ἀγαθὸν ὑπὸ τούτου τοῦ ἀνδρὸς πείσεται. ῥᾴδιον δὲ καὶ 6
ἐντεῦθεν γνῶναι τὸν νόμον πονηρὸν ὄντα· μόνοι γὰρ
αὐτῷ τῶν Ἑλλήνων χρώμεθα, καὶ οὐδεμία τῶν ἄλλων
πόλεων ἐθέλει μιμήσασθαι. καίτοι ταῦτα διέγνωσται
ἄριστα τῶν δογμάτων, ἃ καὶ τοῖς πολλοῖς καὶ τοῖς
ὀλίγοις ἁρμόττοντα μάλιστα τυγχάνει καὶ πλείστους
ἐπιθυμητὰς ἔχει.

Περὶ μὲν οὖν τούτων οὐκ οἶδ' ὅ τι δεῖ μακρότερα 7
λέγειν· πάντως οὐδὲν γὰρ ἂν πλέον εἰς τὸ παρὸν
ποιήσαιμεν· δέομαι δ' ὑμῶν τῶν λόγων ἴσους καὶ
κοινοὺς ἡμῖν ἐπιστάτας γενέσθαι, καὶ πάντας ἄρχοντας
περὶ τούτων καταστῆναι, καὶ μήτε τοῖς λοιδορουμένοις
μήτε τοῖς ὑπὲρ καιρὸν χαριζομένοις ἐπιτρέπειν, ἀλλὰ
τῷ μὲν ἐθέλοντι λέγειν καὶ ἀκούειν εὐμενεῖς εἶναι, τῷ
δὲ ἀσελγαίνοντι καὶ θορυβοῦντι χαλεπούς. ἀκούσαντες

44 ἡγοῦμαι ζημίαν A : ζημίαν ἡγοῦμαι Q 46 add. Emperius^1 : alia alii 47 ἐνθένδε A^1 : ἐνθάδε A^a Q ἀλλ' re vera AQ 48 διαφθερεῖ Ald. : διαφθείρῃ A : διαφθείρει Q 49 καὶ post μᾶλλον add. Reiske 50 ὑμῶν Steph. : ἡμῶν AQ 51 συνειδότας A^1Q : συνειδότες A^a 53 ὑπὸ Dobree : ἀπὸ AQ 61 οὐδὲν γὰρ AQ : γὰρ οὐδὲν Reiske πλέον Lipsius : πλεῖον AQ 64 μήτε A : μήτι Q 66 ἐθέλοντι Q : θέλοντι A 67 δὲ AQ : δ' Blass^3

γὰρ ἑκάστου τῶν ὑπαρχόντων ἄμεινον βουλεύσεσθε περὶ ἡμῶν.

8 *Ἔστι δὲ περὶ τῆς μισοδημίας καὶ τῆς στασιωτείας βραχύς μοι λόγος καταλελειμμένος. εἰ μὲν γὰρ ἄκριτος ἦν, εἰκότως ἂν τῶν κατηγορούντων ἠκροᾶσθε καὶ ἐμοὶ ἀναγκαῖον ἦν ἀπολογεῖσθαι περὶ τούτων· ἐπειδὴ δὲ τετράκις ἀγωνιζόμενος ἀπέφυγον, οὐκέτι δίκαιον ἡγοῦμαι λόγον οὐδένα περὶ τούτου γίγνεσθαι. πρὶν μὲν γὰρ κριθῆναι οὐ ῥᾴδιον ἦν εἰδέναι τὰς αἰτίας, οὔτ' εἰ ψευδεῖς εἰσιν οὔτ' εἰ ἀληθεῖς· ἀποφυγόντος δὲ ἢ καταγνωσθέντος τέλος ἔχει καὶ διώρισται τούτων ὁπότερόν ἐστιν.* 9 *ὥστε δεινὸν νομίζω τοὺς μὲν ἁλόντας μιᾷ ψήφῳ μόνον ἀποθνῄσκειν, καὶ τὰ χρήματα δημεύεσθαι αὐτῶν, τοὺς δὲ νικήσαντας πάλιν τὰς αὐτὰς κατηγορίας ὑπομένειν, καὶ τοὺς δικαστὰς ἀπολέσαι μὲν κυρίους εἶναι, σῷσαι δ' ἀκύρους καὶ ἀτελεῖς φαίνεσθαι, ἄλλως τε καὶ τῶν νόμων ἀπαγορευόντων δὶς περὶ τῶν αὐτῶν πρὸς τὸν αὐτὸν μὴ ἐξεῖναι δικάζεσθαι, καὶ ὑμῶν ὀμωμοκότων χρήσεσθαι τοῖς νόμοις.*

10 *Ὧν ἕνεκα περὶ ἐμαυτοῦ παραλιπὼν Ἀλκιβιάδου τὸν βίον ἀναμνῆσαι βούλομαι. καίτοι ἀπορῶ γε διὰ τὸ πλῆθος τῶν ἁμαρτημάτων πόθεν ἄρξωμαι, ἐμποδὼν*

10 *ἐμποδὼν* Harp. ε 45.2–3 s.v.

---

68 *ἑκάστου* AQ : *<περὶ> ἑκάστου* Reiske : *ἕκαστον* Maidment *βουλεύσεσθε* A : *βουλεύσασθαι* Q : *βουλεύσασθε* Redondo i Sànchez[2] 70 alt. *τῆς* A : om. Q *στασιωτείας* Steph. : *στασιωτίας* A, et re vera Ald. : *ἀσωτίας* Q 71 *λόγος* A^{c}Q : *λόγος καὶ* A^{a} 72 *ἂν* A : om. Q 73 *τούτων* A : *αὐτῶν* Q 75 *τούτου* AQ^{it} : *τούτων* Q^{1sv} *γίγνεσθαι* A : *γενέσθαι* Q 76 *ἦν* del. Blass 76–7 *ψευδεῖς εἰσιν οὔτ' εἰ ἀληθεῖς* A : *ψευδὴς οὔτ' εἰ ἀληθὴς εἰσὶν* Q 77 *ἀποφυγόντος* Ald. : *ἀποφεύγοντος* AQ 78 *ὥστε* Steph. : *ὡς* AQ 80 *δημεύεσθαι* Muret apud Lipsium : *δημεύειν* AQ : *δημεύειν <ὑμᾶς>* Reiske *τοὺς δὲ νικήσαντας* Muret apud Lipsium : *τῶν δὲ νικησάντων* AQ : *τῶν δὲ νικησάντων <τινὰς>* vel *<ἐνίους>* Dover apud Albinium[5] 84 *τῶν αὐτῶν* Q : *τοῦ αὐτοῦ* A 85 *ὑμῶν* A : *ἡμῶν* Q *ὀμωμοκότων* Steph. : *ὁμωμοκότων* AQ *χρήσεσθαι* Hirschig[1] : *χρῆσθαι* AQ 88 *ἄρξωμαι* maluerit Blass[2] : *ἄρξομαι* AQ

ἁπάντων ὄντων. περὶ μὲν οὖν μοιχείας καὶ γυναικῶν ἀλλοτρίων ἁρπαγῆς καὶ τῆς ἄλλης βιαιότητος καὶ παρανομίας καθ' ἕκαστον εἰ δεήσειε λέγειν, οὐκ ἂν ἐξαρκέσειεν ὁ παρὼν χρόνος, ἅμα δὲ καὶ πολλοῖς ἀπεχθοίμην τῶν πολιτῶν, φανερὰς τὰς συμφορὰς ποιῶν αὐτῶν. ἃ δὲ περὶ τὴν πόλιν εἴργασται καὶ τοὺς προσήκοντας καὶ τῶν ἄλλων ἀστῶν καὶ ξένων τοὺς ἐντυγχάνοντας, ἀποδείξω.

Πρῶτον μὲν οὖν πείσας ὑμᾶς τὸν φόρον ταῖς πόλεσιν 11
ἐξ ἀρχῆς τάξαι τὸν ὑπ' Ἀριστείδου πάντων δικαιότατα
τεταγμένον, αἱρεθεὶς ἐπὶ τούτῳ δέκατος αὐτὸς μάλιστα
διπλάσιον αὐτὸν ἑκάστοις τῶν συμμάχων ἐποίησεν,
ἐπιδείξας δ' αὑτὸν φοβερὸν καὶ μέγα δυνάμενον ἰδίας
ἀπὸ τῶν κοινῶν προσόδους κατεσκευάσατο. σκέψασθε
δὲ πῶς ἄν τις κακὰ μείζω τούτων κατασκευάσειεν, εἰ
τῆς σωτηρίας ἡμῖν πάσης διὰ τῶν συμμάχων οὔσης,
ὁμολογουμένως νῦν κάκιον ἢ πρότερον πραττόντων,
τὸν φόρον ἑκάστοις διπλασιάσειεν. ὥστ' εἴπερ ἡγεῖσθε 12
πολίτην ἀγαθὸν Ἀριστείδην καὶ δίκαιον γεγονέναι,
τοῦτον προσήκει κάκιστον νομίζειν, ὡς τἀναντία περὶ
τῶν πόλεων ἐκείνῳ γιγνώσκοντα. τοιγάρτοι διὰ ταῦτα
πολλοὶ τὴν πατρίδα τὴν αὑτῶν ἀπολιπόντες φυγάδες
γίγνονται καὶ εἰς Θουρίους οἰκήσοντες ἀπέρχονται.

91 δεήσειε Baiter : δεήσει AQ 92 πολλοῖς A : πολλῆς Q 97 ὑμᾶς A : ἡμᾶς Q 98 τὸν Q : τῶν A 99 τούτῳ A^{c}Q : τούτων A^{a} 100 αὐτὸν AQ^{it} : αὐτῶν Q^{sv} ἑκάστοις Blass : ἑκάστω AQ 101 αὑτὸν Ald. : αὐτὸν AQ 102 προσόδους A^{1} : προσόδων fort. A^{a} (υς in ras.) : προδοὺς Q 103 τούτων A : om. Q κατασκευάσειεν A^{1}Q : παρασκευάσειεν A^{a} εἰ AQ : <ἢ> εἰ Meier 106 ἑκάστοις Turr. : ἑκάστης AQ : ἑκάστῳ Schiller διπλασιάσειεν Q : διπλάσειεν A : ἐδίπλασεν Blass 107 πολίτην ἀγαθὸν ἀριστείδην A : ἀριστείδην πολίτην ἀγαθὸν Q 108–9 περὶ τῶν πόλεων A : om. Q 109–10 διὰ ταῦτα πολλοὶ A : πολλοὶ διὰ ταῦτα Q 110 αὑτῶν Steph. : αὐτῶν A : ἑαυτῶν Q ἀπολιπόντες A : καταλιπόντες Q 111 οἰκήσοντες ἀπέρχονται A : ἀπέρχονται οἰκήσοντες Q

δηλώσει δὲ ἡ τῶν συμμάχων ἔχθρα, ὅταν πρῶτον ἡμῖν καὶ Λακεδαιμονίοις γένηται ναυτικὸς πόλεμος. ἐγὼ δὲ νομίζω τὸν τοιοῦτον πονηρὸν εἶναι προστάτην, ὅστις τοῦ παρόντος χρόνου ἐπιμελεῖται, ἀλλὰ μὴ καὶ τοῦ μέλλοντος προνοεῖται, καὶ τὰ ἥδιστα τῷ πλήθει, παραλιπὼν τὰ βέλτιστα, συμβουλεύει.

13 Θαυμάζω δὲ τῶν πεπεισμένων Ἀλκιβιάδην δημοκρατίας ἐπιθυμεῖν, τοιαύτης πολιτείας ἣ μάλιστα κοινότητα δοκεῖ ᾑρῆσθαι, οἳ οὐδ᾽ ἀπὸ τῶν ἰδίων αὐτὸν θεῶνται, ὁρῶντες τὴν πλεονεξίαν καὶ τὴν ὑπερηφανίαν, ὃς τὴν Καλλίου γήμας ἀδελφὴν ἐπὶ δέκα ταλάντοις, τελευτήσαντος Ἱππονίκου στρατηγοῦντος ἐπὶ Δηλίῳ ἕτερα τοσαῦτα προσεπράξατο, λέγων ὡς ὡμολόγησεν ἐκεῖνος, ὁπότε παῖς αὐτῷ ἐκ τῆς θυγατρὸς γένοιτο, προσθήσειν
14 ταῦτα. λαβὼν δὲ τοσαύτην προῖκα, ὅσην οὐδεὶς τῶν Ἑλλήνων, οὕτως ὑβριστὴς ἦν, ἐπεισάγων εἰς τὴν αὐτὴν οἰκίαν ἑταίρας, καὶ δούλας καὶ ἐλευθέρας, ὥστ᾽ ἠνάγκασε τὴν γυναῖκα σωφρονεστάτην οὖσαν ἀπολιπεῖν, ἐλθοῦσαν πρὸς τὸν ἄρχοντα κατὰ τὸν νόμον. οὗ δὴ μάλιστα τὴν αὑτοῦ δύναμιν ἐπεδείξατο· παρακαλέσας γὰρ τοὺς ἑταίρους, ἁρπάσας ἐκ τῆς ἀγορᾶς τὴν γυναῖκα ᾤχετο βίᾳ, καὶ πᾶσιν ἐδήλωσε καὶ τῶν ἀρχόντων καὶ τῶν νόμων
15 καὶ τῶν ἄλλων πολιτῶν καταφρονῶν. οὐ τοίνυν ταῦτα μόνον ἐξήρκεσεν, ἀλλὰ καὶ λαθραῖον θάνατον ἐπεβούλευσε Καλλίᾳ, ἵνα τὸν οἶκον τὸν Ἱππονίκου κατάσχοι,

112 *ὅταν πρῶτον* Reiske viii. 462 : *πρῶτον ὅταν* AQ 115 *χρόνου* A : *χρόνον* Q : *χρόνου* <*μόνον*> Blass : <*μόνον*> *χρόνου* Hertlein[2] 118 *ἀλκιβιάδην* A : *ἀλκιβιάδη* Q 119 *τοιαύτης πολιτείας* in ras. A[1] : *τοιαύτας πολιτείας* Q *ἣ μάλιστα* A : *ἣ μάλλιστα* Q 120 *ᾑρῆσθαι* Valckenaer : *εὑρῆσθαι* AQ 125 *αὐτῷ* del. Blass[3] *θυγατρὸς* A : *θυγατρὸς αὐτοῦ* Q 126 *λαβὼν* A : *παραλαβὼν* Q 131 *αὑτοῦ* Steph. : *αὐτοῦ* AQ *παρακαλέσας* A : *παρεκαλέσας* Q 132 *τὴν γυναῖκα, ᾤχετο* A : *ᾤχετο τὴν γυναῖκα* Q 135–6 *ἐπεβούλευσε καλλία* A : *καλλία ἐπεβούλευσε* Q 136 alt. *τὸν* A : *τοῦ* Q

ὡς ἐναντίον πάντων ὑμῶν ἐν τῇ ἐκκλησίᾳ κατηγόρει·
καὶ τὰ χρήματα τῷ δήμῳ ἔδωκεν, εἴ πως τελευτήσειεν
ἄπαις, φοβούμενος μὴ διὰ τὴν οὐσίαν ἀπόλοιτο. καίτοι
ὅστις ὑβρίζει γυναῖκα τὴν ἑαυτοῦ καὶ τῷ κηδεστῇ
θάνατον ἐπιβουλεύει, τί χρὴ προσδοκᾶν τοῦτον περὶ
τοὺς ἐντυχόντας τῶν πολιτῶν διαπράττεσθαι; πάντες
γὰρ ἄνθρωποι τοὺς οἰκείους τῶν ἀλλοτρίων ποιοῦνται
περὶ πλείονος. ἀλλὰ μὴν οὐδ' ἔρημος οὐδ' εὐαδίκητός ἐστιν,
ἐπεὶ διὰ τὸν πλοῦτον ἔχει πολλοὺς τοὺς βοηθήσοντας.
Ὃ δὲ πάντων δεινότατόν ἐστι, τοιοῦτος ὢν ὡς 16
εὔνους τῷ δήμῳ τοὺς λόγους ποιεῖται αὐτός, ἄλλους
δὲ ὀλιγαρχικοὺς καὶ μισοδήμους ἀποκαλεῖ. καὶ ὃν
ἔδει τεθνάναι διὰ τὰ ἐπιτηδεύματα, κατήγορος τῶν
διαβεβλημένων ὑφ' ὑμῶν αἱρεῖται, καί φησι φύλαξ
εἶναι τῆς πολιτείας, οὐδενὶ τῶν ἄλλων Ἀθηναίων οὔτ'
ἴσον οὔτ' ὀλίγῳ πλέον ἀξιῶν ἔχειν· ἀλλ' οὕτω σφόδρα
καταπεφρόνηκεν, ὥστε διατετέλεκεν ἁθρόους μὲν ὑμᾶς
κολακεύων, ἕνα δ' ἕκαστον προπηλακίζων. ὃς εἰς 17
τοσοῦτον ἐλήλυθε τόλμης, ὥστε πείσας Ἀγάθαρχον τὸν
γραφέα συνεισελθεῖν οἴκαδε τὴν οἰκίαν ἐπηνάγκασε
γράφειν, δεομένου δὲ καὶ προφάσεις ἀληθεῖς λέγοντος,
ὡς οὐκ ἂν δύναιτο ταῦτα πράττειν ἤδη διὰ τὸ συγγραφὰς
ἔχειν παρ' ἑτέρων, προεῖπεν αὐτῷ δήσειν, εἰ μὴ πάνυ

137 ἐναντίον Q : ἐναντίων A κατηγόρει Steph. : κατηγορεῖ AQ 139 μὴ διὰ AQ[2] : μὴ δὴ ut vid. Q οὐσίαν A : ἀπουσίαν Q 141 προσδοκᾶν A : προδοκᾶν Q 144–5 ἀλλὰ … βοηθήσοντας post ἀπόλοιτο l. 139 transponi maluit Fuhr : ἔρημος <ἐκεῖνος> Blass 147 αὐτός, ἄλλους δὲ scripsi : αὐτὸς ἄλλους AQ : αὐτός, τοὺς δὲ Sauppe : καὶ τοὺς ἄλλους Dobree 149 ἔδει Dobree : δεῖ AQ 150 ὑμῶν Emperius[3] : ἡμῶν AQ 152 ἔχειν A : ἐχει Q 153 ὥστε διατετέλεκεν] ὥστε δια in ras. A[1] ἁθρόους Lipsius : ἀθρόους AQ 155–6 τὸν γραφέα A : om. Q 156 οἴκαδε del. Hirschig[1] : τὴν οἰκίαν del. Steph. 158 συγγραφὰς AQ[1] : συγγραφὴς Q[a] 159 ἔχειν παρ' ἑτέρων A : παρ' ἑτέρων ἔχειν Q : παρ' ἑτέροις ἔχειν Dobree

ταχέως γράφοι. ὅπερ ἐποίησε· καὶ οὐ πρότερον ἀπηλλάγη,
πρὶν ἀποδρὰς ᾤχετο τετάρτῳ μηνί, τοὺς φύλακας
λαθών, ὥσπερ παρὰ βασιλέως. οὕτω δ' ἀναίσχυντός
ἐστιν, ὥστε προσελθὼν ἐνεκάλει αὐτῷ ὡς ἀδικούμενος,
καὶ οὐχ ὧν ἐβιάσατο μετέμελεν αὐτῷ, ἀλλ' ὅτι κατέλιπε
τὸ ἔργον ἠπείλει, καὶ οὔτε τῆς δημοκρατίας οὔτε τῆς
ἐλευθερίας οὐδὲν ἦν ὄφελος· οὐδὲν γὰρ ἧττον ἐδεδέκει
18 τῶν ὁμολογουμένων δούλων. ἀγανακτῶ δ' ἐνθυμούμενος
ὑμῖν μὲν οὐδὲ τοὺς κακούργους ἀσφαλὲς εἰς τὸ δεσμω-
τήριον ὂν ἀπάγειν, διὰ τὸ χιλίας δραχμὰς τετάχθαι
ἀποτεῖσαι ὃς ἂν τὸ πέμπτον μέρος μὴ μεταλάβῃ τῶν
ψήφων· ὁ δὲ τοσοῦτον χρόνον εἵρξας καὶ ἐπαναγκάζων
γράφειν οὐδὲν κακόν πέπονθεν, ἀλλὰ διὰ ταῦτα
σεμνότερος δοκεῖ καὶ φοβερώτερος εἶναι. καὶ πρὸς μὲν
τὰς ἄλλας πόλεις ἐν τοῖς συμβόλοις συντιθέμεθα μὴ
ἐξεῖναι μήθ' εἶρξαι μήτε δῆσαι τὸν ἐλεύθερον· ἐὰν δέ τις
παραβῇ, μεγάλην ζημίαν ἐπὶ τούτοις ἔθεμεν· τούτου
δὲ τοιαῦτα πράξαντος οὐδεμίαν οὐδεὶς οὔτ' ἰδίαν οὔτε
19 δημοσίαν τιμωρίαν ποιεῖται. νομίζω δὲ ταύτην εἶναι
σωτηρίαν ἅπασι, πείθεσθαι τοῖς ἄρχουσι καὶ τοῖς νόμοις·
ὅστις δὲ ὑπερορᾷ ταῦτα, τὴν μεγίστην φυλακὴν ἀνῄρηκε
τῆς πόλεως. δεινὸν μὲν οὖν ἐστι καὶ ὑπὸ τῶν ἀγνοούντων
τὰ δίκαια πάσχειν κακῶς, πολὺ δὲ χαλεπώτερον, ὅταν
τις ἐπιστάμενος τὰ διαφέροντα παραβαίνειν τολμᾷ·
φανερῶς γὰρ ἐνδείκνυται, ὥσπερ οὗτος, οὐκ αὐτὸς τοῖς

160 γράφοι A[1] Q : γράφει A[a] 162 ὥσπερ παρὰ βασιλέως] secludenda susp. Albini[4] ὥσπερ A : ὡς Q 163 προσελθὼν A : προελθὼν Q 166 pr. οὐδὲν A : om. Q ἐδεδέκει Emperius[1] : ἐδεδοίκει AQ 168 μὲν A[1] : om. A[a]Q εἰς τὸ δεσμωτήριον ὂν A : ὂν εἰς τὸ δεσμωτήριον Q 169 χιλίας A : χιλλίας Q 170 ἀποτεῖσαι Blass[2] : ἀποτίσαι AQ 174 συμβόλοις A : συμβούλοις Q 178–9 ναι σωτηρίαν ἅπασι πείθεσθαι artiore spatio A[1] 180–1 ἀνήρηκε τῆς πόλεως A[c] (ἀνήρηκεν A[a]) : τῆς πόλεως ἀνῄρηκεν Q 184 φανερῶς Q : φανερὸς A

νόμοις τῆς πόλεως, ἀλλ' ὑμᾶς τοῖς αὑτοῦ τρόποις
ἀκολουθεῖν ἀξιῶν.
Ἐνθυμήθητε δὲ Ταυρέαν, ὃς ἀντιχορηγὸς ἦν Ἀλκιβιάδῃ 20
παισί. κελεύοντος δὲ τοῦ νόμου τῶν χορευτῶν ἐξάγειν
ὃν ἄν τις βούληται ξένον ἀγωνιζόμενον, οὐκ ἐξὸν
ἐπιχειρήσαντα κωλύειν, ἐναντίον ὑμῶν καὶ τῶν ἄλλων
Ἑλλήνων τῶν θεωρούντων καὶ τῶν ἀρχόντων ἁπάντων
παρόντων ἐν τῇ πόλει τύπτων ἐξήλασεν αὐτόν, καὶ τῶν
θεατῶν συμφιλονικούντων ἐκείνῳ καὶ μισούντων τοῦτον,
ὥστε τῶν χορῶν τὸν μὲν ἐπαινούντων, τοῦ δ' ἀκροάσασθαι
οὐκ ἐθελόντων, οὐδὲν πλέον ἔπραξεν· ἀλλὰ τῶν κριτῶν οἱ 21
μὲν φοβούμενοι οἱ δὲ χαριζόμενοι νικᾶν ἔκριναν αὐτόν,
περὶ ἐλάττονος ποιούμενοι τὸν ὅρκον ἢ τοῦτον. εἰκότως
δέ μοι δοκοῦσιν οἱ κριταὶ ὑπέρχεσθαι Ἀλκιβιάδην,
ὁρῶντες Ταυρέαν μὲν τοσαῦτα χρήματα ἀναλώσαντα
προπηλακιζόμενον, τὸν δὲ τοιαῦτα παρανομοῦντα
μέγιστον δυνάμενον. αἴτιοι δ' ὑμεῖς, οὐ τιμωρούμενοι τοὺς
ὑβρίζοντας, καὶ τοὺς μὲν λάθρα ἀδικοῦντας κολάζοντες,
τοὺς δὲ φανερῶς ἀσελγαίνοντας θαυμάζοντες. τοιγάρτοι 22
τῶν νέων αἱ διατριβαὶ οὐκ ἐν τοῖς γυμνασίοις, ἀλλ' ἐν
τοῖς δικαστηρίοις εἰσί, καὶ στρατεύονται μὲν οἱ
πρεσβύτεροι, δημηγοροῦσι δὲ οἱ νεώτεροι, παραδείγματι
τούτῳ χρώμενοι, ὃς τηλικαύτας ποιεῖται τῶν
ἁμαρτημάτων ὑπερβολάς, ὥστε περὶ τῶν Μηλίων γνώμην
ἀποφηνάμενος ἐξανδραποδίζεσθαι, πριάμενος γυναῖκα

185 τῆς re vera Q : τοῖς A αὑτοῦ Turr. : αὐτοῦ AQ 187 Ἀλκιβιάδῃ A : Ἀλκιβιάδου Q 188 δὲ AQ : γὰρ Richards[1] 189 ξένον ἀγωνιζόμενον, οὐκ sic distinxit A (colon posuit Q) : ξένον, ἀγωνιζόμενον οὐκ Turr. 192 παρόντων ἐν τῇ πόλει A : ἐν τῇ πόλει παρόντων Q : παρόντων {ἐν τῇ πόλει} Albini[3] : τῶν ἐν τῇ πόλει Blass 193 συμφιλονικούντων B : συμφιλονεικούντων AQ 195 πλέον M : πλεῖον AQ 199 μὲν τοσαῦτα Q : τοσαῦτα μὲν A 201 ὑμεῖς A : ἡμεῖς Q 202 λάθρα AQ : λάθρᾳ Turr. 208 περὶ A: περί τε Q 209 ἐξανδραποδίζεσθαι A : ἐξανδραποδίσασθαι Q

τῶν αἰχμαλώτων υἱὸν ἐξ αὐτῆς πεποίηται, ὃς τοσούτῳ παρανομωτέρως Αἰγίσθου γέγονεν, ὥστ' ἐκ τῶν ἐχθίστων ἀλλήλοις πέφυκε, καὶ τῶν οἰκειοτάτων ὑπάρχει αὐτῷ τὰ ἔσχατα τοὺς μὲν πεποιηκέναι τοὺς δὲ πεπονθέναι.

23 ἄξιον δὲ τὴν τόλμαν αὐτοῦ σαφέστερον ἔτι διελθεῖν. ἐκ ταύτης γὰρ παιδοποιεῖται τῆς γυναικός, ἣν ἀντ' ἐλευθέρας δούλην κατέστησε, καὶ ἧς τὸν πατέρα καὶ τοὺς προσήκοντας ἀπέκτεινε, καὶ ἧς τὴν πόλιν ἀνάστατον πεποίηκεν, ὡς ἂν μάλιστα τὸν υἱὸν ἐχθρὸν ἑαυτῷ καὶ τῇ πόλει ποιήσειε· τοσαύταις ἀνάγκαις κατείληπται μισεῖν. ἀλλ' ὑμεῖς ἐν μὲν ταῖς τραγῳδίαις τοιαῦτα θεωροῦντες δεινὰ νομίζετε, γιγνόμενα δ' ἐν τῇ πόλει ὁρῶντες οὐδὲν φροντίζετε. καίτοι ἐκεῖνα μὲν οὐκ ἐπίστασθε πότερον οὕτω γεγένηται ἢ πέπλασται ὑπὸ τῶν ποιητῶν· ταῦτα δὲ σαφῶς εἰδότες οὕτω παρανόμως πεπραγμένα, ῥαθύμως φέρετε.

24 *Πρὸς* δὲ τούτοις τολμῶσί τινες περὶ αὐτοῦ λέγειν, ὡς οὐδὲ γεγένηται οὐδεὶς πώποτε τοιοῦτος. ἐγὼ δὲ νομίζω μέγιστα κακὰ τὴν πόλιν ὑπὸ τούτου πείσεσθαι, καὶ τηλικούτων πραγμάτων εἰς τὸν λοιπὸν χρόνον αἴτιον δόξειν, ὥστε μηδένα τῶν προτέρων ἀδικημάτων μεμνῆσθαι· ἀνέλπιστον γὰρ οὐδέν, τὸν τὴν ἀρχὴν τοῦ βίου τοιαύτην κατασκευασάμενον καὶ τὴν τελευτὴν ὑπερβάλλουσαν ποιήσασθαι. ἔστι δὲ σωφρόνων ἀνδρῶν φυλάττεσθαι τῶν πολιτῶν τοὺς ὑπεραυξανομένους, ἐνθυμουμένους ὑπὸ τῶν τοιούτων τὰς τυραννίδας καθισταμένας.

211 *παρανομωτέρως* Reiske : *παρανομώτατος* A : *παραναμομώτερος* Q 215 *γὰρ* A : *δὲ* Q 217 *ἧς* A^1Q : om. A^a, susp. Blass^3, del. Dalmeyda 220 *μὲν* A^1Q : om. A^a 221 *οὐδὲν* A^1Q : *οὐδὲ* A^a 224 *παρανόμως πεπραγμένα* Q : *πεπραγμένα παρανόμως* A *ῥαθύμως* Q (cf. Wackernagel 1907, 26 = Kl. Schr., ii. 1057) : *ῥᾳθύμως* A 232 *κατασκευασάμενον* A^1Q : *παρασκευασάμενον* A^a 233 *ποιήσασθαι* AQ : *ποιήσεσθαι* maluit Baiter : *ἂν ποιήσασθαι* Sluiter

Ἡγοῦμαι δ᾽ αὐτὸν πρὸς ταῦτα μὲν οὐδὲν ἀντερεῖν, 25
λέξειν δὲ περὶ τῆς νίκης τῆς Ὀλυμπίασι, καὶ περὶ πάντων
μᾶλλον ἢ τῶν κατηγορηθέντων ἀπολογήσεσθαι. ἐξ
αὐτῶν δὲ τούτων ἐπιδείξω αὐτὸν ἐπιτηδειότερον τεθνάναι
μᾶλλον ἢ σῴζεσθαι. διηγήσομαι δ᾽ ὑμῖν. Διομήδης ἦλθε 26
ζεῦγος ἵππων ἄγων Ὀλυμπίαζε, κεκτημένος μὲν οὐσίαν
μετρίαν, στεφανῶσαι δὲ ἀπὸ τῶν ὑπαρχόντων τὴν πόλιν
καὶ τὴν οἰκίαν βουλόμενος, λογιζόμενος τοὺς ἀγῶνας
τοὺς ἱππικοὺς τύχῃ τοὺς πλείστους κρινομένους. τοῦτον
Ἀλκιβιάδης πολίτην ὄντα καὶ ⟨οὐ⟩ τὸν ἐπιτυχόντα,
δυνάμενος παρὰ τοῖς ἀγωνοθέταις τῶν Ἠλείων, ⟨τὸ
ζεῦγος⟩ ἀφελόμενος αὐτὸς ἠγωνίζετο. καίτοι τί ἂν
ἐποίησεν, εἴ τις τῶν συμμάχων τῶν ὑμετέρων ἀφίκετο
ζεῦγος ἵππων ἔχων; ἦ που ταχέως ἂν ἐπέτρεψεν 27
ἀνταγωνίζεσθαι ἑαυτῷ, ὃς Ἀθηναῖον ἄνδρα βιασάμενος
τοῖς ἀλλοτρίοις ἐτόλμησεν ἵπποις ἁμιλλᾶσθαι, δηλώσας
τοῖς Ἕλλησι μηδὲν θαυμάζειν ἄν τινα αὐτῶν βιάσηται,
ἐπεὶ καὶ τοῖς πολίταις οὐκ ἐξ ἴσου χρῆται, ἀλλὰ τοὺς μὲν
ἀφαιρούμενος, τοὺς δὲ τύπτων, τοὺς δὲ εἱργνύων, τοὺς
δὲ χρήματα πραττόμενος, οὐδενὸς ἀξίαν τὴν δημοκρατίαν
ἀποφαίνει, τοὺς μὲν λόγους δημαγωγοῦ τὰ δ᾽ ἔργα
τυράννου παρέχων, καταμαθὼν ὑμᾶς τοῦ μὲν ὀνόματος
φροντίζοντας, τοῦ δὲ πράγματος ἀμελοῦντας. τοσοῦτον 28
δὲ διαφέρει Λακεδαιμονίων ὥστ᾽ ἐκεῖνοι μὲν καὶ ὑπὸ

236 ταῦτα Meier : τοῦτο AQ 237 τῆς Ὀλυμπίασι Turr. : τῆς ὀλυμπιάσι A : τοῖς ὀλυμπιᾶσι Q 238 ἀπολογήσεσθαι Ald. : ἀπολογήσασθαι AQ 239 ἐπιτηδειότερον A : om. Q 244 τύχῃ AQ : τέχνῃ Schiller 245 add. Steph. 246–7 <τὸ ζεῦγος> ἀφελόμενος Reiske (ζεῦγος ante δυνάμενος posuerat Scaliger) : ἀφελόμενος AQ : ἀφελόμενος <τὰς ἵππους> Hirschig[1] 248 ὑμετέρων A : ἡμετέρων Q 249 ἂν ἐπέστρεψεν (sic) Q : ἐπέτρεψεν ἂν A 250 ἑαυτῷ A[1]Q : αὐτὸν A[a] Ἀθηναῖον Q : Ἀθηναίων A βιασάμενος A : βιασάμενον Q 251 ἐτόλμησεν ἵπποις A : ἵπποις ἐτόλμησεν Q 253 ἐπεὶ A[c]Q : ἐπειδὴ A[a] 256 ἀποφαίνει Reiske : ἀποφαίνων AQ 257–8 τοῦ μὲν … τοῦ δὲ A : τοὺς μὲν … τοὺς δὲ Q 258 τοσοῦτον A : τοσούτῳ Q

τῶν συμμάχων ἀνταγωνιζομένων ἀνέχονται ἡττώμενοι, οὗτος δὲ οὐδ' ὑπὸ τῶν πολιτῶν, ἀλλὰ φανερῶς εἴρηκεν οὐκ ἐπιτρέψειν τοῖς ἀντεπιθυμοῦσί τινος. εἶτ' ἐκ τῶν τοιούτων ἀναγκαῖον τὰς πόλεις τῶν ἡμετέρων πολεμίων

29 *ἐπιθυμεῖν, ἡμᾶς δὲ μισεῖν. ἵνα δὲ μὴ μόνον Διομήδην, ἀλλὰ καὶ τὴν πόλιν ὅλην ὑβρίζων ἐπιδείξειε, τὰ πομπεῖα παρὰ τῶν ἀρχιθεώρων αἰτησάμενος, ὡς εἰς τἀπινίκια τῇ προτεραίᾳ τῆς θυσίας χρησόμενος, ἐξηπάτησε καὶ ἀποδοῦναι οὐκ ἤθελε, βουλόμενος τῇ ὑστεραίᾳ πρότερος τῆς πόλεως χρήσασθαι τοῖς χρυσοῖς χερνιβίοις καὶ θυμιατηρίοις. ὅσοι μὲν οὖν τῶν ξένων μὴ ἐγίγνωσκον ἡμέτερα ὄντα, τὴν πομπὴν τὴν κοινὴν ὁρῶντες ὑστέραν οὖσαν τῆς Ἀλκιβιάδου τοῖς τούτου πομπείοις χρῆσθαι ἐνόμιζον ἡμᾶς· ὅσοι δὲ ἢ παρὰ τῶν πολιτῶν ἤκουον ἢ καὶ ἐπεγίγνωσκον τὰ τούτου, κατεγέλων ἡμῶν, ὁρῶντες ἕνα ἄνδρα μεῖζον ἁπάσης τῆς πόλεως δυνάμενον.*

30 *Σκέψασθε δὲ καὶ τὴν ἄλλην ἀποδημίαν τὴν εἰς Ὀλυμπίαν ὡς διέθετο. τούτῳ σκηνὴν μὲν Περσικὴν Ἐφέσιοι διπλασίαν τῆς δημοσίας ἔπηξαν, ἱερεῖα δὲ καὶ τοῖς ἵπποις ἐφόδια Χῖοι παρεσκεύασαν, οἶνον δὲ καὶ τὰ ἄλλα ἀναλώματα Λεσβίοις προσέταξε. καὶ οὕτως*

29 *τοῖς—θυμιατηρίοις* Ath. *Deipn.* 9.75 408C, ac stp Eust. ad H. *Od.* 1.37 (1.34.29 Stallbaum), qui ambo Lysiae locum attribuunt (*ἐν τῷ κατὰ Ἀλκιβιάδου* Ath.)

---

260 *ἀνταγωνιζομένων* A : *ἀγωνιζομένων* Q 261 *εἴρηκεν* A : *εἴρηκε* Q 262 *οὐκ ἐπιτρέψειν* A : om. Q 264 *διομήδην* AQ : *Διομήδη* Schiller 265 *ὑβρίζων* A : *ὑβρίζειν* Q *ἐπιδείξειε* Emperius[1] : *ἐπιδόξειε* AQ : *ἐπιδείξαιτο* Reiske : *ἔτι δόξειε* Albini[5] 266 *τἀπινίκια* v. Meurs : *τὰ πινάκια* AQ 267 *προτεραίᾳ* Pierson : *προτέρα* AQ *θυσίας* Scaliger : *οὐσίας* AQ *ἐξηπάτησε* A : om. Q 269 *χερνιβίοις* Taylor ex Athenaeo : *χερνιβείοις* Blass[3] : *χερνίβοις* Q : *χερν*ίβοις* A[c] 272 *τῆς ἀλκιβιάδου* QL[csv] : *τοῖς ἀλκιβιάδου* A *πομπείοις* Q : *πομπίοις* A 273 *ἡμᾶς* AQ : *ὑμᾶς* Q[1sv] 274 *ἡμῶν* A : *ὑμῶν* Q 275 *μεῖζον ἁπάσης* Sluiter : *μείζονα πάσης* AQ 276 *εἰς* A : *εἰς τὴν* Q 277 *διέθετο. τούτῳ* sic interpunxit Reiske : *διέθετο τούτῳ* Steph. : *διέθετο τοῦτο* A : *διετίθετο τοῦτο* Q

εὐτυχής ἐστιν ὥστε τοὺς Ἕλληνας τῆς παρανομίας καὶ
τῆς δωροδοκίας μάρτυρας κεκτημένος οὐδεμίαν δέδωκε
δίκην, ἀλλὰ ὁπόσοι μὲν ἄρχοντες ἐν μιᾷ πόλει γεγένηνται,
ὑπεύθυνοί εἰσιν, ὁ δὲ πάντων τῶν συμμάχων καὶ 31
χρήματα λαμβάνων οὐδενὸς τούτων ὑπόδικός ἐστιν,
ἀλλὰ τοιαῦτα διαπεπραγμένος σίτησιν ἐν Πρυτανείῳ
ἔλαβε, καὶ προσέτι πολλῇ τῇ νίκῃ χρῆται, ὥσπερ οὐ
πολὺ μᾶλλον ἠτιμακὼς ἢ ἐστεφανωκὼς τὴν πόλιν. εἰ
δὲ βούλεσθε σκοπεῖν, εὑρήσετε τῶν πολλάκις τούτῳ
πεπραγμένων ἕκαστον ὀλίγον χρόνον πράξαντάς τινας
ἀναστάτους τοὺς οἴκους ποιήσαντας· οὗτος δ'
ἐπιτηδεύων ἅπαντα πολυτελέστατα διπλασίαν οὐσίαν
κέκτηται. καίτοι ὑμεῖς γε νομίζετε τοὺς φειδομένους 32
καὶ τοὺς ἀκριβῶς διαιτωμένους φιλοχρημάτους εἶναι,
οὐκ ὀρθῶς γιγνώσκοντες· οἱ γὰρ μεγάλα δαπανώμενοι
πολλῶν δεόμενοι αἰσχροκερδέστατοί εἰσιν. αἴσχιστον
δὲ φανήσεσθε ποιοῦντες, εἰ τοῦτον μὲν ἀγαπᾶτε τὸν ἀπὸ
τῶν ὑμετέρων χρημάτων ταῦτα κατεργασάμενον,
Καλλίαν δὲ τὸν Διδυμίου, τῷ σώματι νικήσαντα πάντας
τοὺς στεφανηφόρους ἀγῶνας, ἐξωστρακίσατε πρὸς
τοῦτο οὐδὲν ἀποβλέψαντες, ὃς ἀπὸ τῶν ἑαυτοῦ πόνων
ἐτίμησε τὴν πόλιν. ἀναμνήσθητε δὲ καὶ τοὺς προγόνους, 33
ὡς ἀγαθοὶ καὶ σώφρονες ἦσαν, οἵτινες ἐξωστράκισαν
Κίμωνα διὰ παρανομίαν, ὅτι τῇ ἀδελφῇ τῇ ἑαυτοῦ
συνῴκησε. καίτοι οὐ μόνον αὐτὸς ὀλυμπιονίκης ἦν,
ἀλλὰ καὶ ὁ πατὴρ αὐτοῦ Μιλτιάδης. ἀλλ' ὅμως οὐδὲν

284 συμμάχων καὶ A : συμμάχων Q : συμμάχων <ἄρχων> καὶ Meier 289 τῶν πολλάκις τούτῳ Lipsius : πολλὰ τῶν τούτω AQ 292 πολυτελέστατα Q : πολιτελέστατα A 293 ὑμεῖς A : ἡμεῖς Q 298 ὑμετέρων A : ἡμετέρων Q ταῦτα AQ : τοιαῦτα dubitanter Dalmeyda κατεργασάμενον A : κατεργασμένον Q 300 τοὺς στεφανηφόρους ἀγῶνας Q : ἀγῶνας τοὺς στεφανηφόρους A[1] : ἀγῶνας στεφανηφόρους A[a] 301 τοῦτο Steph. : τοῦτον AQ ὃς AQ : ὡς B 305 οὐ μόνον A : μὴ μόνος Q

ὑπελογίζοντο τὰς νίκας· οὐ γὰρ ἐκ τῶν ἀγώνων, ἀλλ᾽ ἐκ τῶν ἐπιτηδευμάτων ἔκρινον αὐτόν.

34 Ἀλλὰ μὴν εἰ δεῖ κατὰ γένος σκοπεῖν, ἐμοὶ μὲν οὐδαμόθεν προσήκει τούτου τοῦ πράγματος (οὐδὲ ἔστιν οὐδεὶς ὅστις ἂν ἀποδείξειε τῶν ἡμετέρων οὐδένα τῇ συμφορᾷ ταύτῃ χρησάμενον), Ἀλκιβιάδῃ δὲ μάλιστα πάντων Ἀθηναίων. καὶ γὰρ ὁ τῆς μητρὸς πατὴρ Μεγακλῆς καὶ ὁ πάππος Ἀλκιβιάδης ἐξωστρακίσθησαν ἀμφότεροι, ὥστ᾽ οὐδὲν θαυμαστὸν οὐδ᾽ ἄτοπον πείσεται τῶν αὐτῶν τοῖς προγόνοις ἀξιούμενος. καὶ μὴν οὐδ᾽ ἂν αὐτὸς ἐπιχειρήσειεν ἀντειπεῖν, ὡς οὐ τῶν ἄλλων ἐκεῖνοι παρανομώτατοι ὄντες τούτου σωφρονέστεροι καὶ δικαιότεροι ἦσαν, ἐπεὶ τῶν γε τούτῳ πεπραγμένων οὐδ᾽ ἂν εἷς ἀξίως κατηγορῆσαι δύναιτο.

35 Νομίζω δὲ καὶ τὸν θέντα τὸν νόμον ταύτην τὴν διάνοιαν ἔχειν· ἀποβλέψαντα τῶν πολιτῶν πρὸς τοὺς κρείττους τῶν ἀρχόντων καὶ τῶν νόμων, ἐπειδὴ παρὰ τῶν τοιούτων οὐκ ἔστιν ἰδίᾳ δίκην λαβεῖν, δημοσίαν τιμωρίαν ὑπὲρ τῶν ἀδικουμένων κατασκευάσαι. ἐγὼ τοίνυν ἔν τε τῷ κοινῷ κέκριμαι τετράκις, ἰδίᾳ τε οὐδένα διεκώλυσα δικάζεσθαι βουλόμενον· Ἀλκιβιάδης δὲ τοιαῦτα ἐργασάμενος
36 οὐδεμίαν πώποτε δίκην ὑποσχεῖν ἐτόλμησεν. οὕτω γὰρ χαλεπός ἐστιν, ὥστε οὐ περὶ τῶν παρεληλυθότων ἀδικημάτων αὐτὸν τιμωροῦνται, ἀλλ᾽ ὑπὲρ τῶν μελλόντων φοβοῦνται, καὶ τοῖς μὲν πεπονθόσι κακῶς ἀνέχεσθαι

307 ὑπελογίζοντο A : ὑπολογίζοντο Q   308 ἔκρινον A : ἔκριναν Q   310 τούτου A : τοῦδε Q   312 Ἀλκιβιάδῃ Valckenaer : ἀλκιβιάδης A : ἀλκιβιάδην Q   314 <δὶς> ἐξωστρακίσθησαν add. Markland ex Lys. 14.39 et Harp. α 75.3–4 s.v. Ἀλκιβιάδης   316 μὴν A : μηδὲν Q   318 παρανομώτατοι AQ : παρανομώτεροι Steph.   318–19 καὶ δικαιότεροι A : om. Q   322 κρείττους A : κρείττονας Q   324 ἰδίᾳ A^cQ : ἰδίαν A^a 325 κατασκευάσαι] κατ in ras. A^1 ἐγὼ <μὲν> Bekker   327 ἐργασάμενος A : εἰργασμένος Q   328 ἐτόλμησεν A : ἐτόλμησε Q   330 αὐτὸν A^1Q : αὐτῶν ut vid. A^a

λυσιτελεῖ, τούτῳ δὲ οὐκ ἐξαρκεῖ, εἰ μὴ καὶ τὸ λοιπὸν ὅ τι
ἂν βούληται διαπράξεται. καίτοι οὐ δήπου, ὦ Ἀθηναῖοι,
ὀστρακισθῆναι μὲν ἐπιτήδειός εἰμι, τεθνάναι δὲ οὐκ
ἄξιος, οὐδὲ κρινόμενος μὲν ἀποφυγεῖν, ἄκριτος δὲ φεύγειν·
ὁ δὲ τοσαυτάκις ἀγωνιζόμενος δικαίως καὶ νικήσας πάλιν
δόξαιμι δι᾿ ἐκεῖνα ἐκπεσεῖν; ἀλλὰ γὰρ ἴσως μετὰ μικρᾶς 37
διαβολῆς ἢ φαύλων κατηγόρων ἢ διὰ τῶν ἐπιτυχόντων
ἐχθρῶν ἐκινδύνευον, ἀλλ᾿ οὐ διὰ τῶν ἐρρωμενεστάτων
καὶ λέγειν καὶ πράττειν, οἵτινες δύο τῶν τὴν αὐτὴν αἰτίαν
ἐχόντων ἐμοὶ ἀπέκτειναν. οὔκουν τοὺς τοιούτους δίκαιον
ἐκβάλλειν, οὓς πολλάκις ἐλέγχοντες εὑρίσκετε μηδὲν
ἀδικοῦντας, ἀλλὰ τοὺς μὴ θέλοντας ὑποσχεῖν τῇ πόλει
περὶ τοῦ βίου λόγον. δεινὸν δέ μοι δοκεῖ εἶναι, εἰ μέν τις 38
ἀπολογεῖσθαι ἀξιώσειεν ὑπὲρ τῶν ἀποθανόντων ὡς
ἀδίκως ἀπολώλασιν, οὐκ ἀνασχέσθαι τῶν ἐπιχειρούντων·
εἰ δέ τις τῶν ἀποφυγόντων πάλιν περὶ τῆς αὐτῆς αἰτίας
κατηγορεῖ, πῶς οὐ δίκαιον περὶ τοὺς ζῶντας καὶ τοὺς
τεθνηκότας τὴν αὐτὴν γνώμην ἔχειν; ἔστι μὲν οὖν 39
Ἀλκιβιάδου μήτε αὐτὸν τῶν νόμων καὶ τῶν ὅρκων
φροντίζειν, ὑμᾶς τε παραβαίνειν ἐπιχειρεῖν διδάσκειν, καὶ
τοὺς μὲν ἄλλους ἐκβάλλειν καὶ ἀποκτείνειν ἀνηλεῶς,
αὐτὸν δὲ ἱκετεύειν καὶ δακρύειν οἰκτρῶς. καὶ ταῦτα μὲν οὐ
θαυμάζω· πολλῶν γὰρ αὐτῷ κλαυμάτων ἄξια εἴργασται·
ἐνθυμοῦμαι δὲ τίνας ποτὲ καὶ πείσει δεόμενος, πότερα
τοὺς νεωτέρους, οὓς πρὸς τὸ πλῆθος διαβέβληκεν

333 διαπράξεται Bekker : διαπράξηται AQ   335–7 φεύγειν· … ἐκπεσεῖν; sic interpunxit Hermann   336 ὁ δὲ A : οὐδὲ Q   τοσαυτάκις] άκις e corr. A[1]   δικαίως καὶ νικήσας AQ : νικήσας δικαίως Blass : καὶ νικήσας, δικαίως Reiske   <ἂν> ante δόξαιμι, ut vid., desiderabant Turr.   338 <ὑπὸ> φαύλων Reiske   346 ἀνασχέσθαι A, re vera Q : <ἂν> ἀνασχέσθαι Reiske   ἐπιχειρούντων A[1]Q : ἐπιχειρησάντων fort. A[a]   349 τὴν αὐτὴν γνώμην post l. 348 δίκαιον Q   οὖν A : om. Q   350 αὐτὸν A : αὐτῶν Q   351 φροντίζειν A : φορτΐζείν sic Q   354 αὐτω A : αὐτῶν Q   355 πότερα A : πότερον Q   post πότερα ras. 4–5 litt. A[c]

ἀσελγαίνων καὶ τὰ γυμνάσια καταλύων καὶ παρὰ
τὴν ἡλικίαν πράττων, ἢ τοὺς πρεσβυτέρους, οἷς οὐδὲν
ὁμοίως βεβίωκεν, ἀλλὰ τῶν ἐπιτηδευμάτων αὐτῶν
40 καταπεφρόνηκεν; οὐ μόνον δὲ αὐτῶν ἕνεκα τῶν
παρανομούντων, ἵνα δίκην διδῶσιν, ἐπιμελεῖσθαι ἄξιον,
ἀλλὰ καὶ τῶν ἄλλων, ὅπως τούτους ὁρῶντες δικαιότεροι
καὶ σωφρονέστεροι γίγνωνται. ἐμὲ μὲν τοίνυν ἐξελάσαντες
τοὺς βελτίστους περιδεεῖς καταστήσετε, τοῦτον δὲ
κολάσαντες τοὺς ἀσελγεστάτους νομιμωτέρους ποιήσετε.
41 Βούλομαι δ' ὑμᾶς ἀναμνῆσαι τῶν ἐμοὶ πεπραγμένων.
ἐγὼ γὰρ πρεσβεύσας εἰς Θετταλίαν καὶ εἰς Μακεδονίαν
καὶ εἰς Μολοττίαν καὶ εἰς Θεσπρωτίαν καὶ εἰς Ἰταλίαν καὶ
εἰς Σικελίαν τοὺς μὲν διαφόρους ὄντας διήλλαξα, τοὺς δ'
ἐπιτηδείους ἐποίησα, τοὺς δὲ ἀπὸ τῶν ἐχθρῶν ἀπέστησα.
καίτοι εἰ τῶν πρωτευόντων ἕκαστος τὰ αὐτὰ ἐποίησεν,
ὀλίγους ἂν πολεμίους εἴχετε καὶ πολλοὺς συμμάχους
42 ἐκέκτησθε. περὶ δὲ τῶν λειτουργιῶν οὐκ ἀξιῶ μεμνῆσθαι,
πλὴν κατὰ τοσοῦτον, ὅτι τὰ προσταττόμενα δαπανῶ οὐκ
ἀπὸ τῶν κοινῶν ἀλλ' ἀπὸ τῶν ἰδίων. καίτοι τυγχάνω
νενικηκὼς εὐανδρίᾳ καὶ λαμπάδι καὶ τραγῳδοῖς, οὐ
τύπτων τοὺς ἀντιχορηγοῦντας, οὐδ' αἰσχυνόμενος εἰ τῶν
νόμων ἔλαττον δύναμαι. τοὺς οὖν τοιούτους τῶν πολιτῶν
πολὺ μᾶλλον ἐπιτηδείους ἡγοῦμαι μένειν ἢ φεύγειν.

42 εὐανδρίᾳ Harp. ε 152.2 s.v.

---

362 τούτους AQ : τούτους <κολαζομένους> Reiske : τοῦτο Dobree 364 καταστήσετε A : καταστήσητε Q 365 ἀσελγεστάτους mal. Sauppe : ἀσελγεστέρους AQ νομιμωτέρους A : νομιωτέρους Q : νομιμωτάτους Emperius^3 ποιήσετε A : ποιήσητε Q 367 pr. εἰς Q : om. A 368 Μολοττίαν mal. Blass : Μολοσσίαν AQ 369 διαφόρους <ὑμῖν> mal. Blass 371 εἰ A : οἱ Q πρωτευόντων AQ : πρεσβευόντων Luzac τὰ A : om. Q 373 λειτουργιῶν AQ : ληπουργιῶν Blass^3 375 alt. τῶν A : om. Q 376 εὐανδρία A Harp : εὐανδρεία Q^1 (ευ e corr., quid fuerit non liquet)

ANDOCIDES INDEX NOMINUM

ANTIPHON INDEX NOMINUM